WHY TRUE LOVE WAITS

WHY

The Definitive Book on

TRUE

How to Help Your Kids Resist Sexual Pressure

LOVE

WAITS

♦ ♦ ♦

Josh McDowell

TYNDALE HOUSE PUBLISHERS, INC.,
CAROL STREAM, ILLINOIS

Visit Tyndale's exciting Web site at www.tyndale.com

TYNDALE and Tyndale's quill logo are registered trademarks of Tyndale House Publishers, Inc.

Why True Love Waits

Designed by Dean H. Renninger

Interior charts by Luke Daab. Copyright © 2002 Tyndale House Publishers.

Published in 1987 as Why Wait? by Here's Life Publishers, Inc.

Revised edition in 2002 by Tyndale House Publishers, Inc.

Library of Congress Cataloging-in-Publication Data

McDowell, Josh.
  Why true love waits : a definitive work on how to help your youth resist sexual pressure / Josh McDowell.
    p. cm.
  Rev. ed. of: Why wait? / Josh McDowell and Dick Day.
  Includes bibliographical references.
  ISBN-13: 978-0-8423-6591-8
  ISBN-10: 0-8423-6591-5
  1. Sexual ethics.   2. Youth—Sexual behavior.   3. Parenting.   I. McDowell, Josh. Why wait?   II. Title.
  HQ32 .M386 2002
  306.7′0835—dc21   2001008714

Printed in United States of America

13   12   11   10   09   08   07
9   8   7   6   5   4   3

CONTENTS

Acknowledgments xiii

How to Use This Book xv

PART ONE: A CRISIS OF PREMARITAL SEX

Chapter 1: Why Does True Love Wait?: Our Youth Want Answers. 3

"We're in Love, So What Are We Waiting For?" 5

God's Description of True Love 7

Premarital Sex and Youth: The Disturbing Facts 9

A Small But Positive Trend Among Youth to Wait. 13

Reasons for the Trend to Wait. 16

Chapter 2: Adolescent Premarital Sex: The High Cost to Youth 29

The Exorbitant Cost for Premarital Sex. 31

Sexually Transmitted Diseases:

The Cost of Infection and Possible Death. 32

    An Epidemic of STDs. 33

    Young Women at Greater Risk 39

    Blind to the Horror of STDs 42

Premarital Sex and Pregnancy: The Cost of Another Life 44

    The Sad News about Teen Pregnancy 45

    The Rocky Road of Teen Birth and Parenting 48

    The Dead-End Road of Abortion 50

Chapter 3: Adolescent Premarital Sex: The High Cost to Society 53

The High Cost to an Unmarried Teenage Mom 55

    The Challenge of Continuing Education. 55

    The Financial Burden. 55

    The Possibility of Another Pregnancy. 56

    The Need for Adult Support 56

The Emotional and Spiritual Price Tag 56
The High Cost to the Child. 57
   Disturbing Risks of STDs 58
   Economic, Emotional, and Psychological Problems 59
   Disappointing Cycle of Teen Births 60
   Abortion: The Ultimate Price 60
The High Cost to Society. 61
   The Cost of STDs 62
   The Cost of Adolescent Pregnancy 63
   The Cost of a "Private Act" 64

PART TWO: REASONS KIDS DON'T WAIT FOR SEX
Chapter 4: The Physical Reasons: Children in Grown-up Bodies 69
   Puberty: A Body Equipped for Sex 71
   Early Dating: Early Sex 73
   Alcohol and Drugs: Weakening Defenses against Premarital Sex 75
   Birth Control: The Myth of "Safe Sex" 77
   Our Culture's Motto: "If It Feels Good, Do It". 79
   Teen Sex Activity: The Fallout of Prior Sexual Abuse 87

Chapter 5: The Environmental Reasons: Growing Up
in a World Where Wrong Is Right. 91
   Biblical Values versus the Postmodern Culture 92
      Disillusioned in a Postmodern Culture 94
      Illicit Sex in Our Culture 96
      The Me-ism Culture 97
      A Society Lacking Foundation 100
   Myths and False Assumptions of the Postmodern Culture 101
      "No One Will Get Hurt." 101
      "It's All Right. We're Engaged." 103
      "I Owe It to Him." 108
      "Having Sex with Me Will Prove Your Love." 110

Chapter 6: The Media's Role. 117
   What Are the Media Trying to Sell? 118

Television 121
Music and Lyrics 125
Pornography 127
Media's Biggest Lie 129
The Deception of Distorted Values 131
Putting the Media in Its Place 133

Chapter 7: The Emotional Reasons: A "Love Famine" at Home 137
Our Kids Need Love, Modeling, and Attention 138
Parental Modeling 139
Searching for a Father's Love 140
Divorce 146
Broken Home, Broken Kids 148
Our Kids Need Clear Instruction about Sex 150
Teaching Sex in Context 152
Lack of Information 154
An Expression of Rebellion 157

Chapter 8: The Relational Reasons: Needy Kids Turn to Sex 161
Searching for Love 161
Searching for Security and Self-Esteem 167
Searching for Intimacy 171
Searching for Companionship 174
Searching for an Escape from Fear of Rejection 175
Searching for a Spiritual Connection 179

**Chapter 9: The Psychological Reasons: Everyone Is Doing It,
So Why Shouldn't We?** 181
Pressure to Conform 185
Pressure to Be Popular 187
Pressure from a Boyfriend or Girlfriend 189
Pressure of a Different Kind: School Sex Education 194

PART THREE: REASONS KIDS SHOULD WAIT FOR SEX
Chapter 10: Abstinence: God's Protection and Provision 199
God's Viewpoint on Premarital Sex 200

"Thou Shalt Not" Is Evidence of God's Love 201
God Gives Laws to Protect Us and Provide for Us 204

Chapter 11: The Physical Reasons to Wait 209
Sexually Transmitted Diseases: The Health Risk of Premarital Sex. . . 211
    Human Immunodeficiency Virus (HIV) and
    Acquired Immune Deficiency Syndrome (AIDS) 214
    Chlamydia 219
    Pelvic Inflammatory Disease (PID). 222
    Gonorrhea 224
    Genital Herpes (HSV). 227
    Genital Warts from Human Papillomavirus (HPV) 231
    Syphilis. 237
    Trichomoniasis 238
    Hepatitis B 239
    Cancer 239
Unwanted Pregnancy. 240

Chapter 12: The Emotional Reasons to Wait 247
Protection from the Emotional Pitfalls of Premarital Sex. 248
    Protection from Guilt 248
    Protection from Performance-based Sex. 250
    Protection from Misleading Feelings about Sex and Love. 251
    Protection from Addiction to Sex 253
    Protection from the Hardships of Breaking Up. 255
    Protection from Poor Self-image. 257
Provision for Emotional Wholeness in Future Marriage 259
    Provision of Maturity. 260
    Provision of Genuine Love 261
    Provision of Respect for One's Body 262
    Provision of Dignity. 263
    Provision for Only One "First Time" 264
    Provision for Intimacy 266

Chapter 13: The Relational Reasons to Wait 269
Protection from Unhealthy Relationships 269

Protection from Communication Breakdown 269

Protection from Difficult Courtships 271

Protection from Comparison. 272

Protection from Sex-dominated Relationships 276

Protection from Damaged Family Relationships 278

Protection from the Pitfalls of Cohabitation. 281

Provision for a Unique Relationship in Marriage 288

Provision of Virginity. 289

Provision of a Bond of Love and Trust 290

Chapter 14: The Spiritual Reasons to Wait 293

Protection from Spiritual Decline. 293

Protection from a Sin against the Body. 293

Protection from God's Judgment 295

Protection from Interrupted Fellowship 296

Protection from Being a Negative Influence 298

Provision for Spiritual Blessing for Sexual Purity 301

Provision of the Blessing of Patience. 301

Provision of the Blessing of Trust 303

Provision of Jesus to Fill the Void 307

Chapter 15: Why "Safe Sex" Isn't Safe 313

The Dangers of Condom Failure 315

Flawed "Protection". 320

The Health Risks 322

Truly Safe Sex 324

Provision of Virginity. 325

PART FOUR: HOW TO HELP OUR KIDS WAIT FOR SEX

Chapter 16: Develop a Nurturing Relationship with Kids 331

A Parent and Child Connection Equals Reduced Sexual Involvement . . 333

Communicate Your Acceptance. 334

Lavish Them with Appreciation. 335

Be Available to Your Kids. 335

Display Your Affection. 336

Establish Accountability with Your Kids. 337
Building Your Child's Self-Image Equals Reduced
Sexual Involvement 339
The Right Perspective of Themselves 340
Fostering Open Communication with Your Child Equals Reduced
Sexual Involvement 344
The Skill of Listening 344
Eleven Principles for Good Communication. 345

Chapter 17: Encourage an Intimate Relationship with Christ. 355
Establishing a Relationship with Christ. 356
Handling Temptation 358
Meditating on God's Word 359
Pleasing Christ. 360
Christ Accepts You Just As You Are 361
Living in the Power of the Holy Spirit. 363
Confess Sin 364
Recognize God's Will 365
Ask for His Filling 365
Follow His Leading 366

Chapter 18: Teach and Model Moral Values at Home 369
How to Model a Context for Sex in Your Marriage 370
The Need to Model Love 371
How My Husband Models Love 373
How My Wife Models Respect 374
The Challenges of a Single Parent 375
How to Reinforce Positive Values 376
Encourage Positive Peer Pressure 377
Get Involved with School and Teachers. 377
Latchkey Kids and Single Parenting 378
The Power of Books. 379
Guidelines for Helping Kids Navigate Cyberspace 379
How to Communicate God's Perspective about Sex. 381
In the Beginning Was Sex. 381
God's Specific Plan for Sex 383

How to Teach Sex at Home. 384
    Where to Begin 385
    What to Say 386
    How to Say It 388
How to Instill Christian Values about Sex. 389
    The Christian Perspective of Relationships 390
    Teach Values Naturally and Casually. 391

Chapter 19: Help Kids Develop the Strength to Say No. 395
    Encourage the Development of Convictions 396
    Encourage a Christian Conscience. 401
    Encourage a Commitment to Abstinence. 403
    How Far Is Too Far? 407
    Strategies for Keeping Sexual Standards 412

Chapter 20: Help Kids Determine Standards for Dating 421
    When Should They Start Dating?. 423
    How to Maintain Control When Dating. 424
    Equip Your Kids with "Escape Routes". 436

Chapter 21: Offer Forgiveness and Provide Hope When Kids Blow It . 443
    The Gift of Forgiveness 444
    A Picture of God's Forgiveness 445
    Biblical Insights for Those Who Seek Forgiveness 451
        Steps to Forgiveness. 453
    What Can Be Done about Lost Virginity?. 457
    Hope Lives On 459

Notes 461
About the Author 491

ACKNOWLEDGMENTS

The research, revision, and rewriting of this book from the original *Why Wait?* work was possible only because of the efforts of so many dedicated and talented people:

- Kathi Macias, who began the revision by folding in research for a Russian edition of the book.
- Ed Stewart, who expertly reorganized, rewrote, and folded in all the current statistics to create a reader-friendly reference text.
- Christy Karassev, who spent tireless days working on the documentation, filing, and coordination of the endnotes and keeping the communication channels between all parties open and clear.
- Marilyn Burns, who e-mailed and faxed more pages than she cares to mention.
- Dick Day, who provided me with so much input, advice, and counsel on the original *Why Wait?* book. His influence in my life and my writings has left a permanent impact.
- Dave Bellis, my associate of twenty-five years, who orchestrated this enormous revision and followed it through the complex maze of details to completion and release.
- Tyndale House Publishers, who believed that this work was an invaluable resource for churches and families and bent over backwards to move it through the system at breakneck speed.

May God richly bless you all for your service to the Kingdom.
Josh McDowell

HOW TO USE THIS BOOK

Why True Love Waits is a reader-friendly, easy-to-use reference text addressing, from a biblical perspective, the crisis of adolescent premarital sex in twenty-first century culture. It is a completely revised, updated, expanded, and rewritten version of Josh McDowell's best-selling book, *Why Wait?* originally published in 1985.

Why True Love Waits is a rich treasure of relevant information, revealing statistics, and pertinent insights on the current adolescent sex crisis. The book contains:

- Up-to-date and comprehensive research and documentation which detail the current adolescent premarital sex crisis and its roots and reveal why this crisis must be urgently and pointedly addressed.
- Poignant letters and gripping anecdotes from scores of actual Christian young people who are being pressured by our sex-oriented culture and media to compromise the Bible's teaching to wait for sex until marriage.
- A crystal clear and rock-solidly documented apologetic of God's promise of protection and provision for those who follow his guidelines for sexual purity.
- Practical, relevant steps you can take to help your youth resist sexual pressure in a postmodern culture which communicates at every turn, "If it feels good, do it."

Why True Love Waits is targeted to a number of individuals who will find the book to be an invaluable resource:

- **Church Youth Leaders:** (1) Use this reference book to help you formulate your response to the adolescent premarital sex crisis in your ministry, prepare talks to youth, develop lessons and Bible studies on the subject of abstinence, prepare for counseling youth who are struggling with sexual pressures, etc. (2) Have your youth prepare presentations to the group using this resource plus other great resources.

- **Pastors and Denominational Leaders:** Use this reference book to help you prepare sermons on the topic of sex in our culture, plan church-wide, regional, or denominational youth conferences promoting biblical abstinence, conduct parents' conferences, etc.
- **Christian Education Leaders, Sunday School Teachers, Christian School Teachers:** Use this reference book to help you formulate or supplement lesson plans when teaching units on Christian sex education.
- **Parents:** Use this reference book to help you enrich your relationship with your children, prepare for questions they may ask about sex, formulate a plan for teaching biblical abstinence in your home, etc.
- **Youth:** Use this reference book to help you find answers to your questions about youth and sex, bolster your own convictions for biblical abstinence, prepare research papers on the teen sex crisis for college or high school classes, etc.

The wealth of research and statistics presented in *Why True Love Waits* reflects the most recent data available in the areas of adolescent sexual involvement, sexually transmitted diseases, teen pregnancy and abortion, and more. However, things change quickly in our culture. By the time this book reaches you, some of this data may have changed. In order to stay current on the adolescent premarital sex crisis, visit www.josh.org/lovewaits.

Information in *Why True Love Waits* is drawn from a wide array of organizations, ministries, individuals, and media resources which address various facets of the adolescent sex crisis. Some of these entities are in wholehearted agreement with the Josh McDowell Ministry and the biblical view of premarital sex and abstinence, but some are not.

> Use of statistics, comments, arguments, or opinions from any source does not necessarily connote an endorsement of that source.

The following information is presented to help you better understand where many organizations and ministries stand on the issues covered in this book and what resources are available.

SEXUALITY INFORMATION AND EDUCATION COUNCIL OF THE UNITED STATES (SIECUS)

- **Mission Statement:** The Sexuality Information and Education Council of the U.S. (SIECUS) is a national, nonprofit organization which affirms that sexuality is a natural and healthy part of living. Incorporated in 1964, SIECUS develops, collects, and disseminates information, promotes comprehensive education about sexuality, and advocates the right of individuals to make responsible sexual choices.
- **SIECUS is a major advocate of abortion:** "Every woman, regardless of age or income, should have the right to obtain an abortion_" (www.siecus.org, About SEICUS, SIECUS Position Statements, August 17, 2001).
- **SIECUS is a major advocate of comprehensive sex education and condom distribution:** "Comprehensive [contraception/abortion] school-based sexuality education_should be an important part of the education program_" (www.siecus.org, About SEICUS, SIECUS Position Statements, August 17, 2001).
- *Citizen* magazine did an exposé on SIECUS in their February 2001 issue, pp.19–21.

PLANNED PARENTHOOD

Planned Parenthood is a very large international corporation which is out in front advocating abortion, contraception, and comprehensive sex education ("This is Planned Parenthood," Fact Sheet, September 17, 2001). The Alan Guttmacher Institute is the research arm of Planned Parenthood.

- **Mission Statement:** "A primary aim is to guarantee the freedom of women to terminate unwanted pregnancies [have abortions]" ("The Alan Guttmacher Institute's Mission," Fact Sheet, September 17, 2001).
- **Key Magazine:** *Family Planning Perspectives*

THE NATIONAL CAMPAIGN TO PREVENT TEEN PREGNANCY

- **Mission Statement:** To improve the well-being of children, youth, and families by reducing teen pregnancy. The Campaign's goal is to reduce the teen pregnancy rate by one-third between 1996 and 2005 (www.teenpregnancy.org/fact.htm, "About the Campaign," August 17, 2001).
- **A Primary Aim:** "Abstinence should be strongly stressed as the best choice for teens because of its effectiveness and its consistency with the beliefs of

adults and teens. But giving teens information about—and access to—contraception is still important" ("Campaign Update—A Prescription for Progress," summer 2001).

The National Campaign to Prevent Teen Pregnancy advocates teen contraception and abortion.

THE MEDICAL INSTITUTE FOR SEXUAL HEALTH (MISH)

◆ **Mission Statement:** The Medical Institute is a nonprofit medical organization founded in 1992 by gynecologist Joe S. McIlhaney Jr., M.D., designed to confront the world epidemics of nonmarital pregnancy and sexually transmitted disease with incisive health care data. Driven by medical, educational, and other scientific data, The Medical Institute informs, educates, and provides solutions to medical professionals, educators, government officials, parents, and media about problems associated with sexually transmitted disease and nonmarital pregnancy.

◆ **A Primary Aim:** Because the problems associated with these twin epidemics are so substantial The Medical Institute believes we must actively promote risk elimination, rather than just risk reduction. The only 100 percent effective way to avoid nonmarital pregnancy and STD infection is to avoid sexual activity outside a mutually faithful, lifelong relationship—marriage. (www.medinstitute.org/about/whatis.htm, "About Us: What is the Medical Institute?" August 17, 2001).

THE ABSTINENCE CLEARINGHOUSE

◆ **Mission Statement:** The Abstinence Clearinghouse is a nonprofit national educational organization that promotes the appreciation for and practice of sexual abstinence through distribution of age-appropriate, factual, and medically accurate materials. The Clearinghouse was founded to provide a central location where character, relationship, and abstinence programs, curricula, speakers, and materials could be accessed. The Clearinghouse serves national, state, and local agencies, as well as international organizations.

◆ **Service Provider:** The Clearinghouse helps to strengthen national, state, and local agencies through the various services it offers, such as:

    1. Hosting educational national and regional conferences

    2. Publication and distribution of the *Abstinence Clearinghouse*

Directory of Abstinence Resources (which contains hundreds of abstinence-until-marriage resources)

3. Publication of *The Abstinence Network*, a national quarterly newsletter to inform and educate those working to help young people to abstain from premarital sexual intercourse

4. Production of materials to provide information on and to promote abstinence education

5. Providing technical assistance to schools and other societal institutions to assist in preventing behaviors that place young people at risk for HIV infection, other STDs, and unintended pregnancy

• **More Information:** "Interested in learning more about the Abstinence Clearinghouse or receiving a newsletter? Let us know! To learn about the many benefits of becoming an affiliate of the Abstinence Clearinghouse, please visit the Affiliations section" (www.abstinence.net/AboutUs.cfm, "Abstinence Clearinghouse: About Us," August 17, 2001).

SEX RESPECT

• **Founder:** Former teacher Colleen Mast

• **Mission Statement:** "Sexuality is more than a physical act; it is a combination of physical, mental, emotional, and spiritual needs. Teaching kids about sexuality is more than passing on facts. It's passing on attitudes and values. It helps kids know they have the freedom to choose not to have sex before marriage, and there are some very good reasons to say no to premarital sex," Mrs. Mast says. "If we say no because I said so, then our reasons for saying no are pretty slim and easy to disregard. But, if we give good reasons and appeal to the intellect and the heart, treating these kids as the intelligent human beings they are, they are much more likely to think about the consequences of premarital sex."

• **Program:** Early results of studies from schools using the Sex Respect curriculum in Illinois, Missouri, Kansas, Michigan, and Wisconsin have shown:

  • Before taking the course, 36 percent of the students said sexual intercourse among teens is acceptable provided no pregnancy results. Only 18 percent agreed after the course, and 65.5 percent disagreed.

  • Before the course 20 percent said sexual urges are "always" controllable, and 62 percent said they are "sometimes." Afterward, 39 percent said "always" and 51 percent "sometimes."

- Before the course, 35 percent said there are "a lot" of benefits to waiting until marriage for sexual intercourse. After taking the course, 58 percent agreed.
- Sex Respect: The Option of True Sexual Freedom curriculum was launched in nine states and Canada in the first year and is currently used in more than 2500 school systems nationwide for the 1996–97 school year.

- The Sex Respect curriculum includes three textbooks: a student workbook, a parent guidebook, and a teacher manual. For more information, see the Sex Respect Web site (www.sexrespect.com, August 17, 2001).

TRUE LOVE WAITS

- **Mission Statement:** True Love Waits is an international campaign that challenges teenagers and college students to remain sexually abstinent until marriage. It was created in April 1993, and is sponsored by LifeWay Christian Resources of the Southern Baptist Convention.

  To date, over a million young people have signed covenant cards stating: "Believing that true love waits, I made a commitment to God, myself, my family, my friends, my future mate, and my future children to be sexually abstinent from this day until the day I enter a biblical marriage relationship."

- **Effectiveness:** True Love Waits works. A scientific study conducted by two sociologists and published in the *American Journal of Sociology* found that teenagers who pledge to remain sexually abstinent until marriage are 34 percent less likely to have sex than those who do not take virginity vows. In fact, Peter S. Bearman, professor of sociology and director of the Institute for Social and Economic Theory and Research at Columbia University, said by age fifteen half the teens in the study had already had sex. Those who took virginity vows, however, usually held off for eighteen more months. He said he believes virginity pledges are an excellent way to give teens a way to say no. He points out that pledging may be a way to bridge some of the difficult years in early adolescence with (unwanted) sexual activity.

- **For more information:** www.truelovewaits.com

CHOOSING THE BEST

- **Mission Statement:** Choosing the Best is an abstinence-focused sex education curriculum that gives teens the information and training they need to discover for themselves that abstinence until marriage is their "best choice."

- **Program:** Choosing the Best helps teens reduce at-risk sexual behavior through:
    - Clear communication of the physical and emotional risks of being sexually active.
    - Small-group directed discussions that encourage abstinence and lead to real changes in attitudes and actions.
    - Self-esteem building exercises that help teens value who they are, the choices they make, and their ability to resist peer pressures.
    - Structured interaction with parents/guardians that opens communication and encourages positive parental influence.
    - Choosing the Best is organized in an easy-to-use format with case studies and questions that encourage active classroom discussions and meaningful parent/teen interactions.

- **Scope:** For three years from 1997 through 1999, over forty school districts purchased and used the Choosing the Best Middle School Curriculum and 850 teachers were trained in abstinence seminars involving over 100 school districts. Assuming each teacher impacted an average of 100 students over the school year, 82,000 students would have been influenced. In 2001, a new high school curriculum, Choosing the Best LIFE, was selected to be used in twenty of the largest school districts representing almost 40 percent of all the ninth graders in Georgia. In 2000 Choosing the Best added WAIT Training, a relationship curriculum, for use in schools. To date over 2000 school districts in forty states are now using Choosing the Best programs.

- **Effectiveness:** A researcher at Northwestern University in Illinois studied over 6000 middle school students who completed the Choosing the Best curriculum and were evaluated in a pre- and post-test survey. Specific results from the study included:
    - 74 percent of all students stated they are now willing to say no to sex before marriage.

- 60 percent of those students who were sexually active are now willing to say no to sex before marriage.
- 75 percent of all students had reliable positive changes toward more abstinent attitudes from pre-test to post-test.

Dr. Bill Roper, former Director of the Centers for Disease Control, served as chairman of the medical advisory board for Choosing the Best. He stated:

> As a pediatrician, and as a person interested in and concerned about teen sexuality issues, I am pleased to commend the program Choosing the Best to you. When I was director of the federal Center for Disease Control and Prevention (CDC), I spent a considerable amount of time on efforts to promote good health among young people, and to prevent the physical, social and economic harm that results from the early onset of sexual activity today. I have reviewed Choosing the Best, and I believe it to be a well-prepared program that gives young people needed information and helps them build the skills they need for making healthful decisions. I hope this is useful to you as you consider these issues.

PROJECT REALITY

- **Mission Statement:** Project Reality, a 501©(3) nonprofit corporation, has been a pioneer in the national field of adolescent health education, developing, teaching, and evaluating abstinence-centered programs in the public schools since 1985. Project Reality has administered three divisions for more than a decade under a grant funded by the State of Illinois Department of Human Services. Two divisions have sites throughout the state. The third is concentrated in the City of Chicago. In addition to abstinence curricula and related materials, in-service teacher training seminars are provided for all participating schools, as well as a variety of motivational speakers for school assemblies.
- **Middle School Division, Statewide, Grades 6–9:** An eight-unit series with a strong medical emphasis. A values-based, abstinence-focused curriculum that gives teens the information and training they need to discover for themselves that abstinence until marriage is the "best choice" and helps them reduce at-risk sexual behavior. Includes a student workbook and a teacher manual. In 1999–2000, it served 31,029 students in 208 schools.
- **Senior High School Division, Statewide, Grades 9–11:** A fifteen-unit program emphasizing the abstinence concept as the healthiest way of living. By stressing the composite approach of saying no to pre-marital

PART ONE

A CRISIS OF ADOLESCENT PREMARITAL SEX

◆   ◆   ◆

CHAPTER 1

WHY DOES TRUE LOVE WAIT?

OUR YOUTH WANT ANSWERS

IF YOU MET DEREK, you would probably like him. He is well-liked and respected by his fellow students and the members of the church college group. And he's a good-looking guy with a great personality. He used to date a lot of girls, but now he has a steady girlfriend. Michelle shares his commitment as a Christian, and in Derek's eyes she is a vision of beauty. They are always together studying, talking about the Bible, or just hanging out. Derek is pretty sure he will marry Michelle someday.

Derek is something of an oddity among twenty-year-old men on his campus. He is still a virgin. He knows that God's Word forbids premarital sex, and he has lived by that standard in the midst of the culture's plummeting moral standards. And it was relatively easy for him to live a pure life—until he met Michelle. Many of their evenings end with long embraces and deep, passionate kisses. But Derek always breaks it off before they go too far. He knows God wants him to reserve sex with Michelle for marriage, but his desire to know her intimately seems to deepen daily.

I was intrigued when Derek told me about an experience he had while sharing his faith with his college friend Colin. During the conversation, Colin asked Derek, "Do I have to stop having sex with my girlfriend in order to become a Christian?" Colin told him how much he loved his girlfriend. She was taking birth-control pills, and they both felt that engaging in sex added a deeper level of meaning to their already good relationship.

This question precipitated a long discussion between Derek and Colin about commitment and the lordship of Christ. "And," Derek said, "Colin's question opened up a fresh dilemma for me: Why am I waiting for sex until marriage?"

For the first time, Derek felt unsure in his understanding of God's prohibitions on premarital sex. "I told Colin what the Bible says, that sex must be saved until marriage," Derek explained to me. "Yet deep in my heart, I began to ask the same question that Colin asked me. Michelle and I are already more committed to each other than many married couples. Why wait?"

In his dorm room after what proved to be a frustrating witnessing experience, Derek began to question God even more. "I had to find an answer," he said. "I argued with God that prohibitions against premarital sex seem a bit archaic in light of advanced birth-control methods and changing views about sex in our culture. Perhaps the apostle Paul's admonitions against fornication need revising."

Finally, Derek realized that God is neither archaic nor blind to twenty-first century practices. "I concluded that I just had to be patient and wait for his answer . . . even though I could not understand the reasons." So Derek gamely waited for God's answer, though his mind was filled with turmoil. And his hunger to experience sex with Michelle continued to grow.

Annie is another person you would be proud to claim as a relative or a friend. Even though she's only a junior in high school, Annie's heart is set on serving Christ as a nurse on the foreign mission field. It is what God has called her to do, and she is eager to follow.

Attractive but shy, Annie hasn't dated much in high school. And when she did date, the boy had to be a Christian with a passion to serve God that matched her own. Since there weren't many boys like that in her small community adjacent to an army base, Annie was content to wait for the man God would choose for her. Premarital sex was totally out of the question for Annie. She knew what the Bible said and was deeply committed to remaining a virgin until marriage.

Then Annie met Jeff, a ruggedly handsome Green Beret from the base who kept coming into the card shop where she worked part-time. Jeff was five years older than Annie, and he wasn't a Christian. So whenever he asked her out, Annie declined politely as she had done with many other soldiers who happened into the shop. Instead, she quietly prayed for Jeff's salvation and shared a word of witness when she could.

Undaunted, Jeff kept coming into the store. To Annie's surprise, after a few months Jeff announced that he had trusted Christ. He started attending Annie's church and became an active part in the college-career group. Jeff's life seemed transformed. He couldn't get enough of church and Bible study.

When he asked Annie to go out again, she suddenly didn't have a reason to refuse. Jeff was quickly becoming the kind of guy she had been asking God to find for her. The rush of attention from the new, on-fire believer melted Annie's heart, and she fell in love—and she fell hard.

After a few weeks of the intense, thrilling romance, Annie went to see the youth minister's wife. "Before I met Jeff," Annie confessed, "premarital sex wasn't even a temptation for me. Whenever I dated, the guys weren't . . . well, they weren't anything like Jeff.

"But being with Jeff has awakened all kinds of desires in me. He doesn't understand why the Bible says we should wait for sex until marriage. When he asks me, I tell him God says it's wrong. But when I'm with Jeff, everything and everyone else—including Jeff—says it's right for two people so deeply in love. And in three weeks, Jeff's unit is shipping out for a tour of duty overseas. He'll be gone six months. He says that having sex together before he goes away will help him make it through our long separation. Funny thing. I'm starting to feel the same way.

"I have never questioned God's directives on sex until now. Why did God say wait until marriage, especially when you're so deeply in love? If I can't find a reason beyond 'Thou shalt not,' I don't think I can say no much longer."

"WE'RE IN LOVE, SO WHAT ARE WE WAITING FOR?"

Derek and Annie are representative of thousands of Christian young people who struggle with the question, "Why does true love wait until marriage for sex?" Sexual pressures on our kids are at an all-time high. Their friends, peers, and many of their adult role models are succumbing to the pressures of a sex-crazed society that mocks biblical abstinence as puritanical and irrelevant. As one young woman told her father, "When I see how casually sex is treated by my classmates, when they make it all sound so natural and inevitable, there are times when I wonder what I'm waiting for."

Surrounded by a permissive society that accepts and even glorifies casual sex, students today are wrestling with sexual decisions that previous generations never had to face. For many of our kids, those decisions are made with little thought about the consequences. According to one fourteen-year-old high school student, "All they think is that they really want this guy to like them, and so they're going to 'do it.'"

Derek and Annie are struggling with the "Why wait?" question in the face of their passions and temptations. But many other Christian students are not struggling much at all—because they are *not* waiting. Here's what some of them said:

Sure, I'm a Christian, and I know the Bible says no sex until after marriage. But the Bible also talks about not eating shellfish and women not wearing pants in church and a lot of other cultural rules we don't follow today. My girlfriend and I prayed about it, and we feel that sex before marriage is no different in God's eyes than fried shrimp for dinner. It was important in the past, maybe, but doesn't apply to today. We really love each other, and sex is bringing us even closer.

◆   ◆   ◆

Is sex before marriage wrong for a Christian? It really depends. Sleeping around, one-night stands, just seeing how many people you can have sex with—that's wrong. Playing Russian roulette with sexually transmitted diseases and putting others at risk—that's wrong. Being careless and getting pregnant or having an abortion—that's wrong. But when two people are really in love with each other and committed only to each other, then sex is natural and beautiful. Travis and I were both virgins when we had sex last summer. And we haven't been—and won't be—with anyone else. What's wrong with that?

◆   ◆   ◆

What is marriage anyway? It's just a legal piece of paper and a formal way of saying "I do." The lifetime commitment, which is much more important, comes long before that. Four months ago, when we were alone at my parents' cabin by the shore one afternoon, Jana and I said our own vows to each other before God. It was our own secret wedding, and we celebrated by having sex. We'll get married the traditional way in a few years, but we love each other and our commitment has never been deeper than it has been these last four months. We're following the spirit of God's law about sex, not the letter of the law. I think the Bible says that's what we're supposed to do.

These are Christian kids who know very well *what* the Bible says about premarital sex. As parents, pastors, youth leaders, and teachers, we have not failed to lay down the law to them: no sex until marriage. But what most Christian youth are lacking is the *why* behind the Bible's restrictions on sex. Even those deeply committed to the Lord struggle to find answers about sex that make sense to them. As seen in the previous examples, Christian young people are stumped by two main issues: the antiquity of the Bible and the element of true love.

The Antiquity of the Bible

Christian youth accept the Bible's authority on many issues but struggle when it comes to morality and lifestyle choices. They are aware that the Bible places clear limitations on sexual activity, but they consider these limitations merely old-fashioned, overly strict rules for a different time and a different culture. They may believe the rules and moral precepts God laid out in the Old Testament had a purpose for that particular time and place, but they have a hard time accepting that God would intend these same precepts to apply to them in the twenty-first century.

To answer their objections, we must help our youth understand the reason surrounding God's rules. Behind every negative commandment in the Bible, there are two loving motivations. One is to protect us, and the other is to provide for us. The "thou shalt nots" of the Bible come not from a tyrannical ruler who wants to spoil our fun but from a loving Father who has our best interest at heart.

For example, when God says, "Thou shalt not commit adultery," he is not being a cosmic killjoy. He is being a cosmic *lovejoy*. He is saying, "I don't want you to do something that will bring you and others pain. I love you, and I have better things planned for you."

Likewise, God does not prohibit illicit sex to spoil our fun. He knows the devastating consequences of extramarital sex—consequences such as guilt, pain, unwanted pregnancy, and even death and disease—and he wants us to avoid those heartbreaking consequences. In talking to our young people about sex, we've got to help them see that the precepts of the Bible were given out of purest love. Beyond that, we must make it clear that these same precepts are still relevant today for all the same reasons. God says no to premarital sex because he loves us enough to protect us from harm and provide for our good. (You'll find more on the protect and provide principle of God's love in chapter 10.)

GOD'S DESCRIPTION OF TRUE LOVE

Most Christian youth have a moral standard. They agree that promiscuous sex with anyone, anytime is wrong. But sex between two people in a committed relationship who really love each other somehow seems different. We saw that Derek believes he and his girlfriend are deeply in love and are more committed to each other than many married couples. And all of the examples above expressed "true love" as their justification for engaging in or considering premarital sex. Does true love make sex right? When young couples are truly in love and plan on getting married someday, what's to stop them from having sex now?

I shock many parents and church leaders when I say that I agree, in a way, with today's young people—I believe that true love *does* make it right. Now, before you put the complaint letter in the mailbox, hear me out. True love *is* the biblical standard for sex. The problem is, most youth are working from a counterfeit standard of love—one that says love permits sex without boundaries, outside of God's definition of love.

What is God's definition? In 1 Corinthians, the apostle Paul gives a good description of what love does and does not do. "Love is patient and kind. Love is not jealous or boastful or proud or rude. Love does not demand its own way. Love is not irritable, and it keeps no record of when it has been wronged. It is never glad about injustice but rejoices whenever the truth wins out" (1 Cor. 13:4-6, NLT).

Paul also wrote that "love does no wrong to anyone" (Rom. 13:10, NLT). Instead, we are to treat all people as we would like to be treated. Remember the Golden Rule? "Do for others," Jesus commanded, "what you would like them to do for you" (Matt. 7:12, NLT). Again, Paul put it this way: "Each of you should look not only to your own interests, but also to the interests of others" (Phil. 2:4).

With these verses and others as a guide, we can derive a concise statement defining love. *Love is making the security, happiness, and welfare of another person as important as your own.* It is really an imitation of God's love, the kind of love that protects the loved one from harm and provides for his or her good. True love is giving and trusting, secure and safe, loyal and forever. And because its priority is to protect and provide for the loved one, true love will not do things that are harmful to the security, happiness, and welfare of another person.

Throughout this book, we will provide comprehensive evidence of how waiting to have sex until after marriage provides for the spiritual, relational, emotional, and physical health of a person, and how such waiting can protect a person from a host of negative consequences. You will be able to demonstrate and document to your young people that anyone who uses love as a justification for premarital sex is not speaking out of love at all. You will be able to teach your young people how living in harmony with God's loving prohibitions is for their ultimate good.

PREMARITAL SEX AND YOUTH: THE DISTURBING FACTS

Without solid reasons for saying no to premarital sex, today's kids are vulnerable in times of temptation, doubt, and questioning from their friends and peers. Many are responding by getting involved sexually, as evidenced in the following survey results from the *Journal of Youth and Adolescence*.[1]

PERCENT OF NONVIRGIN STUDENTS ("EVER HAD SEX") FOR ALL STUDENTS, MALES, AND FEMALES			
Ages of students	Percent of all students who "ever had sex"	Percent of males only who "ever had sex"	Percent of females only who "ever had sex"
12–13 years	12.4%	11.5%	13.3%
14 years	13.9%	17.4%	9.7%
15–16 years	34.8%	32.4%	39.1%
17–18 years	61.1%	65.2%	58.5%
Total Ages	**24.8%**	**24.3%**	**25.3%**

NUMBER OF STUDENTS REPORTING AGE AT FIRST SEX FOR ALL STUDENTS, MALES, AND FEMALES			
Ages	All Students	Males	Females
12 and under	13.1%	19.8%	7.3%
13–14 years	43.3%	46.6%	40.4%
15 years and older	43.6%	33.6%	52.3%

VOLUNTARY OR FORCED SEX REPORTED BY MALE AND FEMALE STUDENTS

Forced Sex	All Students	Males	Females
Forced	3.5%	2.2%	4.6%
Pressured	13.3%	4.4%	21.2%
Both wanted	81.1%	91.1%	72.2%
Pressured partner	1.0%	.7%	1.3%

RELATIONSHIP WITH PARTNER AT FIRST SEX AS REPORTED BY ALL STUDENTS, MALES, AND FEMALES

Relationship with partner	All Students	Males	Females
Spouse	1.4%	3.0%	——
Fiancee	2.5%	.8%	1.3%
Steady	54.4%	43.6%	63.8%
Dating	13.7%	18.8%	9.2%
Knew well	12.6%	14.3%	11.2%
Just met	11.6%	12.8%	11.2%
Stranger	5.3%	7.3%	3.3%

STUDENT REPORTS OF LOCATION OF FIRST SEX

Where had sex *first time*?	All Students	Males	Females
Own home	20.4%	18.7%	21.9%
Partner's home	36.8%	35.8%	37.7%
Friend's home	17.5%	17.2%	17.9%
Somewhere else	25.3%	28.4%	22.5%

TOTAL NUMBER OF SEXUAL PARTNERS FOR ALL STUDENTS, MALES, AND FEMALES			
Total number of *sexual partners*	All Students	Males	Females
One	50.2%	44.3%	55.2%
Two	14.7%	13.0%	16.2%
Three	15.4%	16.0%	14.9%
Four	6.7%	8.4%	5.2%
Five or more	13.0%	18.3%	8.4%

A recent *Los Angeles Times* article, "Talking to Teens about Sex—It's in the Details," further documents the practice of sexual activity among teenagers. Fifty-five percent of fourteen- to nineteen-year-old males said they had had vaginal sex. Two-thirds of these males reported having engaged in oral sex, heterosexual anal intercourse, and/or masturbation by a female.[2]

The National Longitudinal Study of Adolescent Health states, "Seventeen percent of seventh- and eighth-graders report having had sexual intercourse. Among adolescents in high school, the figure is almost three times as high (49.3 percent). . . . Males and females in the seventh–twelfth grade report having had intercourse just about equally: 39.9 percent of boys, 37.3 percent of girls."[3]

Consider these additional statistics reflecting the current level of premarital sex among our youth:

◆ The 1995 Youth Risk Surveillance System Survey showed that 53 percent of this nation's high school students were sexually active.[4]
◆ One study reported that almost one-third of ninth grade girls had had sex at least once.[5]
◆ Another study reported that 25 percent of all ninth grade students were already involved in sexual intercourse.[6]
◆ According to a March 1, 1997, article in the *Los Angeles Times*, "56 percent of girls and 73 percent of boys have had intercourse by the age of eighteen. The average teen is sexually active for about eight years before marrying."[7]

◆ Although the world average for the onset of sexual intercourse is 17.6 years, the United States has the earliest average, at 16.2 years.[8]

◆ In Baltimore's public schools, the median age of first sexual intercourse is 13.5 years for girls, 12.5 years for boys.[9]

A study was conducted at Southern Baptist Carson-Newman College and reported to the Southern Baptist Ethics Conference in 1992. The following is the percent of students at the college reporting premarital intercourse over a seven-year period (1984–1991). For males, premarital sexual intercourse increased from 55 percent in 1984 to 70 percent in 1991. For the females, the change was even more dramatic. Only 27 percent of the females admitted that they had engaged in premarital intercourse in 1984, but 53 percent in 1991 said they were sexually experienced. In the most recent data collected (fall semester 1991), 66 percent of the males and 65 percent of the females said that they had experienced premarital sexual intercourse.[10]

Notice the increase of sexual activity in older teenage women since the seventies:

Though there has been a slight drop recently, rates of sexual intercourse among U.S. teens have increased dramatically in the last few decades. Between 1971 and 1988, the proportion of sexually active adolescents and young women ages fifteen to nineteen with "more than one lifetime sexual partner increased nearly 60 percent. In the United States, nearly 70 percent of students in the twelfth grade have had sexual intercourse, and 27 percent of twelfth-grade students have had four or more sex-

PERCENT OF WOMEN 15–19 WHO HAVE HAD PREMARITAL SEX[11]	
Years	Percentages
1971	31.7
1976	39.0
1982	45.2
1988	52.6
1995	49.6

ual partners. . . . A 1992 survey of 2,248 students in grades six, eight, and ten, from an urban public school district found that 28 percent of sixth-graders and half of eighth-graders reported having had sexual intercourse."[12]

One in seven sexually experienced high school girls surveyed by the CDC reported having four or more lifetime partners, and the number of lifetime partners has been shown to be strongly associated with risk of STDs (sexually transmitted diseases). A teen is in even greater jeopardy of acquiring an STD if her first intercourse occurred at an earlier age, her pattern of partner selection is poor, or she uses drugs or alcohol.[13]

In another study, 17 percent of seventh and eighth graders report having had sexual intercourse. Among adolescents in high school, the figure is almost three times as high at 49.3 percent. Males and females in the seventh through twelfth grades report having had intercourse just about equally: 39.9 percent of boys, 37.3 percent of girls. Teens living in the South and rural areas, and teens whose parents receive welfare were most likely to have experienced sexual intercourse. Of girls who are sexually experienced, 11.8 percent of younger teens and 19.4 percent of older teens report having been pregnant.[14]

The Institute for American Values conducted a nationwide study of one thousand college women over a period of eighteen months. The findings show that many college women prefer to "hook up" rather than to date. Hooking up is a new phenomenon in many universities. Hook-ups are defined as physical encounters ranging from kissing to sexual intercourse without emotional involvement or any kind of commitment. Both participants expect nothing further after the encounter. The ambiguity of the phrase hooking up and the zero commitment are part of the reason for its popularity. "Saying we've hooked up allows women to be vague about the nature of the physical encounter while stating that it happened."[15]

Teen sexual activity is highly associated with other health risk factors. Compared with students who never had intercourse, those who reported ever being pregnant or getting someone pregnant were

- twelve times more likely to have been treated for a suicide injury;
- ten times more likely to have been treated for a fight injury;
- five times more likely to have driven drunk;
- three times more likely to binge drink.[16]

I'm not rolling out these statistics to make our kids look bad or to attack their behavior. Our young people don't need our condemnation; they need our forgiveness and love. This is why, wherever I go today, one of my most important talks for young people is on self-image. I tell them, "In God's eyes, you are special!" And within the context of our love and acceptance, our kids need reasons to wait. It's not enough to tell them "no sex"; we must lovingly and clearly share with them why.

A SMALL BUT POSITIVE TREND AMONG YOUTH TO WAIT

In the midst of the alarming statistics about teenage premarital sex, there are some hopeful signs. A 1995 national survey found that 50 percent of young women fifteen to nineteen years of age had experienced intercourse, the first decline ever recorded by the periodic survey.[17] Additional research indicates a similar trend for teenage males. The percentage of never-married males age fifteen to nineteen who had experienced sexual intercourse declined from 60 percent in 1988 to 55 percent in 1995, reversing a trend measured since 1979.[18]

Another study of teens showed that 44 percent had made a conscious decision to delay intercourse; 76 percent had a friend or close acquaintance who had made this decision; 74 percent said that among their peers "it is considered a good thing to decide to remain a virgin."[19] According to the Centers for Disease Control and Prevention, "The latest data show that nearly 52 percent of high school students are still virgins."[20]

Since 1991 the number of teens who have had intercourse has dropped from 54 percent to 48 percent, according to the Centers for Disease Control, and teen pregnancy is down slightly as well. Abstinence initiatives are now commonplace around the country. In the last two years, the federal government and various states have cofunded 698 new programs, which are clearly making inroads. "Project Reality," an Illinois-based abstinence group, recently asked 10,000 teenagers the question, "Can sexual urges be controlled?" Fifty-one percent said "always"; just 3.5 percent said "never."[21]

The number of teens in high schools across the country who are virgins has been increasing since 1990. Today approximately 52 percent of teens in high schools are still virgins. Another 13 percent have not had sex in the past three months and are not considered to be sexually active.[22] A decline in teen pregnancies has also occurred during the same period. Pregnancy rates for teenagers have decreased 17 percent from 1990, and abortion rates have dropped by 31 percent since 1986.[23] This information should encourage and support policy makers and parents who believe that adolescents can understand and respond to messages about abstinence and marriage.

In a nationwide study of 1,000 college women, 39 percent said "they have not had sexual intercourse"; that is, they have remained virgins.[24]

In a recent report, the government's National Center for Health Statistics said the teen pregnancy rate for females aged fifteen to nineteen declined 19 percent from 1991 to 1997, the most recent year for which data are available. That trend reversed an 11 percent increase in teen pregnancies from 1986 to 1991.

The report says that most pregnant teens are eighteen or nineteen years old—40 percent are seventeen or younger. More than three-fourths of all teen pregnancies are unintended and out of wedlock. More than half of the pregnancies result in birth, and very few of those babies are put up for adoption. Of the rest, 30 percent are terminated by abortion; 14 percent end in miscarriage.[25]

The most recent trends show the overall birthrate to teens aged fifteen to nineteen declined by 18 percent from 1991 to 1998 and teen birthrates have fallen in every state and across ethnic and racial groups. In 1998, for girls aged fifteen to seventeen, the birthrate of thirty births for every 1,000 was a record low. In addition, pregnancy rates for this group are at the lowest level since 1976, the earliest year for which such data are available. For fifteen to nineteen year olds, the pregnancy rate decreased by approximately 15 percent between 1991 and 1996 (the latest year available). The abortion rate declined by 22 percent over the same period and the share of pregnancies ending in abortion fell. Similarly, repeat births among teens declined by 21 percent from 1991 to 1998, when nearly 18 percent of teen mothers had a second child.[26]

At least one poll found that, regarding sexual matters, the majority of the more than 1,000 teens questioned held conservative opinions.

- Almost half said that sex before marriage is "always wrong" (53 percent of girls, 41 percent of boys).
- Fifty-eight percent of boys and 47 percent of girls said that homosexuality is "always wrong."
- Fewer than 25 percent admitted to ever having had sex, but 71 percent said "a lot" or "some" of their peers were sexually active.[27]

The following findings come from 18,462 high school students aged fifteen to seventeen who voluntarily participated in the 1999 Oregon Youth Behavior Survey, a study conducted by the Oregon Health Division. Here are a couple of interesting highlights:

- Sexual abstinence among teens is increasing. Nearly two-thirds (65 percent) of students surveyed said they have not yet had sexual intercourse. In 1991, 54 percent of students surveyed reported never having intercourse.
- More students would advise others to wait. Seventy-three percent of survey respondents would advise classmates to postpone sexual intercourse until they are older or married. In 1995, 62 percent of survey respondents said they would give postponement advice.[28]

A recent survey of teens, published in the May 1998 issue of *YM (Young and Modern)*, revealed the pleasantly surprising results that many teens are indeed learning to say no to premarital sex. Sixty-eight percent of the teens surveyed said they were virgins. Eighty-seven percent of the girls said that, among their closest peers, being a virgin is admired, and 62 percent of the boys said the same. Most encouraging of the survey's results was the fact that 44 percent of the teens said they had made a conscious decision to delay intercourse until they are "majorly in love or married."[29]

We would much prefer that "majorly in love" had been omitted from the statement. But even as it stands, the statement indicates that teens are at least re-thinking the free-love philosophy that has prevailed over the last generation. As responsible parents, pastors, teachers, and youth workers, we need to come alongside our young people and help them move even further away from the dangerous "anything goes" view in our culture and bring them back into line with God's best for their lives.

REASONS FOR THE TREND TO WAIT

What are the reasons for the slight decline in premarital sex? There are many. In a survey of college-age men and women, all virgins, respondents gave four basic reasons they had not engaged in sexual relations. They were:

- ◆ too early in the relationship (22 percent of women, 14 percent of men)
- ◆ moral or religious reasons (31 percent of women, 11 percent of men)
- ◆ fear of pregnancy (almost 50 percent of both men and women)
- ◆ partner wasn't willing (11 percent of women, 64 percent of men)

In addition, many of the women interviewed indicated "lack of a loving or committed relationship" as a major reason for abstaining from sex, while a large number of both male and female participants said "they had not yet met the 'right' person." However, those who had abstained from sex solely because they felt they had not yet met the right person were less likely to feel good about their virginity than those who maintained their virginity for moral or religious reasons. "Both male and female virgins who were satisfied with their sexual status reported greater religious commitment than did virgins who were frustrated by their sexual status." None of the virgins indicated they abstained from sexual intercourse be-cause of lack of sexual desire, which "belies the stereotype of the 'frigid' virgin."[30]

According to one study, "Half of the teens surveyed (50 percent) said that fear of pregnancy and STDs is the main reason why teens don't have sex. . . . One quarter of teens surveyed (26 percent) said the main reason why teens don't have sex is because of religion, morals, and values."[31]

The following statistical study reveals an even greater breakdown of reasons students give for abstinence. The numbers in parentheses represent the rank order of the reasons given.

REASONS FOR BEING A VIRGIN[32]			
Reason	Total Sample (289 polled)	Virgin Men (97 polled)	Virgin Women (192 polled)
I have not been in a relationship long enough or been in love enough.	3.21(1)	2.78(1)	3.43(1)
Fear of Pregnancy	3.00(2)	2.66(2)	3.16(2)
I worry about contacting AIDS.	2.84(3)	2.59(3)	2.96(3)
I worry about contracting another STD.	2.73(4)	2.53(4)	2.83(6)
I have not met a person I wanted to have intercourse with.	2.61(5)	2.00(9)	2.91(4)
I do not feel ready to have premarital intercourse.	2.60(6)	2.12(7)	2.84(5)
It is against my religious beliefs.	2.13(7)	2.02(10)	2.18(8)
I believe that intercourse before marriage is wrong.	2.09(8)	1.91(11)	2.18(7)
I have been too shy or embarrassed to initiate sex with a partner.	2.06(9)	2.39(5)	1.89(11)
Fear or parental disapproval	2.02(10)	1.73(12)	2.17(9)
I don't feel physically attractive or desirable.	1.96(11)	1.98(8)	1.96(10)
My current (or last) partner is (was) not willing.	1.85(12)	2.24(6)	1.65(12)
I lack desire for sex.	1.33(13)	1.31(13)	1.35(13)

Hearts Broken, Hopes Shattered

Before you break out the sparkling cider and toast the demise of the sexual revolution, be aware that the promising trend is still quite small. While we are encouraged that the abstinence message has made some headway among our youth, we are not out of the woods by any means.

A few more may be waiting, but those who choose not to wait are yet in peril of the physical, emotional, spiritual, and relational dangers of premarital sex. For example, the National Campaign to Prevent Teen Pregnancy recently reported: "While the percentage of high schoolers who say they've had sexual intercourse is falling (55 percent in 1999, compared to 68 percent in 1995), more are catching sexually transmitted diseases, especially gonorrhea and chlamydia."[33] In other words, the declining rates of premarital sex among youth are not good news to those who do not wait—and pay the consequences.

Without solid reasons to wait, too many of our young people are still plunging headlong into sexual activity unaware of the harvest of pain and heartache they will reap. Many of them started out like Derek and Annie, whose stories opened this chapter. They had been told that premarital sex is wrong, but they struggled to understand *why* true love waits. So they eventually gave in and found their answers the hard way.

The effects of premarital sex can be detrimental. I talk to the victims everywhere I go. These students are crying out because they are hurt, disillusioned, and despairing after premarital sex. My heart breaks for them and for the countless numbers of students who, like Derek and Annie, are yet teetering on the precipice, needing answers to the driving question, Why should true love wait?

Look into the pain-filled hearts of several young people who have intimately shared with me the emotional pain they have suffered after deciding not to wait for sex until marriage. The poignant comments below can be multiplied by literally thousands of students who have written our ministry to express similar heartbreaking experiences with premarital sex:

> Premarital sex gave me fear as a gift . . . and shame to wear as a garment. It stole my peace of mind and robbed me of hope in a bright future. Sex smashed my concentration in class to smithereens. My desire for church activities was ground to a pulp. It made crumbs of the trust I had known in Christ . . . and in men and women. Sex gave me a jagged tear in my heart that even now, seven years later, is still healing.

◆ ◆ ◆

Dear Mr. McDowell,

Can you help me? I'm thirteen and I've just ruined my life. I thought Mike really loved me, but last night we had sex for the first time and this morning he told my girlfriend that he didn't want to see me anymore. I thought giving Mike what he wanted would make him happy and he'd love me more. What if I'm pregnant? What am I going to do? I feel so alone and confused. . . . I can't talk to my parents, so could you please write me back and help me. I don't know how I can go on.

◆ ◆ ◆

Having premarital sex was the most horrifying experience of my life. It wasn't at all the emotionally satisfying or the casually taken experience the world perceives it to be. I felt as if my insides were being exposed and my heart left unattended.

◆ ◆ ◆

It's not a pretty picture. It's not a TV soap opera either. The reality of pregnancy outside of marriage is scary and lonely. To have premarital sex was my choice one hot June night, forcing many decisions I thought I would never have to make. Those decisions radically changed my life.

◆ ◆ ◆

It took losing my virginity at a very young age, losing my self-respect and possibly my fertility, helping to ruin another person's marriage and family life, acquiring a non-curable virus, not getting the fulfillment that sex should provide in marriage, and living with the guilt that Satan always tries to make me feel . . . for me to realize how detrimental sex before marriage can really be.

◆ ◆ ◆

I love him. He said he loved me too. But after we did it, he called me all sorts of names and left me. The reason I am writing is, I don't understand this. We went together for months and I thought we had something special . . . I really need help. I have this feeling that no one cares about me, and no matter what I do I am not able to make any man happy. If it's not too much trouble, could you write me back and tell me what to do? I'd appreciate it.

◆ ◆ ◆

The reason I'm writing this is I'm alone and confused. My boyfriend kept pursuing me for sex . . . I had sex with him thinking that I owed it to him. . . . Later when I learned I was pregnant he blew up, said to get an abortion, and that it was all my fault. So, to save my parents heartache and to keep Matt, I had an abortion. Now Matt has left me. . . . How can God love me after all I have done?

Could you please write back? I'm just so confused. Can God really love and forgive me?

◆ ◆ ◆

It's so hard sometimes—like last week, when I was over at Bill's, and his roommate Tom started talking to me again. He knows Bill and I haven't slept together, and he's basically told me I'm too Victorian. But what really hurt was his accusation that there's something wrong with anyone who doesn't want to have sex before marriage. I didn't know what to say.

The following student told her story in the third person. Consider the heartache she felt when her lips said yes as her heart was saying no:

She was extremely young, but she didn't feel young. It seemed like such a mature jump . . . from the immature age of twelve to the much more exciting, official-teenager age of thirteen. She really loved being and "acting" older. She thought everything was great!

She was an honor student and was also very involved in extracurricular activities. She loved to do things and share deep, dark secrets with her best friend. She had a good family and her parents taught her well the difference between right and wrong. She was sensible and had a good head on her shoulders . . . so it seemed.

He was older than she and extremely popular. He was very talented and was always the center of attention. She was overwhelmed with joy when he started to pay special attention to her. She was so pleased when he picked her as a girlfriend, rather than any of the other girls who would have died for the chance.

One day he told her, "I love you." But she had nothing to say in return. She did not love him, yet she adored the popularity he gained for her. She was blinded by the new attention she received from that newly discovered "popularity." Everyone said "Hi" to her. Everyone wanted to know her.

He asked her if he could express his love to her. She said she wasn't ready. He said, "I love you." She did not reply.

Later he told her something had happened. He said he showed his "love" to someone else. She said it was all right. He said, "I love you." She was naive. She looked down and said nothing.

She had never had so many friends before. So many people wanted to talk to her. In fact, she noticed that boys were paying a lot more attention to her. But, she stayed with him . . . because he loved her.

Then he told her it had happened again. He showed "love" to someone else, yet he did not really love that someone else. He even told her who the girl was. She looked away. She felt threatened. But he told her, "I love you." She looked down and quietly replied the same. He told her to show her love for him. She didn't want to, but she didn't want to lose him to someone else. So she "showed her love."

She was violated. She was innocent no longer. She broke up with him. He asked her to take him back. He told her, "I love you." But she rejected him.

A few days later, he was "in love" with someone else. She was impure and unwholesome. She was used. She was drowned with shame. She was swallowed up by guilt. She was very alone.

She is afraid to love ever again. She is afraid to ever be loved again. She knows she can never change the past. She has stained her life . . . a stain that will never come out.

She was extremely young. She finally realized how young.

This girl no longer needs answers to the why wait question. What she does need is an understanding of God's cleansing forgiveness and grace.

"If Only I Had Waited"

She is not the only young person to regret her decision to become involved in premarital sex. A number of studies and surveys have uncovered widespread remorse and regret among students who decided not to wait for sex.

- Sixty-three percent of teens surveyed who have had sexual intercourse wish they had waited longer. More than one-half of teen boys (55 percent) and the overwhelming majority of teen girls surveyed (72 percent) said they wish they had waited longer to have sex.[34]
- Nearly two-thirds of teens who have had sexual intercourse wish they had waited, according to a poll released by the National Campaign to Prevent Teen Pregnancy.[35]
- Nearly eight out of ten teens surveyed (78 percent) agreed that teens should not be sexually active.[36]
- In a study of 1,228 parochial school students, nearly half wished they had waited longer before having sex, especially females and the more religious students.[37]
- According to a report titled "Teenagers Under Pressure," 76 percent of

girls and 58 percent of boys agreed that the most common reason for teenagers to initiate sex is because the boys want it. The report also said that 81 percent of the teenage girls who had sex said they wish they had waited until they were older, and 60 percent of the boys said they hadn't been mature enough.[38]

◆ One study found that "84 percent of girls age sixteen or younger want to learn how to say no without hurting the other person's feelings."[39]

◆ A 1994 poll by ICR Survey Research Group for *USA Weekend* asked more than 1,200 teens and adults what they thought of "several high profile athletes [who] are saying in public that they have abstained from sex before marriage and are telling teens to do the same." Seventy-two percent of the twelve- to seventeen-year-olds and 78 percent of the adults said that they agree with the pro-abstinence message. Moreover, 44 percent of those under the age of eighteen agreed that "today's teenagers hear too little about saying no to sex."[40]

STUDENT REPORTS OF WISHING THEY HAD WAITED LONGER FOR SEX[41]			
Wish waited longer for sex	All students	Males	Females
No	57.3%	72.2%	44.5%
Yes	42.7%	27.8%	55.5%

On the television news program *Prime Time America* in 1992, Diane Sawyer interviewed a number of teenage girls who had been sexually active and had gotten pregnant. At the close of the segment, Sawyer asked a penetrating question to each girl: "If you had it to do all over again . . . let's say, starting right now, you'd never been with a boy at all, how long would you wait?" Here are the answers she received:

Christy: "Till I got married."

◆ ◆ ◆

Brandy: "Uh-huh" (agreeing with Christy).

◆ ◆ ◆

Andrea: "Till I got married."

◆ ◆ ◆

Bethany: "I think I would be better off if I was still a virgin."[42]

You can feel the regret in the words of this young man, who shared his story with me.

If only I had waited. I see now how uncluttered my life would have been, how my mind would have been free from this burden that besets me even years later.

If you want to know what it is really like, get two pieces of paper and glue part of one to the other. After it has dried, pull them apart. What you have in your hands is a vivid picture of two people after a premarital sexual relationship—both torn, both leaving a part of themselves with the other.

All my relationships had two things in common: one was we made love a lot, and the other was that they always ended and I always went through (and am still going through) incredible pain. I don't know if the breakups were because God didn't want us having sex or because of other reasons, but they hurt worse than anything ever has.

I finally got this girl into bed (actually it was in a car) when I was seventeen. I thought I was the hottest thing there was, but then she started saying she loved me and started getting clingy. I figured out that there had probably been a dozen guys before me who thought they had "conquered" her, but who were really just objects of her need for security. This took all the wind out of my sails. Worse yet, I couldn't respect someone who gave in as easy as she did, and I was amazed to find that after four weeks of sex as often as I wanted, I was tired of her. I didn't see any point in continuing the relationship. I finally dumped her, which made me feel even worse, because even I could see she was hurting. At least one of her parents was an alcoholic (maybe both were) and her home life was a disaster, and just when she thought she could hold on to someone, I ditched her. I didn't feel very cool after that. I felt pretty low.

I gave no thought to what I would tell my future wife about those months when my girlfriend and I engaged in all the pleasures of the marriage bed with none of the commitment. A wife was a nebulous figure in the far-off future, not a person with feelings or someone who would care that I had been intimate with anyone besides her.[43]

Perhaps this man could have saved himself and his partner a lifetime of pain and regret if someone had only provided him with good reasons to wait.

After hearing me speak about waiting for sex, a young man at a university told me, "What you said really hit me. If I could have just one wish in life, it would be for me to be twelve years old again and hear this same lecture. I have made some wrong decisions and now I'm feeling pain from my choices."

Somehow we have to get the word to these young people before they scar their lives with behavior they will regret for a lifetime.

Searching for Reasons to Wait

Month by month and year by year, I hear young people expressing their confusion about premarital sex. Most of them, like Derek and Annie at the opening of this chapter, are Christians who attend church, read their Bibles, pray, and share their faith. And most of them know that sex before marriage is wrong, but they don't know *why* it's wrong. They understand that God says no, but they don't know *why* he says no. "I was looking for reasons not to have premarital sex," confesses Michael, a university student, "and I didn't receive answers."

A coed writes, "I knew [premarital sex] wasn't 'right' but I never knew why."

After interviewing thousands of young people, I am convinced that many teens and young singles are sexually active, not because they really want to be, or don't know how to say no, but because they don't have any deep personal reasons for waiting until they are married. Listen to the cry of the following students who struggle with how and why to say no to premarital sex:

I had been told all my life that sex before marriage was wrong, but no one ever told me why. In the twelfth grade I found myself dating one boy for a long period of time. We spent a lot of time alone, and as a result our relationship became more physical. I felt guilty, bitter, frustrated, and dirty. Because of those feelings, I would say to him, "We need to stop having sex, or at least slow down." Well, we tried to slow down, but that didn't work. Instead of getting closer, we grew further apart. After two years of dating I finally said, "No more sex," and he said, "Good-bye." Since then, whenever I dated another person for a length of time, sex became a part of the relationship. Tears always came because I knew I had blown it again.

◆ ◆ ◆

I had already achieved the impossible. I was almost eighteen and I was still a virgin. I had just never wanted to "do it." . . . I was very much in love, or thought I was, with a dashing college man, and from time to time he would mention that he had never dated a girl who said no as many times as I had. After a while, my resolve weakened, and since I had no reason to say no, I decided that I would do it to show how much I loved him. I didn't really want to, but in my own mind I couldn't rationalize not having sex. I gave in to pressure because saying yes was easier than saying no and trying to explain why not.

◆ ◆ ◆

I feel like sex is OK as long as you don't get pregnant, but if you get pregnant, then you should get married to the guy. I disagree with the statement that a person should wait until marriage to engage in sex. My question is, Why? I know God will show me, but I have a real hard time getting it all straight. Sometimes when I get to the point where I want sex, I run to this certain guy. Most of the time it's not his fault but mine that we have sex. I really love this guy and I pray that I marry him, but I want it to be OK in God's eyes. Why isn't it?

Our young people desperately need to know more than just the difference between right and wrong. They need to know and understand why right is right and wrong is wrong. They clearly need and want more information, especially on the *why* of sexual relationships rather than the *how*. They need those reasons now. One of my major concerns is the urgency behind these cries for help. How many more beautiful lives will be damaged if we fail to provide our young people with "Why Wait?" answers—and soon?

If our kids are going to be able to say no to sexual pressure, they need to know more than Bible verses like 1 Thessalonians 4:3 ("abstain from sexual immorality," NASB). They need to understand that God's precepts are in their best interests and the best interests of those they love. As parents, youth leaders, pastors, and teachers, we must equip ourselves with solid answers to the question of *why* true love waits, and equip ourselves to provide young people with down-to-earth answers that make sense spiritually, socially, psychologically, emotionally, and physically.

The so-called sexual revolution of recent decades has created a dangerous moral precipice from which many are falling to destruction. We must do more than just erect a barbed wire fence at the top of the cliff or put a fleet of ambulances at the bottom to care for the wounded. *We must keep our young people away from the cliff in the first place.* To do so requires that we flood their lives with the truth about morality, for truth will help buoy them up and destroy the very foundations of the sexual revolution.

Youth Want to Know

Our church young people are not immune to the dire problems incurred by those who dabble in premarital sex. On the contrary, many of them are included in the stories and statistics in this book. When it comes to our kids and premarital sex, their church attendance seems to have limited value as a deterrent.

How do we adequately refute this "get-it-now" approach? If sex is truly satisfying—and it can be—why should adolescents wait to enjoy it? Why shouldn't the young in heart and body explore this fascinating dimension of their humanness as soon as they feel the "urge to merge"? How do we tell students like Derek and Michelle, Annie and Jeff to buck the trend and save sex until marriage, especially when no one else seems to be waiting?

The why wait question demands a forthright and complete answer. We cannot afford simply to tell our young people no and try to deal with sex as a negative.

I have found that most adolescents don't know the biblical basis for waiting until marriage for sex. They don't know the whys of their moral beliefs. And a generation without moral conviction will crumble under the pressures of a secular worldview. Consequently, when they face the tremendous temptations to give in to their sexual drives, they lack the necessary foundation for the conviction to abstain. They are ignorant of the devastating emotional, physical, relational, and medical reasons to wait. *We must equip them with that foundation. We must give them the answers they need!*

A while back I ran into an old friend who shared an interesting story. She had begun teaching eighth-grade girls in her local evangelical Bible church. "Several weeks ago I had seven of them over to the house for a sleepover. Just before everyone went to bed I asked them, 'How many of you plan on being a virgin when you get married?' Not one of them said yes. Finally one girl spoke up and asked, 'How many of us are virgins?' They all were. That night I went to bed in turmoil, wondering what to do."

The next morning my friend asked the girls to watch one of our ministry's videos that documents the many possible painful consequences of getting involved in premarital sex. The video also provides solid reasons for saving sex for marriage. After watching and discussing the program with the girls, she again asked, "How many of you now intend to wait until marriage for sex?" This time all seven said they did.

Before leaving, one of them came back to thank her. She said, "Mrs. Duke, no one ever gave us any reasons for waiting."

For the first time in my memory, teenagers are seeking solid reasons for waiting. In a study done in the Atlanta, Georgia, school system, students were asked what they wanted most in a sex-education program. The overwhelming majority answered, "How to say no to physical involvement."

The stories and statistics in this chapter vividly illustrate why I feel the need to address this issue. Parent, pastor, youth leader, or teacher, your young people are asking, "Why wait for sex?" They want to know why they should save sex for marriage and how they can say no in the meantime. If you don't tell them, where will they get the answers?

This book has the answers you can and must share with your young people.

In part 2, we will detail and document the many reasons kids become sexually involved today. If you don't know what motivates them to participate in premarital sex, you will be ill-prepared to help them say no to it.

In part 3, we will lay out the reasons why true love waits for sex until marriage. These reasons are biblically based and relevant to your kids. This section will give you the insights you need for combating the immorality and permissiveness that engulf this generation.

In part 4, you will learn practical, proven steps for helping your young people say no to premarital sex and instead, choose to save themselves for marriage. You're reading this book, so you obviously want to become more involved in their lives and their decisions regarding their sexuality. Part 4 will equip you for that involvement.

◆   ◆   ◆

But first we must count the cost of adolescent premarital sex to our young people. Encouraging and helping them to wait for sex until marriage is not just a biblical issue. It is also a serious health issue. Sexually active kids are playing with a live hand grenade. Every encounter of casual sex places them at great risk physically, emotionally, and relationally. By answering their why wait questions you will do more than satisfy their curiosity. Your timely intervention on the matter of premarital sex could possibly save their lives.

CHAPTER 2

ADOLESCENT PREMARITAL SEX

THE HIGH COST TO YOUTH

A MAN IS SITTING in the family room watching the evening news when his teenage son walks in. "Hey, Dad," the kid says, "do you know anything about Russian roulette?"

"Russian roulette?" the dad says casually. "You mean where someone loads a revolver with only one bullet, spins the cylinder, lifts the barrel to his head, and pulls the trigger?"

"Yeah, that's what I'm talking about," the kid says, excited.

"Sure, I've heard of Russian roulette," the dad acknowledges, glancing between his son and the TV. "What about it?"

The boy explains. "Well, all the guys at school are talking about it. They think playing Russian roulette is really cool . . . and I agree with them."

The dad looks back at his son with a knowing smile. "You've played Russian roulette, then, have you, Son?"

"Yeah, with the guys—four times this week already," the kid says, nodding vigorously.

"How many guys?" Dad inquires.

"Well, there *were* five of us," the boy explains, "but Zack goofed up. I'm really going to miss him."

"Yes, I kind of liked Zack," Dad puts in.

The kid hurries on. "Dad, I get such a rush when I squeeze the trigger!"

"I've heard there's nothing quite like it," Dad says.

"And it only gets better when you start putting more bullets into the cylinder."

Dad nods with interest. "Oh, you're up to two bullets already?"

"Naw, that's for babies," the boy says. "I'm up to three, and next week I think I'll try four."

"You mean you're going to fill four of the six chambers of the gun and play Russian roulette?"

"Doesn't that sound exciting, Dad?" the kid says with a laugh.

Dad studies him for a moment. "Well, Son, it's great to see you having so much fun, but . . ." His voice trails off.

"But what, Dad?" the boy asks with concern.

Dad grips the boy by the shoulder. "Well, I just want you to be careful, Son. Russian roulette can be dangerous if you're not careful. Don't forget about Zack."

"No problem, Dad. I'll be real careful. It won't happen to me."

"Great!" Dad says with pleasure. "I knew I could count on you. I'm glad we had this little talk together."

"Me too, Dad," the kid says, leaving the room. "Good night."

"Good night, Son."

I tell this ludicrous story to make a point. What would you think of a parent with such a careless attitude toward his child's involvement in a potentially deadly "hobby"? It is unthinkable that any parent with an ounce of intelligence or compassion would condone such an activity with a blasé, "Be careful, Son." Being careful won't do it. If that was your child, you would forbid him from playing that game even once more. And you would do whatever you could to separate your child from that gun and any friends who were influencing him to play Russian roulette. Why? Because you know that just one pull of the trigger can be fatal.

This is the reality of premarital sex among our young people. It may be thrilling and exciting to them. But every casual sexual encounter is like a game of Russian roulette, and increasing the frequency or the number of partners is like adding more bullets to the cylinder. I'm not saying that dabbling in casual sex will kill a young person, although the possibility of contracting a potentially fatal disease is always present. But young people don't come away from a sexual experience unscathed either physically, emotionally, spiritually, or relationally. It's as sure as playing Russian roulette with a bullet in every chamber. If they pull the trigger, they will get hurt in some way.

THE EXORBITANT COST FOR PREMARITAL SEX

Young people who get involved in premarital sex will pay a price—guaranteed. The consequences of guilt, pain, heartache, and possibly disease or death are too costly. But in the rush of passion, peer pressure, and temptation, our kids don't think about what their promiscuity will cost them. That's why we must thoroughly answer their questions about sex and proactively impress upon them God's reasons for waiting for sex until marriage.

One significant cost of premarital sex is the negative impact it has on a young person and his or her "lifetime partner"—the person or persons to whom he or she may make a lifetime commitment. Sadly, early sexual activity is linked to a tendency for unstable relationships with lifetime partners. A young person who begins sex at age sixteen has a greater than 80 percent chance of having more than one lifetime partner. Note in the following table that the younger the age at first intercourse, the less likely young people are to remain with one lifetime partner and the more likely they are to have multiple partners.

AGE AT FIRST INTERCOURSE AND LIFETIME PARTNERS[1]		
Age at First Intercourse	1 Lifetime Partner	2–5 Lifetime Partners
Under 16	11.3%	58.1%
16	18.6%	44.6%
17	17.35%	44.4%
18	26%	37%
19	37.6%	27.4%
20 or greater	52.2%	15.2%

Young people who wait for sex have a better chance of enjoying a lasting, fulfilling marriage than those who do not.

In the rest of this chapter I want to focus on two of the most exorbitant costs of premarital sex to our kids: (1) the threat of sexually transmitted diseases; and (2) the possibility of, and complications from, pregnancy. These are significant problems in our society, as anyone in the health field will verify. For example, the Medical Institute for Sexual Health (MISH) recently reported, "Approximately 12 million new cases of STDs occur annually, three million of them among teenagers. Each year, nearly one million teenagers become pregnant, about one-third of whom decide to abort their babies."[2] Since this report was released, the incidents of STDs have risen to 15 million a year.[3] We expect that the other figures are higher also.

Adolescent sexual activity is more prevalent than at any other time in American history. As a result, sex and its consequences have become a major health problem. Are our kids concerned about the high costs of STDs and pregnancy? Yes, but girls are significantly more concerned than boys, as reflected in the following survey results from the Kaiser Family Foundation:

CONCERNS ABOUT STDS AND PREGNANCY[4]		
How concerned are the *girls/boys* you know about . . .	Girls Percentage	Boys Percentage
HIV/AIDS	61	51
Other STDs	53	43
Getting pregnant	58	39

The study also revealed that "concerns about HIV, other STDs, and pregnancy do not increase with age, nor do they grow much as the level of sexual activity that a teen and his or her friends engage in increases."[5]

Yes, many young people are alert to the cost of premarital sex in the form of STDs and unwanted pregnancies. But do these potential outcomes deter kids from getting involved sexually? The answer is no, as documented in the previous chapter. Far too many young people are ignoring the imminent dangers of STDs and pregnancy for the momentary thrill of a sexual escapade. And our young people are paying a steep price long after the thrill has evaporated.

There are so many other costs of premarital sex to consider, and we will discuss them later in the book. But if STDs and pregnancy were the only dangers of premarital sex, they are reasons enough to do whatever it takes to get our kids to wait.

SEXUALLY TRANSMITTED DISEASES: THE COST OF INFECTION AND POSSIBLE DEATH

A young married man who isn't a Christian—I'll call him Kevin—came to see me. He knew that I was actively involved in warning young people and adults about the dangers and heartache of premarital sex. "Please keep telling people what you're telling them about sex," Kevin urged me. When I asked him why, he told me his sad story:

> I lived a pretty loose lifestyle when I was younger. I had plenty of casual sex with plenty of women. When herpes came on the scene, I knew I could never get rid of it if I got it. But it didn't really change my lifestyle. Fortunately, I never got it.
>
> Then a new strain of herpes started showing up. Nobody had heard much about it because it doesn't have any symptoms—no blisters or anything. But you can still pass it on. The one way you know for sure that you're infected is if you produce a child with a birth defect. But even that didn't change my lifestyle.
>
> Then AIDS came on the scene. That really got my attention. It's fatal. So I finally decided to change my lifestyle, stop the casual sex, fall in love, get married, and have children. So that's exactly what I did. Then my wife gave me herpes.

John has a similar story. Soon after he had sexual intercourse with his girlfriend, John noticed some small bumps on his penis. His doctor told him he had genital warts, caused by human papillomavirus (HPV), a sexually transmitted disease John had never heard of. Despite acid treatments, laser techniques, and excisional surgery, John still suffers from venereal warts and is concerned about developing cancer. He also fears that he will never be able to marry.[6]

Sad stories. Kevin and John and countless numbers of young men and women are still paying a high price for the promiscuity of their youth. They are the victims of an epidemic that is ravaging our population.

An Epidemic of Sexually Transmitted Diseases

One of the most destructive and permanent results of premarital sex is acquiring a sexually transmitted disease. During the past decade in North America there has been "an unprecedented STD epidemic, particularly in adolescent and young adult women."[7]

Consider the extent of this epidemic. Over 15 million people contract a new STD each year. One in four of these new infections occur in individuals under twenty years of age. Sixty-eight million Americans are currently infected with a sexually transmitted disease.[8]

According to a 1995 *Los Angeles Times* article, every year in America

- 1.1 million people are infected with gonorrhea;
- 500,000 new cases of genital warts occur (there are about 40 million cases overall);
- 100,000 to 200,000 Americans get hepatitis B;
- 120,000 cases of syphilis are diagnosed;
- about 450,000 new AIDS cases are reported;
- nearly 3 million Americans are infected with trichomoniasis.[9]

The U.S. Department of Health and Human Services reports that sexually transmitted diseases "affect more than 65 million people in the United States."[10]

A 1996 SIECUS report came up with another chart of statistics on the most common STDs. This estimate may vary somewhat from the previous list, but the numbers are just as sobering.

THE MOST COMMON STDS[11]		
STD	Annual Estimated Incidence	Curable?
Chlamydia	4 million	Yes
Trichomoniasis	3 million	Yes
PID	1 million	Yes
Gonorrhea	800,000	Yes
HPV or Genital Warts	500,000–1 million	No
Genital Herpes	200,000–500,000	No
Syphilis	101,000	Yes
HIV/AIDS	80,000	No

Five out of the ten common reportable infectious diseases in the United States are sexually transmitted diseases. The Centers for Disease Control (CDC) indicated that chlamydia is the most common reportable infectious disease in the United States. Gonorrhea ranked second and AIDS third. Syphilis and hepatitis B were also included in the top ten. These five STDs accounted for 87 percent of all cases of infections caused by the top ten infectious diseases found in this country.

Fifty percent of the cases of chlamydia reported by the CDC were in teenagers. Gonorrhea was the most commonly reported infectious disease among people fifteen to twenty-four years old. The more common diseases of herpes and HPV are not included in the list because they are not designated as reportable by the CDC.[12]

At least one person in four will contract an STD at some point in his or her life. *As many as 56 million American adults and teenagers are infected with an incurable STD.*[13] At least 24 million people are infected with human papillomavirus (HPV), or genital warts, and as many as one million new infections occur each year. HPV is associated with cervical and other genital and anal cancers.

While the dangers of HIV/AIDS are becoming more well-known, there are other dangers involved with less commonly known STDs. For example, the human herpes virus type 8 is associated with Kaposi's sarcoma, one of the most aggressive human cancers, and may eventually be found to cause it. Some studies are discovering that this particular virus is present in the semen of many men.[14]

P. D. Hitchcock, author of *AIDS Patient Care*, paints a graphic picture of the STD epidemic. He writes that the accumulation of incurable sexually transmitted infections in a population over time is analogous to a faucet dripping water into a beaker. Each infection is like a single drop of water. Not only do the incurable infections—herpes simplex virus (HSV), human papillomavirus (HPV), and human immunodeficiency virus (HIV)—accumulate in the population, so do untreated infections such as chlamydial infection. As the beaker fills up, a promiscuous individual's chances of encountering an infected partner increase.[15]

One student who wrote to me summarized the Russian roulette nature of sexual activity and STDs this way:

> If you have multiple sex partners or the person you sleep with is promiscuous, not only have you reduced the value of a human being to nothing, using sex only for pleasure, but you also open yourself up to many kinds of diseases. They may be bothersome or chronic or fatal, depending on what you get, but if you sleep around enough, you will probably get something.

What will the promiscuous individual get? Dr. John Diggs, M.D., medical consultant for the Family Research Council, has itemized many of the physical consequences of premarital sex, most of them related to sexually transmitted infections.

- Any of thirty different STDs
- Early funeral plans (cervical cancer, HIV, hepatitis B, hepatitis C, depression)
- Expensive medicines with severe side effects and high rates of allergic reaction
- $16,000 per year in medicines (HIV/AIDS)
- Depression
- Itching (crabs)
- Inability to climax (Antiorgasmia)
- Sterility
- Abortion
- Cryosurgery
- Proctitis
- Chronic joint pain (Reiter's syndrome)
- Need for antibiotics during pregnancy
- Painful intercourse (dyspareunia)
- Pregnancy
- Must tell future mate of sexual disease if you have an incurable STD
- Painful urination (urethral syndrome)
- Ugly warts requiring prolonged chemical or laser treatment
- Need for expensive infertility treatment
- Delayed parenthood
- Severe abdominal infection (Fitz-Hugh-Curtis syndrome)
- Recurring painful sores (genital herpes)
- Hospitalization for surgeries
- Other sexual dysfunction[16]

Consider the following statistics documenting the prevalence and danger of sexually transmitted diseases:

- Today more Americans are infected with sexually transmitted diseases (STDs) than at any other time in history.[17]
- There are as many as 45 million cases in just the U.S. of genital herpes.[18]

- The latest estimates indicate that there are 15 million new STD cases each year in the U.S., about half of which contract lifelong infections that are incurable.[19]
- An estimated 56 million Americans have an *incurable viral* STD other than HIV, such as genital herpes or human papillomavirus (HPV). That is more than one in five Americans.[20]
- Dr. W. Cates estimates that a staggering 65 million Americans have an incurable STD.[21]
- Worldwide, an estimated 333 million new cases of four curable STDs (gonorrhea, chlamydial infection, syphilis, and trichomoniasis) occurred among adults fifteen to forty-nine years of age in 1995.[22]
- An estimated one million Americans are infected with human immunodeficiency virus (HIV).[23]
- An estimated 5.5 million new infections occur each year with at least 20 million people currently infected.[24]
- *There is no single STD epidemic, but rather multiple epidemics.*[25]

Now let's narrow the focus and look at how STDs are specifically impacting the adolescent population. To get a better picture, come with me on an imaginary trip to the local mall, perhaps the largest one in your area. It's Saturday afternoon and the place is crawling with students aged fifteen to nineteen. Take a peek into the arcade. There are about forty kids pumping coins into the machines and whooping it up playing video games. Do you have the picture in mind? Now let me tell you something about these kids.

According to statistics, roughly half of them—twenty or so—are sexually active. They're either having sexual intercourse, practicing mutual masturbation and "outercourse," or performing oral sex. And the more they talk about their sexual exploits, the more pressure they bring on their peers who are not yet "doing it."

As you look at them, you probably can't tell which ones are already into sex. But imagine that you can. Imagine that the twenty standing on the left side of the arcade, both boys and girls, are sexually active. I have some especially alarming news about this group. Conservatively, five to six of them, whether they have discovered it yet or not, are already infected with a sexually transmitted disease. Eventually they will require medical treatment to cure or cope with the virus they have picked up, though some will have to deal with an incurable infection for the rest of their lives. One of them may even die as a result of his or her disease.

But before you begin to feel happy for the thirteen or fourteen uninfected kids hanging out with the infected kids, remember that they are also sexually active. Every time one of them sneaks off to have sex, he or she may do so with someone who is already infected. The more they continue to play sexual Russian roulette, the more likely they are to find the chamber with the bullet.

Anywhere we go in the mall, the numbers are about the same. Roughly half of the adolescents we see are having sex, and a quarter to a third of those are carrying a sexually transmitted disease. This realization may change how you look at the crowds of kids you see in your community, at the mall, around the schools, and in the youth group.

We are currently seeing an unprecedented outbreak of sexually transmitted diseases among American teenagers. The following facts break my heart. I trust that they motivate you to share the truth with your kids about the cost of premarital sex.

- The latest estimates indicate that there are 15 million new STD cases in the U.S. each year. Approximately one-fourth of these new infections are in teenagers.[26]
- Teens comprise about 10 percent of the population, but account for 25 percent of the STDs in America.[27]
- Three million teenagers—about one in four sexually experienced teenagers—acquire an STD every year. By the end of 1995, there were more than 2,300 teenagers diagnosed with AIDS.
- Young adults are the age group at greatest risk of acquiring an STD for a number of reasons: They are more likely to have multiple sexual partners; their partners may be at higher risk of being infected; female teenagers are more susceptible to cervical infections, such as gonorrhea and chlamydia, due to their cervical anatomy.[28]
- Teens are up to ten times more susceptible to pelvic inflammatory disease (PID) than adults.[29]
- Of all new HIV infections, 25 percent are found in those under the age of twenty-two.[30]
- More teenagers have chlamydia than any other age group.[31]
- Recent studies suggest that human papillomavirus (HPV), the most common STD among U.S. teens, is present in anywhere from 15 to 46 percent of these young people.[32]
- Of teens who have had sex, one out of every three will graduate from high

school with a diploma *and* a sexually transmitted disease. As many as 40 percent of our school enrollment have contracted serious infectious STDs.

- One in every four young people has already been infected with an STD by the age of twenty-one. The diseases vary from chlamydia to syphilis to gonorrhea.[33]
- Sixty-three percent of newly infected people are less than twenty-five years old.[34]
- Eighty-six percent of all STDs occur among persons aged fifteen to twenty-nine years.[35]
- STDs and AIDS rates are 2.5 times higher among females under age twenty than can be predicted from rates among males under age twenty.[36]
- Three out of five Americans living with HIV were infected as teens.
- Gonorrhea rose 13 percent among teens between 1997 and 1999, with teenage girls having the highest rate of any female age group.
- An estimated 3 million people contract chlamydia each year in the United States; 40 percent of cases occur in fifteen- to nineteen-year-olds.[37]
- Approximately two-thirds of people who acquire STDs in the United States are younger than twenty-five.[38]
- According to the Centers for Disease Control and the Kaiser Family Foundation, approximately 65 percent of all sexually transmitted infections contracted by Americans this year will occur in people under twenty-four. One in four new HIV infections occurs in people younger than twenty-two.[39]

Having multiple sex partners greatly increases the risk of contracting an STD. One study found that 75 percent of teenagers who initiate intercourse before age eighteen have two or more partners, and 45 percent have four or more partners. However, of those young people who postpone sex until age nineteen, only 20 percent have two or more partners in their twenties, and only one percent have four or more partners.[40]

The number of infected teens continues to spiral upward at an alarming rate. Dabbling in sex is like a game of Russian roulette. The cost is too high. We must show our kids how true love can wait.

Young Women at Greater Risk
Single and nineteen years old, Linda was experiencing severe pains in the lower left side of her abdomen. She went to a doctor, who found a huge pelvic mass

the size of a cantaloupe—a dilated, blocked fallopian tube, obstructed from a pelvic infection due to chlamydia or gonorrhea, and filled with pus and fluid. The fallopian tube was removed. Her other fallopian tube was scarred and, although it was microsurgically repaired, Linda has little chance of ever bearing children, a dream she had cherished for years. It was a heavy price to pay for her sexual experiences with multiple partners.[41]

This story touches me deeply because I have three daughters. Think about the adolescent girls in your family, youth group, congregation, or classroom. Most of them are sweet, innocent, and full of life. Like Linda, the exciting, fulfilling experiences of college, career, marriage, and mothering are yet ahead of them. But tragically, these young women stand to pay an especially high price for casual sex. Boys are more sexually active than girls. But due to their physical makeup, females are generally more susceptible to sexually transmitted diseases than young men. We must protect these precious girls and young women by encouraging them to wait for sex until marriage.

Allow the sobering facts about young women and STDs to sink in:

- For some STDs, e.g., chlamydia trachomatis, adolescent women have a physiologically increased susceptibility to infection due to increased cervical ectopy and lack of immunity.[42]
- Another review showed that adolescent women are biologically more susceptible to sexually transmitted disease because they have lower antibody levels and therefore are more likely to become infected with STDs.[43]
- Kathleen Ethier, a behavioral scientist in the CDC's division of STD prevention, points out that cells on the face of a girl's cervix are especially infection-prone. Also, she says that adolescent females tend to incur more trauma to the genital region during intercourse, making infection more likely after exposure to an STD bug.[44]
- Women are particularly vulnerable to STDs because they are . . . more likely to have asymptomatic infections that commonly result in delayed diagnosis and treatment.[45]
- Chlamydial infection has been consistently high among adolescents; in some studies, up to 30 to 40 percent of sexually active adolescent females studied have been infected.[46]
- According to the Institute of Medicine, "The cervix of female adoles-

cents and young women is especially susceptible to infection by certain sexually transmitted organisms."[47]

◆ Using data from the National Hospital Discharge Survey[48] from 1979 to 1988, more than 80,000 women between the ages of fifteen and twenty-four were admitted annually for pelvic inflammatory disease (PID). Current rates are estimated to be higher because of the rising level of sexual activity and rate of STDs among adolescents.[49]

◆ Cervical cancer rates are also increasing among young women, which may reflect an increased exposure to STDs such as human papillomavirus (HPV).[50]

◆ Certain types of sexually acquired human papillomavirus are now believed to cause nearly all cancer of the cervix, vagina, vulva, anus, and penis.[51]

◆ Nearly half of the female college students tested in one study had evidence of genital HPV.[52] A three-year survey at Rutgers University . . . found that 60 percent of female students had been infected with HPV.[53]

◆ A study reported in the *American Journal of Obstetrics and Gynecology* found that 38 percent of sexually active women, thirteen to twenty-one years of age, were already infected with HPV, an incurable viral infection that has been linked to certain cancers of the genital tract.[54]

◆ Approximately 16,000 new cases of cervical cancer are diagnosed each year, making cervical cancer the third most common reproductive tract cancer in women and the seventh most common type of cancer overall in women.[55]

◆ There appears to be a trend in our patient population toward younger women presenting with squamous carcinoma [cancer] of the vulva. Human papillomavirus [HPV] infection appears to be more common in young women with vulvar carcinoma. There may be a difference in the etiologies producing squamous carcinomas of the vulva. Education encouraging the early detection and prevention of sexually transmitted diseases might alter the rising incidence of this disease in younger women.[56]

◆ Perhaps most well documented in some ways are the increased risks adolescents have assumed in contracting cervical cancer and cervical dysplasia by engaging in early intercourse with multiple partners. Harris, as early as 1980, noted a fourteen-fold increase in cervical dysplasia in persons who have three or more sex partners, compared to those having fewer.[57]

◆ A recent study showed a statistically significant difference in the risk of developing cervical intraepithelial neoplasia (CIN) between those beginning sexual coitus before age eighteen and those whose age at first coitus was over eighteen.[58]

◆ Women who are infected with an STD while pregnant can have early onset of labor, premature rupture of the membranes, or uterine infection before and after delivery. . . . It is estimated that 30 to 40 percent of excess preterm births and infant deaths are due to STDs.[59]

For the sake of our daughters and other young women at risk, we must help young people say no to sexual pressure and premarital sex.

Blind to the Horror of STDs

Even more tragic, it appears that many of our adolescents, especially these vulnerable young women, are unaware of the potential cost of their promiscuity. With widespread media information and "safe sex" being taught in our public schools today, it would seem that Americans especially would be well educated about STDs. Unfortunately, this is not the case. "In a 1993 national survey of 1,000 women from eighteen through sixty years of age, almost two-thirds knew nothing or very little about STDs other than HIV/AIDS and only 11 percent were aware that STDs can be more harmful to women than to men. The lack of knowledge among young women in high-risk groups was dramatic: 65 percent of young women reported 'almost none' or 'very little' knowledge regarding STDs."[60]

Only 11 percent of teenagers surveyed reported receiving information about such diseases from their parents, and yet 70 percent of twelfth-grade students were sexually active and 27 percent had engaged in sexual relations with four or more partners each.[61]

One report states:

> Many educators carried a 1960's and 1970's ethos with them in developing sex education curriculums that focused upon "individual freedom of action" and broad tolerance for a wide range of sexual behaviors. This was coupled with reliance upon "values clarification" as a teaching method in which "right or wrong" have no universal meaning, and students (even in early adolescence) are urged to make decisions themselves concerning sexual involvement based upon "their own" values.[62]

As a result of the above, most sexually active Americans have underestimated their risk of infection. For example, one survey showed that "84 percent of women surveyed were not concerned about acquiring an STD, including 72 percent of young women (age eighteen to twenty-four) and 78 percent of women who reported having had 'many' sexual partners."[63]

It's obvious that our young people are not receiving adequate information and guidance in their homes, schools, youth groups, and churches. We must get the word to them before they "pull the trigger" by becoming sexually active.

Outercourse and Oral Sex: Dangerous Alternatives

A number of our young people think they can enjoy the thrill of sex and still skirt the dangers of sexually transmitted diseases. They practice "outercourse"—genital stimulation without penetration—and oral sex, reasoning that they cannot catch STDs without intercourse. But that's a painful and possibly fatal error of logic, as Amy discovered.

Thirteen-year-old Amy had a boyfriend, but she insisted to her mother that she had never had sex. The girl was worried about blemishes on the skin of her vulva, so her mother took her to the doctor. Biopsies of the skin showed a severe precancerous condition that, if left untreated, would certainly develop into cancer. Amy was treated with laser surgery, but it was unsuccessful. The doctor then removed the skin of her vulva and replaced it with grafted skin.

Amy admitted to the doctor that she had participated in "outercourse" with her boyfriend, which she didn't consider to be sex. Outercourse is often promoted as "abstinence" and labeled as "safe sex." What students like Amy fail to realize, however, is that secretions containing sexually transmitted germs can be spread from one person to another without sexual penetration.[64] STD organisms can be found in a woman's secretions, and even a small crack or cut on the skin or a skin rash is enough to allow the infection to enter.[65]

Amy's supposedly "safe" sex play with her boyfriend had reaped her a serious infection, and it will cost her for the rest of her life.

Another way young people try to sidestep the problems of both STDs and pregnancy is by substituting oral sex for intercourse. While the number of teens who say they are sexually abstinent is on the rise, so too is the number who admit to having oral sex. The proportion of boys who have never had intercourse, yet received oral sex from a girl, rose from 10.3 percent in 1988 to 16.9 percent in 1995. While the data are about boys, they support what newspapers have been reporting anecdotally—that young girls who aren't having intercourse may nonetheless be giving oral sex.[66]

In one sampling of Christian students at a Baptist college, 65 percent of the males and 56 percent of the females admit that they have engaged in oral/genital stimulation of their partners. For some this becomes a substitute for sexual intercourse. As one female put it, "If I do that for him, he doesn't pressure me for intercourse, and I don't have to worry about getting pregnant."[67]

As with outercourse, young people don't consider oral sex to be "real" sex, nor do they fear the same negative consequences from their promiscuity. They assume that oral sex poses a much lower risk of HIV transmission than vaginal or anal intercourse. They do not understand, however, that oral transmission of non-HIV STDs is becoming increasingly common. Doctors are beginning to see more cases of oral gonorrhea as well as oral herpes.[68]

With oral sex among teens on the rise, so are the risks linked to the practice. Oral herpes, pharynegeal gonorrhea, and a kind of oral-wart virus are the main culprits. The study also notes troubling psychological fallout: giving oral sex can make girls feel exploited, and they do it out of a desire to be popular and to "make boys happy."[69]

The debilitating and potentially fatal reality of sexually transmitted diseases far outweighs the momentary pleasure our young people may receive from promiscuity. But if they don't realize the cost, they will continue to put themselves and others in harm's way. In chapter 11, we will explore in greater detail the most prevalent sexually transmitted diseases, their symptoms, their prognoses, and their possible cures—when such cures exist.

PREMARITAL SEX AND PREGNANCY: THE COST OF ANOTHER LIFE

Tina and her boyfriend, both juniors in high school, had been together for almost a year. Tina loved Wade and hoped they would marry some day. Wade told Tina he wanted to "prove" his intention to marry her by having sex. Tina, who was a virgin and a Christian, had allowed him to kiss and fondle her intimately, but she always stopped their making out before sex. Tina thought getting pregnant was the worst thing that could happen to her. She knew a couple of girls at school who had gotten pregnant, and they were miserable now. It was their own fault, she knew. They had been "doing it" since junior high. No wonder they got pregnant.

After the winter formal, Wade took Tina to a secluded cabin in the woods he had borrowed for the night. Once inside, Wade built a fire in the stone fireplace and lit a few candles. Then he surprised Tina with an expensive ring, an "engaged to be engaged" ring, he told her. Tina was overjoyed and filled with love to the point of tears.

As they began making out, Wade whispered, "Just once, Tina. After all, we're almost married." The romantic cabin, candles, and ring had weakened Tina's resolve. *Just once—what could it hurt?* she thought. Besides, she wanted to thank Wade for his generosity. So she gave in.

Two months later, Tina confessed tearfully to her mother that she was pregnant. The whole story poured out. "I didn't think it would happen," she sobbed. "I don't sleep around, Mom. I only did it once. It's not fair."

The Sad News about Teen Pregnancy

Unplanned and unwanted pregnancy is one of the biggest heartaches resulting from premarital sex among students. Admittedly, the majority of single, unwed mothers in this country are in their twenties, not their teens. But the fact remains that sexual promiscuity among adolescents does result in unwanted pregnancy.

Tina's story is replayed countless times in some version or another among teenaged women. Listen to the pain and disillusionment of teen pregnancy as expressed by several students who wrote to me.

> The tragic reality among pregnant girls at my school is that many believed they would not conceive because they had sex only once, or they felt that only bad girls get pregnant.
>
> ◆ ◆ ◆
>
> When I left my baby at the hospital the day after he was born, I left part of me with him. The problems and hurt caused by premarital sex far outweighed the benefits. I learned this the hard way. The one good thing that happened because of my pregnancy is that I received Jesus as my Savior.
>
> ◆ ◆ ◆
>
> I learned the hard way. Abortion resolves one situation for the moment, but it never resolves the guilt or breaks the bond between a mother and her baby.
>
> ◆ ◆ ◆
>
> I used to think, ten years from now I'll be a woman of twenty-four. Now I think, I'll be twenty-four and my child will be ten.
>
> ◆ ◆ ◆
>
> Even if a couple decides to marry after conceiving a child, the woman often feels cheated and carries resentment toward her husband. I know someone like that.

It's my grandma. Their marriage was the pits. And the child, my aunt, still throws
it in Grandma's face. Even after all these years, the reminder is still there.

◆ ◆ ◆

My friend is now married, but she still lives with regrets, especially of her past
abortion: "Even after you're married, you have so many scars. It follows you everywhere, even though it has been forgiven. You go to the doctor and are required to
write out your medical history, and you have to write *abortion*. The thought patterns, too, do not suddenly go away. They have to be erased over and over."

◆ ◆ ◆

When you are a teenager and you become pregnant, you have several options
open to you, none of them favorable.

You may say, "But Josh, I've read that teen pregnancies, births, and abortions are steadily declining." You're right. The overall birthrate to youth aged fifteen to nineteen declined by 18 percent from 1991 to 1998, and teen birthrates
have fallen in every state and across ethnic and racial groups. For girls aged fifteen to seventeen, the 1998 birthrate—thirty births for every 1,000—was a record low. In addition, pregnancy rates for this group are at the lowest level since
1976, the earliest year for which such data are available.

More generally, for fifteen- to nineteen-year-olds, the pregnancy rate decreased by approximately 15 percent between 1991 and 1996. The abortion rate
declined by 22 percent over the same period, and the share of pregnancies ending
in abortion fell. Furthermore, repeat births among teens declined by 21 percent
from 1991 to 1998, when nearly 18 percent of teen mothers had a second child.[70]

But we must receive this encouraging news guardedly. Although the birthrate to unmarried adolescent females declined slightly between 1994–1995, the
overall trend has been upward:

- During the 1970s, the birthrate to unmarried adolescents increased by
  23.8 percent.
- During the 1980s, the birthrate to unmarried adolescents increased by
  52.3 percent.
- During the 1990s, the birthrate to unmarried adolescents increased
  only 4.5 percent.
- From 1994 to 1995, the birthrate to unmarried adolescents *declined* by
  4.2 percent, the first drop in at least 25 years.[71]

Here is an interesting sidebar on teen pregnancy. What is often discussed as the problem of teenage pregnancy in the U.S. may more appropriately be described as the problem of *unmarried* teen pregnancy. Actually, teen pregnancy rates are not much different now than they were twenty-five years ago, although the rates were elevated a few years in the early 1990s.[72] The problem is that teenagers who become pregnant today are less likely to be married than in years past. In 1950, less than 15 percent of the births to women fifteen to nineteen years old were to unmarried women. In 1970, the proportion was 30 percent. By 1997, it had risen to over 75 percent.[73]

Since 1970, the birthrate for married teenagers declined more than 20 percent (from 444 per 1,000 to 344 per 1,000) while the birthrate for unmarried teenagers almost doubled (from 22 per 1,000 to 43 per 1,000).[74]

The following chart contrasts the recent decline in teen births with the steady increase since 1970. It is clear that the small positive trend is just a drop in the bucket compared to the overall trend.

I don't mean to put a damper on this positive trend, because it suggests that the message of abstinence is taking hold to some degree among our youth. But we cannot become complacent. Saying that the teen pregnancy and birthrates are steadily declining is a little like a country at war saying that the mortality rate in combat is declining. It may be good news at first glance, but if soldiers are still dying in battle, the war is definitely not over.

Similarly, unwed adolescent females continue to get pregnant at a high rate. And with every unwanted teen pregnancy, there are at least three "casualties": the girl, the guy who impregnated her, and the child they have created. Whether they marry or not, Tina and

UNMARRIED BIRTHS TO ADOLESCENTS 15-19[75]	
Years	Rates Per 1,000 Unmarried Women
1970	22.4
1975	23.9
1980	27.5
1981	27.9
1982	28.7
1983	29.5
1984	30.0
1985	31.4
1986	32.3
1987	33.8
1988	36.4
1989	40.1
1990	42.5
1991	44.8
1992	44.6
1993	44.5
1994	46.4
1995	44.4

Wade will have to deal not only with the pregnancy but with the many emotional and relational consequences of their night in the cabin. And if Tina allows her child to be born, that innocent person's life will be impacted by the conditions of his or her conception. As long as girls like Tina are getting pregnant, the war is not over. So we must continue to urge our kids to wait for sex until marriage.

Yes, birth and pregnancy rates for teens of all races have been steadily declining. But high rates remain one of the most serious challenges facing our nation. One report states that as many as four out of ten American girls get pregnant at least once by the time they're twenty.[76]

Statistics from the Minnesota Organization on Adolescent Pregnancy, Prevention, and Parenting show that 66 percent of teen women nationwide are sexually active by the time they are seniors in high school, or by the age of eighteen. Twenty percent of those girls, according to Planned Parenthood, become pregnant and half of those will give birth. Of the rest, 40 percent choose abortion and 8 percent miscarry.[77]

Another study came up with slightly different yet parallel numbers. "Each year . . . approximately 10 percent of all fifteen- to nineteen-year-old females . . . become pregnant. About one-third of those teens abort their pregnancies, 14 percent miscarry, and 52 percent (or more than half a million teens) bear children, 72 percent of them out of wedlock."[78]

From 1950 to 1992, nonmarital births increased 490 percent. This trend has held steady for the last twenty years and shows little sign of abatement. Additionally, 40 percent of teenage pregnancies are aborted; as a result, looking at the number of teenage births does not show the magnitude of the increase in unwed pregnancies.[79]

Whenever adolescent girls like Tina become pregnant, there is a high price to pay. As the previous studies reflect, pregnant girls stand at a fork in the road, and each of the two paths before them is difficult. About half of these girls travel the rocky road to giving birth, and most of those will go on to parent the child. Abortion is the road less traveled, but only slightly. In each case, the physical, emotional, and financial cost of pregnancy to the girl and others can be significant. It's a burden they should never have to carry.

The Rocky Road of Teen Birth and Parenting

If Tina elects to give birth to the child, she will be in a large segment of young women in our country. One writer commented insightfully, "In 1960, one out of twenty American kids was born outside of marriage. Today, it's almost one out of three. If we fail to act, in ten years it will be one in two—and half the rest will lose their dads through divorce."[80]

The following statements give us a picture of teen births:

- A 1996 report to Congress on out-of-wedlock childbearing indicates that 35 percent of all single-mother births are to women over age twenty-five; 35 percent are to women ages twenty to twenty-four; 30 percent are to teenagers.[81]
- The teen birthrate in the United States is the highest of any industrialized nation, nearly twice as great as that of the United Kingdom and fifteen times that of Japan.[82]
- More than 80 percent of those who are seventeen or younger when they have their first child are unmarried. Fewer than half of them will get married within ten years.
- Today, over 75 percent of teen births and 32.8 percent of all U.S. births are out-of-wedlock births.[83]
- In fifteen- to nineteen-year-olds who deliver their first child, the likelihood that the child was conceived outside of marriage has increased from 28.2 percent in the 1930s to 89 percent in 1990–1994. Among African-American women fifteen- to nineteen-year-olds in 1990–1994, 91.8 percent of first births occurred out-of-wedlock, while during 1930–1934, the rate was 37 percent.[84]
- Unwed birthrates rose 78 percent among teenagers from 1975 to 1990 and 79 percent among female adults.[85]
- Of all teen births, 72 percent are to unmarried women.[86]
- The birthrate for unmarried black women ages fifteen to nineteen has increased 16 percent in the last fifteen years. The birthrate for unmarried white women has more than doubled.[87]
- Twenty percent of never-married women of childbearing age had at least one child by 1994. In the last twelve years the percentage of the nation's never-married women giving birth has risen from 15 percent in 1982 to 19 percent in 1988 to 20.2 percent of the total 22.7 million women in 1994.[88]
- The number of unmarried teens who had children rose from 5.6 percent in 1992 to 6.5 percent in 1994.[89]

◆ In 1970, there were 3.8 million single parents, in 1990 there were 9.7 million, and in 1994 there were 11.4 million.[90]

Young people like Tina and Wade are woefully unprepared for childbearing and parenthood. Let's say that Tina (and Wade, in the unlikely event that he stays with her) decides to keep her baby instead of give it up for adoption. The pressures of parenting at such a young age are great and the repercussions are costly financially, emotionally, and relationally. We will examine some of those costs in the next chapter. And we will discuss the heartache of adolescent births in greater detail in chapter 11.

The Dead-End Road of Abortion

Tina has another very costly way to respond to her pregnancy. As untold millions of young women before her, Tina can choose to abort her unborn fetus, and our immoral society will bend over backward to help her do it. In many states a sixteen-year-old girl cannot receive aspirin from the school nurse without parental consent, yet the same girl can receive an excused absence from school officials to have an abortion performed without her parents' knowledge.

But abortion comes with a staggering price tag to the young woman—and I'm not talking about the doctor's fee. In the process of killing their unborn children, women have died on the abortion table. For those who survive, there are the obvious health risks. Many are unable to have children when they want to. Then there is the devastating emotional scarring that results—guilt, remorse, haunting nightmares. Consider the sad situation of a young woman whose story was sent to me.

I had an abortion when I was sixteen. Later, when I got married, I was anxious to have my own family. After a period of time of trying to get pregnant and not succeeding, I went to the doctor, and his discovery left me brokenhearted. Evidently the abortion had caused scar tissue to build up and closed the Fallopian tubes leading to my uterus. My body had formed its own defense against any future abortion—or pregnancy. The doctor had no other explanation.

What a terrible price to pay for a few minutes of sexual pleasure. In chapter 11, we will take a closer look at the tragedy of adolescent abortion.

◆ ◆ ◆

The toll exacted from our youth for premarital sex is virtually incalculable. They are playing Russian roulette with their health, their futures, and their very lives, and we must do whatever we can to take this loaded gun from their hands. But somebody else is paying when our kids are promiscuous. In the next chapter we will examine the high price of the adolescent premarital sex crisis on the rest of us—the families, churches, schools, and communities involved with these young people.

CHAPTER 3

ADOLESCENT PREMARITAL SEX

THE HIGH COST TO SOCIETY

DON'T YOU SOMETIMES WISH you could step into a time machine and zoom several years into the future to see what your life will be like? Apart from a stupendous and unforeseeable breakthrough in technology, such a feat can't be done, of course. But I would like you to use your imagination with me to fast-forward about ten years into the future and find out what happened to Tina, the girl from the previous chapter who had sex with her boyfriend Wade and became pregnant. I want to show you how Tina's life was impacted by those few hours of romantic and sexual bliss with Wade in the cabin after the winter formal. The following scenario is fictional, but it is based on a number of factual studies tracking adolescents with unwanted pregnancies.

As we look in on her now, Tina is twenty-seven years old and single. With her parents' help, she made two very important decisions in the first three months of her unplanned pregnancy. First, she decided not to abort the baby. As a Christian, she felt terrible about having sex outside of marriage and getting pregnant. She wasn't about to add murder to her mistakes through abortion.

Her second decision was to break up with Wade. He had secretly pressured her to get an abortion, and when Tina firmly declined, he got angry. "If you really love me, you'll do what I want," he said threateningly. "We can have children later, but I don't want that responsibility now." Tina saw Wade in a new light, and she didn't like what she saw. So she gave back the expensive ring he had given her, and they never spoke again. Tina has dated only a few times since then.

The ten-year-old girl with Tina is her daughter, Kristin. They live together in a rented duplex eleven miles from Tina's parents' home. For the first three years after Kristin was born, Tina and her baby lived with her mom and dad. When Tina finally moved out on her own, she supported her daughter with the meager wages she earned as a receptionist and whatever money her lower-middle income parents could spare. She has been laid off twice in the last seven years and has had to rely on food stamps and skimpy unemployment checks. Tina was embarrassed about being on welfare, and she yearns for the day she will make enough money to support her daughter and even buy a home. But that day is still in the distant future.

Tina, a bright and industrious student, tried to finish high school after Kristin was born. But the rigors of caring for a baby daughter pushed her scholastic career to the back burner. She still vows to get her GED someday and even go to college. In the meantime, Tina's child and job occupy all her time, and rent and living expenses take every penny of her income. If not for occasional cash gifts from Tina's parents, her situation would be even worse.

Her mom and dad have invited Tina to come back and live with them. Tina has resisted so far, valuing her independence. But her resistance is beginning to weaken. Living with her parents would greatly reduce her expenses and allow her to start saving money. And Kristin would have more exposure to Grandma and Grandpa's love and care, especially during summertime and school vacations when Tina is at work. Tina is going to talk to her parents about it again this weekend. She could be back home by the end of the month.

Despite her difficult situation, Tina realizes that she has a lot to be thankful for. She knows other girls who got involved in premarital sex and are much worse off than she is. For one thing, Tina is greatly relieved that she doesn't have a sexually transmitted disease. Wade was her first and only sexual partner, and they were both virgins and disease-free at the time. One of Tina's friends from high school has been in and out of the hospital suffering from cervical cancer related to an STD.

Furthermore, Tina loves Kristin very much and has no regrets about deciding to give birth and raise her. Even so, she is grateful that she did not remain sexually active and get pregnant again. She can only imagine the stress of raising two or three children in her financial situation.

Tina's circumstances are all too common in the lives of countless girls like her. They have written to tell me their sad stories. The cost of premarital sex in the lives of the adolescents who get involved extends far beyond the onset of sexually transmitted diseases and unwanted pregnancy. And the ripple effect goes far beyond the participants to touch family and community. Let's take a closer look at how the additional costs of adolescent premarital sex become a burden to society.

THE HIGH COST TO AN UNMARRIED TEENAGE MOM

To say that having a baby can turn an unmarried adolescent girl's life upside down is an understatement. Writing in the *Wall Street Journal*, Charles Murray stated, "Illegitimacy is the single most important social problem of our time— more important than crime, drugs, poverty, illiteracy, welfare, or homelessness, because it drives everything else."[1] Consider four significant obstacles facing girls like Tina.

The Challenge of Continuing Education

There is a 70 percent chance that the single, teenage mom will never finish high school or go on to college. Having a child out of wedlock is a common reason that young women drop out of school.[2] Think of how dropping out at age sixteen or seventeen will significantly impact a young woman's potential for career and wage earning. And since a prospective suitor must be willing to take on a child as well as a wife, the prospects for marriage are diminished.

The Financial Burden

There is a strong probability that the single, teenage mom will end up on the public dole. According to the Medical Institute for Sexual Health (MISH), of all unmarried teen mothers, 77 percent will apply for and receive welfare within five years of giving birth.[3] The probability is even greater for younger girls. More than 80 percent of mothers seventeen years old or younger end up in poverty and reliant on welfare.[4]

During their first thirteen years of parenthood, adolescent moms earn an average of about $5,600 annually, less than half the poverty level.[5] In her report, "Kids Having Kids," Rebecca Maynard states: "Of the half a million teens who give birth each year, roughly three-fourths are giving birth for the first time. More than 175,000 of these young mothers end up in poverty and reliant on welfare."[6] One study showed that 28 percent of women who become mothers as teenagers are poor in their twenties and early thirties, whereas only seven percent of women who first give birth after adolescence are poor at those ages.[7] And the financial burden is only half the story. Consider the mental and emotional cost of scrabbling along at a poverty level trying to make ends meet.

The Possibility of Another Pregnancy

There is the possibility of an unmarried adolescent mom getting pregnant again. According to the National Campaign to Prevent Teen Pregnancy study titled "Whatever Happened to Childhood?" there is a 25 percent chance that a single teen mom will have a second child within two years of the first birth. The conditions which precipitated previous sexual escapades may still be present or may reappear.

The Need for Adult Support

As Tina's story illustrates, it is almost a sure thing that the unmarried adolescent mother will end up living with her parents, grandparents, or other adults instead of having her own home. Studies show that fewer than five percent of teen mothers live in homes without adults.[8] Forced into an adult role before they are ready, these girls need the financial and emotional support of mature adults for months and possibly years to come. The cost of adolescent premarital sex to adults like Tina's parents comes in the form of the financial and emotional burden of caring for adult children as well as grandchildren.

The Emotional and Spiritual Price Tag

In addition to these substantial burdens, there is a mental and emotional price for promiscuity. A young person's mind and emotions are affected whenever he or she engages in sexual activity. The mind has the capability to play "reruns" of past sexual experiences, often prompting the person to compare a current sexual partner with a previous one. This can occur even after entering into a genuine, committed marriage relationship. These ghosts of past sexual relationships are not easily dismissed. And they can be devastating to future intimacy in marriage.

Apart from Jesus Christ, it is virtually impossible to overcome the guilt feelings that result from selfish, illicit sex. All of us, Christian or not, are created in the image of God. As such, it is unnatural for us to harm the dignity of another human being without experiencing remorse. Most of us cannot use or abuse another person for self-gratification without feeling some guilt. This emotional burden only makes a promiscuous young person's life more difficult, especially for the girl who is also dealing with the difficulties of an unwanted pregnancy.

There is also a spiritual price tag for promiscuity. A Christian young person like Tina who gets involved in sex before marriage—even once—has violated God's principles and commandments. How damaging that is to any disciple of Jesus Christ. The young person who remains in that state cannot witness effectively and cannot experience God's blessing. Christians who engage in premarital or extramarital sex pay a high price in lost fruitfulness for the kingdom of God.

Some call it "casual sex" or "free sex." Sounds rather innocent and harmless, doesn't it? In reality, adolescent premarital sex is anything but innocent and harmless. Promiscuity taxes a young person's total being—body, mind, soul, and spirit. This is no way for a kid to begin adult life. We must do our part to protect girls like Tina from the overwhelming costs of premarital sex.

THE HIGH COST TO THE CHILD

Before we leave Tina's future, let's take a closer look at Kristin, the little girl born out of wedlock to Tina and Wade. How has she been impacted from growing up as the product of her parents' premarital sex? What price will she pay for her parents' promiscuity?

For one thing, she doesn't know her father. Tina has explained to Kristin the basic details of her family background: that her mommy and daddy loved each other once, but they didn't love each other enough to get married. Tina has told her a little about Wade, that he had sandy hair and green eyes like hers. But Wade disappeared from Tina's life before Kristin was born and has never taken the initiative to ask about his child. Kristin sometimes talks about her wish to meet her daddy some day. And whenever her mother is angry with her, Kristin threatens to run away and live with her father—as soon as she finds out where he is. It's an empty threat, Tina knows, but it still hurts.

Kristin struggles in school, earning below-average grades and frequently failing to follow instructions. Kristin also has been in trouble for hitting other students who call her names. The school counselor explains that Kristin's profile is rather common in children from homes where a single parent's attention and energy is divided between parenting and a full-time job. The counselor also asked curious questions about Tina's relationship with Kristin. Tina finally realized that he was trying to discover if she had physically abused her daughter. Indignant, Tina insisted that she would never do such a thing.

Tina is concerned about Kristin's choice of friends. The ten-year-old seems to gravitate toward troublemakers at school and rowdy kids in the neighborhood. Tina has tried to control her daughter's relationships, but it only results in a shouting match between them. So Tina has backed off, knowing Kristin's friends help fill the void after school before Tina gets home. Unknown to Tina, Kristin's best friend, also the product of a single-parent home, has been tutoring her in such subjects as sex, drugs, and the occult.

Do you see the storm clouds gathering on the horizon for Kristin and her mother? Doesn't your heart go out to this little girl who has struggled under the disadvantages of a single-parent home? It's a sad situation. It wasn't Kristin's fault that Tina and Wade conceived her outside of marriage. But she is also sharing the cost of her parents' premarital sex.

Kristin is an example of only some of the complications besetting the children of unmarried teen parents. A number of studies in this area give a more complete picture of the potential disadvantages these innocent children face. Here are the four most prominent.

Disturbing Risks of Sexually Transmitted Diseases

So many reports that I read from the U.S. Centers for Disease Control and Prevention are heartbreaking. But one of the studies in particular brought tears to my eyes as I read it. The report told about the rising number of pregnant women who must give birth by Cesarean section because of sexually transmitted diseases. If their babies were delivered vaginally, they would be born blind. What a tragedy!

Since adolescents who become pregnant out of wedlock may also be careless in other areas, their innocent children are at risk to be born with a sexually transmitted disease. In addition, there is evidence that "certain sexually transmitted diseases are strongly associated with prematurity and preterm labor. . . . The leading cause of neonatal morbidity and mortality, premature delivery is associated with 60 percent to 80 percent of neonatal deaths."[9] Many of these premature deliveries are caused by bacterial vaginosis (BV). "The prevalence of the condition is high: at least 10 percent in the general population and 30 percent or more in selected population."[10] Eighteen percent of those who tested positive for BV but who were not treated gave birth prematurely, compared with only nine percent of those in whom the infection was diagnosed and treated.[11]

Other infants of unmarried adolescent mothers come into the world drug addicted or plagued by fetal alcohol syndrome. These babies are in trouble even before they are born. They pay a steep price for their parents' undisciplined living and casual sex.

Disadvantages of Abuse and Neglect

Pregnant adolescent moms do not take care of themselves as well as more mature mothers. As a result, their youngsters are at greater risk of low birth weight, infant mortality, mental retardation, and physical and emotional disabilities. Furthermore, children born to teen mothers are twice as likely to be abused or neglected than children born to mothers older than twenty.[12] The chances of these children being physically abused and becoming drug addicted are much greater than if they were born to older women.

In addition, "children of adolescent moms are two to three times more likely than the children of their older childbearing counterparts to report having run away from home during those years. . . . Many of these children end up spending a percentage of their lives in foster care, resulting in a taxpayer burden as high as $900 million a year."[13]

Economic, Emotional, and Psychological Problems

The majority of the children of adolescent mothers grow up in single-parent homes, most without a father present physically and emotionally. According to the U.S. Bureau of the Census, 55 percent of children in Detroit live in single-parent homes, 53 percent in Washington, D.C., and 49 percent in Atlanta; 90 percent of all single-parent homes are homes without a father.[14] And when there is no father, the young family struggles financially.

William Galston, in "A Progressive Family Policy for the 1990s," writes, "The economic consequences of a parent's absence are often accompanied by psychological consequences, which include higher than average levels of youth suicide, low intellectual and education performance, and higher than average rates of mental illness, violence and drug use."[15] Children growing up in these conditions are two to three times less likely to be rated 'excellent' by their teachers and 50 percent more likely to repeat a grade. The sons of adolescent moms finish an average of only 11.3 years of school by the age of twenty-seven. As teenagers, they are 2.7 times more likely to land in prison than the sons of mothers who delayed childbearing until their early twenties.[16]

Disappointing Cycle of Teen Births

It is very likely that Kristin will unwittingly follow her mother's example and become pregnant as an adolescent, thus perpetuating the cycle of physical, emotional, and financial difficulties of her own upbringing. Studies reveal that adolescent moms produce more adolescent moms. According to the New York-based charity Robin Hood Foundation, daughters born to teen mothers are 83 percent more likely to become teenage mothers than those born to women twenty years old and older.[17] And even if they don't bear children in their teen years, the daughters of teen moms are 50 percent more likely to bear children out-of-wedlock at some point in their lives.[18]

The children of unwed adolescent moms are often born with two strikes against them. They face an uphill battle to overcome the many disadvantages that are stacked against them. The cost is too much. These little angels don't deserve such a difficult and unfair start. So for their sakes too we must urge our young people to wait for sex.

Abortion: The Ultimate Price

To her credit, Tina stood firm in the face of Wade's pressure to end her pregnancy through abortion. Tragically, tens of thousands of unmarried, pregnant young women don't take the stand Tina did. In our society, countless unborn human beings pay the ultimate price for their parents' sexual irresponsibility: death through abortion. I don't know about you, but that makes my heart ache. It also must break God's heart to see his innocent creatures, born or unborn, paying the price for their parents' wrongdoing. When we ignore God's loving, protective commandments, someone always pays the price. No sexual encounter is free if others have to pay for it.

The general trends for the number of abortions performed nationally as well as the percentage of young women ages fifteen to nineteen who have had premarital sex have, with few exceptions, been upward. "A teenager in the United States is twice as likely to have an abortion as a teenager in the United Kingdom, the industrialized country with the next highest abortion rate. American teens were more than 13 times as likely to have an abortion as Japanese teens."[19]

As you can see from the chart below, the numbers of abortions rose steadily between 1972 and 1990. And even though abortions seem to be on the decline, consider the shocking reality that the lives of more than a million unborn babies are terminated every year through abortion. Among these numbers are countless unborn babies like Kristin who never have a chance.

It is unconscionable that defenseless children should have to pay for their parents' mistake with their lives. The cost is too great. It is imperative that we help our young people count the cost and say no to premarital sex.

THE HIGH COST TO SOCIETY

When the treatment for sexually transmitted diseases acquired by our adolescents through casual sex requires public involvement, who pays for it?

When unmarried teens deliver their babies in a public health facility, who foots the bill?

When adolescent mothers go on welfare, who provides their weekly income?

When the abandoned, neglected, or abused children of teen moms must be cared for by a county, state, or federal agency, where does the money come from?

The answer to all these questions is the same: you and I. American taxpayers are paying an exorbitant cost for the fallout from adolescent premarital sex. When society must step in to underwrite the expenses associated with sexually transmitted diseases, teen pregnancy and abortion, teen mothers on welfare, or the care of their children, Uncle Sam dips into your pocket and mine. Granted, this cost cannot be compared to the sacrifice of human lives through abortion. But the monetary outcomes from adolescent premarital sex are a staggering cost to society nonetheless.

Here's an idea of how the general costs of

ABORTIONS PERFORMED ANNUALLY[20]	
Year	Abortions
1972	586,760
1973	615,831
1974	763,476
1975	854,853
1976	988,267
1977	1,079,430
1978	1,157,776
1979	1,251,921
1980	1,297,606
1981	1,300,760
1982	1,303,980
1983	1,268,987
1984	1,333,521
1985	1,328,570
1986	1,328,112
1987	1,353,671
1988	1,371,286
1989	1,396,658
1990	1,429,577
1991	1,388,937
1992	1,359,145
1993	1,330,414
1994	1,267,415
1995	1,210,883

government spending for social issues in our country have risen over the past three decades. These figures reflect all social services, including the costs associated with STDs and pregnancy among our youth.

TITLE X SPENDING (GOVERNMENT SPENDING ON SOCIAL ISSUES)[21]			
Year	Amount Spent (in millions)	Year	Amount Spent (in millions)
1971	60.0	1985	142.5
1972	61.8	1986	136.4
1973	100.6	1987	142.5
1974	100.6	1988	139.7
1975	100.6	1989	138.3
1976	100.6	1990	135.7
1977	100.6	1991	144.3
1978	135.0	1992	150.0
1979	135.0	1993	150.0
1980	162.0	1994	180.9
1981	161.0	1995	193.3
1982	124.0	1996	192.6
1983	124.0	1997	198.5
1984	140.0	1998	203.5

The Cost of Sexually Transmitted Diseases

Each year, the cost of dealing with STDs in adolescents greatly impacts our taxes and our overall health-care costs. Most sexually transmitted diseases come with a hefty health-care price tag:

- syphilis (annual cost: $106 million)
- hepatitis B ($156 million)
- genital herpes ($178 million)

- gonorrhea ($1 billion)
- chlamydia ($2 billion)
- HPV ($3.8 billion)[22]

Each year in America approximately $10 billion is spent on major STDs (other than HIV/AIDS) and their preventable complications. This figure rises to approximately $17 billion if sexually transmitted HIV infections are included. And this does not include indirect costs, like time lost from work. Think of the billions of dollars we could save each year if we could convince our young people and others to implement God's guidelines for sexual purity. I'm certainly not against paying taxes to keep our country functioning efficiently. But when we must pay to correct a problem that is easily preventable, the cost to society is too high.

The Cost of Adolescent Pregnancy

Do you realize that nearly 60 percent of adolescent mothers giving birth for the first time have their delivery costs paid by public funds?[23] And do you know that it costs federal and state governments an average of $100,000 in medical and welfare costs for every single teen who has a child? Are you aware that taxpayers spend $2,831 a year per teen mother?[24] That's not free sex; that's expensive sex. And you and I are paying for it.

Adolescent childbearing itself costs the taxpayers $6.9 billion each year. The higher public-assistance benefits—welfare and food stamps combined—caused by adolescent childbearing cost the taxpayer $2.2 billion. The increased medical-care expenses cost is $1.5 billion. The combined cost of adolescent childbearing and other disadvantages faced by adolescent mothers is between $13 billion and nearly $19 billion per year. For example, it costs U.S. taxpayers roughly $1 billion each year to build and maintain prisons for the criminal sons of adolescent mothers.

These figures represent the amount taxpayers would save if a policy successfully delayed adolescent childbearing and addressed other disadvantages. Factoring in all costs related to adolescent childbearing, the gross annual cost to society is calculated to be $29 billion.[25] I could find plenty of other worthwhile places to spend my tax dollars, couldn't you? Most of these expenditures would be unnecessary if our kids waited for sex. By helping them in this way, you will not only save them some grief, you will save yourself a lot of money.

The Cost of a "Private Act"

According to many, sex is a private act between two individuals. And anything that happens behind closed doors is nobody else's business. No one has the right to tell other people how they should behave. We are told, for example, that the government has no right to enact or enforce laws that affect a person's private sexual conduct. And schools should not be allowed to teach principles to guide sexual behavior.

Even many Christians may say, "I guess that's right. Whatever someone wants to do in private is their business and not mine. After all, they'll suffer the consequences, not me. Right?"

Wrong!

If sex is merely a private act behind closed doors, why does the government annually pay large sums of money for abortions?

If sex is a private act behind closed doors, why did a former surgeon general advocate the use of public funds for sex education in all our schools beginning at the third grade?

If sex is a private act behind closed doors, why is the U.S. government spending so much money on AIDS research? Why does the U.S. Centers for Disease Control and Prevention spend so much of its time, at taxpayer expense, on sexually transmitted diseases?

Ironically, many groups that pressure for public funding of abortions and for public care for victims of STDs also defend their absolute right to have unlimited sexual freedom behind closed doors. Their position is a gross philosophical contradiction.

Sex at public expense is not a private act. It is no longer private when people who practice casual sex behind closed doors come out and demand that the government spend billions of dollars on AIDS research. It is no longer private when teenagers who become pregnant behind closed doors pass the costs of those children on to taxpayers.

Even worse, sex is no longer private when one or both partners contract a sexually transmitted disease that is then passed on to others in subsequent "private acts." And many times these partners are unaware that they are carrying, transmitting, and/or receiving a potentially incurable disease. Even an honest answer from a sex partner about sexually transmitted diseases—"Me? No, I'm not infected"—is no guarantee of safety. While dormant in one person, an STD can be transmitted to another.

Since the private act of sex has become so tainted, we who are parents are faced with a grim task. We must explain to our children that they cannot have peace of mind on their wedding night (or afterward) unless they know the detailed sexual history of the person they marry. It wasn't easy telling that to my three daughters and my son. But I had to tell them.

Think of the implications within a marriage if the husband has an extramarital affair. What if he repents and goes back to his wife? She could become frigid because of legitimate fear: "If I have sex with my husband now, it's as if I'm having sex with that woman he had sex with—plus everyone she's had sex with for the last seven to eight years." When we break God's loving commandments, the cost to us can be staggering.

A businessman approached me recently and explained that he had been having an affair with several women. When his wife found out, she was deeply hurt and angry. So to get back at him, she had sex with their neighbor. That man gave her herpes, and then she passed the disease on to her husband. He was devastated and was painfully aware that he was paying a high price for his sin.

God said long ago that illicit sex carries potentially widespread and horrendous physical, social, political, economical, emotional, and moral implications. And yet, if you study history, you will find that it was not primarily religious groups like the Puritans who originated legislation to regulate the sexual activities of a given culture. It was often secular governments who had enough common sense to realize that casual sex is not an innocent private act but rather an act with appalling public consequences and costs.

The only certain way for our young people to avoid the high cost of sexually transmitted diseases and out-of-wedlock pregnancy is for a monogamous man to enter into a monogamous relationship with a monogamous woman. Monogamy is the only way to keep sex truly private. And it is the only sure way to eliminate the high cost of casual sex to those who practice it, their children, and society at large. Only in the context of a marriage commitment—"for better or for worse, for richer or for poorer, in sickness and in health, as long as we both shall live"—can sex between two individuals even come close to being considered a private act.

After a meeting with a group of high school students in Orlando, Florida, I was approached by a big, husky, handsome young man whom I'll call Jed. Tears were streaming down his cheeks as Jed told me he had spent his entire life striving for his father's love. "I did everything I could to get my father to put his arms around me, to hug me, to tell me 'I love you.' He never did. So, about six months ago I finally joined the Marines.

"But I got so lonely in the Marines," Jed continued, "that when I met this girl, I went to bed with her. I'm a Christian. I know Christ personally, and it's the only time in my life I've done something like that. She gave me herpes."

Then Jed's tears really began to flow. "Josh," he said, "will anyone ever love me?"

My heart was broken for this young man. Jed will pay a heavy price for his moral failure. He will have to deal with his disease for the rest of his life. He may end up living a single, celibate lifestyle for fear of infecting a potential wife. He may miss out on the joys of being a father and grandfather. His one moment of weakness may lead to physical, emotional, and relational bankruptcy.

What if Jed had been one of your children or one of the young people in your church, youth group, or classroom? What would you have done or what would you have given to prevent him from paying the high cost of premarital sex? It may be too late for Jed, although God has forgiven him and can still use him. But it's not too late for many of your young people. You can save them from the high cost of promiscuity by helping them wait for sex until marriage.

◆ ◆ ◆

How can we get them to wait? First, we must understand why they are *not* waiting. The reasons are many and complex. But by exploring the reasons kids get involved in premarital sex we will be much better equipped to provide the reasons they should wait. Part 2 of this book will explore in detail why our kids don't wait for sex.

PART TWO

REASONS KIDS DON'T WAIT FOR SEX

◆ ◆ ◆

CHAPTER 4

THE PHYSICAL REASONS

CHILDREN IN GROWN-UP BODIES

FOURTEEN-YEAR-OLD CRAIG stands in front of the bathroom mirror after his morning shower, admiring the image staring back at him. He notices with pleasure the broad shoulders, the hint of muscle definition in the arms and chest, and the new swirls of dark body hair. And he can no longer see the top of his head in the mirror without stooping down a little. *How much I have changed in the last year*, he thinks. He's tall enough to play post on the freshman basketball team; on the eighth grade team he was a puny little guard. He also moved from the soprano section to the bass section in the boys' chorus at school. And only a couple of weeks ago an adult at the mall guessed that he was seventeen instead of fourteen. Yes, he looks and sounds more like a man than a boy now, and the thought makes him grin.

Craig is also beginning to *feel* like a man, especially when girls are around. He no longer wants to pick on them, pester them, and make them mad like he did in middle school. Now he really likes being around them, looking at them, and being close to them—especially the new girl in his German class, Drew. What a rush! He could tell at first glance that Drew was more woman than girl—*much* more. Craig has overheard some of the older guys in the locker room brag about how great sex is. Craig is a virgin, but he also knows guys his age and younger who aren't virgins anymore. Men have sex, and Craig knows he is every bit a man. At times Craig finds himself daydreaming about what sex with Drew would be like.

Walking through the mall, Drew notices the furtive glances. Lots of men look at her, not guys from school very often, but men in their twenties and thirties. Some of them even try to hit on her. That's been going on for a couple of years already. And are those guys ever embarrassed when they find out she is only fourteen! It makes Drew laugh inside, but she doesn't want it to stop. She likes being noticed for her good looks—her *womanly* good looks—even by older men.

Passing a large display window, Drew catches a glimpse of herself in the reflection. She pauses to look, as if interested in the luggage on display behind the glass. She knows she has a great body, even though she doesn't dress to show it off. The guys in her class, especially the wimpy guys whose bodies haven't fully matured yet, seem intimidated by her.

Then there's Craig in German class. What a good-looking guy! Craig has noticed her, she knows, though he doesn't leer at her like some older guys. And Drew has definitely noticed Craig, but she has made sure not to appear very interested. A couple of Drew's friends already have had sex with their boyfriends, but not Drew—who hasn't really been that close to any boy. But if she could be close to a boy, and if she decided to see what sex is like, Craig might be a worthwhile candidate.

Craig and Drew are fourteen-year-old high school freshman. They are too young to apply for a driver's license. They can't get into an R-rated movie without an adult. They are several years shy of meeting the age requirement to vote, to serve in the military, and to buy cigarettes or alcohol. They are just kids, only a few months removed from middle school. But they are kids living in adult bodies. They are physiologically capable of engaging in sexual intercourse and even conceiving and bearing a child. And many kids their age are doing it.

In the next several chapters we will explore a number of reasons why adolescents get involved in premarital sex at such a young age. Craig and Drew illustrate the first reason: *Because they are hormonally and physically capable of having sex.*

It's something like the young man who borrowed his dad's sports car for a date, leaving his old beater car at home. On his way to pick up the girl, he got out on the highway and pushed the accelerator to the floor. A policeman finally caught up with him and pulled him over.

"Young man, I clocked you at 120 mph," the cop said.

"Yeah, I know," the kid replied with a big smile.

"Why in the world were you going 120?"

The kid pointed to the number 120 on the speedometer. "Because in this car I can."

Kids have sex because they can. They have the physiological "equipment" and the hormones to energize those organs. They are also falling under the spell of attraction to the opposite sex, which pulls boys and girls together like magnet and steel. And with sex being glorified in the movies, on TV, and in the music they listen to, kids want to try it out. Since the media is such a driving influence on adolescent sexuality, we will treat it separately in the next chapter.

I have frequently asked young people why the kids they know get into premarital sex. Here is what a couple of them wrote:

> Curiosity is one of the reasons teenagers become sexually active. They want to know what it is like. They hear about it in songs, read about it in books and magazines, and watch it on TV and in the movies. With their curiosity aroused, they go out to try it for themselves.

◆ ◆ ◆

> With all the movies, TV shows, books, and public lifestyles portraying sex as something exhilarating, it is no wonder that teenagers are curious. "What does it feel like?" "Is it really as great as they say?" When such questions bother young people long enough, they are going to seek answers.

Adolescents have a natural curiosity about the unknown, which is the basis of the problem here. If teenagers have a healthy, biblical view of sex, they do not have to do their own research.

A young adolescent may be maturing physically, but he or she is still emotionally immature. This puts a childlike curiosity about sex into the body of an individual capable of sex. The result of this merger is not hard to foresee.

There are obvious physical and hormonal reasons why kids get involved in premarital sex. Let's look at several of the elements which encourage kids to act on their curiosity about sex and "test drive" their sexually capable bodies.

PUBERTY: A BODY EQUIPPED FOR SEX
Puberty is that time of life when a young person's body undergoes changes in preparation for sexual activity and biological reproduction. Craig and Drew have watched this process occur both in themselves and in the opposite sex. Basically, two kinds of changes occur in the process of sexual maturing. Some

changes are called primary or internal; other changes are secondary or external. Primary changes are largely hormonal and center on the development of the reproductive organs, equipping the individual to conceive children. Secondary sexual characteristics involve external physical appearance.

Before puberty, boys and girls may be quite similar in physical appearance. But with the onset of sexual maturity, certain physical distinctions become obvious. Both boys and girls experience a growth spurt in puberty, growing taller and filling out. A young man's voice drops an octave or two, his frame becomes more angular and muscular, and body hair sprouts in abundance, particularly on the face, underarms, chest, and pubic area. A young woman's breasts develop, her hips round out, her legs become shapely, and underarm and pubic hair appears.

The timetable for secondary changes varies from person to person. Some kids mature quickly; others develop more slowly. Girls tend to start puberty about two years earlier than boys, which explains why girls in middle school and early junior high years are sometimes taller, stronger, and better coordinated than boys their same age. The average age at which young girls reach puberty is 12.8 years among Caucasians and a year younger among African-Americans. . . . Nearly half of all African-American girls and 15 percent of Caucasian girls begin to develop sexually by the age of eight.[1]

These radical physical changes have considerable effect on a young person's sense of identity. Generally, boys who develop quickly feel more confident and secure, largely because our society places a great deal of importance on the physical stature of the male. Every time he sees his manly physique in the mirror, Craig's self-confidence swells. At the same time, the boy who is late in developing secondary sexual characteristics is often looked down upon by parents and peers as immature and unmanly.

Most girls are delighted to see their bodies transform from "figure one" to a "figure eight." However, some girls who develop early may feel insecure. They may be the first among their peers to experience the drastic changes of puberty, and they don't quite know how to handle it. The young woman who develops slowly may feel awkward and undesirable. These late bloomers may experience the pain of being left out as their peers begin dating.

The onset of puberty has changed over the last century or so. Because the general health of the population is so much better than one hundred years ago, young people are maturing sexually at an earlier age. In a survey of seventeen thousand girls ages three through twelve, it was found that American girls are reaching puberty earlier than ever before. Almost 50 percent of black girls and 15 percent of white girls begin to mature sexually at age eight. By the twelfth year, most are menstruating.[2] This means that children today face a much longer interval between sexual maturity and marriage than their grandparents did.

Young people today are physically equipped and hormonally charged for sexual activity very early in their teen years, capable of conceiving and bearing children. They may also be more intellectually prepared for sex than any previous generation. Today's youth are considered the best educated generation to date when it comes to quantitative knowledge. This is largely the result of the information explosion in the media, particularly the Internet. Our kids can log on to the information superhighway and research any subject imaginable for a school report or project. And they can also find plenty of information about sex—much of it, like pornography, they don't *need* to know about. The Internet, along with the proliferation of sex in other media, accounts for a very high sexual IQ among our kids.

But do our kids know how to handle what they learn about sex? Not very well. Young people have never before been more physically or intellectually equipped for sex. Yet at the same time, they are emotionally and relationally unprepared to handle the pressures of their sexual hormones, function wisely as sexual beings, or make decisions about sexual activity, marriage, or parenting. This emotional immaturity is rooted in the breakdown of the family, especially in its nurturing functions. Emotional maturity cannot be taught in school. It can be learned only in the context of loving, supportive relationships with adults who are themselves emotionally mature. Sadly, this quality is often lacking in American families.

EARLY DATING: EARLY SEX

I want to caution you to be extremely reluctant to let even a child who seems mature start dating early. Adolescents mature quickly, and each year that a child waits will help him or her be better prepared for the experience. Statistics bear this out clearly. Research shows that 91 percent of all girls who start dating at age twelve have had sex before graduation from high school. This is true of only 56 percent of those who start dating at thirteen, of 53 percent who begin at fourteen, of 40 percent of those who start at fifteen, and only 20 percent of those who begin dating at age sixteen.[3] So be cautious in deciding when to let your child begin. It's better by far to err on the side of making your child wait a little longer than seems necessary.

So, what's next for Craig and Drew? If the sexual attraction continues to build, one of them will probably find the courage to suggest a date: meet at the mall for a movie, go to a school dance, go roller-blading on a Saturday afternoon, or something else. And even though neither of them may begin dating with the intent of having sex, the likelihood that they will have sex increases when they begin dating this early.

Dating will bring the couple closer together physically and emotionally. Closeness prompts physical contact — holding hands, caressing, kissing — which revs the powerful sexual engine in both of them. These elements, combined with their emotional immaturity and natural curiosity about sex, are a formula for disaster. All they need is an opportunity, such as meeting at Drew's house after school two hours before her parents come home from work.

A recent study on teen dating revealed that "romantic attachments are a part of life for teens age thirteen to eighteen, but not a *necessary* part." Nine out of ten teens (89 percent) said they had some romantic involvement with a member of the opposite sex. Teens ages fifteen and sixteen said the physical intimacy of dating is more intense and the emotional aspects more important than when they were younger. The major difference between younger teens and teens of seventeen and eighteen is that the older group said petting and even intercourse are the norm.

About three-quarters (77 percent) of all the teens surveyed said they had an "intimate encounter" with someone of the opposite sex and that the "*possibility* of kissing or other intimate physical activity" had been present. Those claiming to have had an intimate encounter include:

- Sixty-three percent of thirteen- and fourteen-year-old girls who have had a boyfriend;
- Seventy-three percent of thirteen- and fourteen-year-old boys who have had a girlfriend;
- Ninety-two percent of fifteen-, sixteen-, seventeen-, and eighteen-year-old boys and girls who have had a romantic relationship.[4]

Other findings in the study revealed:

- Only three in ten (31 percent) teens said they were "sexually experienced."
- Sexual intercourse became common for boys by age sixteen (55 percent).

- Sexual intercourse became common for girls by age seventeen (51 percent, with only 40 percent of those age sixteen).
- Cases of intercourse among young teens were rare (13 percent for boys and 3 percent for girls ages thirteen and fourteen).
- Of those who considered themselves sexually experienced, fifteen was the average age for first sexual encounter for both boys and girls, although, on average, boys admit to thinking about having sex at age fourteen.
- About 23 percent of teen boys say their same-sex peers start thinking about sex at twelve or younger, while only 7 percent of girls believe this is true about their same-sex peers.
- Approximately 46 percent of sexually active teens have had only one sexual partner; 18 percent have had two partners; 13 percent have had three partners; the remaining 18 percent have had four or more partners.[5]

One additional element must be mentioned when talking about adolescent dating and premarital sex. Parents play a significant role in a young person's decision to become sexually active. I have talked with literally thousands of kids and many of their parents over the years. Here's what I have discovered. Kids with very strict parents tend to rebel and overreact to parental prohibitions, leading many into the forbidden area of dating and sexual experimentation. Kids with very permissive parents have more freedom and thus greater opportunity to get into trouble sexually. But parents who play it down the middle—not too strict, not too lenient—are least likely to see their kids getting involved in sex. We will look more closely at the impact of home and parents on adolescent sex in later chapters.

ALCOHOL AND DRUGS:
WEAKENING DEFENSES AGAINST PREMARITAL SEX

People under the influence of alcohol or drugs do things they may not do when thinking and acting rationally. They lose a measure of control over their actions because they lose the ability to think clearly and make appropriate decisions. A person under the influence may even violate his or her own values because of confused thinking and blurred judgment.

Imagine a teenager stirring to consciousness the Sunday morning after her junior prom. She looks at the clock, squinting because the light shining through her bedroom window is too much to bear. It's 11:30, and she smiles to herself, mildly surprised that her parents didn't wake her up for church. She's so glad they didn't; her head is throbbing, and she has a bad taste in her mouth. Her mind is a haze, and she doesn't want to get out of bed.

Closing her eyes again, she tries to piece together the previous night's activities. She remembers that after the prom, she and Denny went to a friend's party at a hotel room. There was a lot of alcohol, and they played drinking games until the early morning. Coming home, she remembers Denny stopping the car in a deserted lot. She knows they kissed, and she vaguely remembers his hands touching her body. The rest of the night is a blur; she doesn't even remember coming home. But there is a sickness in the pit of her stomach—not so much from the alcohol, but from the realization that she most likely lost something that night, something she could never have back.

People frequently step over the line sexually when drunk or high on drugs, something they would not do when sober.

This is also true of forced sex. A large number of cases of date rape—or rape by a friend, boyfriend, or acquaintance—are also influenced by the use of alcohol and drugs. Linda Fairstein, sex-crimes prosecutor in Manhattan and author of *Sexual Violence: Our War Against Rape*, says, "Drink—the abuse of it, the abuses that occur because of it—is key. In up to 70 percent of acquaintance rapes, alcohol plays a role. And because alcohol poses such a powerful problem, it is the rule at almost every school (and the law in most states) that '[sexual] consent is not meaningful' if given while under the influence of alcohol, drugs, or prescription medication."[6]

The realities of alcohol, drugs, and sex are especially applicable to adolescents, who are emotionally immature and whose judgment is unproven even when sober. Kids who partake of alcohol or drugs are more likely to participate in premarital sex than those who do not, as the following studies attest:

- A 1998 study found that the early onset of substance abuse is a strong predictor of adolescent sexual risk activity.[7]
- Another study found that 13 percent of both boys and girls said they had done something sexual while under the influence of drugs or alcohol that they might not otherwise have done.[8]
- Other research supports the idea that "sexual risk taking often takes place in the context of substance use."[9]

◆ Among children fifteen years of age or older, alcohol or drug use raised risks for sex by seven and five times, respectively, compared with teens who do not drink or abuse drugs.[10]

◆ Studies show that 16.6 percent of college students used drugs or alcohol the last time they had sexual intercourse.[11] In high school students the proportion is even larger—24.7 percent. The group most likely (30.5 percent) to use alcohol or drugs before having sex is high school males.[12]

According to Joseph A. Califano Jr., chairman of The National Center on Addiction and Substance Abuse (CASA), "Those [teens] who drink and use drugs will have sex earlier and with more people, hiking their risk of contracting sexually transmitted diseases or becoming pregnant." CASA researchers based at Columbia University in New York examined data on more than 34,000 U.S. teenagers, consulted over 100 experts, and reviewed the findings of hundreds of studies on youth substance abuse and sexual activity. They write that "63 percent of teens who use alcohol and 70 percent of teens who are frequent drinkers have had sex, compared to 26 percent of those who never drank."[13]

The physical and hormonal changes of puberty provide plenty of sexual spark for the maturing adolescent. When alcohol or drugs are added to the mix, it's like putting gasoline next to that spark. It can lead to a raging blaze of sexual passion that kids are ill-equipped to handle. Inhibitions and sound judgment melt away in the heat, leaving an aftermath of guilt, regret, and pain.

BIRTH CONTROL: THE MYTH OF "SAFE SEX"

Craig and Drew's first "official" date was at the German Club's midterm party. Craig asked his mother to drive them to the party, which was held at the teacher's home, and Drew's dad agreed to pick them up and drive them home. They didn't have a single minute alone, so Craig never even got to hold Drew's hand.

Craig was elated when Drew agreed to meet him at the mall multiplex for a movie the next weekend. He was nervous about taking her hand in the dark theater, but when he did, she responded eagerly and held his hand tightly for the rest of the movie. They shared their first kiss on the next date at the county fair. Huddled on the grass during the fireworks display, Craig pecked her gently on the cheek. In response, Drew turned and surprised him with a long kiss full on the lips. Craig was really disappointed when Drew's dad arrived just then to take them home.

For the next few months, Craig and Drew spent a lot of time together. They had dates—movies, bowling, hiking, school dances, and parties—and hung out together after school two or three afternoons a week. Whenever they were alone, they spent increasing amounts of time "making out." Every advance Craig made seemed to be welcomed and returned eagerly by Drew, which only left him hungry for more of her.

The weekend before Craig's fifteenth birthday, Drew invited him over to her house for a celebration. Drew's parents were gone for the weekend, so Craig lied to his mom about where he was going Saturday afternoon. Mom was thrilled about him dating Drew, but he knew she would never approve of them being alone together at Drew's house. So he told her he was meeting two of his guy friends at the mall.

Riding his bike to Drew's house, Craig stopped at the service station rest room. Assured that he was alone, he inserted coins into the wall dispenser and pushed the tab for a packet of condoms. He didn't know if Drew was ready to go all the way—or even if he was ready. But he decided to be safe just in case. He had heard that condoms prevented pregnancy and sexual diseases, so he slipped the packet into the back pocket of his jeans.

Drew had put up a few streamers over the kitchen table and baked a birth-day cake for Craig. She barbecued hamburgers for both of them and served them with cold, bottled wine coolers her parents kept in the refrigerator. The coolers were as sweet as fruit punch, so they each had two of them. They started making out passionately before Drew even cut the cake. When Drew found the packet of condoms in Craig's pocket, she squealed with delight. With his head spinning from the alcohol and sexual excitement, Craig had a little trouble opening the package and getting the condom in place. But he finally did; then he and Drew had sex on the sofa in the living room.

As Craig and Drew illustrate, the raging hormones of puberty and the physi-cal closeness encouraged by early dating, sometimes intensified by alcohol or drugs, facilitate adolescent premarital sex. The ever-present threat of sexually transmitted diseases and pregnancy may have been a deterrent to sex in another generation. But easy access to birth control devices such as condoms, plus the dangerous generalization that condom use equals "safe sex," has created a false sense of security among our kids. Pop a few quarters into a condom dispenser and you don't have anything to worry about, so why wait for sex?

This casual attitude tends to oversimplify the potential dangers of casual sex. As one student wrote:

> If you don't want the consequences, use birth control. If the girl gets pregnant, hey, just get an abortion. If one of them contracts a sexually transmitted disease, no problem, just get a shot.

It may seem that the availability of condoms and medication would prevent or cure sexually transmitted diseases. Yet society is being overrun not only by all the old diseases but also by a multitude of new strains that defy treatment. It must also be noted that contraceptives, even when readily available and used properly, are no guarantee against pregnancy or STDs. The only real guarantee is abstinence.

A report from the Medical Institute for Sexual Health declared, "['Safe sex' education] is not working. . . . Clearly a change in behavior is needed to stem the current epidemic." The report also pointed out that, although condoms are generally promoted as a means to "safe sex," the method failure rate is about 2 to 4 percent, although many studies show a much higher failure rate, particularly when it comes to preventing pregnancy.[14] And, of course, some STDs can be transmitted even when condoms are used properly and consistently.

We will delve into the myth of safe sex more thoroughly in part 3. Suffice it to say at this point that the illusion of safe sex and the availability of birth control devices are reasons kids like Craig and Drew don't wait for sex.

OUR CULTURE'S MOTTO: "IF IT FEELS GOOD, DO IT"

Let's be honest: Sex feels good, whether the participants are married or just a couple of hormone-driven young adolescents like Craig and Drew. God designed sex to be enjoyed within the context of marriage, but the exhilaration of intercourse isn't activated by a marriage license or a wedding ceremony. Any two people can participate and revel in the ecstasy. The reality that sexual intercourse feels good, that it produces a physical thrill and emotional high, is another reason adolescents get involved—and stay involved—in premarital sex.

Here's what a few kids told me about the pleasure factor of sex:

To most kids, sex is really nothing. So they go ahead and have it just because they like it.

◆ ◆ ◆

I used to know a guy who had sex many times and saw nothing wrong with it. One day I asked him what he did that weekend, and he said he had a girl over for the weekend. I asked if his mom knew, and he said no, she was out of town. Then I asked if he saw anything wrong with what he did. He said, "No. If it feels good, do it."

◆ ◆ ◆

Where I live, many of my girl friends and guy friends are involved in sex because they just want to do it. When I ask them why, they say it usually makes them feel good, although some say they do it because their friends are doing it.

◆ ◆ ◆

Sex is a cheap thrill. Having sex is one date that costs very little money and can be done almost anywhere. Life is empty anyway, so go for it!

Sex not only feels good, it sometimes brings two people closer emotionally and relationally. God designed this element of sex for marriage, but it even works outside the marriage relationship. And in our culture, which glorifies thrills and pleasure, many of our kids are falling to the temptation to put their moral values on the shelf in order to cash in on the pleasures of premarital sex.

Why do young people seem so ready to compromise their morals for a momentary thrill? In order to understand how "feeling good" can override an adolescent's values about sex and prompt premarital sexual activity, we need to look at the search for pleasure in a larger context.

All of us, including our kids, live in a fallen world that brings us a great deal of disappointment, heartache, and pain. Nobody likes suffering, so we often try to alleviate it in some way. The Bible points out repeatedly that we have two choices in dealing with our problems: the wrong way and the right way; the world's way and God's way; the irrational way and the rational way; the illegitimate way and the legitimate way. We see this choice clearly in Ephesians 5:18: "Don't be drunk with wine. . . . Instead, let the Holy Spirit fill and control you" (NLT).

In what we often refer to as the great commandment, Christ says we should love him and love our neighbors as we love ourselves (see Matthew 22:37-40). Notice that there are only two commandments here: Love God and love our neighbor. God does not have to tell us to love ourselves because we do that anyway. Even people who don't really like themselves still love themselves. They prove it by consistently looking out for their own best interests, safety, security, and happiness.

Humankind in its fallen state does not love God. Some of us respond to God's love in the course of our lives, but it is still a struggle to maintain our love for him or our neighbor because we are so busy loving ourselves. And this consuming self-love moves us to seek out pleasure to deaden the pain of life either rationally according to God's truth or irrationally according to our own desires.

One of our God-given desires is for intimacy. Genesis 2 tells us that man was created to be intimate with other human beings as well as with God. We feel emotional pain when that desire for intimacy is not met, and self-love drives us to alleviate that pain in some way. But instead of finding God's solution, we often look to our physical senses for relief. It is irrational to attempt to eliminate emotional pain through the physical senses. It's like taking pain medication to fix a broken bone instead of going to the hospital to get the bone set. The pills will block the pain for a while, but when they wear off, your arm is still broken because pills don't mend broken bones.

Just as pills can temporarily deaden physical pain, sensory experiences can temporarily deaden emotional pain. That's why many people turn to alcohol, drugs, overeating, or sex when they are upset, depressed, or lonely. The sensory high masks the emotional low—but only for a brief time. Our culture has generalized this response by glorifying sensory experience. People say, "If it feels good, do it" or "It can't be wrong if it feels so right."

Our kids have picked up this fascination with physical pleasure in our culture. It's one of the reasons they are not waiting for sex until marriage. In an attempt to soothe the pain in their lives—conflicts with parents and peers, school pressures, the struggle to find their identity—they turn to anything that brings them physical pleasure: alcohol, drugs, food, sex. If it feels good, they go for it, sometimes at great expense to their moral principles and the welfare or happiness of others.

If you asked Craig or Drew what made them have sex at fourteen, they might say something like, "We couldn't help it. The feelings were too strong to control. We were in love, and love means sex." Like many other adolescents, they don't understand that sex is not an uncontrollable desire. We are not animals who respond to primal urges without thinking. We are rational beings, created in the image of God, possessing the dignity, worth, and importance he gave us.

Love for adolescents and adults is not just a feeling, an urge. Love is primarily an act of the will, a choice to make the welfare and happiness of another individual more important than our own. And since sex is an act of love, not a primal response, our most important sex organ is not found below the belt; it is the mind. It is here we make decisions. The brain takes in information, sifts through it, accepts some elements, rejects others, and arrives at conclusions. It is in the brain, not in some primal instinct, that the choice is made to engage in sex or to say no to sex. Therefore, to claim that sex is only an uncontrollable urge is to deny our ability to make choices.

Kids like Craig and Drew need to understand that sex is more of a desire than a drive. It is conditional; we can say no. We are not at the mercy of our sexual urges. But when we give in to the popular notion that sex is merely an act of nature, a physical thrill just for the taking, we encourage the desire for sex to extreme degrees.

Our young people need to know that there are sexual thrills that transcend the urge for instant gratification. Compare the following scenarios:

Scene 1: He picks her up in his mom's car; they drive out to a secluded spot and have sex. They think the spot is secluded, but they freeze up whenever they see headlights. A quick thrill, then it's over. Later, they go home, she to her house, he to his house. He's pretty sure she was on the pill or something, but he's not really at ease about it. He hopes she won't start calling him all the time now. She is home, trying to prove to herself that she can have casual sex and not let it bother her. But it does. She feels lonely and uncertain about the relationship. She hopes he hasn't had sex with any sleazy girls lately. She wonders if she should call him.

Scene 2: They have the house all to themselves. It has been their house since they were married two years ago. He helps his wife finish the dishes as they both try to keep the grins of anticipation from their faces. There is much playful touching and kissing. They both know how the evening will end, but in the meantime, they are enjoying every minute. Later, in a bedroom lit by a single candle, they rediscover the thrill that seems to get better every time. When it's over, they enjoy just being close and whispering sweet, loving words to each other. When they wake up in the morning, they will still be together. Nothing to hide, nothing to fear, nothing to change. And it will be like this for the rest of their lives.

Which thrill is the best, the most enduring? Which is worth looking forward to and waiting for? Which of these is a thrill that lasts? Sex is a thrill—no doubt about it. But the true pleasure of sex cannot be enjoyed unless each person can be completely open with the other. There must be complete trust, complete commitment, and complete acceptance. Such attitudes are possible only in marriage. It is worth waiting for.

Release Valve for the Pressures of Life

Craig and Drew experienced the thrill and pleasure of premarital sex on Craig's fifteenth birthday. It was the first time for both of them, so they don't have to worry about infections. And they used a condom, which prevented Drew from getting pregnant—at least it worked this time. Will they have sex again? Chances are they will. Why? Because the pleasure, excitement, and thrill of sex is regarded as a kind of release valve for the pressures of adolescence. One student explained it this way:

> One of the most overlooked reasons kids have sex is pressure. Not the pressure of friends, either. I'm talking about the pressure of getting good grades, making an athletic team, going out with a certain girl, planning a career after high school. The list goes on and on. The problem is that some kids find themselves not performing up to everyone else's standards, and this reflects on them. They feel like they're not capable of doing certain things. As this vicious cycle progresses, the one thing a teen can do is have sex, whether it be to release tension or to have a sense of doing something right or succeeding at something.

Kids today live under many forms of stress. Parents are often unaware of how intense this stress can be. When emotional and mental pressures begin to mount, sex can provide an immediate sense of satisfaction. It involves body, mind, and emotions, and gives a short-term release of tension.

The pressure adolescents are under is real, and the momentary release that sex provides is also real. Sex does not resolve a stressful situation, of course, but it does supply a temporary escape. And when life gets hectic, stressful, or painful for Craig or Drew, they likely will seek each other out for the comfort and relief of a sexual encounter.

Desire to escape stress through sex—or alcohol, drugs, food, etc.—is a sign of immaturity. A mature person has a healthy sense of self-worth. A mature person shows self-control. A mature person can make decisions that will not necessarily alleviate the stressful situations but will help him or her deal with stress without having to run away from it. A mature person has a solid set of values on which he or she bases behavior, even when pressure is intense.

Sexually active adolescents may blame their actions on stress, but they are responsible for their actions. They cannot control the future, their relationships with parents or friends, or the decisions of a teacher or a coach. But they can control themselves. When teenagers are better able to deal with stress through personal discipline and self-control, they won't feel the need to resort to sex as a release. When they begin to focus on the quality of their own character instead of a "quick fix" for their problems, they will be able to establish and strengthen their personal values.

One Thing Leads to Another

Physical and emotional closeness between a boy and girl is like a drug: the more you get, the more you want. You need increasing levels of activity to bring the same pleasure. When the initial thrill of holding hands wears off, the couple rekindles it with a kiss. When one kiss no longer satisfies, they kiss longer, deeper. Prolonged kissing leads to caressing the body and heavy petting. Once the momentum is underway, it is difficult to slow down or stop. If the couple keeps reaching for a high, they will end up having sex.

Another reason kids get involved in premarital sex—and stay involved—is because they can't get enough of the thrill. They become addicted to the kissing, the petting, and finally the sexual intercourse. It's like a powerful freight train going downhill: Once you get it started, it takes powerful brakes to get it stopped.

But when the relationship is based mainly on sexual gratification, the couple will soon hit a painful ceiling, as the following couple discovered:

We were in love—commitment made, ring bought, date set, gown ordered, attendants fitted, reception planned, invitations addressed, showers given, and apartment rented. Renting the apartment before the wedding was our first mistake. We no longer had to spend time in my parents' basement or his car. The apartment was ours. We combined hand-me-down furniture from each side of the family with special pieces of our own. It was now our future home together and mine to care for in the meantime.

The privacy was more than we could handle. Hand-holding turned into embraces. Kisses found their way down the neck. No longer could we just sit in the same room; we had to be next to each other, wrapped in each others' arms. Hands began to wander up and down the back. Hugs involved the entire body. His excitement was obvious and my pleasure verbal.

I don't know what I felt or what I was thinking. I guess our being married shortly was the easiest rationalization. After all, marriage is a commitment, not a ceremony. Or maybe because, clinically, virginity has to do with the actual culminated sex act. Since that never happened, all the other acts of foreplay seemed harmless. But whatever the reason, night after night we engaged in physical foreplay, but not the emotional "lovemaking" needed for a strong marriage.

Then something happened. I don't know quite when, just that it did. The arguments started. We'd yell for a while and then kiss and "make out," but that solved nothing. We saw each other in a different light. When he saw my fears and insecurities, he tried to cover them with authority and knowledge.

Soon, in tears, the ring came off. The wedding plans waned. Then finally the announcement, first to my parents, then to close friends. The news spread by itself. Gifts were returned. Invitations destroyed. Plans and reservations canceled. The gown prepared for storage. The rings returned. The commitment shattered.

Have I hurt any future relationship by experiencing with one man what will never be the same with any other? Maybe if we would have prayed more, maybe if we hadn't been so afraid, maybe if we would have loved each other more than we loved ourselves, maybe if we could have said no to our desires, maybe if the apartment hadn't been rented. . . .

The addiction of sexual activity is another issue of self-control. First Corinthians 7:9 reads: "If [the unmarried] cannot control themselves, they should marry, for it is better to marry than to burn with passion." Some young people end up having sex because they are undisciplined emotionally and spiritually. They don't have the willpower to say no. Once they start kissing and petting, they can't stop themselves. So it is better for them not only to wait for sex but to wait for the activities that lead to intercourse.

However, it is possible for kids to stop once they have started, as this Christian girl explained to me in her letter.

I felt pressure to have sex when I was dating Mike. My folks stressed good morals and values all my life. I knew right from wrong, so it wasn't too difficult to do what was right. At least until I had gone out with Mike for two years.

Mike and I had really gotten to know one another well by then and realized we were in love. I remember one night, though, when he started "using his hands." I was really embarrassed, but I enjoyed it too.

After that date, things kept progressing. One night Mike told me he wanted to show how much he loved me by making love to me. I couldn't believe it! I remember just sitting on the couch, silent for a couple of minutes. I was shocked; I wouldn't even consider it. I realized that what he wanted to do was definitely morally wrong. I told him I just couldn't give in like that and disappoint my parents.

Our young people don't have to be addicted to sex. They can "kick the habit" and reserve sex until marriage.

Craving for a Child

Most adolescents who are sexually active want desperately to avoid pregnancy. And yet there are some girls who feel so unacceptable to themselves and unloved by others that they intentionally have sex to become pregnant and have a baby. One study showed that 7 percent of teenage pregnancies were intended.[15] Many of these kids crave a child to love, but they especially want someone to love them in return. That's their reason for premarital sex.

These young women are immature. A girl who wants a baby mainly to meet her own need for love and security is unprepared to be a good mother. By expecting the child to resolve her own emotional problems, she puts unrealistic expectations on the baby even before it is born. Parents are to meet the needs of their children. When parents rely on their children to meet their own needs, you have a very dysfunctional family.

Some girls want to get pregnant as a means of forcing a boy to marry them. One girl told me that when her boyfriend broke up with her, she found another guy who had similar physical features, had sex with him, and became pregnant. Then she used her pregnancy as leverage, telling her former boyfriend that he was the father, hoping to trick him into marrying her. It didn't work because she had a miscarriage. But her story reveals the extent to which some girls will go in order to save a relationship.

TEEN SEX ACTIVITY: THE FALLOUT OF PRIOR SEXUAL ABUSE

Here is another reason for adolescent premarital sex, perhaps the most heart-breaking reason of all. Kids who have been sexually abused are more likely to become sexually active at a young age and participate in other high-risk behaviors. What a tragedy! Kids who are scarred by sexual abuse are emotionally predisposed to the pain and dangers of adolescent premarital sex.

Sadly, sexual abuse is all too frequent in our culture. In a 1996 survey of 10,868 adolescent females, 10 percent had experienced sexual abuse by an adult or someone older than themselves—9 percent in the past and one percent in an ongoing situation. These sexual abuse victims had all had a higher number of sexual partners during the past year than the girls who had not been sexually abused. If the sexual abuse victims had also experienced physical abuse, their risk of having multiple sex partners was further increased.

However, regardless of whether or not the girls had experienced sexual abuse, those teens who received high levels of parental support and whose parents disapproved of teenagers having sex had fewer sexual partners than other adolescents. Teens who had been sexually abused by someone other than their parents and who had supportive families had fewer sexual partners than those teens whose families were not supportive.[16]

The following studies underscore the reality of sexual abuse and its impact on adolescent premarital sex:

- Women with a history of involuntary sexual intercourse are more likely to have voluntary intercourse at an earlier age (a risk factor for STDs).[17]
- In 1991, 3.1 million children were abused or neglected and 970,000 were born into poverty.[18]
- Intake surveys in detention centers around the country show that between 50 percent and 70 percent of girls in custody have experienced some form of physical or sexual abuse.[19]
- Surveys of young female offenders show a background of abuse in 50 to 70 percent of cases.[20]
- In 1994 there were 139,980 cases of child sex abuse, up 15 percent from 1990.[21]
- A recent Gallup study found that sexual and physical abuse are three times as high in one-parent households as in two-parent households. That same survey reported that about three million children are physi-

cally abused and one million are victims of sexual abuse every year. These findings suggest that the amount of physical abuse cases is sixteen times higher than reported by the government, and the number of sexual abuse cases is ten times greater.[22]

◆ In a 1992 Washington State Survey of Adolescent Health Behaviors, data on 3,128 girls in the eighth, tenth, and twelfth grades showed that those with a history of sexual abuse were more likely to report having had intercourse by age fifteen (odds ratio, 2.1) and having had more than one sexual partner (1.4). This study concluded that the association between sexual abuse and teenage pregnancy appears to be the result of high-risk behavior exhibited by adolescent girls who have been abused.[23]

A study analysis published in the *Journal of the American Medical Association* in 1998 is based on a review of 166 students from 1985 to 1997. The analysis, as reported in the *Modesto Bee*, concluded:

Sexual abuse in boys is underreported and undertreated. When sexually abused boys are not treated, society must later deal with the resulting problems, including crime, suicide, drug use, and more sexual abuse, said the study's author Dr. William C. Holmes of the University of Pennsylvania School of Medicine.

The earlier studies found that one-third of juvenile delinquents, 40 percent of sexual offenders, and 76 percent of serial rapists report that they were sexually abused as youngsters.

The suicide rate among sexually abused boys was one-and-a-half to fourteen times higher, and reports of multiple substance abuse among sixth grade boys who were molested were twelve to forty times greater.

Holmes said a review of the studies leads him to believe that 10 percent to 20 percent of all boys are sexually abused in some way.[24]

Adolescents who get involved in premarital sex are children driven by adult hormones and the urge to try out their adult bodies. They may appear to be adults, they may feel mature in many ways, and they may believe that their "love" qualifies them for sex. But they are still kids, emotionally unprepared for a mature, committed marriage relationship and the responsibilities of parenting for which God reserved sex. We must help our kids navigate safely through the physical temptations to sexual activity and encourage them to wait.

◆ ◆ ◆

Such a task is daunting, however, when the culture in which we live often encourages, rather than discourages, premarital sex. In the next chapter, we will look at another significant reason why our kids don't wait for sex: a culture that asks, "Why wait?"

CHAPTER 5

THE ENVIRONMENTAL REASONS

GROWING UP IN A WORLD WHERE WRONG IS RIGHT

WHEN I WAS A TEENAGER, many influential voices in my life informed me that premarital sex was wrong. If my parents said anything about it, they would say, "It's a sin; don't do it!" If my pastor preached anything about it, he would say, "It's a sin; don't do it!" If I turned on the radio or television, I would hear, "It's wrong; don't do it!" Teachers and administrators at school said, "It's wrong, don't do it!" Even most of my peers would say, "Don't do it!" If you grew up in a Christian home a generation or so ago, you know what I mean. Sure, some people were involved in premarital and extramarital sex back then. But at home, at church, in school—just about everywhere you went—most of society reinforced the biblical view of premarital sex: It's wrong, it's a sin, don't do it.

How things have changed in a few decades! You know as well as I do that society no longer comes down on premarital sex as it did in previous generations. Young people growing up today may hear their Christian parents say, "It's a sin; don't do it!" And they may hear their pastor say, "It's a sin; don't do it!"—if he says anything at all. Some ministers no longer take a stand on this issue because it might make them unpopular with the congregation. But that's about where the similarity between generations ends. Our kids switch on television, and everybody's doing it—even a former president of the United States! They tune into their music and hear, "Oh, baby, let's do it!" They go to school and hear administrators say, "If you're going to do it, visit our clinic so you can do it safely." They hear many of their peers say, "We're doing it, and it's great!"

Why are kids getting involved in premarital sex? One significant reason is the culture in which they are growing up. An ever-widening circle of public opinion no longer views premarital and extramarital sex as wrong. Rather, such activities are accepted, condoned, even glorified and encouraged. Today's adolescents are participating in premarital sex because more and more voices around them are saying it's okay.

We cannot help young people deal with the Why wait? question unless we understand the changing culture in which they live and the impact of today's culture on their behavior. First Chronicles 12:32 states that they understood the times in order to know what to do (my paraphrase). That's what we must do: understand the culture, so we will know how to respond to it. Many issues in our culture significantly affect the attitudes and behavior of our young people. I want to share with you what kind of world our kids live in today and how this world impacts their thinking, feeling, and behavior—especially in the realm of sex. The more we understand about where kids are, the better equipped we will be to help them wait for sex.

First, we will look at the clash of two cultures—the one many of us grew up in and the one our kids are growing up in. As you read this section, I trust you will be moved by the tremendous pressures society puts on our teens to be sexually active. I also hope you realize that the cultural influences toward adolescent sexual activity are both profound and extensive. Today's teenagers desperately need our help and love. Many of the messages encouraging premarital sexual involvement seem so right to them when in reality the consequences are devastating. Proverbs 14:12 warns, "There is a way that seems right to a man but in the end it leads to death." We must be aware that kids are being duped into believing that premarital sex is right instead of wrong.

Second, we will examine the many myths about sexual behavior that permeate the culture our kids know so well. The influence of the media is significant in shaping today's culture. We will focus on that influence separately in the next chapter.

BIBLICAL VALUES VERSUS THE POSTMODERN CULTURE

We live in an interesting and challenging period in Western civilization. We are experiencing a transition between two cultures. Most of us who are parents grew up in a time when Judeo-Christian values and morals were generally accepted or strongly promoted, especially in the area of sexual behavior. Moral absolutes were a given. Our culture, including Christian and non-Christian people alike, derived sexual principles from the Old (Judeo) and New (Christian) Testaments of the Bible.

But our young people are growing up in a predominantly post-Judeo-Christian culture. The sexual principles of this culture are derived largely from secular humanism and moral relativism. There are no moral absolutes. Right and wrong concerning sexual activity (as well as everything else) are subjective and conditional. If it works for you, if it feels good to you, if it brings you an edge or advantage, it must be right. If not, it must be wrong.

Here's the big problem: These two cultures often coexist within the same household and the same church. The older generation is still living in the Judeo-Christian culture of moral absolutes. Premarital sex is wrong, period, end of discussion. The persons who speak into our lives most authoritatively—our peers, our church, the media we allow in—reinforce that view.

But the younger generation is living in the post-Judeo-Christian culture of moral relativism. And the voices speaking into their lives most forcefully— peers, media—reflect the same culture. What's more, there is little or no communication between the two cultures in the household. In most cases, parents treat their young people as if they are living in the same culture. It's not a generation gap; it's a cultural gap. You might say that parents exist in the modern era and that kids are living in a postmodern era. In a culture where Judeo-Christian values have been almost totally forsaken, those pastors and parents who tell their children that premarital sex is sin and that they should wait for marriage are seen by teens as spoilsports, villains, or total fools.

As Christian pastors and parents, we are in the minority. Because the Judeo-Christian framework no longer prevails in the world beyond our homes, we can no longer guide our young people in the area of sex by simply saying, "It's sinful; don't do it!" or "It's wrong; don't do it!" We can't do that anymore and expect it to work. They want to know—and deserve to know—why. (For a greater understanding of the dual cultures, see my book *The New Tolerance*, Tyndale, 1998.)

Before you accuse me of watering down my message, consider my reasons. Differences always exist between generations, which makes communication difficult. But today, when teens actually live in two cultures at the same time, communication may be close to impossible—particularly if parents are unaware that two cultures exist.

How can we adults ever understand how different things are for young people today from what they were when we grew up? At home and at church their environment may be similar, but at school, with their friends, and when they watch and listen to media, it's a totally different world. Different languages are spoken. Words even have different meanings. No one is more vulnerable than Christian teenagers who live on the "cutting edge" between the parallel cultures.

What can Christian leaders do? On one hand, we need to help Christian parents. The family that holds to Judeo-Christian values needs all the help it can get to strengthen the faith and morality of its children. During this difficult and risky time, struggling parents desperately need the church's support.

The church should provide not only wholesome activities but clear teaching to counterbalance the totally unchristian emphases our young people are exposed to every day. We need to do more for our church young people than "socialize" them. Our purpose in church should be more than just giving them some place to go on Sunday or Friday nights. I agree with Tony Campolo: We must give teens something worth living and dying for.

Disillusioned in a Postmodern Culture

Young people in the postmodern era are without guidelines and adrift in a world they neither made nor chose. Caught in a crush of teenage gods, each making his or her own decision independent of others, they find themselves in chaos. Several students phrased it this way:

> The majority of teens desperately want guidelines and restrictions. Ask a teenager if he wants rules, and he will probably laugh at you. Deep inside, however, teens want someone in authority to say, "No further." Yet, for many, no one does. Consequently, they become their own god.

♦ ♦ ♦

> Another reason some people have premarital sex is that they get confused. They get in the wrong crowd and are brainwashed by the group until they believe things are right that they know are wrong. Pretty soon they don't know any better.

♦ ♦ ♦

> Teenagers today are confused and disillusioned. Virtually every relationship leaves them stabbed in the back. They wonder, "Who can I trust?" The big difference between this generation and the rebellious generations before is that the previous rebellion was for a cause. This generation has no cause. We have given up. We have no vision.

In one sense, the young man who wrote the preceding passage is correct: The generation currently coming into adulthood does not have a crusading cause, a unifying point. But in another sense, teenagers today have a very real cause: survival.

In a dangerous, fragmented society where there is no truth, and right and wrong are interchangeable, teenagers feel tossed about like driftwood. And so we see their actions. They are saturated with information but told there are no real truths. They are told they are the result of a cosmic accident, but they are to think positively and feel good about themselves. Their actions are the result of the contradictions swirling in their minds. Unable to come to any conclusions about their lives, they resort to things they can understand—to sensory pleasures.

Throughout most of history, people have had only one vital question to answer: What am I going to do? Faced with the prospect of survival or death, they focused their attention on what they needed to do to stay alive. Only those fortunate few, the elite, whose basic needs were taken care of, had time to ask: Who am I? Modern society is unique in history because of its enormous affluence. Today, hundreds of millions of people, no longer faced with mere survival, now have time to ask, Who am I? before deciding what their actions will be.

But modern men and women are faced with a dilemma. Unwilling to accept God's truth, they turn to dozens of other concepts now on the market. Overwhelmed and disillusioned, they conclude that they are nothing more than a fluke of chemical happenstance. Whether they recognize such a conclusion does not matter; their acceptance of it is played out in their actions.

Those actions reflect a lack of form in their individual world. Without a recognition of right and wrong or good and bad, without a structure by which to measure themselves and their actions, they are left in despair. To placate the despair, they look to entertain themselves. They look to amusement (which literally means "without thinking"), which always leads to seeking pleasure in temporal, sensory ways: materialism, drugs, and sex.

People are trying to put together the jigsaw-puzzle fragments of their lives. What they don't know is that someone has switched the tops of the puzzle box. In order to assemble the puzzle, we should be looking at the picture of our Creator and the Word of God that points to significance, individual worth, truth, meaning—all the things that give us the dignity God designed us to have. But the pieces given us by our culture—materialism, drugs, and sex—

are so dehumanizing and degrading that we eventually quit trying to figure out the puzzle. We lose ourselves even further in temporal pleasures.

Young people looking on feel this confusion acutely. They need role models at home to teach them right and wrong. If they are instructed in the ways of right and wrong but do not see their parents living this way, they will reject their parents' words as hypocrisy. They need the anchor of God's truth to make sense out of the mayhem confronting them. They need a basis, a standard by which to make decisions. They need a worldview they can put into words.

A caring youth pastor shared with me that "there just aren't many good role models left and very few positive heroes. Because of this, teenagers model themselves after rock stars, movie actors, and athletes. They are being led by people who are incapable of leading, and they are suffering for it."

The desire for parental role modeling was expressed by a young teenager who came to a counselor with her parents. The father made a profound statement on "godly parenting" and his daughter replied in all sincerity, "Dad, I wish you could hear what you just said and do it." This father later left his wife and children for another woman.

It is not what parents preach that kids hear clearly; it's what they do. All parents are role models. Modeling is not the question. The question is, What are they modeling? Are they dispelling a child's confusion or adding to it?

Illicit Sex in Our Culture

Our young people are growing up in a culture which regards adolescent sex as too strong an urge to control. Dr. Ruth, the American sexual guru for so many around the world, was speaking at the University of Cincinnati. She said to a crowd of 1,200 university students that it is unrealistic to expect young people to wait. Their libido [or sex drive] is too strong. In essence, she was saying that we are no different than animals. But the basic difference between an animal and a human being is that the human being was created in the image of God, with the ability to make right moral decisions and to act upon them. When we surrender that, we truly are nothing more than animals.

Here is what Dr. Ruth is really saying to the young person in a culture of moral relativism: "If you want to have sex with your girlfriend and she wants to have sex with you, then it's unrealistic to wait. Your sex drive is too strong." However, if you went to Dr. Ruth for counseling and said, "I want to have sex with my girlfriend, but she doesn't want to have sex with me," she would undoubtedly advise you to wait. But she has already stated that it is unrealistic to wait because your sex drive is too strong. Isn't this a contradiction? If you both want to have sex, go ahead because your sex drive is too strong to wait. But if you want sex and your girlfriend doesn't, you should wait regardless of your sex drive. This is the kind of faulty thinking influencing today's culture. And we allow her—and others like her—to get away with that!

Dr. Ruth's answer challenges any standards regarding right and wrong because according to her philosophy we are only animals acting from an urge we are unable to control. If that kind of thinking is true, then why do we have laws against rape? Isn't it unrealistic to expect a rapist to wait? Their libido is too strong; they can't wait!

Lance Morrow, writing for *Time* magazine, characterizes the animalistic premise for adolescent sex rather colorfully: "Teenagers will no more abstain from sex than will the frisking neighborhood dogs, and it is fatuous, punitive, Neanderthal to expect them to; the best that adult authority can do is to distribute condoms to the beasts and hope they will pause long enough to slip one on before their urgencies of crotch propel them into the hedge." Yet Morrow takes exception to this premise, concluding, "The condom-slinger's mentality takes a ruthlessly unennobled view of human nature. The young tend to fulfill expectations. Government-sponsored condom distribution announces that the society officially expects to get copulating dogs."[1]

When the culture expects kids to act like animals, even encourages it in many ways, guess how they will begin to act. They will sink to the lowest level of our expectations.

The Me-ism Culture

Most people would agree that we are living in a "me-ism" culture, one preoccupied with self. It is clear that advancing and pleasing self is the number-one priority in our world today. Our kids are growing up with a warped sense of entitlement that prompts them to demand, "I want what I want when I want it."

Rampant me-ism has significantly affected the climate of our world's morals. Kids today simply don't view morality and values as they did a couple of generations ago. In an article titled "The Way of the Wise: Teaching Teenagers about Sex," Paul David Tripp writes:

The view of life from which modern sexual expression emerges holds these "truths" to be self-evident:

- That people are ultimate and autonomous. That is, there is nothing more important than the individual. I am self-sustaining and free from any authority I do not choose to follow.
- That the highest of human values and experiences is personal satisfaction and pleasure. I am entitled to my share of pleasure and comfort.
- That I must constantly be vigilant that my "needs" will be met.
- That the most important of loves is the love of self. Without this I will be unable to function.
- That bigger pleasure is better—a constant desire for greater, more effective stimulation.
- That what is important is the here and now, leading to a constant pursuit of instant gratification.
- That the physical person is more important than the spiritual person, leading to an inordinate body focus.[2]

No wonder our young people are out to pursue sex as fast and hard as they can. The present culture has encouraged them to do so.

Compare the values of two teenage girls as found in their diaries, one dated over a century ago in 1892 and one dated 1982. The stark difference illustrates the paradigm shift of morals and priorities during that time period:

FROM THE DIARY OF A TEENAGE GIRL	
in 1892	in 1982[3]
Resolved, not to talk about myself or feelings. To think before speaking. To be self-restrained in conversation and actions. Not to let my thoughts wander. To be dignified. Interest myself more in others.	I will try to make myself better in any way I possibly can with the help of my budget and baby-sitting money. I will lose weight, get new lenses, already got new haircut, good makeup, new clothes and accessories.

You may hope that Christian youth are not as easily influenced by the me-ism culture, especially in the area of sexual behavior. But that hope is unfounded. For example, Dr. M. B. Fletcher of Carson-Newman College, a Southern Baptist school, states:

I am convinced that many in the church believe that the Christian values we teach our children are controlling their sexual behaviors. The evidence suggests that this is simply not the case. . . . This point raises some interesting questions. Do Christian adolescents who are sexually active become less "religious"? Or do they rewrite their theology to permit a sexually active lifestyle? How do teenagers cope with religion and sex?

The following excerpts are from Dr. Fletcher's report, "The Adolescent Experience: Sex Happens," delivered at the Southern Baptist ethics conference in 1992:

The following percent of students reporting premarital intercourse over a seven year period (1984–1991): For males, premarital sexual intercourse increased from 55 percent in 1984 to 70 percent in 1991. For the females, the change was even more dramatic. Only 27 percent of the females admitted they had engaged in premarital intercourse in 1984, but 53 percent in 1991 said they were sexually experienced. In the most recent data collected (Fall Semester 1991), 66 percent of males and 65 percent of females said that they had experienced premarital sexual intercourse. . . .

The average age at first intercourse for both groups was about 17. . . .

Interestingly, 65 percent of the males and 56 percent of the females in the sample [at Carson-Newman College] admit that they have engaged in the oral/genital stimulation of their partners. For some reason this becomes a substitute for sexual intercourse. As one female put it, "If I do that for him, he doesn't pressure me for intercourse and I don't have to worry about getting pregnant."

Do you get the idea that our Christian youth are taking their cues about sexual behavior from the self-centered culture in which they live? Dr. Fletcher's report continues:

[Our students] are still under the influence of religious values but appear willing to compromise their values if an acceptable excuse can be found. . . .

"If you are in love, sex is a natural, meaningful way to express your feeling for your partner." They reconcile this notion with biblical teachings about love, sex, and marriage by equating love with marriage. If you love someone and are committed to them, it is the same as being married—it is just not official. To them, therefore, a loving relationship and commitment to each other are the necessary preconditions for a sexual relationship. . . .

I ask the students, "How does one make a moral decision?" Their first responses are always quite predictable. First, they say, "Everyone must make his or her own decision." When prompted to continue, they say, "What is right for one person may not be right for another." It is my impression that this is the extent of their thinking on moral decision-making. After some discussion to clarify this ethical position, I then ask, "Are there no moral absolutes?" Almost always they say, "No, there are no moral absolutes."[4]

The postmodern culture is a me-ism culture. Today's adolescents are getting into premarital sex because the culture encourages them to satisfy themselves even when their me-ism conflicts with morals.

A Society Lacking Foundation

Another identifying factor of the culture surrounding our adolescents is the transient nature of American life. We live in a highly mobile society. This year 35 million Americans will move to a different home. And when kids don't experience a secure, stable, predictable home life, they will act out that insecurity in a number of ways. They will test the rules and boundaries imposed on them from the authority figures in their lives—parents, teachers, youth leaders, even God.

People relocate for a variety of reasons: to find better jobs, more favorable weather, lower rent or property taxes; or because they are transferred by their employers. The moving may be from coast to coast or merely from one housing development to another, but the results are the same. Very few people today "put down roots." But without roots, our young people are vulnerable to drifting in their morals and convictions.

It is also an isolated society. In many areas—like California, for example—homeowners are becoming more isolated from their neighbors by cinder-block walls, chain-link fences, and other barriers. Even when neighbors don't erect fences, the isolation can be just as real. For example, how many of your neighbors do you know personally? These days, particularly in new communities, most people rarely become acquainted with their next-door neighbors.

As each family faces the various crises of life, they often do so alone. Their neighbors never know their joys or sorrows. A friend of mine once told me a sad story. He learned from a newspaper article that the sixteen-year-old son of a family living across the street had been killed in a car accident. Prior to reading the tragic news story, he didn't even know the name of the family or that they had a teenage son.

When I was a boy in Michigan, everyone in our neighborhood knew everyone else for miles around. Of course, our entire county had fewer residents than the high-density housing developments of today. Not only did people know each other from living in the same area so long, but many of us were related. Within the radius of a few miles I had uncles, aunts, cousins, and grandparents. When any crisis arose, we supported each other.

Meaningful relationships take time to develop. But many young people today have never lived in any one place long enough to develop the solid relationships that can help carry them through their stressful adolescent years. They do not have the traditional support systems to fall back on that so many of us had.

Our kids also are growing up in an uncertain society. A majority of today's young people view the future with apprehension. The uncertainty in our society leaves our young people with diminished hopes for the future. A sixteen-year-old in Oakland, California, said, "I feel like I'm preparing for nothing." Another student said, "I think I'm going to grow up, and there won't be anything to live for." With such bleak hopes for the future, most young people are easily influenced to make decisions on short-term pleasure rather than long-term consequences.

Why should a teenager who believes he or she lives in a "doomsday world" follow the Christian advice to wait for sex until marriage? They have been taught that with one push of a button the world can be blown apart. Tomorrow they may be gone, so "Why not?"

MYTHS AND FALSE ASSUMPTIONS OF THE POSTMODERN CULTURE

Today's culture has its own beliefs about adolescent premarital sex. Notice that I used the word *beliefs* instead of *truths*. That's because the party line on premarital sex is riddled with myths, false assumptions, and lies. And they are so prevalent in our culture that our kids are buying into them big time. If we are to help our young people say no to premarital sex, we must clear away the smoke screen and help them see the truth.

"No One Will Get Hurt."

Teenagers today have been duped into believing that premarital sex is OK because it doesn't hurt anybody. They assume they can do whatever they want with their bodies, and if that means sex, it's all right. They further argue that sex is a lot better than being involved in drugs or alcohol. And they insist that with proper care they can avoid pregnancy and disease.

When teenagers try to rationalize sex by claiming that it doesn't hurt anyone, two main elements are at work. First, these people willfully turn a blind eye to the pain that premarital sex already has caused in countless lives around them. Second, they give in to relativistic thinking and rely on situational ethics to guide them rather than an absolute standard of right and wrong.

It doesn't take a sociological genius to know how seriously people are hurt by premarital sex. All you have to do is read a newspaper. Our society is hurting terribly from unwanted pregnancies, sexually transmitted diseases, abortion, and so on. All a teenager has to do is look around the classroom to see broken relationships and emotional wreckage caused by premarital sex. Teenagers who think they will be spared this pain are lying to themselves. They are being willfully ignorant. They think the rules don't apply to them.

A Christian who understands God's system of values does not have to grope around to find right and wrong. God's loving standards are unchanging. They reflect his very nature and character and apply to any society and to any person at any time in history. There is no guesswork. But those who do not accept the definitions of right and wrong as set forth in the Bible have to find some other way of determining their values. They have to approach a situation and set a course of action based on something. If they listen to the relativistic thinking of our society, they will look to themselves for answers. They will say, "The right thing to do in this situation is to do what makes me feel good or is to my advantage."

This is situational ethics, a make-it-up-as-you-go morality that has no basis in anything. It allows a young person to justify premarital sex by saying, "It won't hurt anyone," when he or she really means, "I think I can get out of this without being hurt, so it must be all right." Such ethics fly in the face of the righteous standards God has given us in his Word.

The extreme danger in this was spelled out by Paul when he said, "So I tell you this, and insist on it in the Lord, that you must no longer live as the Gentiles do, in the futility of their thinking. They are darkened in their understanding and separated from the life of God because of the ignorance that is in them due to the hardening of their hearts. Having lost all sensitivity, they have given themselves over to sensuality so as to indulge in every kind of impurity, with a continual lust for more" (Eph. 4:17-19).

So many Christian young people have fallen into the cultural trap of thinking all truth is relative. Christians who have fallen into relativistic thinking have two choices. They can turn back to God and to the truth, which has remained constant since time began. Or they can continue as they are, in which case they will move further away from any semblance of righteousness, and their heart will become more and more hardened toward God.

"It's All Right. We're Engaged."

A lot of young people see engagement as just the first stage of marriage. The only thing missing is a little piece of paper, so why not begin to enjoy the sex? This was the approach one couple took, and it backfired in their faces. Their story was shared with me by a student.

> Lori and Jeff, a strong Christian couple, had been dating seven months when they fell into the trap of the enemy. "I thought it wouldn't be that bad to consummate our relationship, because, after all, we were engaged, and we knew we were going to be married." That was Lori's excuse. She didn't realize that God doesn't look at future promises when dealing with present sin.
>
> The father of lies will try to convince you that if you really love a person, God understands your need to express that love in a physical manner. Not true. After a time of being sexually active, Lori and Jeff went through a terrible two-month period that could have destroyed their relationship. Although they repented, the scars are still there. Lori speaks of the time they were "engaged in sin." "Our prayer life went downhill. So did everything else. I felt, 'Now Jeff is coming over to see me—for just one reason.'"

Studies show that 50 percent of people who get married have been engaged at least once before. So being engaged really means nothing as far as having the security of knowing that you will be married to that person soon. In addition, a 1992 random-sample survey found that 78 percent of those who have been divorced participated in sexual intercourse prior to marriage. The study also found that those who had sexual relations before marriage were more likely to commit adultery than those who had no premarital sexual experience.[5]

To further illustrate the potential negative consequences of believing this myth, here is a letter written by a Christian leader to a girl, warning her not to repeat the mistake of others.

Dear Kelly,

Congratulations on your engagement! You've just entered into a very special stage of life, no longer single but not quite married. Mike seems to be a perfect match for you. The more I get to know him, the more I believe that your match was made in heaven.

However, one area of your relationship has been troubling me for a while, but I haven't known how to talk to you about it. It's your increasing sexual involvement with Mike. You've told me he sometimes puts pressure on you to go further in your physical relationship than you feel comfortable with and that you often give in because of your desire to please him. As a Christian, you know that God has reserved sexual intercourse for the marriage bed, so I have no worries about your becoming pregnant or contracting a sexually transmitted disease. What does worry me is this: I know from counseling many young women that the commitment of engagement often makes it easier to rationalize heavy sexual involvement that stops just short of what is expressly forbidden.

Let me warn you that by engaging in that kind of sexual activity you are risking spiritual, emotional, and psychological consequences. Our vision always seems to be clearer in hindsight. For that reason, I want to tell you the story of a young woman I know who was once almost exactly where you are now.

Pat first had sex when she was 16. She became a Christian the next year, and although she eventually learned that sex outside marriage was wrong, she was often frustrated by her inability to break an established pattern of exchanging sex for "love." Finally, Pat decided to stop dating for a couple of years so she could get her thoughts together. It was a time of incredible spiritual growth, and it seemed God was giving her victory in an area that had been a "thorn in the flesh" for so long. At last she felt ready to start dating again. After a few brief relationships, she met Bill.

A mature Christian and leader in her church, Bill was quite different from any guy she'd ever dated. He rarely touched her, but instead spent time discovering her secret plans and aspirations. For the first time, Pat sensed a genuine interest in herself as a person and not as a sex object. Bill even asked Pat's permission before he first kissed her. When they became engaged, Pat felt that her dreams had come true.

But even the sweetest dreams can turn sour. As their love intensified, so did their physical affection. Each kiss seemed a little longer than the last, each embrace a little more passionate. At first, Pat wasn't at all concerned. She thought,

Hey, I don't have a problem with lust anymore. I'm perfectly capable of controlling myself, and besides, Bill would never pressure me for sex.

But just as the kisses were losing their excitement, Bill's hands started reaching down Pat's chest. The first time it happened, he apologized for losing control, but soon his fondling her breasts became a regular part of their romance. One night things went further than either of them planned. As they were making out, Bill reached for Pat's pelvis. She angrily broke away from him.

When he tried to comfort her by saying that his goal was to give her pleasure by trying to manually bring her to orgasm, she tearfully replied she didn't want that kind of pleasure—not yet. They asked each other's forgiveness, prayed to the Lord for His forgiveness, and Bill promised, "This will never happen again." But it did happen, again and again and again.

Pat would try to resist Bill's advances gently. When his hands moved toward her most erogenous areas, she would firmly put them elsewhere. She explained why she didn't want to have her body sexually aroused, why she believed it was wrong, but Bill never seemed to hear her words. Pat often felt as if she was fighting a battle; their sexual involvement was most intense when she became too weary to fight.

At that point Pat came and talked to me. She expressed a desire to have a pure relationship, although she often fell short of that desire. She said, "Normally, I would advise someone in my situation to get out of the ungodly relationship, but how do you get out of the relationship when it's with the person you want to spend the rest of your life with?"

I met again with Pat two months later. This time her desire to strive for godliness was gone. In its place was strong rationalization. I sensed she had grown tired of fighting Bill, had given in, and was desperately seeking to find some way to justify to herself the sexual activity she knew was wrong. She said, "I realize now that this is different from my past sexual activity. I used to buy love with sex. I know I don't have to buy Bill's love; it's already mine. Now I share my body out of my love for him. Plus, being engaged really makes things different. Bill and I love each other, and we are committed to each other, and that's the context God wants sex in, right? Besides, we will be married in three months, and if we get familiar with each other's bodies now, we will feel much more at ease on our wedding night. We will also have some knowledge of what is sexually pleasing to each other so our sexual adjustment in marriage will be easy."

Pat's rationale sounded good on first hearing, but her life betrayed the lie she was living. The first thing to go was her spiritual life. She lost all desire to spend time in God's Word or in prayer. She no longer confessed her sin to God because she felt that nothing needed forgiving. Pat gradually stopped going to church and fellowship groups. She wasn't getting anything out of them, she said. I suspect it was because she felt like a hypocrite. When friends would ask if anything was wrong, she would answer, "No, nothing. I'm just going through a dry spell with God right now."

Mentally, Pat began to experience depression. Sometimes she would start crying for no apparent reason. The radiant joy that had once characterized her life was replaced by a lethargic "blue" feeling and a constant lack of energy.

Slowly, even the dream relationship with Bill began to change. She would get irritable and snap at him without provocation. She was increasingly critical of him. It became difficult for her to trust him or to believe his promises. Though Pat and Bill still verbally professed their love for one another, the feelings they once had were slowly growing cold and were at times replaced by revulsion and even hatred.

Throughout that time, the whirl of wedding plans and parties offered a convenient busyness into which Pat could throw herself. Occasionally, when her schedule slowed down enough to allow a quiet moment alone, she would wonder if she was doing the right thing by marrying Bill. But she attributed her fears to prenuptial jitters.

When Pat's sister Karen came home from college a month before the wedding, she noticed a marked difference in Pat. Lovingly, Karen began to question her sister until she got a full account of the relationship. Karen convinced Pat that starting a lifetime commitment under the present circumstances could be disastrous and the best thing to do would be to postpone the wedding. It was good that Pat had the courage to follow Karen's advice. She realized it would be better to put the relationship on hold than to terminate it years later in divorce court.

Pat and Bill never did marry. It has been several years now, and Pat only recently has acknowledged that sexual involvement was the root of the problems. She told me, "As I think back, I know that the effects of our unwise sexual activities were deadly. The mutual loss of respect, the guilt, and the anger at myself and him were all things we tried to ignore but eventually could not. Using our engagement as a rationale was never enough to excuse our actions, though we often tried to do so. I thought I could isolate my sex life from the rest of my life, but I quickly learned that, like a rope woven together, all the areas of my life are intertwined and affected by each other. I still wonder how something that started off so great could become such a nightmare. Where did we go wrong? It's hard to admit, but I'm now convinced that our premature sexual intimacy ultimately caused our engagement to be broken."

Kelly, I hope you can see why I've taken the time to write all this to you. I want to help keep you from making similar mistakes and suffering the same pain as Pat. I do get worried about you because I see many similarities between you and Pat in situation, background, and mindset. However, I know that at this point your basic desire is to live a life pleasing to God. That's why I believe you can avoid taking the path Pat took.

The story of Pat and Bill was included here in its entirety because it gets the point across better than a hundred sermons could. People can argue and justify themselves all day long, but the pain brought about by consciously violating God's command is terribly real. Sex before marriage cannot help the marriage in any way.

If every engagement ended in marriage, it might be difficult, apart from the Bible, to refute sexual activity during this period. But, as has been noted, the reality is that over half of all engagements are broken off. And those who think living together before marriage will better equip them for living together afterward are in for an even greater letdown. Studies have shown that couples who live together before marriage have more problems than married couples do. In fact, many couples who live together with the intention of marrying later often break up before they marry. One researcher found this to be the case in 40 percent of the couples he studied. Even those couples who eventually marry have a 50 percent higher divorce rate than couples who did not live together before marriage.[6]

God established sex for the marriage relationship. As a couple builds toward the point of officially sealing their commitment in front of God, friends, and family, they find more and more opportunities to strengthen that commitment. The engagement period should be a wonderful time of supporting, loving, and honoring one another.

Sex before marriage doesn't build up, it breaks down. It doesn't show love, it shows selfishness and self-centeredness. It doesn't honor, it uses. In one sense, a rush for sex before marriage embodies everything an engagement shouldn't be.

Those who insist on becoming familiar with each other's bodies for the sake of the wedding night are not only denying themselves the thrill of discovery on that night, the first night in which they can do what only a husband and wife may do, they also disregard a basic knowledge of anatomy. In the words of Tim

Downs, a Christian cartoonist and speaker, "Rest assured the plumbing works." There is no need to try it out in advance.

But despite the pain that sex may have brought to almost-married couples, there is good news. God heals. I have counseled a number of couples who were involved sexually, and I have seen great things happen when they gave control of the relationship back to God. Couples in much the same situation as Pat and Bill have reestablished trust and mutual respect by totally abstaining from physical contact. Even though they may have felt they couldn't go back to a nonphysical relationship, they knew they had to choose between putting off gratification for the moment and losing each other. Engagements then turn from being a time of insecurity and distrust to a time of purification. It can be done.

When trust is rebuilt in such a close relationship, it causes the individual partners to trust themselves again. Whereas the sexual activity had caused each to feel insecure and to have a poor self-image, stopping the activity brought about a new sense of self-control, responsibility, and dignity. As they each experienced a new, healthy self-image, they were also able to view the other person as worthy of dignity and respect.

"I Owe It to Him."

If a girl thinks she owes a boy sex (it is rarely the other way around), it is because he wants her to think that. Otherwise, she would know by his words and actions that he cares for her regardless of how she responds. He either cares for her and acts in a loving and respectful way, or he is concerned about himself and acts in a manipulative way.

It all comes back to the dignity of each person and how our worldview influences our actions. To treat people with dignity is to show them God's love by our actions. The Christian worldview is not compatible with manipulation; manipulation indicates people are there to be used, not loved. God's love longs to give, not get.

A graduate student about to be married writes:

> God has graciously given Jane and me physical self-control in our three years of dating. I have never asked or expected her to perform in any way. She owes me nothing, especially her own body. By my having that attitude, she respects me and in marriage will want to give herself totally and freely to me. It is a love with no strings attached and no wrong and deceptive motivations. She knows that I respect her and this builds her up as a woman of God.

The story is told of a man who approached a woman and asked if she would go to bed with him for a million dollars. She said she would.

He then asked, "Would you do it for ten dollars?"

"No!" she said, "What do you think I am, a prostitute?"

"Well," the man said, "we have already established that. Now we're just haggling over the price."

In a sense, we prostitute ourselves when we allow others to manipulate us. We give them what they want in order to get what we want. A girl manipulated into sex by a boy because "she owes it to him" is selling her body for whatever she wants out of the relationship, be it security, popularity, or some semblance of love. God is grieved when we thus destroy the dignity he has given us.

The cause of this mentality of "giving something in order to get something" is insecurity. If a boy feels he must have sex with a girl, regardless of how he gets her to say yes, he is showing insecurity. He has made sex a requirement for feeling right about himself or feeling good about her. Likewise, a girl who gives in to his manipulation in order not to lose him does not have a self-image grounded in the Word of God. She values the relationship more than her own importance, and she acts out her insecurities.

Sex is not a chip for bartering. You don't buy it in the market. When it becomes something to be obtained by making strategic moves, sex becomes an end in itself.

A manipulative boy does not want sex with this particular girl, he just wants sex. When he indicates that she owes it to him if she wants to keep the relationship, he shows that he is out to take, not give. He's not seeking to cement a lifelong commitment of love and sharing and looking out for the other person's best interests; he wants to make it with anyone who will say yes. A girl who offers herself at such a price doesn't feel she is of great value, which is tragic in light of so much that God says to the contrary.

This myth that a girl "owes" sex to her boyfriend is one of the lies that is fueling the increase of date rape across the nation. The following data bear this out:

* A startling new study published in the *Journal of the American Medical Association* revealed that "nearly one in five girls surveyed had been physically or sexually abused by a date."[7]
* Between 1993 and 1994, forcible sex offenses, such as sodomy and rape, on college campuses increased by 12 percent.[8]

◆ In one particularly lengthy study of students in the seventh through ninth grades, it was found that 23 percent had experienced some form of unwanted sexual activity on dates; 15 percent had experienced date rape.[9]

◆ Sexual force or coercion or the possibility of it is a critical part of sexual experiences for some adolescent girls.[10]

◆ One study found that 16 percent of girls whose first intercourse was before age sixteen reported that first intercourse was not voluntary.[11]

◆ Studies indicate that youth who have been sexually abused are more likely to become sexually active at a young age and participate in other high risk behaviors. . . . This risk factor is important because a substantial proportion of young people, particularly women, have experienced sexual abuse or rape. Child sexual abuse is also common. In a national sample of women eighteen or older, 15 to 32 percent (depending on the criteria used) report having been sexually abused as a child. Additionally, 20.4 percent of college women report having been forced to have sexual intercourse. Overall, almost 13 percent of women in the United States report having been raped, and about 25 percent report having been sexually coerced.[12]

This problem of sexual coercion does not necessarily end when a girl passes from her teens into adulthood. Studies show that "31 percent of married women report violence in their most recent relationships."[13]

Another commonly believed lie that fuels the "justification" of forcible sex offenses is that women who say no really mean yes. Some men think that a girl's resistance is just part of the game, that she doesn't really mean it. Even some women who had experienced these forcible sex offenses tended to place the blame on themselves. Five of the twenty-six subjects who discussed their experience reported being under the influence of alcohol at the time and thus felt responsible for their abuse.[14] Furthermore, according to a study on sexual violence, rape victims nationwide have a 2 percent chance that their story will be believed.[15]

Sex is a gift two people give each other lovingly after marriage. Kids who provide sex feeling that they owe it to another are lost in the fog of a lie.

"Having Sex with Me Will Prove Your Love."

"If you really love me, you will prove it by having sex with me." How many young people, especially girls—even Christians—fall for that line? They reconcile this notion with biblical teachings about love, sex, and marriage by equating love with marriage. They rationalize, "If you love someone and are committed to them, it is the same as being married—it is just not official." To them, therefore, a loving relationship and commitment to each other are the necessary and essential preconditions for a sexual relationship.[16]

How many young people have been drawn into premarital sex by the false assumption that illicit sex is proof of true love? Nowhere in the Scriptures do we find someone demonstrating love by manipulating and causing another person to sin. When the Bible talks about love, it always refers to actions and attitudes that draw people closer to God and each other and demonstrate his character. Remember: True love regards the security, happiness, and welfare of another to be as important as one's own.

Sex without marriage can never demonstrate the love of God. People who fall for "proving their love" with sex are buying into a lie with their bodies and emotions. They are squandering something priceless on a cheap product.

But what about non-Christians, people who don't measure right and wrong by God's standards? Perhaps their personal definition of love allows for this kind of activity. Such a question can be answered only by that person's value system, which, without an absolute standard as its base, is foggy to begin with. If a non-Christian girl believes that the most loving thing she can do is give somebody something he wants, she is caught. If he wants sex, she can give him that. But what if he wants her to help him commit suicide? Must she, out of love, push him off a cliff?

A deficient value system is one that contradicts itself. It lets people think, in some instances, that right and wrong actions (or loving and nonloving actions) are based on how they will make someone feel; yet it also may prohibit certain actions because they are "just plain wrong." Without a measuring rod to determine right and wrong, standards become arbitrary. And when right and wrong are arbitrary, they are meaningless.

Christian teenagers who think sex is a way to show love have lost sight of God. They aren't filtering their thoughts and actions through the Bible. If they were, they would know that acts of love can only do good and draw others to God. Premarital sex does not fit that description.

"Sex Proves That I'm an Adult, Not a Child."
The teenage years are times of transition from being a dependent child to becoming an interdependent adult. Interdependent persons believe that they have

something worthwhile to give to others, and that others have something worthwhile to give to them.

While this transition from childhood to adulthood involves every facet of a young person's life, we must remember that the different areas of that individual's life develop at different rates of speed. For example, one person may seem more "mature" than another of the same age because he or she is more mature socially and emotionally than the other. But the second person may be more mature physically than the first.

Regardless of their actual level of development, many teenagers see sex as a way to speed up their total passage to adulthood. After all, sex is not something children do. It is for adults. The logic behind this way of thinking is not hard to see. So kids begin to mimic adults by engaging in so-called adult activities: smoking, drinking, and sex. By doing these things, they mistakenly think they will magically become adults. A youth worker shared with me that

> high school girls I know try to act like married persons in a relationship, and having sex is one of the ways they do it. Girls have dreamed of marriage and the perfect man from an early age and they often like to pretend. I, however, have heard girls say that when they gave away their virginity they felt they gave away their youth, which they are very sorry about. This is especially true if they got pregnant.

Although teenagers may be interested in instant physical maturity, they often ignore or are unaware of other aspects of their lives that need to be developed in order to mature as a whole person. They usually don't realize that those facets of their lives are just as affected by sexual activity as the physical aspect is, if not more so.

The physical ability to have sex cannot make up for a lack of maturity in other areas of a young person's life. One type of maturity needed is moral maturity. Dr. Urie Bronfenbrenner of Cornell University has done extensive research on adults' inability to transmit moral values to their kids. He points out that part of the reason is our cultural tendency to segregate people by age groups. This segregation has happened as a result of the mobility of our society, lack of extended-family influence, single parenting that has created latchkey kids, and so on.

A young person is forced to spend time with his or her peers, whose influence shapes his or her moral thinking (among other things). Combine this peer exposure with an educational system that does not teach moral values, the lack of contact with preceding generations, and the desire of teenagers to achieve adulthood through sex, and you have young people who are physically capable of sex, yet with little more moral understanding of it than two dogs in an alley.

The intellectual maturity of today's youth seems to have surpassed that of previous generations because of the enormous amount of information available. But many educators are questioning the validity of what passes for intellectual maturity in our educational system. Memorizing data and repeating it does not bring about intellectual maturity. Young people need to be challenged to reason, to deduce, and to be creative.

Yet this type of maturity—the ability to solve problems, to reason through and foresee the consequences of one's actions—is not necessarily taught in schools. Educators call it intellectual or cognitive maturity. Everyone else calls it common sense. The Bible calls it wisdom. Many teenagers are trying to become adults without it.

Young people are also making their transition to adulthood with less emotional maturity than in years past. Our society affords less freedom to express emotions. It doesn't mean that emotional outbursts are not possible; it means that teenagers do not often find help in understanding how they feel, and so are unable to develop the maturity needed to handle emotional stress and to be responsible for emotional reactions.

Family tensions contribute to teens' immaturity. School counselors are seeing more and more students with behavioral and self-image problems caused by such stress in the home as fighting or absent parents, lack of love and acceptance by parents, a single parent (usually the mother) having a live-in lover, and so on. Such students are generally referred to the counselor by a teacher, since the parents do not communicate with their kids and are unaware of the stunted emotional growth caused by family stress.

Regrettably, these emotional and self-image problems make it difficult for teenagers to go against what the crowd is doing. Conformity is a haven for emotionally immature and insecure people, and it is hard for such people to say no to sex, even when intellectually and morally they know it is wrong.

A sign of emotional maturity, then, is having enough confidence to stand up for one's values. A person's value system is a vital part of his or her worldview. To understand another's worldview and value system, we can observe that person's behavior—because people inevitably act out their values.

If they do not live according to their stated value system, we can conclude that they don't really believe what they say they do. If, for example, they say that God designed sex for the completion of marriage, yet are sexually active before marriage, their true worldview is in conflict with their claimed beliefs. Their physical maturity overrides their lack of emotional, intellectual, social, and moral maturity.

One of the hallmarks of any kind of maturity is the ability to delay gratification until a future time. When young children are given two pieces of candy, they want to devour both of them. They don't understand why they should put one aside for later—they are not mature enough to understand. Likewise, a physically mature yet otherwise immature teenager does not understand that sex does not make instant adults.

We see in our culture today a great deal of sexual immaturity among our youth. Feeling that they have to express sexual desire right now indicates that immaturity. The basic issue is not sexual expression, but rather the whole personality development. Somewhere along the line, our kids have to start establishing some healthy patterns in their lives and relationships.

Just remember: A twelve-year-old boy can have sex, but it doesn't make him a man. My German shepherd can have sex, but it doesn't make him more of a dog—let alone a man!

"Once You've Had Sex, There's No Turning Back."

Adolescents mistakenly believe that once they have become sexually involved, they cannot stop or turn back. Having already lost their virginity, they see no way to get it back, so they keep making things worse by perpetuating their sinful behavior. A Christian who is sexually active before marriage and falls into this kind of thinking has given up on God's forgiveness. It doesn't mean that God's forgiveness no longer applies or is no longer complete; it means the Christian has developed an improper view of God the Father. The beauty of God's forgiveness is that it is never-ending. We can come to him in repentance at any time, for any reason, no matter how long we have been straying from him.

Sexually active teenagers know that once they have started down a path, it is easy to keep going. But God offers us the opportunity to leave the old ways behind and start on a new path: a renewal that can start at the time of our choosing. If we have walked ten steps away from God, he has already walked nine steps toward us. But we have to take that final step to a restored relationship with him.

Continuing to have sex often tears down one's self-esteem. The young person feels cheap, used, and unworthy of God's love. A girl commented that she felt God could not use her because she wasn't a virgin—and so she might as well blow it again. She was miserable. She had more trouble forgiving herself than accepting God's forgiveness.

Reestablishing a damaged relationship with God requires two things: repentance and forgiveness. Both of these simply mean to agree with God. Repentance means to agree that sin is sin, with no rationalizations and no intent to commit it again. Forgiveness means to agree that God's grace—evident in Christ's death on the cross—is sufficient payment for our sins.

To reject God's forgiveness is to say that his grace is inadequate to cover our sin, and nothing grieves him more than such an attitude. When we consider ourselves beyond forgiveness, we say that God is not all-powerful, that he is unable to cope with the magnitude of what we have done. Nothing hurts him more than rejecting his grace when he has paid such a tremendous price for it.

Once we agree with God unconditionally that our sin is wrong (repentance) and that his grace is sufficient to erase our sins (forgiveness), we are free to turn around and start over. God forgives, and he doesn't keep a scorecard.

Viewed in a different light, continued premarital sex presents a real danger, something everyone needs to consider. The path of teenage sex is full of all kinds of traps, and the longer the young person stays on it, the less likely he or she is to escape unharmed. Emotional trauma, ruined relationships, ruined reputations, ruined self-image, unwanted pregnancies, and sexually transmitted diseases are all there—the path is dangerous. To emphasize those consequences is neither sensationalism nor an attempt to panic anyone. It is the hard truth. Staying on the wayward path simply because one is already there is a foolish gamble.

For a more in-depth look at what it means for a young person to find forgiveness and new direction after sexual sin, see chapter 21.

✦ ✦ ✦

The message and influence of today's culture to youth is, "Go ahead, enjoy sex now; it's foolish to wait." Perhaps the loudest voices in this culture come through the media: television, movies, music, the Internet, etc. In the next chapter we will explore how the media is giving our kids other strong reasons not to wait for sex.

THE MEDIA'S ROLE

REMEMBER DEREK FROM CHAPTER 1, the committed Christian university student who is wrestling with the question "Why should true love wait?" after a discussion with his friend? Let me tell you a little more about him. One of the things Derek and Colin enjoy doing together is going to movies. They like "guy flicks"—action stories, cops and bad guys, blazing machine guns, exploding cars. Going to the movie and watching someone save the world single-handedly is a welcome diversion from the pressures of Derek's studies.

Derek won't attend a movie where the primary story line glorifies adultery or an illicit sexual affair. And he won't go with Colin to see overt "skin flicks," R-rated movies full of nudity and sex that were labeled outright pornography a generation ago. Derek is careful about what he sees because he knows he can be negatively influenced by raunchy films.

The guns, guts, and glory movies Derek watches occasionally show flashes of female skin, and there is usually a gratuitous sex scene or two—featuring the unmarried hunky hero and his voluptuous girlfriend. But Derek can overlook this stuff because it's not what the movie is about. He wishes the movie producers wouldn't clutter up a good action movie with such stuff, but seeing a few seconds of exposed breasts or a sweaty sex scene doesn't really affect him.

Or does it?

I can tell you a little more about Annie, too, the Christian student being pursued by Jeff, the Green Beret. Her escape from the rigors of school and work are romance novels. Most of the time she reads Christian romances, love stories where the hero and heroine come closer to God—but never get into bed with each other before marriage. But Annie will occasionally pick up a secular romance in which the morals of the main characters are questionable or downright embarrassing. But everything turns out fine by the end of the story, and

Annie excuses their immoral behavior because the characters are not Christians in the first place. Such stories haven't made a lasting impression on her.

Or have they?

Like Derek and Annie, our young people are growing up in a media-saturated society. Unless you pack up and move to an uninhabited island in the middle of the ocean, you will have difficulty preventing your kids from being influenced by television, videos, movies, radio, the Internet, music, books, magazines, etc. And for the most part, the media is not neutral. Whether they are trying to entertain us, inform us, motivate us, or sell us something, those using the media are either actively or passively communicating something to us—and to our kids.

What is the media telling our young people? In the area of sex and morality, the media mostly tells them lies. And these lies often address valid physical, emotional, and relational needs. In her article for Inter-Varsity Christian Fellowship, "Why Wait for Sex?" Alice Fryling writes:

> Our society is starved for intimacy. And many of the lies we believe in our culture have to do with our hunger for relationship. We want acceptance, loving relationships, and deep intimacy, and yet we believe the lie that sex will satisfy our hunger. . . . We are people who long to be loved, touched, and understood in a world of declining family ties and epidemic dysfunction. Our desires are certainly not new; they are as old as humanity. The difference in our world today is that people are trying to fulfill these longings in strange ways.[1]

No wonder Derek, Annie, and countless other Christian young people exposed to the media begin to say, "We're truly in love. Why wait?" Media lies about sex are another major reason why young people become involved in premarital sex.

WHAT ARE THE MEDIA TRYING TO SELL?

The media bombards us daily with messages about sex. Sex is a primary ingredient in most advertising. It is used to sell everything from automobiles to deodorants. Our radios, television sets, movie screens, CD players, books, magazines, and newspapers graphically and convincingly tempt us to sexual fantasy and experimentation apart from morals or responsibility.

We are often told that television doesn't affect behavior very much. The tobacco industry, at a time of public pressure to remove tobacco ads from TV, declared that media commercials don't effect a change in a person's lifestyle and that media ads would not cause a person to take up smoking. That's about the craziest thing I've ever heard! If advertising doesn't influence people, why did the tobacco industry spend hundreds of millions of dollars on TV commercials? Marketing and advertising people are not stupid. *If there is no relationship between TV commercials and viewers' behavior, why do American businesses spend billions of dollars on advertising each year—for prime-time television alone?*

Entertainment is even more influential than advertising in communicating to our kids about sex. Picture this scenario. Boy meets girl. Boy and girl find each other attractive and want to know each other better, so they set aside an evening to be together. Do they sit and talk to each other? No. They rent a DVD and sit side by side staring at a big-screen TV in boy's home theater while Mom and Dad are out for the evening.

On the screen, boy meets girl. Boy and girl find each other attractive and want to know each other better, so they set aside an evening to be together. Do they sit and talk to each other? No. They take off their clothes and engage in mad, passionate sex to the sound of violins blaring from eight speakers around the room. There is a happy ending. Movie boy and girl stroll hand-in-hand into the sunset to live happily ever after.

Following the DVD movie, real-life boy and girl still want to get to know each other. But by now, their hormones are raging. They have been entranced by a movie that communicates, "Sex is a great way to get to know someone." Their minds are flooded with the sights and sounds of passionate kisses, naked bodies, romantic violins, and a happy ending. Boy and girl look deeply into each other's eyes. Then they take off their clothes and engage in mad, passionate sex in boy's bedroom.

In only a few days, boy thinks girl is easy. Boy dumps girl. Girl wonders what went wrong.

Does that sound possible? far-fetched? familiar? Read part of a letter I received from a girl in West Virginia:

I accepted Jesus as Savior when I was nine. I have been going to church all my life and still do. At age seventeen I began dating a boy who had graduated and gotten work with a factory in town. I thought he was cool. Well, one night we went to see [a sexually explicit movie]. On the way home we took a detour and had intercourse in the backseat of his mother's car. After five months of dating, he broke up with me. I was crushed.

This sad story is being repeated countless times in the lives of our young people. And one of the primary culprits behind this human tragedy is the media and the lies it feeds to our kids about sex. A guy's mind remembers scenes of sex so vividly that when he is with his girlfriend, it is easy for him to act them out. "My memory is so vivid that I have to guard what I watch because I can easily recall those scenes," laments one student.

What is the damaging message about sex so frequently communicated through the media, either directly or indirectly? Abbylin Sellers, author of *The Sexual Abstinence Message Causes Positive Change in Adolescent Behavior*, identifies six media lies about sex. For each lie, Sellers gives us the truthful message our kids need to grasp.

LIE 1: *Sex creates intimacy*.
True intimacy is built on commitment to honesty, love, and freedom. A prostitute may expose her body, but her relationships are hardly intimate.

Ask the question: is a prostitute intimate?

LIE 2: *Starting sex early in a relationship will help you get to know one another and become better partners later*.
Sex is an art that is learned best in the safe environment of marriage.

LIE 3: *Casual sex without long-term commitments is both fun and freeing*.
A satisfying sexual relationship requires trust, trust that grows only in the context of the lifelong commitment of marriage.

LIE 4: *If you don't express your sexuality freely, you must be repressed, sick, or prudish*.
This can be a very intimidating lie, but the fact is that premature sex is bad for your emotional, physical, and cultural health.

LIE 5: *Sex is freedom*.
Young people who become sexually active in response to peer pressure to be sophisticated and independent are actually becoming victims of current public opinion. No one is really free who engages in any activity to impress the majority.

LIE 6: *Surely God understands that this is the twenty-first century!*
God did not give these rules because he is a spoilsport. Quite the contrary. Because he is God and because he loves us more than we can ever know, he has told us how to have the best, most satisfying sexual experiences: in marriage.[2]

TELEVISION

Maybe you don't agree. Perhaps you think I'm exaggerating to make a point. After all, we all watch television, listen to the radio, and attend movies. Is the media really communicating "lies"? Let me show you what I mean by focusing in on the medium of television. Consider the research regarding the impact and effects of TV on our personal and societal lives.

Notice first the prominence of television in the daily experience of our families and kids:

- Americans spend about one-third of their free time, more than the next ten most popular leisure activities combined, watching television.[3]
- The average teenager spends more time in front of the television than on any other activity besides sleeping.[4]
- Television viewing increases in preteen years and declines after age twelve.[5]
- Youth ages nine to fourteen spend over 20 percent of waking hours watching television, compared to 9 percent on hobbies and 3.5 percent on homework.[6]
- The average American teen spends about twenty-three hours a week watching television, with the heaviest viewers coming from low-income households.[7]
- African-American households watch 50 percent more television than other groups in the U.S.[8]; Latino teenagers watch more than thirty hours per week.[9]
- By age eighteen, a teenager will have seen 350,000 commercials; 100,000 may be advertisements for beer.[10]

What impact does the deluge of television viewing have on kids? It is anything but neutral, as several studies have documented. Television can and does influence behavior, often in a bad way:

◆ Adolescents who watch a lot of television consistently score lower on academic achievement tests. Researchers have found that high levels of television viewing have a negative impact on school performance.[11]

◆ Adolescents who were sexually active or used alcohol, tobacco, or other drugs listened to the radio, watched music videos, and viewed movies, cartoons, and soap operas on television more often than teens who did not participate in these behaviors.[12]

◆ Those fifth and sixth graders who had a greater awareness of alcohol advertisements in the media than their peers intended to drink as adults, had positive associations with drinking, and were more aware of beer brands.[13]

It's not just that our kids are glued to the television for hours on end, it's what they internalize as they watch. A number of recent studies reveal the high sexual content in today's television programming. The numbers may vary a little from study to study, but the overall message of this research is sobering.

◆ Prime-time television contains roughly three sexual acts per hour, including deep kissing and petting.[14]

◆ Only one of every six acts of intercourse [on TV] is between married couples. In daytime serials, favored among junior and senior high school students, there are more than three sexual acts per hour, and nonmarital intercourse is portrayed twice as often as marital intercourse.[15]

◆ A 1993 study of nineteen prime-time shows viewed most often by ninth and tenth graders counted just under three sexual references per hour, usually long kisses or unmarried intercourse. In action-adventure series, most of the sex involved either unmarried intercourse or prostitution.[16]

◆ In a study of television viewing patterns of African-Americans and whites, African-American teenagers watched ninety more minutes of television per day than did white teenagers. There were approximately thirty-nine sexual acts or references per week in the programs watched by African-Americans, compared to twenty-four per week in those watched by white adolescents.[17]

◆ Adolescent females watch more television with sexual content than do

adolescent males. Each year a female teen could view 1,500 sexual acts or references including intercourse, prostitution, and rape.[18]
- Pregnant teens watch more television overall than their non-pregnant peers, but the programs they select contain less sexual content.[19]
- Another study determined that teens were more attracted to programming with portrayals of prostitution and intercourse outside of marriage than those of marital intercourse and homosexuality.[20] A clear and understood values system, open communication within the family, and active viewing of television by teenagers, however, alter these effects on values.[21]

One significant study, conducted by the Kaiser Family Foundation, examined 1,114 programs that aired between October 1999 and March 2000 on ABC, CBS, Fox, HBO, Lifetime, NBC, TNT, PBS, USA, and KTLA (the Los Angeles WB affiliate). Here are a number of points from that study as reported in various resources:

- Half the characters having intercourse were in established relationships, while 16 percent had just met.[22]
- Sixty-eight percent of all shows included sexual content, up from 56 percent in 1997–1998. These shows averaged more than four scenes with sexual content per hour. About one out of every four shows (27 percent) on television included *sexual behaviors*; the remainder featured characters *talking about sex*.[23]
- Over two-thirds of all television shows (68 percent) had some kind of sexual content. This was a jump from the preceding year, in which over half of the programs (56 percent) found a way to get sex into their shows, from dialogue innuendoes to showing couples in bed.[24]
- The most widely viewed shows—those airing in prime time on the major broadcast networks—were even more likely to include sexual content. Three out of four of these shows included sexual content, up from two out of three during the 1997–1998 season.[25]
- Two-thirds (68 percent) of the characters involved in the intercourse-related scenes were adults appearing to be twenty-five or older, about a quarter (23 percent) appeared to be young adults ages eighteen to twenty-four, and 9 percent appeared to be under eighteen.[26]

◆ Three years ago, 3 percent of all characters involved in intercourse were teens; by 2000 that figure had jumped to 9 percent.[27]

◆ Most disturbingly, of those shows that featured sexual intercourse, 9 percent of the participants were under the age of eighteen. (This is up from 3 percent the previous season.)[28]

◆ Nearly 85 percent of sitcoms had something to do with sex. This was a 28 percentage point jump from the preceding season (56 percent), which was bad enough.[29]

◆ Most of the sex on TV is talk, not nudity or pornography as such, but 10 percent of all programs depicted or implied sexual intercourse (up from 7 percent the previous season).[30]

And how does the constant stream of sexual subject matter affect our kids? Again, the statistics tell the story.

◆ College students exposed to large amounts of sexual behaviors on television were more likely to believe that their peers engaged in those same activities.[31]

◆ In a study of thirteen- to fourteen-year-olds, heavy exposure to sexually oriented television increased acceptance of nonmarital sex.[32]

◆ Viewing of daytime serials and MTV is a predictor of sexually permissive attitudes and behavior among college students. Older adolescents in one study tended to mimic the sexual themes from the shows they watched.[33]

◆ In a *U.S. News and World Report* poll last year, just 38 percent of the Hollywood elite was concerned about how TV depicted premarital sex, compared with 83 percent of the public. "Hollywood has glorified adult premarital sex," argues Sen. Joseph Lieberman. "And that is unhelpful if your goal is to reduce teen pregnancy and out-of-wedlock births."[34]

Television is a powerful influence in the lives of our kids. On daytime and nighttime soaps, glamorous stars pass from one sex partner to another like a game of musical chairs. Radio and TV commercials suggest that our sex life will improve if we wear designer jeans, drive sporty cars, splash on a certain cologne, or use the right toothpaste gel. "Adolescents who rely heavily on television for information about sexuality may believe that premarital and extramarital intercourse with multiple partners . . . is the norm. Believing that such behavior is normative may make adolescents more susceptible to pressure from their partners."[35]

Here's what some of our kids are saying about the negative impact of television in their lives:

> When I was a youngster, the soap operas were a part of my daily entertainment. What a mistake to fill the young mind with such thinking! I also purchased sexual-type magazines at a very young age. My mother never monitored what we read. Thoughts of petting, kissing, and sexual intercourse were planted in my mind during a very crucial point in my adolescent life.
>
> By the eighth grade I was already acting out, by kissing and petting during recess, what had been planted in my thoughts. This continued during high school. When I moved away from home to go to college, I began having intercourse.

◆ ◆ ◆

> Many teenage girls and even a few boys are hooked on soap operas. In most soaps almost every person in the cast is involved in sex without marriage. Teenagers watch this and learn through those programs that premarital sex will make them happy and content.

When was the last time you saw anybody on television say no to sex? Think about it. You can see why a sixteen-year-old girl who had just lost her virginity wrote me to say, "Mr. McDowell, I couldn't compete with television."

And not everything we see on television is make-believe. Young people see glamorous actresses talking about having a big rock star's out-of-wedlock child and saying what a wonderful life she has. And there seems to be an endless procession of unmarried media stars living together and boasting about great sex. The line between their own lives and the characters they often play on the screen is hard to distinguish.

Doesn't the portrayal of sex on television seem seriously overbalanced to the permissive side? This is the message our kids are receiving from the hours and hours they spend watching. No wonder they go out and experiment with sex.

MUSIC AND LYRICS

I have asked young people how the music they listen to affects them and their peers. Their answers are always candid and revealing:

Another reason teenagers engage in premarital sex is the music they listen to. The lyrics in rock and country music are suggestive, they talk freely about sex. Countless song lyrics allude to one-night love affairs, part-time lovers, "this night will be a night of magic" and so on.

◆ ◆ ◆

Some teenagers may think nothing of it and say, "Oh, I don't listen to the words, I just like the rhythm and the tune." Subconsciously, though, they take in those suggestive lyrics. They may come to think any kind of sex is all right—which is not good.

◆ ◆ ◆

Over Christmas my brother cranked up the song "French Kissing in the USA," and to get me riled, he told me what a great song it was. The glorification of a song such as that leads teenagers to French kiss without even questioning it. This applies to music openly talking about having sex, etc.

The music kids listen to today conveys another strong message about sex. Popular music on the radio and CDs bombards them with explicit lyrics of sexual invitation and conquest. And as if hearing the words was not enough, cable networks like MTV and VH1 provide the suggestive images through their music videos. Kids don't just hear and see the music; they feel it through high-tech sound systems and booming speakers. They are persuaded by what they hear through constant repetition. Studies show that teenagers who listen to hard rock and heavy metal music are more likely to participate in high-risk behaviors, including drug use and sexual intercourse without contraception or with casual partners.[36]

When the music that teenagers find most appealing contains a barrage of encouragement toward sex, it is no surprise they are affected by it. Psychologist Abraham Maslow researched what he called "peak experiences" in human lives. He pointed out that of hundreds of cases studied, there were many different experiences that people singled out as their life's highlight. "Peak experiences" involving music ranked second in the list—surpassed only by sex. From such a statement one can deduce the dynamics when sex and music are combined.

Frank Zappa wrote an article on the role of rock in the sociosexual revolution. His conclusions were that rock music is sex. The big beat matches the body's rhythms, and the lyrics reinforce it.

A teenager's worldview, his value system, and his attitude toward human dignity will determine the role music plays in his life. If he knows the effect the lyrics have on him, he must make a choice about which music he will allow to influence him. If he chooses to listen to music that degrades rather than dignifies men and women, he is not only showing what his true worldview is but which influences he wants to shape his future actions.

PORNOGRAPHY

The darkest lies about sex told in the media are found in pornography. Pornography promotes sexual promiscuity, incestuous sexual relationships, marital infidelity, sexual deviancy, and "no-consequence" sex. Not only do pornographic videos, magazines, Web sites, etc., arouse sexual appetites and illicit desires, they graphically demonstrate the how-to's for a variety of sexual acts and perversions. Soft-core porn has been termed the "marijuana" of pornography that leads its users to desire harder, more bizarre "heroin" versions of sexual explicitness.

It can be tenably argued that increasing occurrences of date rape are linked to increasing exposure of males to nonviolent, soft-core pornography. I am convinced that the attitudes, perceptions, values, and sexual aggressiveness of teenagers are altered in the same or in an even greater way than those of adults as a result of their exposure to pornography. It is reasonable to assume that soft-core pornography and its themes would be especially appealing to adolescents discovering their own developing human sexuality. Teenagers are less equipped and less experienced than adults to understand and properly control their developing human sexuality and related sexual drives.

One of the most popular and accessible instruments of pornography at the dawn of the twenty-first century is the home computer and, more specifically, the Internet. Thousands of pornographic Web sites can be accessed from the same computer your kids use to research term papers and exchange e-mail. And many of these sites are free and can be located through most search engines.

Donna Rice Hughes, author of *Kids Online: Protecting Your Children in Cyberspace* (Revell, 1998), hosts a Web site with the URL www.protectkids.com. The following information about the extent of Internet pornography was posted on this site recently:

- There are now at least 40,000 porn sites on the World Wide Web and probably more. No one has been able to count them all. (*U.S. News & World Report*, 3/27/2000)
- Web surfers spent $970 million on access to adult-content sites in

1998. That number is expected to rise to more than $3 billion by 2003, according to the research firm Datamonitor. (*U.S. News & World Report*, 3/27/2000)

◆ Thirty percent of all unsolicited e-mails contain pornographic information. (Choose Your Mail.com study, October 1999)

◆ Cybersex is the crack cocaine of sexual addiction. (Dr. Robert Weiss, Sexual Recovery Institute, *Washington Times* 1/26/2000)

◆ Sixty percent of all Web site visits are sexual in nature. (MSNBC/Stanford/Duquesne Study, *Washington Times* 1/26/2000)

◆ Sex is the number one searched for topic on the Internet. (Dr. Robert Weiss, Sexual Recovery Institute, *Washington Times* 1/26/2000)

◆ Of all "born again" Christian adults (in America), 17.8 percent have visited sexually-oriented Web sites. (Zogby survey conducted for Focus on the Family, 2000)

Even more alarming, since the Internet is so easily accessed on the home computer, our young people are coming into contact with pornographic Web sites. Kids are taking advantage of the vast resources available to them on the Internet. In the process, they encounter—sometimes intentionally—material depicting sexual material of every description.

Protectkids.com adds the following information about kids, the Internet, and on-line pornography:

◆ A May 1999 survey found that 47 percent of American teens are on-line—the top two activities being e-mail (83 percent) and search engines (78 percent). (*Newsweek*, 5/10/99)

◆ The majority of teenagers' on-line use occurs at home, right after school, when working parents are not at home. (Arbitron New Media Study, October 1999)

◆ Fifty-three percent of teens have encountered offensive Web sites that include pornography, hate, or violence. Of these, 91 percent unintentionally found the offensive sites while searching the Web. (Yankelovich Partner survey, The Safe America Foundation; 9/30/99)

◆ Fifty-eight percent of teens say they have accessed an objectionable Web site: 39 percent offensive music, 25 percent sexual content, and 20 percent violence. (*USA Today*, 10/2/1999)

- Sixty-two percent of parents of teenagers are unaware that their children have accessed objectionable Web sites. (Yankelovich Partners Study, September 1999)
- Pornographers disguise their sites (i.e. "stealth" sites) with common brand names, including Disney, Barbie, and ESPN, to entrap children. (Cyveillance Study, March 1999)

Sadly, the Internet has placed pornography literally at the fingertips of our kids. In chapter 18, we will share some specific strategies for parents and other adults to help kids avoid the pitfalls of pornography on the Internet.

MEDIA'S BIGGEST LIE

But you may say, "Yes, excessive examples of illicit sexual activity on television, in movies, in music lyrics and videos, and on the Internet is undoubtedly a bad influence on our young people. But in a society as sexually permissive as ours, where's the lie?"

You can see it yourself by answering this question: In all the casual sex you have seen portrayed in the media, how many times has a character contracted a sexually transmitted disease? You are unusual if you can think of at least one occurrence. I often ask that question of the audiences to whom I speak. Even in crowds as large as 5,000, I rarely find someone who can remember even one bad outcome from casual sex.

From a medium that self-righteously expresses its concern for "the public's right to know," what we have been getting in this area is definitely a lie. A recent study found an average of ten incidents of sexual behavior per hour on network television during prime time. Yet references to adverse consequences are rare; there are approximately twenty-five instances of sexual behavior portrayed on prime-time television for every instance of protective behavior shown or comment regarding STDs or unintended pregnancy.[37]

Here is my point in bold letters to underscore its importance: **Hardly anyone on TV or in the movies pays a price for illicit sex. But in real life, people often pay dearly.** A number of studies bear out my contention that the media is lying about the dangers of casual sex:

- A University of California at Santa Barbara study found that "sexual content crops up in 75 percent of programs during the 'Family Hour,' the first hour of prime time when most kids are watching." The report's sponsors say that "while a rise in such content may not be surprising, parents may be shocked to learn that only one in 10 of such discussions addresses the risks and responsibilities of sex."[38]

◆ In a study of daytime serials, 50 hours of selected programming included 156 acts of sexual intercourse and only five references within three episodes to contraception or safer sex. The only mention of HIV/AIDS referred to contraction through IV drug use and not sexual activity.[39]

◆ In his book *Prime Time*, Robert Lichter and his colleagues at the Center for Media and Public Affairs found that prime-time television now by implication endorses unmarried adults' intentions to have sex in about three out of four cases and raises concerns only about 5 percent of the time.[40]

◆ Only 10 percent of the shows studied in the Kaiser report mentioned any possible consequences of having sex, such as unintended pregnancy—not to mention how illicit sex can lead to AIDS or the judgment of God.[41]

When Derek sees a scene of tender, casual sex in a war movie, he may consider it innocent and relatively harmless. The sex is great, and the characters go on with their lives (and subsequent loves) enriched from having met and mingled bodily fluids. Derek is left with the subtle impression that casual sex isn't so bad.

But that's not real life. It's fiction. It's fantasy. It's a lie. In real life, such encounters often end with the participants diseased and dying. But we almost never see that in the movies. No wonder Derek has begun to question God's prohibitions on premarital sex. He is falling under the influence of the lie.

The last secular romance novel Annie read portrayed a young woman "coming of age" in the arms of a dashing, romantic man who introduced her to the glories of sex in the bedroom of a romantic Victorian mansion. But books like that rarely describe the guilt and emotional trauma many young women suffer after being conquered and eventually discarded. So when Annie's boyfriend stirs up her passions with his loving words and tender kisses, what reason does she have to delay the bliss she expects from yielding to his advances?

Our actions are the result of our thoughts, and our thoughts are the result of what we have put into our minds. We cannot think something unless we have a basis for it in our minds. Granted, human beings are creative, able to think abstractly, able to stretch the limits of thought to new areas. Yet we require certain images with which to build those thoughts.

If people had never seen pornography, would they be able to conceive it and dwell on evil thoughts? Possibly. But if all they had ever heard of sex was how it forms a beautiful bond in a marriage, they would be hard-pressed to warp those thoughts.

But our society has been spared the work of having to create evil thoughts. We just buy a magazine, go to a porn theater (and hope no one sees us), pay for a sexually explicit channel on the cable or dish, or log on to a XXX Web site that brings degradation and exploitation into the comfort of our living room or bedroom. It all looks so professional and nicely done that we forget what we are really seeing: a gift of God being perverted for profit. And our kids have greater access to these evils than we want to believe. You may have the sex networks blocked on your television system, but the parents of your child's friend may not.

The pornographers walk away with our money, but their patrons—including our young people—walk away with the opinion that people are objects to be used for personal gratification instead of God's beautiful creation. The longer and more intensely we dwell on these thoughts, the more likely we will be to act them out.

When our thoughts are out of sync with the truth, our actions will be also. That is why the Bible tells us to guard our minds, not to tempt ourselves, not to be conformed to the garbage the world offers us, but rather to be transformed by the renewing of our minds, that we may understand God's good, pleasing, and perfect will (see Rom. 12:2). And when we get a grip on his will, we can act in accordance with it.

THE DECEPTION OF DISTORTED VALUES

What are the results of the media's lie? Bombarded by thousands of messages promoting "harmless" casual sex, millions of adolescents are getting pregnant and/or contracting STDs every year. By and large, the secular media does little to reinforce moral values or demonstrate the consequences of irresponsible moral behavior.

The current alarm regarding the spread of AIDS, however, has triggered some healthy signs of change. You rarely see anyone in the media acquiring an STD from promiscuity, but there appears to be a trend toward recognizing that possibility. The trend seems to be toward portraying more monogamous relationships and expressions of regard for safety, both for oneself and for the other person.

While these trends could bring some positive changes, we must be aware of the subtle ways in which they also will promote promiscuity and premarital sex. The expected changes will not bring a godly morality with its fulfilling expression of genuine love. Rather, they will make the changing values appear respectable.

For years now we have allowed the media to misrepresent casual sex and free love. Young people have been shown that the cure for everything is to jump into bed. Sex is proclaimed as a cure-all. It's the remedy for emptiness and loneliness. It's the answer to a lack of significance. All lies. Sex is not a cure-all. There's no such thing as casual sex. There's no such thing as free love.

For the most part we have allowed our young people to determine who they are as sexual beings on the basis of these lies propagated by the media. This deception is crucial, because our sexuality affects everything we say, hear, think, and do. Sexuality is at the core of our human existence. And we have allowed our young people, who are growing up right now, to base their sexuality on lies.

Enticing, erotic scenes on TV and in the movies communicate to our teens, "Be sexually active." The focus is on immediate sexual gratification. Yet the concerned parent says, "Wait" and promotes abstinence as the standard for young people. Our kids are getting mixed signals about sexual behavior—no wonder there is so much confusion.

The media not only distorts sexual realities, but it also cultivates feelings of inadequacy among young viewers. When judging the value of a person, tremendous emphasis is placed on the physical. The media communicates that the value of a person is primarily his or her physical attractiveness. We are blitzed in the media with an endless parade of beautiful women, which gives teenage girls a very unrealistic standard by which to judge their own attractiveness.

I hope you know that the media's standard for beauty is not realistic. What's more, it is constantly changing with regard to which body types, hairstyles, fashions, etc., are "in." Think what that does to the average young woman. Often it totally distorts her sense of self-worth. If by comparison to the latest standards of physical beauty she is not attractive, she sees herself as without worth or value, which results in tremendous feelings of inadequacy.

The young male is also affected. He develops totally unrealistic ideas about a woman's true beauty. Why do most men place physical attractiveness above all other considerations when they seek relationships with the opposite sex? Because of the media, of course. All the male heroes on TV have "beautiful women."

What gives the media such power over young people? It's the amount of time they spend listening, watching, reading, and absorbing what it purveys. Consequently, young people spend less time interacting with real adults. Their heroes and models are fictional characters on a screen living lives that are fantasy, not reality. They end up believing and emulating a lie.

Sad to say, most young people, even from church families, have not learned about their sexuality in church. Even a greater tragedy, most did not learn about their sexuality at home. They have learned it from television, movies, music, and the Internet.

The sexual "freedom" portrayed in today's entertainment media is a joke made at the expense of human dignity. Sex without marriage so often leads to self-doubts, diseases, unwanted pregnancies, shattered emotions, manipulation, and exploitation. Such results are rarely portrayed on TV or in the movies because people don't want to hear about those things. They want to be told that somehow, someday, their promiscuity will lead to happiness, even though it hasn't up to this point. And since our culture demands entertainment that reflects its hopes—not its realities—our TV and movie screens will continue to bring us lies about sex.

The Scriptures admonish us to flee youthful temptation. If a teen knows that and still takes his girlfriend to see an R-rated movie with plenty of skin, he will probably act out his aroused feelings when the movie is over. He can blame society all he wants, but he chose to see the movie, despite the warning in the Bible. Or if a teen girl invites her boyfriend over to watch an R-rated video or cable movie, she shouldn't be surprised when she violates her own limits of physical contact.

PUTTING THE MEDIA IN ITS PLACE

If the attitudes of our young people toward sex are going to change, either the media must change or the listening and viewing habits of young people must change. While we have been permissively silent, the media of our culture has been telling our children that intimacy is found through sex and that casual sex and free love are valid expressions. As a result, most of our young people have developed their concept of sexuality from the media's message without realizing that premarital sex comes with a staggering price tag. One young lady wrote to me about the high price she paid:

> What the movies and the soap operas don't tell us about is the devastation and the broken hearts that occur due to affairs and premarital sex. I do not make light of the consequences of wrong sexual involvement. Without a doubt, the hardest and most painful thing I've gone through, more than major surgery, tests for cancer, a broken family, and numerous job rejections, is getting over a sexual relationship with a married man.

Before placing all the blame on the media, however, we must examine our role in this problem as parents, teachers, pastors, and youth leaders. Many of us share in the blame because of our permissiveness. Often we regard television as a harmless "electronic baby-sitter." We send our young people off to the local multiplex theater without reading up on the movies they are going to see. We turn our kids loose on the computer without monitoring the sexually explicit Web sites that can be accessed with only the click of a mouse.

How much guidance have you given your children and youth about what television programs and movies to watch? What about the music they listen to? Have you ever written a letter of protest to your local television stations when they broadcast inappropriate programming? In most cases we have lost the battle without even putting up a fight. Many of us have been silent both inside and outside the home concerning the dangerous effects of what our kids watch and listen to.

No, I'm not advocating that we throw out our TVs and radios, destroy our computers, boycott movie theaters or video rental stores, and toss all paperbacks and magazines into the furnace. These avenues of communication all have a positive upside. We just need to help our kids sort through what they watch and listen to, recognize the lies that are being communicated, and put appropriate filters in place.

Parents have the task of bringing their children up in the admonition of the Lord and the influence of the Scriptures, yet they cannot go on dates with their kids to keep them in line. Parents always must be a resource of God's standards when a young person needs an answer, but kids ultimately make their own decisions. The more they are taught from their early years to make proper choices, the easier it will be for them to stay on the right course when temptation comes.

Sure, you may have to expend more time and energy to guard yourself and your children against the onslaught of lies being propagated through the media. And you may need to mount a personal campaign to confront your local television stations and the advertisers who sponsor them. But if you don't make an investment in your kids now, you may have to later, after the unchallenged lies of the media have made a shambles of their personal lives. (Part 4 of this book will offer a number of strategies to help adults provide the guidance and help kids need in the area of sexual behavior.)

We point our fingers at the media as being responsible for the sexual bombardment we endure on every page and every channel. The media point their fingers back at us and say they are only giving us what we want. "As a person thinks, so he is," say the Scriptures. So as our minds fill with sexual thoughts, we buy magazines containing articles about sex and we contribute to the ratings of TV shows with sexual encounters. Our minds become more filled with sex, and we demand more from the media. It is a snowball effect—a vicious cycle.

In a way, the amusement we seek in the media (by the way, the word *amusement* literally means "without thinking") is a denial of God's creation of us. We are created in his image: intelligent, clever, able to reason. By replacing mental nourishment with mental chewing gum, we turn our backs on one of the major elements that sets us apart from animals. When that mental sedative fills us with sexual suggestions and images, we associate sex with amusement.

From there, it is a simple step to seek out sex as a form of amusing escape, a sensory entertainment. Teenagers are doubly susceptible to this because of the hormonal and emotional upheavals they are going through. Without a knowledge of right and wrong, without standards, without the Holy Spirit to fill the void, young people are open to the quickest counterfeit escape our society can provide.

The number one barrier we can erect against the influence of the negative media is an emotional attachment, a loving bond, and an intimate connection with our children. From this positive relationship you may then discuss the issue of the impact of media in their lives and in your home. This is much more effective than categorically blasting the media and forbidding your children from movies, TV, or the Internet. Such a response is often an attempt to compensate for the lack of a close family relationship.

◆ ◆ ◆

When our young people immerse themselves in the media and allow sexually charged images and sounds to fan the flames of adolescent hormones, there is often a deeper reason for it. Kids are looking for something to satisfy their deep, God-instilled needs: love, acceptance, approval, affirmation, and intimacy, to name but a few. And when those needs go unmet in home, church, and school, adolescents intensify the search in other, less healthy areas. In the next chapter we will explore how some of the significant adults in a child's life—those who should be part of the solution—are actually a large part of the problem.

CHAPTER 7

THE EMOTIONAL REASONS

A "LOVE FAMINE" AT HOME

STUDENTS AT CERTAIN UNIVERSITIES are not known for their benevolence toward visiting speakers, especially those with conservative and/or Christian views. As I waited my turn to speak at the outdoor free-speech platform of one of these schools, I felt butterflies in my stomach. What I say had better be right on or it would be shoved back down my throat. If the students were not interested in my topic or how I developed it, they would simply ignore me.

As I stepped up to speak, the crowd was noisy and not particularly hospitable. There was no public address system so I had to rely on old-fashioned lung power to be heard. I had only a few seconds to grab their attention. The butterflies were still there as I began. "Almost every one of you has two fears. First, you are afraid you will never be loved. Second, you are afraid you will never be able to love."

The noise suddenly evaporated and everyone turned in my direction, suddenly eager to hear where I was going with my bold opening. I wasn't surprised because I knew my statement would strike a nerve. Most students readily identify with these two deep fears.

Psychologists believe that this "love famine" is one reason many young men and women get involved in premarital sex. Lisa, who is sixteen and pregnant, would agree:

My mother kept asking me, "Why? Why?" My answer was simple: Because I want to be loved, that's why. Is that so terrible? I wanted someone to tell me that I'm pretty, that he cared about me. Finally, someone did.

n this chapter we will look at two specific ways a love famine in the home may prompt adolescent premarital sex: (1) a lack of parental love, modeling, and attention and (2) a lack of parental instruction about sex.

OUR KIDS NEED LOVE, MODELING, AND ATTENTION

Young people are adrift in their sexual beliefs, convictions, and behavior because they don't know how to love. Learning to love is not something that happens automatically. We don't just grow up, reach puberty, and find that all of a sudden we know how to love. I'm not talking about sex here; I'm talking about the essence of love—caring, transparency, vulnerability, and intimacy.

Love is not primarily a feeling. If love were a feeling, God could not command it because you can't make someone feel something. For example, you can tell your child, "You are going to eat broccoli and you are going to like it." You may be able to get your child to eat it, but you can't make him or her like it. Similarly, you can command someone to love another person—which is an act of the will, but you cannot make him or her like that person because you cannot force an emotion.

Love is first and foremost an action. Paul makes that clear in 1 Corinthians 13. Telling someone "I love you" has no meaning if it is not supported by loving actions. We can't teach love to our kids. Love is not a lecture class; it's a lab course. Young people learn to love by seeing love modeled, experiencing love from others, and replicating the example. Love is learned by responding to its expression.

God intended for kids to learn to love in the home by seeing both parents first love each other and then love them unconditionally. When young people learn love at home, they won't have to go out looking for it in the backseat of a car. According to Sarah Brown, director of the Washington, D.C., based National Campaign to Prevent Teen Pregnancy, "We know from studies that close relationships between parents and their children over many years reduce sexual risks."[1]

When loving relationships in the home break down and the parental model of love ceases to function, children grow up ignorant of how to give or receive love. For these children, developing close, intimate relationships may be impossible. Despite a desperate need for love, young people who grow up experiencing a love famine at home are afraid they will never find it. So they often settle for a cheap imitation: sexual experiences that will only make their pain and hunger for love worse.

After listening to one of my talks in England, a sixteen-year-old wrote to me:

> I wish someone would just love me. I want someone to show me they care. I just wanted you to know that. I want love but I don't know how to accept it or give it.

I could show you scores of letters just like that one. Our kids are starving for genuine parental love. That's why so many of them search out or fall into sexual relationships at a young age. They don't know how to love because they have not seen love modeled, so they settle for sex, which the media portray as love.

What happens when parents pay little or no attention to their children? What happens when work stress is allowed to pollute relationships at home? What happens when adult role models are gone or absent from the home? Our Judeo-Christian values are not communicated effectively, if at all. Children and young people are left starved for love. Many young people are uncertain of their parents' love. I personally know many parents who definitely love their children, but whose actions don't always show it.

Where teenage premarital sex is concerned, the only foolproof solution is prevention. This begins with parents spending time with their children long before hormones, peers, and the media begin pressuring them about sex.

Parental Modeling

I often am asked to give one single reason why kids get involved in premarital sex. Of course I always reply that there are many reasons, and we are covering most of them in this section of the book. However, if I had to narrow it down to just one reason, it would be this: inattentive parents.

According to research, "Nearly one in three parents in America is seriously disengaged from his or her adolescent's life, and especially, from the adolescent's education."[2] Parental inattentiveness creates a love famine that affects both parents and children. It also creates a vicious, self-perpetuating cycle in which parents who are starved for love raise children who are even hungrier for love. The results are devastating.

On the other hand, a healthy home environment makes a significant difference in the health of American youth. When teens feel connected to their families and when parents are involved in their children's lives, teens are protected. Teens also are protected by their parents being present at key times during the day (in the morning, after school, at dinner, and at bedtime), and by their parents' high expectations for school performance. When parents are more frequently present in the home at key times of the day, older youth (grades nine to twelve) are less likely to smoke cigarettes or drink alcohol, and both older and younger adolescents are less likely to smoke marijuana.[3]

Close parental involvement and connection is also a key ingredient in preventing premarital sex. Adolescents who receive warmth, love, and caring from parents, and whose parents openly disapprove of adolescent premarital sex and contraception, are less likely to become sexually active. In other words, loving, involved parents who give clear messages about delaying sex have children who are less likely to have early intercourse. Providing teens with a sense of connectedness is one of the most important things we can do as parents to help them learn to say no to destructive behaviors.

One of the greatest securities of a child comes from the love of the parents for each other. Young people today are longing for relationships that will last. They are crying out for role models of men and women who have it together — in love, marriage, sex, and family. They are desperately looking for relationships that work. One of the greatest things parents can do for their children is to love one another and let their children know it.

Searching for a Father's Love

Even though love from both parents is important, most young people especially crave love and attention from their fathers. Why is this so? One reason is that men have real problems with showing their emotions. Some men even hide any tender feelings they might have by pretending to be cynical about love. They are uncomfortable with any serious discussion of love. And those who can't talk about love usually have difficulty expressing it. I really believe that lots of hugs between fathers and their teenage children—especially their daughters— would do more to stop adolescent premarital sex than any other single factor.

An essay written by a young woman in her twenties illustrates the critical importance of a father's love and attention:

> When I was fourteen, I dated an eighteen-year-old boy. After a month or so of dating, he told me that he loved me and had to have me. He said if I loved him I would have sex with him. And if I wouldn't, he would have to break up with me. What did I think at fourteen years of age? I knew sex was wrong before marriage, yet I so desired to have a man love me.

I was so insecure about my father's love; I always felt like I had to earn it. The better I was at home with my chores, the more my father loved me. The more A's on my report card, the more my father loved me.

So here's my boyfriend, whom I really liked and thought I loved, telling me he loved me. Well, I needed that love. And if the condition to keep that love was to have sex with him, I felt I had no choice. I didn't want to lose my virginity, but I also didn't want to lose the man who loved me. So I finally gave in.

After two years I broke up with my boyfriend, and soon had another and went through the same cycle with him, and then another, and another. Was I more secure? No. I was a puppet in the hands of any man who said, "I love you." I wanted so desperately to find someone who would love me unconditionally. Isn't that ironic? The main thing I searched for, unconditional love, was being offered to me conditionally. "If you love me, you'll have sex with me."

At the age of twenty-one I found that unconditional love.

This young woman found Jesus Christ, who accepted her just as she was. She ended her essay with an entry from her personal diary. In it we see the inner self of a beautiful human being who has suffered immeasurably in her search for her father's love:

I felt lonely tonight, and I thought about the many times in my life that I have felt lonely . . . intense loneliness, as though I were here in life all alone. And I realized that what I was lonely for was a daddy, to be able to call him up when I hurt, have him listen to me, hear him say he understands. But I never had that with my dad, so I'm lonely without that link to my past.

Yet tonight God spoke to me in that still, quiet way and said He was there for me. As my tears poured, I said, "Will You be my daddy? Will You be there to talk to . . . just to talk to? And will You listen? Yes, I know You will. And the most wonderful thing about You as my daddy is that I can be with You all the time."

Then I thought about the girl who this very night will lose her virginity because she is searching for her daddy's love. And I want to be able to stop her somehow and tell her that she'll never find it in another man.

How my heart is wrenched when I think of this girl . . . when I think of myself, so many years ago. My life has been a search for my daddy's love. And in Jesus, I am found and I am loved. Forever.

The results of one survey suggest that most sexually active girls are looking for something other than sex in their romantic relationships. The survey reported that 72 percent of women prefer being held close and treated tenderly than having sex.[4] Had their fathers been a continuing source of acceptance and affection, these girls would not have had to seek them in illicit relationships.

I receive letters from kids like this all the time. Here are four of them that touched me deeply:

I realize that you don't know me, and I'm only a face in a crowd of teenagers. Why don't I have a father like you? You made me cry today when, in my high school assembly, you talked about your relationship with your daughter and how you show her you love her. I never cry. You learn not to in my family. All I want is a chance. I wish I had a father. I wish someone loved me like you love your family. You don't know how badly I want to understand things, how much I want a chance to. And it may sound stupid but if someone would hold me just for a minute—no strings, no games—well, I can't really explain it.

◆ ◆ ◆

I am fifteen years old. I'm one of those teenagers that is in search of their father's love. Could you please pray for me, and also for my dad and mom? Just pray that they will see that teens do spell love T-I-M-E. I wish so much that my daddy would do half the things with me that you've done with yours. He hasn't done anything since I was about five. And I've really needed it, the past eight years especially.

◆ ◆ ◆

My name is Jennifer. I am fifteen years old. I watch your show every time I can. Thank you so much for just caring. I know you have never met me, but it's almost like you're the daddy I never had. You see, my real dad left me and my mom when I was a baby, and when I was just three years old my stepdad left. Neither one of them would fall under the name "father."

The other night you said that most kids don't want to have sex, they just want someone to care. That is so true! I have almost fallen into the "sex trap" because I just wanted a man to love me.

◆ ◆ ◆

In Birmingham, when I shook hands with you and gave you the letter, and you gave me a "peck" on the cheek, I must say, it made me feel "loved." A peck on the cheek is a "fatherly" expression. I've never had a kiss! I wish I'd had a father to phone me and say, "I love you, honey."

Perhaps some of you fathers are feeling that I'm being unfair. "I thought you said the problem was inattentive parents. You seem to be focusing only on fathers. What about inattentive mothers?"

Of course there are inattentive mothers, and they undoubtedly have a damaging effect on their children. But I think that we men must shoulder much of the blame for our teens being where they are. Most of us are very busy. We are gone from home a lot because of our jobs. When we come home tired, it is easy to neglect our children. What we men need to realize is how important it is to our children that we have a close, loving relationship with them. Sure, mothers are important, but they can't do the job of loving our children *alone*.

I held a one-week youth conference at the largest (and one of the wealthiest) evangelical churches in our country. I had counseling appointments with forty-two junior and senior high school students. Their number one question was, "Josh, what can I do about my dad?" When I asked what they meant, they made statements like, "He never has time for me"; "He never takes me anywhere"; "He never talks to me"; "He never does anything with me."

I asked all forty-two of them, "Can you talk with your father?" Only one said yes.

I also asked all the girls, "If you got pregnant, could you go right to your father and share this with him?" Most of them didn't feel they could. That's heartbreaking, isn't it? If ever there is a time when a young woman ought to be able to go to her father and talk to him, it is in a situation like that.

Teens as young as thirteen or fourteen years of age "struggle with complex sexual situations, involving pressure, drinking and drug use, or relationships that are moving too fast, which they are often not prepared to handle."[5] Slightly over one-third (36 percent) say they have done something sexual, or have felt pressure to do something sexual, that they did not feel ready to do.

Broken Families

Divorce — its prevalence in our society, the fear that it will happen to their parents, or the pain of a family already shattered by it — is another key reason young people reach out for sex as a substitute for the warmth of parental love. I learned about this fear firsthand many years ago.

One day, when my now married son, Sean, was only six years old, he came home from school a little bummed out. I asked what was wrong.

"Aw, nothing, Dad."

Sean and I communicate pretty well, so I said, "Come on, share with me what you're feeling."

He hesitated and then asked, "Daddy, are you going to leave Mommy?"

I knew that question would come up someday. "What makes you ask that?" I said.

Three of his friends' dads had just divorced their mothers, Sean told me, and he was afraid I might do the same.

I sat down with Sean, looked him in the eye, and said, "I want you to know one thing. I love your mother very much. I'm committed to her, and I'll never leave her. Period."

That little six-year-old heaved a big sigh of relief. Then he smiled at me and said, "Thanks, Dad." He didn't need reinforcement of my love for him; he needed the security that comes from knowing that his mother and I love each other and are committed to a permanent relationship. Like all young people today, Sean needed to be part of a lasting relationship.

Evidence of the emotional consequences of divorce on young people is everywhere. One of the great fears of many young children and teenagers is the loss of a parent through divorce—and with good reason. You may have heard that the national divorce rate has slowed in recent years. It's true. The divorce rate peaked in the early 1980s, and by 1991 the divorce rate had dropped to its lowest point since 1979.[6] Yet married couples continue to divorce in alarming numbers. The following research indicates that divorce is a problem that does not seem to be going away:

- According to the National Center for Health Statistics, the number of divorces in America has increased nearly 200 percent in the last thirty years, while today the percentage of people marrying is at an all-time low.
- According to the U.S. Bureau of the Census, in 1960 there were 73.5 marriages for every 1,000 unmarried females and 9.2 divorces for every 1,000 married females. By 1987, there were only 55.7 marriages per 1,000 unmarried women and 21 divorces per 1,000 married women.
- In 1960, 70 percent of all marriages were first marriages while today about 50 percent are first marriages.[7]
- Almost one-third of all American families with minor children—63 percent of the nation's black families—are headed by single parents, and the percentages are rising, the Census Bureau reports.[8]

- In 1970, there were 3.8 million single parents, in 1990 there were 9.7 million, and in 1994 there were 11.4 million.[9]
- One million children have been affected by divorce every year since 1972; that's 25.5 million children.[10]
- At least 37 percent of American children live with divorced parents.[11]
- Tonight about 40 percent of American children will go to sleep in homes where their fathers do not live. Before they reach the age of eighteen, more than half of our nation's children will spend at least a significant portion of their childhoods living apart from their fathers. Never before in our nation's history have so many children grown up without knowing what it means to have a father.[12]
- Research shows that 60 percent of all new marriages now end in separation or divorce.
- Divorce is a primary factor in as many as three in four teen suicides.
- Young people from the ages of eighteen to twenty-two are twice as likely to show high levels of emotional distress and have poor relationships with their parents if they come from divorced families compared to intact families.[13]
- The U.S. Census Bureau reports that between 1980 and 1990, the number of stepfamilies increased 36 percent to 5.3 million. There are 7.3 million children in stepfamilies.[14]
- In a seven-year study of 198 stepfamilies and nuclear families, it was found that 20 to 30 percent of stepchildren had significant behavior problems, while 10 to 15 percent of those in nuclear families did.[15]
- Children who are raised "outside of intact marriages" are at high risk for serious problems in their lives. These children are two to three times more likely to become criminals, to experience psychological disorders or to drop out of school, and five times more likely to live in poverty.[16]
- Studies show that women, who usually end up with custody of minor children, experience an average of a 73 percent decline in living standards during the first year after a divorce.[17]
- Fewer than 60 percent of today's children live with their biological, married parents, while the percentage of children living with a divorced parent has risen from 2.1 percent in 1960 to 9.5 percent in 1990.[18]

David Poponoe, a professor of sociology at Rutgers University, says, "In three decades of work as a social scientist, I know of few other bodies of data in which the weight of evidence is so decisively on one side of the issue: on the whole, for children, two-parent families are preferable. . . . If our prevailing views on family structure hinged solely on scholarly evidence, the current debate would never have arisen in the first place."[19]

More emphasis on closer family ties is desired by 86 percent of teens, with only slightly greater emphasis on this value noted among young women (90 percent) than among young men (82 percent). Is it surprising then that 75 percent of the surveyed teenagers felt that it is too easy to get a divorce in this country? Of teens from divorced homes, 74 percent said that their parents didn't try hard enough. A research institute study showed that out of a list of twenty-four values, the two most important to young adolescents in grades five through nine are "to have a happy family life" and "to get a good job when I am older." The "State of the Nation's Youth" survey showed that "84 percent of the teens' . . . future success will be defined by whether they have close family relationships."[20]

When divorcing parents ask their children, "Do you want us to continue our painful relationship for your sake?" the answer is almost universally, "Yes, we do!" Young people today want to be part of a loving, lasting relationship.

One reason divorce is so damaging to young people is that it generally removes fathers from day-to-day contact with their children. Today men spend much less time in the home than they did in past generations, either because of heavy workloads or because of divorce. Ninety percent of the children of divorce live with their mothers. By the time a child today is eighteen, the odds are that he or she will have spent some part of life living with the mother alone. In almost every case, divorce means a fatherless home. One-half of the children with divorced parents do not see their fathers regularly.

DIVORCE

I believe that divorce has a greater negative impact on a child than the death of a parent. There are several reasons why it is easier for most children to lose a parent through death than through divorce.

First, when children lose a parent through death, they usually will not feel personally responsible. But when they lose a parent through divorce, they often blame themselves, even though in most cases they had nothing to do with it. Almost every child of divorce goes through life carrying that heavy load of guilt that sounds like this: "Mom and Dad split up, and it's my fault."

A boy of ten said to me in all seriousness, "If I had kept my room clean, my dad wouldn't have left my mother." I asked him what he meant. He said his dad used to complain (as I think most dads do) that his room was always messy. Then one day his dad and mother separated, and the boy assumed it was his fault. I'm afraid this boy will go through high school, college, and into a career believing he was personally responsible for the breakup of his parents' marriage. What a terrible burden to carry!

I counseled a young woman whose parents were divorced when she was sixteen. She said, "If I had been a better cook, my father would never have divorced my mother." Because her mother worked outside the home, it was Debbie's responsibility to keep the house clean and prepare the evening meals. Her father often complained about her cooking. Then one night this man, whom she loved and admired more than anyone on the face of the earth, packed his bags and left. Seven years later, Debbie remains convinced—no matter what anyone tells her—that "my father divorced my mother because I was a lousy cook." Her cooking had nothing to do with the divorce of her parents. But regardless of how many counselors she may see (she's now with her fifth psychologist), Debbie continues to go through life blaming herself.

After I had spoken at a conference, a woman came to me asking for my help. She told me that two weeks earlier her husband had served her with divorce papers. That afternoon, as she was driving to the conference with her fourteen-year-old son, the boy said to her, "Mom, I'm sorry. I'm sorry. Forgive me!" Then he began crying. When she asked what he was sorry about, he answered, "I'm sorry for making Dad divorce you." The woman assured him that the breakup was not his fault. But he kept insisting, "Yes, it is my fault." When she asked why, he answered, "If I hadn't loved soccer so much, he would never have left you."

I see it all the time. Young people feel responsible for their parents' divorce.

The second reason it is more difficult to lose a parent through divorce than through death is the lack of finality. When a parent dies, it is painful, but the child eventually realizes Mom or Dad is gone and experiences a measure of closure. After a period of mourning, he goes on with his life.

But there is no finality with divorce. It isn't over in the lives of the kids when the papers are signed. There is no mourning period after which he or she picks up the pieces, goes on with life, and begins the healing process. The reality of divorce returns every holiday, every summer vacation, and—for many young-sters—every weekend. The pain of separation goes on and on. Christmas with Mom, New Year's with Dad. Easter dinner at Dad's house, Thanksgiving dinner at Mom's. Spring break with one parent, summer vacation with the other. There's no end to it.

I hear so many divorced fathers and mothers say, "You know, my kids really handled the divorce well." These parents try to find comfort in the apparent strength of their children. And it may seem that the kids are doing well on the outside. Teens can often do that—fool us about what's happening on the inside. But you know they have to be hurting.

Social scientists can provide us with volumes of statistics on divorce. But they cannot quantify its emotional impact on our children. Divorce is a major cause of the diminished hope in our kids and one reason why they may start looking for love in all the wrong places.

Broken Home, Broken Kids

A Chinese proverb says, "In the broken nest there are no whole eggs." What a pro-vocative summary of the negative impact of divorce.[21] The U.S. Census Bureau gives the following statistics regarding the increase of divorce in our culture:

- In 1900, one divorce for every ten marriages.
- In 1920, one divorce for every seven marriages.
- In 1940, one divorce for every six marriages.
- In 1960, one divorce for every four marriages.
- In 1972, one divorce for every three marriages.
- In 1976, one divorce for every two marriages.[22]

When God said, "Let us make man in our image," he didn't just make a male. He made a female also. Although each individual is handcrafted by God, the complete image of God is shown in the relationship of a man and a woman. When that relationship is broken, the image of God in the home is shattered.

God the Father is the model for earthly fathers. Earthly fathers are to point their families to God the Father. This is the design, yet it has all but disappeared from American society in the last two decades. We are seeing many results of this in our kids, one of which is being early sexual involvement.

Mary is a seventeen-year-old with two younger brothers and a married sister.

Her parents have been divorced for almost a year. Mary and her brothers have been living with their mother, who works outside the home all day. Mary's boyfriend is the dream of every girl. Erick is a senior and a very popular football player. He has been Mary's only source of comfort for months now. As a result, Erick feels entitled to ask Mary to have sex. Mary's loneliness for her own father enhances her fear of rejection, so she consents.

A broken home is a major influence in adolescent premarital sex. I have received letters from countless numbers of kids whose parents are divorced. And many of these kids tell me that they have become involved in premarital sex.

In addition, the increased divorce rate has influenced teens' decisions when they find themselves in an unplanned pregnancy situation. "An obvious reason so many teenagers are rejecting marriage [when they discover they are pregnant] is because of the emotional pain they have suffered from their parents' failed marriages. The divorce rate has increased 400 percent since 1963, leaving today's youth with deep-seated emotional scars."[23]

Even when they do consider marriage, the outlook is grim. "Nearly one-third of first marriages among teens end in divorce within five years," according to the Alan Guttmacher Institute.[24]

Broken homes can lead to premarital sex in at least four ways. One is the lack of value structure that results from such a family. Children are taught to say, "I'm sorry," to put things back where they got them, to be polite, to be nice to their little sisters. Yet Mom and Dad are unforgiving, unaccepting, and mean to each other. Without adult role models, the concepts of right and wrong disappear.

A broken home also can lead to premarital sex as the influence and pressure from peers becomes stronger than that in the home. The closeness and sharing that should take place in the family is sought elsewhere.

In addition, a lack of security in the home may motivate a teenager to look for intimacy in irrational ways. Physical closeness will not provide true intimacy, but it gives a temporary and sensory substitute for security.

A fourth reason is the effect of divorce on the child's self-image. Children of divorced parents not only feel rejected by the parents, but they also usually hold themselves accountable for the divorce, as though their actions caused it. The feelings of rejection and guilt may cause a teenager to seek a boost in his or her self-image through sex. Sex allows that teen to feel important and attractive to someone.

If there was something you could do to prevent your son or daughter, or the young people in your church or school, from experiencing the pain and heartache that accompany premarital sex, would you do it? I can't imagine anyone answering that question in the negative. Any parent, pastor, or teacher with any compassion at all would jump at the chance to save his or her kids from pain.

There *is* something you can do, and it is within your reach. I often say it this way: One of the best things you can do for your kids is to love your spouse. You can combat the love famine in your child's life by purposely modeling love in your relationship with your husband or wife. Make your marriage a growing example of a loving relationship. Let your respect, kindness, faithfulness, and friendship show in how you talk to each other, care for each other, and even disagree with each other. Then determine to demonstrate that same quality of love toward the young people under your care. It will make all the difference in the world.

OUR KIDS NEED CLEAR INSTRUCTION ABOUT SEX

When there is a love famine in the home, positive, nurturing communication suffers. As a result, adolescents lack parental instruction about sex. They must gain their sexual education elsewhere, through self-discovery, peers, or the media. As a result, sex education is at best incomplete and at worst erroneous.

A couple of students summarized the situation this way:

> Teenagers are ignorant about what they are doing. All they know is that they were made with certain body parts, so they might as well find out what they're used for. Sort of like test-driving a car just to see how well it performs.

> ◆ ◆ ◆

> Lack of accurate information about sex, although less of a problem than in our parents' adolescence, is still quite common, and young people often don't realize how far they are going. Before they know it, they have an unexpected pregnancy on their hands. It must be pointed out that some parents are much to blame since they have not informed their children on the topic of sex, either because they are too embarrassed to discuss it, are irresponsible, or are ignorant themselves.

Sex education begins at home, whether parents are aware of it or not. When sex is honestly discussed, the home becomes a source of both objective facts and moral understanding. When sex is a taboo subject, kids discern that it is something mysterious and forbidden, and therefore something probably worth exploring.

The Kaiser Family Foundation agrees that parents play the most important role in a child's sexual education. Even though I disagree on the type of information children need, I agree with the foundation's conclusion: "Parents are the number one influence on their children's sexual decisions, and the more information you give a child, the more likely he or she is to abstain. Yet only 44 percent of moms and dads have discussed the topic with their preteen."[25]

So the process of educating children about sex in an intelligent and open manner must begin at home. Teenagers need to know that the changes in their bodies and the changing emotions that accompany them are normal. They need to know that their increased sexual awareness is also normal.

This is especially important among Christians. The church also must be involved in the education of its young members. Teenagers are going to find out one way or another how their bodies work, and when parents and the church deny kids the information they so vitally need, they set their young people up for trouble.

Sex education at home must begin at a very young age and continue as the child grows up. It is an eighteen-year course of love and insight, sharing and listening. If you wait for the "big talk," it probably will come too late. By the time you get around to it, your child probably already knows more than you do (or at least he or she will think so).

It is one thing for someone to say, "Teach your kids about sex," and quite another to find parents eager to do so. But we must respond to the needs of our children. Secular educators and family planning organizations are more than happy to fill the void that many Christian parents are leaving, and our kids are paying the price for learning sex without morality.

What many parents don't realize is how much of an impact they have on the sexual attitudes and behavior of their children. According to a YMCA parent and teen report, teens say that the majority (80 percent) of their sexual values come from their parents.[26] To me, a challenging finding by the YMCA study is that "not having enough time together" with their parents is the *top* concern among teenagers today.[27]

According to the White House study on adolescent behavior and parental involvement, "a majority of sexually active teens — boys and girls — say that they wished they had waited [for sex]." The report shows that "having a close relationship with one's children and spending time with them . . . is strongly related to whether teens engage in risky behavior such as . . . having sex at early ages."[28]

The report continues its admonition to parents to spend time with their children to protect them. "The likelihood of having had sex is strongly correlated . . . with being close to a parent." More than 50 percent of fifteen- and six-teen-year-olds who don't feel close to parents are sexually involved, while only 32 percent of those who do feel close are involved. For seventeen- to eighteen-year-olds it's even greater: 68 percent who do not feel close to parents are sexually active.[29]

A research report published in the *Journal of the American Medical Association* reveals, "Teens who have relatively higher parental involvement in their lives are somewhat protected from emotional stress, suicide thoughts or attempts, substance abuse, becoming sexually involved at young ages, and, to a lesser extent, involvement in violence."[30]

Kids don't want to discuss something they feel guilty about, because they don't want to let their parents down. Nor do they want their parents to add to their guilt. They want their parents to be happy with them, yet the actions that led to the guilt may have resulted in part from a lack of instruction from Mom and Dad.

Kids really want to find the answers they need—at home. What often turns them off is that parents jump to conclusions or overlecture instead of really listening to what their teens are trying to say. If parents show an interest in their children when they are young, the kids will show an interest in their parents later. Good communication with teenagers and younger children requires a lot of time and thought, but it is the start of a lifelong family relationship. The right time to start is now. For more information on communicating with your teen, see chapter 16 of this book.

Teaching Sex in Context

A parent's most vital role is in explaining the proper context for sex. During health class at school, kids may learn the basic anatomy of reproduction, but they usually won't learn about the sanctity of sex or God's plan for sex in their lives. They need to know about both sex *and* love—and the difference between them. As the following lines from students suggest, kids can get confused about these two issues.

> Too often sex and love are confused. Granted, they should go together in the right context, but they are not synonymous. They are two separate concepts. Sex should be an act performed by two people committed to loving each other for life; love, in varying degrees, can be felt by anyone.

♦ ♦ ♦

Teens misunderstand what real love is. Today's teenagers think love is an act instead of a commitment. Ninety percent of all guys and 80 percent of all girls will
lose their virginity by age twenty. They have no example of real love in their lives,
and many have been taught sex education without morals from grade school on.

Every person has an innate desire for love, a desire given by God. But love is
something that must be learned. It can't be written out as a definition and have
an impact. It must be acted out by role models. When people see a model of
love, they learn how to respond to love and act in love. This is why the Scriptures say, "We love because he first loved us" (1 John 4:19).

The Bible, for the most part, doesn't define love. Rather, it shows us love in
action, as in the deeds of Christ, the explanation of active love given in 1 Corinthians 13 and Matthew 25, God's boundless love for a stubborn and rebellious
Israel, and so on.

Since love is learned from role models, the family is the most important influence on how a child perceives love (followed by peers and society in general).
When parents are to an appreciable degree acting out the imagery of God, displaying to a perceptible extent the attributes of Christian love, children will
grow up learning that love.

Children in such homes grow up learning to be accepted and appreciated,
which leads them to a feeling of security and significance. These children, in
turn, will respond to that love in obedience to the parents' authority and will begin internalizing the principles taught by the parents.

This is why the destruction of the family is so devastating. Children grow
up learning from their parents that love means, "Get what you can from the
other person, and when that person doesn't perform properly, get out of the relationship." Such is the feeling of "love" that many kids today are confusing
with sex.

Children can grow up desiring to love their parents, but still not feel secure
in the relationship. Often in order to get the love of their parents, they fall into
the "flight syndrome." That is, they put themselves on a performance basis for
their parents' love, and when they do something they think won't be pleasing,
they cover it up. They run from honesty. They are afraid that their shortcoming
will lead to rejection.

This can happen when well-meaning children try to please Mom and

Dad, but it has a stifling effect. Open communication is blocked when children think that honesty will lead to parental disappointment. They may cease trying new things for fear of failure. They may stop taking risks to stretch their horizons.

These kids then enter their teenage years equating love and performance. When they say, "If you love me, you'll have sex with me," they are only keeping in line with their own distorted definition of performance-based love.

The biblical picture of love is one of giving without expecting anything in return, accepting another person without conditions, and experiencing a security in the relationship that is not dependent on performance. This is a far cry from the shallow and self-centered type on the market today. And it is in the home where this love must be modeled.

I have three daughters and a son. One of the greatest heritages I can leave for my children, and one of the greatest responsibilities I have for them, is to love their mother—to give my children a model of what it means for a man to love a woman. Most kids are growing up today not knowing what love between a man and woman actually is. God intended that children learn this from their mother and father.

For example, when a young man says to one of my daughters, "I love you," how is she supposed to know what that means? By watching television? By watching a movie or a video? No! God intended for my daughter to know what it means for a man to love her because she has seen me model that love toward her mother. She will be able to think through this and reason, *If this guy truly loves me, then he will treat me like my father treats my mother.*

That is the heritage I want to leave my children.

Lack of Information

A loving home and good parental modeling are essential to sex education, but they are not enough. At some point you have to impart some information about the physical, emotional, and spiritual dynamics of sex. Kids don't learn about sex by osmosis. They need practical, comprehensive instruction. If they don't get it at home, they will get it somewhere—the locker room at school, a pornographic TV channel, video, or a magazine.

Where and how teens get advice on sex is not much different than it was twenty years ago, as illustrated in the following chart:

WHERE DO TEENS GET IDEAS FOR TALKING ABOUT SEXUAL ISSUES?			
Have you ever gotten any good ideas about talking about sexual issues from . . .[31]	Boys	Girls	Total
A friend or sibling	60%	63%	62%
A sex education or health class	39%	48%	44%
A TV show or movie	42%	38%	40%
A magazine	12%	59%	36%
One of your parents	25%	38%	32%
A book or brochure	18%	30%	24%
A religious leader	15%	15%	15%
Never turned to any source	17%	12%	15%
MTV	13%	16%	15%
A counselor or therapist	9%	13%	11%
Any other source	4%	6%	5%

Another study discovered that both male and female teens (40 percent versus 31 percent) and younger and older teens (36 percent versus 35 percent) say they have not had a single helpful conversation with their parents about sex.[32]

One young woman who wrote to me suffered greatly because her parents did not share with her important information about sex.

I guess you could say I was a direct by-product of modern secular society. I grew up in a non-Christian family, and when the divorce phenomenon began in this country in the 1970s, my parents jumped on the bandwagon.

My mother completed her master's and got a job, and my brother and I began to come home in the afternoons by ourselves. We got our own snacks and watched TV until Mom got home. We were very mature kids for our age (about 11 and 12), and we enjoyed being on our own.

As I got into high school, I started to make plans for college, and I wanted to be far enough away from home to "be my own person."

I remember my visions of an exciting, jet-setting career, complete with expense account. My favorite magazine was *Cosmopolitan,* and I dreamed of being just as elegant and attractive as the women pictured in it. Not exposed to anything but the world's view of sex, I naturally assumed I would be sexually active before I got married, if I got married at all. Since sex outside of marriage was acceptable, marriage seemed to be a somewhat old-fashioned option.

Despite growing up in the Bible Belt and having many Christian friends, no one ever told me premarital sex was wrong. Not even my mother. She didn't want to bias me with her opinion, so she never told me one way or the other.

I believe this is one major reason people of any age participate in premarital sex. They are never given God's definition of love, marriage, and sex. I had people tell me sex before marriage was a sin (what's that?) and that God had told them he wanted them to wait, but they never explained what sin was, and they never said God didn't want me to have sex before marriage either.

I was asking questions about Christianity and not having them answered. I was asking (looking) for reasons not to have premarital sex, and I didn't receive any answers I could apply to my situation.

God admonishes parents to instruct their children in a healthy, biblical view of sex. This is not a simple task, and you may even find it embarrassing to teach your kids about the proper place of sex. But if you don't teach them, who will?

Raising a family is not a simple task. Although Western society is the result of Christianity, our culture now attacks and erodes its influence. Rather than reinforce Christian morals as was done in generations past, our schools disavow God's truth and teach a relativistic outlook. Instead of teaching moral absolutes, our culture teaches relativism and situational ethics.

As the influence of Christianity diminishes in our society and families, the devastating results will continue to show up in our kids. Without direction, they clutch at false securities. Without the solid self-image of a child of God and loving, intimate relationships at home, they grab at anything to make them feel a little better about themselves. Without a knowledge of God and his love, they settle for anything that resembles love, even if they are exploited and hurt by it. Without the Word of God taught in the family and the love of God shown in the family through nurturing relationships, kids are adrift. They have no basis on which to make decisions. They have no security.

Along with the necessary information about sex, parents must convey that premarital sex is not the unforgivable sin. Even kids from Christian homes make wrong choices about sex. These kids need to know they can turn to their parents. They need to hear their parents say, "No matter what you've done or what you do, we love you and will never turn our backs on you. Nothing you have done wrong is beyond repair. We will help you through any trouble. We are here for you to turn to. Talk to us."

An Expression of Rebellion

Some young people are going to pursue premarital sex no matter what the adults in their lives do. Kids occasionally rebel against their parents' authority, and sex is one avenue of rebellion. It certainly happens in homes where parents and children are in constant conflict. But it also can happen when parents are doing their best to teach and model biblical love and sex. Here's how the kids who write to me talk about it.

Jessica liked to be around her friends, because when they were together, she didn't have to think about all the hurt her mom had caused her.

One night Jessica had a party at her house. She met Joe, a cute, intelligent guy, and was immediately attracted to him. They talked a lot and got to know each other over the course of the evening. Nearly everyone at the party was paired off in different parts of the house. Jessica led Joe to her parents' bedroom, and they had sex that night in her parents' bed. It was the ultimate way Jessica could think of to rebel against her mother and the hurt.

◆ ◆ ◆

Many times young people engage in sex out of spite or rebellion against parents or authority. They simply choose a lifestyle based on what Mom and Dad don't want from them. This is an act of the will, not of the intellect, I am convinced. Usually, the young person learns a lesson from this rebellious attitude somewhere down the road.

◆ ◆ ◆

The people in my age group become sexually active before marriage mostly because of peer pressure or rebellion against parents. From what I see at my school, some parents don't care about their children, much less whom they are with and what they are doing. The kids, not totally excluding me, rebel by doing something they think will harm their parents, not realizing they are harming themselves more than anyone.

◆ ◆ ◆

The main attraction to premarital sex, I think, is that it is not allowed. Many teens do things just because Mom and Dad said no.

A youth pastor writes:

One of my high schoolers is an only child whose mother writes books and speaks on family relationships. He once told me that he could greatly hurt his parents and ruin his mother's career if he rebelled. Since then he has been in trouble with the law, switched schools for his own personal safety, and has greatly grieved his parents. Even though his parents are wonderful, he seems to be rebelling to hurt them.

Rebellion is a reaction generally caused by a lack of relationship. Counselors see again and again how the rebellious child is reacting to poor relationships, both between the parents and child and between the parents themselves.

One marriage and family counselor estimates that in as many as 95 percent of the cases regarding a rebellious child, marriage counseling for the parents is required. Family counseling is included, too, but the marriage counseling is the crux. He reports that amazing results in the children's behavior take place once the parents get their act together.

Imposing rules on a young person will not work if a positive relationship has not been established between him or her and the one making the rules. The kid will rebel against authority, since he or she is not convinced the authority figures have the kid's best interest at heart. To counter the rebellion, parents often lay down even more rules. It becomes a battle, with parents and children pitted against each other rather than working together toward understanding. That rebellion can take the form of active resistance or passive indifference.

Sex as a form of rebellion signifies faulty relationships within the student's family. However, concerned parents can take some initial steps to reestablish the relationship.

First, there is one basic principle a parent needs to remember: Rules without relationships lead to rebellion. If you are not nurturing a relationship of love, acceptance, and affirmation with your child, he or she will throw your rules back in your face in some form of rebellion.

Second, back off on as many rules as possible, especially grounding. Let the kids know you want to rebuild mutual trust. You are still in charge, but you can't show your kids you trust them if they have no opportunity to prove themselves trustworthy.

You need to exercise caution, however, because a sudden switch from rules can lead to anarchy and could confuse the situation. Don't overplay the suspension of rules. Relationships that have eroded over the course of years won't instantly change, and kids won't respond just because you expect them to.

What needs to happen now is what should have been happening all along: You need to focus on the kids and listen to them. One of the most powerful ways to build a relationship is to listen. You have to know what is going on in their heads. In some ways it is no different from establishing a friendship. When you listen to someone, you are telling that person that he or she is important to you. As you and your teenager become more important to each other, you will want to spend more time together. When you feel you are reaching this point, begin working on some activities together.

As the relationship and trust are gradually (or sometimes quickly) reestablished, the rebellion will become less of an issue. Your kids don't have to hurt you now, because they like you and may even love you. They don't have to rebel against what appears to them as your stupid rules anymore, because now they know you love them and have their best interest at heart. They don't have to have sex with someone now just to be rebellious—they trust your judgment more.

We will explore in much greater detail the topic of developing a healthy parent-child relationship in chapter 16.

◆ ◆ ◆

Adolescents get involved in premarital sex when certain needs go unmet. In the next chapter we will identify many of those specific needs and why kids' love-need-hunger leads to sexual experimentation.

CHAPTER 8

THE RELATIONAL REASONS

NEEDY KIDS TURN TO SEX

ANOTHER REASON KIDS DON'T WAIT until marriage for sex is that they unwittingly attempt to meet a variety of emotional and relational needs through sexual activity. Just like the rest of us, adolescents are created with the need for love, security, intimacy, companionship, affection, spirituality, etc. When these needs go unmet—as they do occasionally for everyone—many young people turn to sex, hoping to fill the void.

SEARCHING FOR LOVE

For many young people, *love* is the magic word when it comes to having sex. A poll of 5,000 children in grades four to twelve, conducted by Louise Harris for the Girl Scouts, revealed that 54 percent of boys and 22 percent of girls in junior and senior high school said they would have sex with someone they loved; 11 percent of boys and 22 percent of girls would "try to hold off" if they could.[1]

In another survey, kids were asked, "What are the reasons kids you know have sex?" Sixty-three percent of the girls and 50 percent of the boys responded, "They were in love."[2]

Most adolescents say they have been in love at some point. But when they try to tell their parents, they hear something like, "What can you possibly know about being in love? You're only a kid." Maybe some kids *don't* know much about being in love. But they still reach out for it in ways that bring them heartache. The following stories, shared with me by heartbroken teenagers, painfully illustrate this point:

I trusted Bobby to know how far we could go without making love. He was in the driver's seat. He was also insecure, and he would tell me over and over how he loved me, how he was sure I didn't love him as much as he loved me. It was then that I set out to prove it. I was his—110 percent his. The first time we made love, I had no idea what was going on. Afterwards, he didn't speak—he passed out. I was so alone. I've never hated myself more. But it was done, my virginity was gone. Never could I get it back. It didn't matter after that, so sex became an everyday occurrence. My only fear was losing Bobby. He was the first, and even if he treated me badly (and there were those times) I was going to do anything I could to hang on to him.

Slowly we drifted apart. He wanted to go out with other girls. I loved him and he fooled me into thinking he loved me too. But he didn't love me. He tricked me into thinking he loved me. Bobby's "love" was a conditional, selfish kind of love, not anything like love as it's described in 1 Corinthians 13:4-7:

"Love is patient and kind. Love is not jealous or boastful or proud or rude. Love does not demand its own way. Love is not irritable, and it keeps no record of when it has been wronged. It is never glad about injustice but rejoices whenever the truth wins out. Love never gives up, never loses faith, is always hopeful, and endures through every circumstance" (NLT).

◆ ◆ ◆

It was near Thanksgiving, and she was baby-sitting. "Mind if I come over?" Well, one thing led to another, and in a strange house on an old beat-up sofa I was no longer a virgin.

Virginity gone, innocence gone, the floodgates of immorality were now open, and in poured masturbation, prostitutes, marijuana, speed, a couple of acid trips, crabs, and a few bouts with gonorrhea. Love and acceptance were all I was looking for.

How could the world be so rotten? I hadn't found love. I'd found casual sex with all kinds of strings attached. Acceptance? No one really cared. They were too worried about getting burned themselves.

From beginning to end, the Bible shows us what God's love is like. Remember what we said in chapter 1? *Love makes the security, happiness, and welfare of another as important to us as our own.* This type of love is not selfish, considers others more important than ourselves, and seeks to guard and strengthen the dignity God has given each person. It is a reflection of God's love for us.

Unfortunately, many of our young people have lost sight of God's kind of love. As a general rule, many have reduced love to one of two things: (1) a warm feeling or emotional reaction, or (2) a positive response to a relationship that makes them feel good. Both of these are self-directed, not outer-directed, and stand in juxtaposition to the biblical model.

It is no wonder teenagers become confused about love. Teenagers are in the process of maturing and establishing their own identities; yet they must contend with a force that baffles and defies definition even by adults.

"Love," however, seems to be a justifiable cause for premarital sex, perhaps more so than any other reason. Even Christian teenagers, lacking a solid understanding of love, may be firmly convinced that unmarried people who are "in love" may engage in sex. As one researcher states:

> Kids believe that love carries moral weight. Yet the "in love" standard is extremely encompassing. Even at the age of thirteen, more than half of all teens (53 percent of boys, 52 percent of girls) say they have been in love, and the percentages rise to include 85 percent of eighteen-year-old boys and 83 percent of seventeen-year-old girls.
>
> A fifteen-year-old New York City girl, a virgin only because her father called downstairs to her at a crucial moment and interrupted her last night with a summer boyfriend she felt she loved, told us that once she "wanted to have sex with someone I loved. Right now, I don't think it really matters if I have sex with someone I love. I think after I have sex for the first time, then it'll matter." Later on in our interview, she added that "if I was to go out and have sex with someone whom I didn't love, I wouldn't be a virgin anymore, but I still wouldn't have made love."
>
> This distinction, though it is perhaps a rather tortured effort to justify some future scratching of an itch caused as much by curiosity as anything else, also represents a not unusual effort to establish some standard for right and wrong in a world where inherited rules seem unconvincing_
>
> We have to remember what the survey showed about teens' conservatism. Teens do want their friends to think well of them, and most do want to be "good." That combination can make the generous standard of love a flag of convenience. In the absence of notions like commitment and responsibility, horniness can look an awful lot like "love."[3]

The pressure on young adolescents today is intensified by confusion. Teens look at love and sex as being synonymous. Much of this confusion is encouraged by television, videos, and movies.

This confusion about sex and love can cause a young adolescent to feel acute pressure to have sex when he feels he loves someone. Another danger of this confusion is the pressure to respond sexually when the other person says "I love you." The conclusion of many teens is, "If you don't have sex with me, you don't really love me."

The Josh McDowell Ministry commissioned Barna Research to do one of the largest studies ever of evangelical, fundamental church kids. The findings of the study showed this astonishing result: 46 percent of evangelical Christian kids truly believe that if you love someone, it justifies sex, it makes sex "right." These are Christian kids! Obviously, they are confused about the true meaning of love and the purpose of sex.[4]

The Kaiser Family Foundation study gives some very interesting insights on how and why teens have sex. It found that teen girls who have already had sexual intercourse feel that love or being in love is the predominant reason. The major-

WHY TEENS HAVE SEX[5]					
		BOYS		GIRLS	
	TOTAL	Sexually Active	Not	Sexually Active	Not
He or she has met someone he or she really loves	31%	23%	27%	54%	31%
He or she is engaged or married	19%	2%	21%	8%	31%
He or she has the opportunity to do it with someone he or she likes	19%	43%	21%	11%	7%
He or she has reached a certain age or maturity level	14%	15%	16%	11%	14%
He or she feels pressure to do it because everyone else is	10%	15%	12%	6%	8%
His or her girlfriend or boyfriend is pressuring him or her	5%	1%	1%	6%	9%
Don't know	2%	1%	1%	4%	0
Total	100%	100%	100%	100%	100%

ity of teen boys, especially those who have had sex, will often say "it is simply a matter of opportunity." However, 25 percent of all teenage boys, whether virgins or nonvirgins, will say "love is the main consideration."[6]

The encouraging insight from the above study is that "almost half (44 percent) of all teens age thirteen to eighteen say they have made a conscious decision to delay intercourse, three-quarters (76 percent) hang out with someone who has made this decision, and the same proportion (74 percent) say within their group it is considered a good thing to decide to remain a virgin."

A university counselor relates that one of his clients, a college student, discovered "she was pregnant after having casual sex with a friend. Both had been drinking too much, she said. After weeks of painful deliberation, she decided to have an abortion. As she waited in the clinic, another student whom she knew entered the lobby. Both were embarrassed to see the other, but when they began to talk, they discovered to their mutual horror that the same man had fathered their children. Were the two tiny bodies that were expelled that day and tossed into an incinerator the result of love?"

The pressure line is: "If you love me, you will have sex with me," or "If you love me, you'll prove it." Sex is never a test of love. The true nature of love is seen in how we treat people (see 1 Cor. 13:4-7). The result of this pressure is that the person pressured begins to feel that his or her willingness to take the next step into sexual involvement becomes a test of true affection or love for the other—not trust, respect, caring, sensitivity, but sex.

Usually the two discover later that what they thought were feelings of love were only charged-up sexual sensations, and now they must live with the consequences. The "I love you" of one person can be significantly different for another. Sex is often given in the name of love with the anticipation of marriage and commitment. But for the partner, sex is simply saying, "You're someone very special," with no anticipation whatsoever to marry.

That pressure line, "If you love me, you'll have sex with me," should be considered in the light of the following replies by teens:

If you love me, you'll respect my feelings and not push me into doing something I'm not ready for.

◆ ◆ ◆

Having sex doesn't prove you're in love. I have too much self-respect to get sexually involved before it's right. I've decided to wait.

◆ ◆ ◆

OK, prove how much you love me by understanding and respecting my feelings.

◆ ◆ ◆

Love or no love, anyway you slice it, it can result in a baby and that does matter.

◆ ◆ ◆

I love you. But I'd feel better showing you in another way.

What's Love Got to Do with It?

Many young people today are so desperately crying out for love that *they will believe anything and fall for anyone.* The truth is often ignored in the heat of the moment. This is true not only of girls but of boys as well. A recent teen survey indicated that 25 percent of the boys surveyed said they had lost their virginity because of love.[7] The following story, told by Dr. Liana R. Clark of Philadelphia, Pennsylvania, so vividly illustrates the desperate lengths to which teenagers are willing to go to get the love they need, I felt it was worth printing in its entirety.

Anitra was a patient with pelvic inflammatory disease whom I recently had on the adolescent ward. She was a sweet sixteen-year-old who was the mother of a seven-month-old infant. The baby's father was in jail. Anitra admitted that she had been trying to conceive a child with her new boyfriend of one month. The residents were aghast and did not know how to counsel this young woman effectively. I spent about two hours with her one Saturday afternoon where we explored her reasons for wanting another child. The truth was that she felt a child would make her boyfriend stay with her. She was incredibly needy and lacked self-esteem. When I asked her about her needs and wants for the future, Anitra turned to me with tears welling in her eyes and said, "Without babies and men, what else is there for me?"

Although I wanted to put my head down and cry with her, I instead decided to do something more positive. She was to create a list of activities and interests she had thought about but never tried to do. The only condition was that they have nothing to do with men or babies. The next day, Anitra had a fifteen-item list waiting for me, which included acting, singing, nursing, law, even surfing. We then designed a plan to help her begin some of these activities. Since her discharge, she has put off her plans to get pregnant and has returned to her church activities. She is trying very hard to make a future for herself and her child.[8]

People throughout time have tried to understand love, define it, and experience it. If our young people cannot adequately define love, how in the world can they know if they are in love? They can't. If they can't define love, how can they know if they are being loved? They can't. If they can't define love, how can they even know if they are in a loving relationship? They can't. The confusion about love weakens a young person's resolve to wait for sex.

Our society, to a great extent, has stopped passing biblical morality on to its kids. Without clear standards of right and wrong, teenagers are left to find their own. Many come up with "love" as the justification for sex. But they don't know what love is. I took a survey of 4,000 college students at Campus Crusade for Christ conferences, asking them to write their definition of love in two minutes. When I examined all the cards they turned in, I found that only seven of these Christian students were able to give a definition. No wonder so many Christian kids are getting involved sexually in the name of "true love." They have no idea what they're getting into.

SEARCHING FOR SECURITY AND SELF-ESTEEM

In an adolescent relationship, the search for security, acceptance, and self-esteem often takes the form of premarital sex. Let the following personal accounts from kids just like yours sink in.

Sins against God lead to ugly consequences. In the case of my girlfriend and me, premarital sex not only scarred us individually, but also damaged our relationship and ultimately hurt others outside the relationship.

Individually, I used premarital sex to deal with my lack of self-esteem. Because my partner was hesitant, I saw each encounter as a chance to be persuasive, domineering and accepted by at least one beautiful girl. Each session proved to me that I was a man and equipped me with good stories for the locker room. I looked to premarital sex to bolster my self-image instead of looking for worth in the eyes of my Creator. When my fiancée became pregnant, my self-worth deteriorated even further.

◆ ◆ ◆

People confuse sex with love. They think the compatibility of two people is in the pelvis rather than in the head. Insecurity breeds this type of thinking. An insecure person is afraid of losing the person of his (or her) affections and may see sex as a way to hold on to him. Using sex for manipulation and control is also typical of insecure people.

◆ ◆ ◆

Low self-esteem may drive teenagers to gain approval through sex rather than through acceptance of the truth that they are persons of worth because God says so.

◆ ◆ ◆

With a pizza face, a small frame, and a germ-sized self-esteem, I entered into puberty. I mention this in no way to inspire a pity party on my behalf or to make half-baked excuses for what followed in my life, but to show the interrelated nature of one's self-image and sexual behavior.

As a junior high student I bought every put-down that came my way, at a very high price. I became completely convinced that I was basically dumb, hopelessly homely, essentially a weakling, and conclusively a reject. Once I bought that image, I set about to live up to the details of the contract—and others responded to me in kind.

Then, early in my high school days, a change began that brought with it both good news and bad news. The good news is that I finally found someone who really believed in me. A Christian math teacher became vulnerable himself to get through to me. It was through his persistent demonstration of Christlike love that God began to form a new image for me to live up to. My freshman year in high school was definitely a mile marker, as things began to improve in every area of my life. By the time I was a senior, I was a leader in sports, a better-than-average student, and was elected student body president by my classmates. Even though this should have provided the much needed self-worth, I continued to have an undercurrent of doubt and fear.

Herein lies the bad news. I looked to female attention for proof of my worth as a male. The attention I received from a young woman became the gauge for my own worth. It didn't take long to discover the enjoyment of making out and the immediate gratification that comes in lustful exchange. As I got more physically involved, I found it more difficult to stop at necking and petting, and my life became increasingly filled with guilt. I was a miserable Christian, knowing that my dating was far from the biblical standard.

By the time I enrolled in Bible college I was tired of my double standard and resolved to establish a higher standard of behavior. Then I met Shirley. We began with a wholesome relationship centered around spiritual things, but it didn't last long. About halfway through the year we had decided we were made for each other and wanted to plan our wedding as soon as possible. To accommodate school rules we put our wedding off until summer break. With this mental arrangement we could justify anything.

"After all, we are practically husband and wife."

At this point we had also adopted a philosophy that stated, "It can't be wrong when it feels so right." I remember sneaking into one of the prayer rooms late one night after hours. Following a short prayer and an even shorter "sharing time," we became passionately involved. Then the back door of the chapel opened and closed. We quickly went back to praying, asking God to keep us from being caught in the position we were in. For being right, it sure felt wrong all of a sudden.

Only a short time after this experience I happened to catch Shirley feeling right with another guy. That closed the last chapter on the novel called Shirley and I: The Couple That Felt Right.

For close to a year I didn't date at all. Then I became interested in another young lady. This time I was aware that God had directed me to the one I was to spend my life with. This leading wasn't based on physical attraction or an insecure ego, but on a common calling and desire to serve the Lord together.

As much as I wanted a completely different kind of relationship with Melody, I led her, too, into a compromise of her standards, causing a breach of trust and a great deal of guilt. Once a physical standard is let down, it becomes extremely difficult to raise a new banner.

Never be fooled into thinking that getting what you want from a guy or a gal is going to increase your sense of self-worth. The Word of God says, "He who saves his life shall lose it and he who loses his life for my sake shall find it." I found that trying to bolster my ego through exploitation left me with an even greater sense of worthlessness. Since that time I have found that basing my self-worth on anything apart from the acceptance of God leaves me empty. If you want to find yourself, get to know God. In discovering him, you'll discover yourself.

◆ ◆ ◆

Being a jock, I had many sexual relationships, but the one thing that really stung me was the hatred that came out of these relationships later. Deep down inside I was really insecure about whether or not I was accepted by girls and whether or not I was a man. . . . The pressures were very strong, so strong that I felt very lonely many times if I "failed" to attract a girl when all of my friends did.

◆ ◆ ◆

Sex provides some kids with a sense of security, a feeling of acceptance; it gives them the assurance they are liked and wanted.

For instance, a girl's family is really having problems and she needs someone to listen to her, care about her and, most of all, love her. In her eyes, she needs someone who will just make her forget her problems, someone she can hold on to for security. She meets the "perfect guy," but really this guy is having basically the same problems and is looking for security as well. Because neither one of them knows what real love is, they may mistake it for sex. This is where a lot of people my age get into trouble.

Our needs are compounded by the breakdown of the family. God intends for our inner needs to be met by him first, then by other people. In times past, even without a relationship with God, people could find relative security and significance within the family. They had at least one place where they could be themselves and not have to perform.

But that is not true in most cases today. Rather than being a haven from the world, the family setting is often a place of discord and unrest, a place where spouses are put on a performance basis, knowing they will be discarded if they do not continually please their husband or wife. Any element of security the family may have held is removed, since people within the family are not loved for who they are, but rather for how they perform. Kids growing up in that kind of environment lack acceptance and security, which leaves them with an unhealthy sense of worthlessness. They don't feel free to be themselves. They believe that if they were, no one would like them.

When young people seek acceptance, they will do what other people do in order to be like them. They have to perform, to do the right things, to live up to the standards of those whose acceptance they seek. Some may do it through joining gangs, others by being top athletes and keeping up with the crowd, and others by fulfilling the sexual desires of a boyfriend/girlfriend or date.

Suffering from poor self-images brought about by lack of acceptance of them as unique individuals, teenagers may grab for the first thing that resembles security. Often this means sex. Kids so desperately want love, acceptance, and care that they will violate their moral values to get it. And when a young person discovers acceptance brought about by pleasing another person, regardless of how shallow and fickle that acceptance may be, it leads to a cycle of seeking security in performance and trying to impress others.

One of the keys to developing personal significance is the freedom to fail, the freedom not to be perfect. Such freedom can be present only when a person feels secure, when a person feels accepted for who he or she is, not for what he or she does. This kind of security is what young people need to develop in their relationships. And when they do, it will pay off in their marriages.

When two people are committed to each other, they both have freedom. They don't need to put on a show to gain the other's approval. Then, when they are married, they have the security to be themselves, to admit what they do not know. They don't have to be experts at sex on their honeymoon because they are admitted amateurs. Part of the thrill of beginning a life together is learning about sex together, guiding and helping each other. It forms an extremely strong bond in the marriage since they are doing it together. That's worth waiting for.

Apart from marriage, there is no security. There may be a spoken commitment, but if one partner refuses to make the commitment final through marriage, words are just words. Sex without commitment automatically bypasses the stages of acceptance, security, and significance and goes straight to putting someone on a performance basis. That person is not accepted as a unique person who is loved no matter what, but instead he or she only has value for performance. It is degrading and dehumanizing. It is counter to everything God wants in relationships between people. It takes teenagers who are searching for security and dangles in front of them a carrot they can never reach, no matter how hard they try.

If you want more information and insight on the biblical view of self-image, see my book *See Yourself As God Sees You* (Tyndale House Publishers, 1999).

SEARCHING FOR INTIMACY

Another reason adolescents rush into sex is the attempt to find intimacy in a relationship. Kids want to feel close to another human being, to make an emotional connection, and to feel specially cared for. Many young people mistakenly equate physical intimacy with emotional or relational intimacy. Getting close in bed or in the backseat of a car makes them think they are really starting to get close.

The excessive sexuality among adolescents indicates our culture's inability to experience true intimacy. A young person who has been involved sexually with various men wrote: "It is far easier to 'bare your bottom' than to 'bare your soul.'" Emotional contact is the goal; sex is often the means. Obviously, a physical act cannot help someone reach an emotional goal. But for an insecure teenager hungry for intimacy, it seems plausible.

A young university coed called me long-distance. I could tell by her voice that she was distressed. "Mr. McDowell, in the last five nights I have gone to bed with five different men. Tonight, I got out of bed and asked myself, *Is that all there is?*"

Then she began crying. When she regained her composure enough to speak, she said, "Please tell me there's something more."

I said, "There certainly is. It's called intimacy."

What is intimacy? A fifteen-year-old girl once described intimacy as "a place where it's safe to be real." A sixteen-year-old girl told me that intimacy is "the capacity to be real with another person." Wow, that's powerful! That's what we all want—no superficiality, no barriers, no facades, but rather to be real.

The sexual revolution of the past decades has not been as much a search for sex as a search for intimacy. Most young people today do not want sex nearly as much as they want a close and caring relationship with someone. They just don't know how to find it.

The main problem in our culture is not sexual; it's relational. We have embarked on a false quest for intimacy because we don't understand what real intimacy is all about. We have allowed our culture to dictate to us that the only way you can find intimacy is through the physical. Our kids are only reflecting the responses of the culture in general. I am personally convinced that most young people use sex as a means of achieving intimacy. They don't want sex as much as they want closeness with another human being. The tragedy is that people are jumping from one bed to another in their search for intimacy. At best they find a sense of caring for the short duration of an orgasm. Then they are left feeling worse than they felt before.

Today we see people getting involved in sexual activity, often promiscuous sexual activity, for the simple reason that they don't understand what true intimacy is. Sexual experience becomes a substitute for intimacy. We use phrases like "making love" and "being intimate" when talking about sexual intercourse. Yet most sexual involvements, outside the loving commitment of marriage, express very little genuine love or closeness.

Not only do many people misunderstand what real intimacy is, but they are afraid of it. Why do people fear intimacy? Because intimacy inevitably brings vulnerability. Emotional sharing requires self-disclosure, and for many of us the idea of opening up our innermost selves is a scary prospect. Many young people repeatedly share their bodies because they are afraid to share themselves. They participate in countless "one-night stands" because they are afraid to be vulnerable. Most teens and adults mistake the ecstasy of an orgasm for the intimacy of love.

Real intimacy is the result of letting another person see who you are. But if you don't feel good about yourself and your identity, you will keep yourself hidden and never achieve intimacy. Only a person with a relatively good sense of security and identity can fully enter into the experience of intimacy.

We can never enjoy the full potential richness of a meaningful relationship—for which we were created—without becoming intimate with at least one other person. Again, I am speaking primarily about psychological and spiritual intimacy, which is the result of being open and transparent. It is more a matter of communication and sharing than of any kind of grand passion. When two people confide in each other about their innermost dreams, hopes, and thoughts, they are "being intimate." True intimacy involves being able to remove all the masks and disguises we hide behind, without fear of rejection, and be known and loved for ourselves.

Are today's young people capable of finding real intimacy? Absolutely! Here is one who wrote to tell me how it happened.

I used to search for intimacy by latching onto a "special someone" because I felt that as long as I had his love and approval everything would be OK. Yet there was usually a high price tag: the giving of my body. The penalty I paid was that of feeling cheap, used, and guilty. I began to wonder if there would ever be someone who would love and accept me without demanding that I do something to earn that love.

Then I learned about the unconditional love that God has for me. I decided to ask Jesus Christ to come into my life and teach me what true love is all about. I can say with certainty that he has made a difference! Instead of feeling cheap, used, and guilty, I now know that I am valuable, forgiven. I have a new life that began the moment I asked Christ into my life. Because I have experienced an intimate love relationship with God first, I am now able to develop lasting, meaningful relationships with those around me. I also know that when I do marry and can enjoy sex in its proper context, my sex life won't be mediocre. It will be excellent because that's what God desires for those who choose him: excellence in all areas of their lives!

For young people or anyone, the first step to real intimacy is a life-changing relationship with Jesus Christ.

SEARCHING FOR COMPANIONSHIP

The search for intimacy is a search for companionship. People are desperate to escape the loneliness that plagues our culture. And adolescents are among the most vulnerable to the pain of loneliness. It's another reason kids get involved in premarital sex. A sexual encounter is at least a momentary escape from loneliness.

Girls are most vulnerable to loneliness. The following student got an up close look at loneliness and how her friend tried unsuccessfully to escape it through sex.

I used to think it would be OK to have sex with a steady boyfriend; at least then you would be doing it with someone who really did care about you. I thought that until I lived with my roommate, Liz. Liz dated Chris for two years. They went to high school homecomings and proms together, they drank beer and ate Oreos together, and they made love together in the back of Chris's car.

And afterward, Chris would drive Liz back home, and sometimes Liz would cry, because she was in her bed back home, and she was alone. When Liz found out she was pregnant, she was alone, too.

Chris said he couldn't marry her because he had a good football scholarship, so Liz went to a clinic to have an abortion, and she went by herself.

Once again, she was alone.

Usually, adolescent sex is a quest for a steady relationship, not sex. Steady relationships can remove aloneness for months. Yet the fear of losing that person and being lonely again prompts one to have sex to keep that person. But what he or she is really looking for is affection and companionship. After I returned from a speaking tour in England, a student wrote me a letter in which she said, "I just want someone to love me (not physically)." Then she made a statement which I think communicates where most young people are today, not just in our Western culture, but around the world: "I want someone who cares. I want to love and I want to be loved, but I don't know how to do either."

Some girls want to have a baby in hopes that their boyfriend will marry them, and then he and the child will take away their loneliness. Even in the case of teenage pregnancies where marriage does not follow, approximately 96 percent of unwed teenage mothers who do not have an abortion end up keeping their children. This is generally done in order to meet their own emotional need for companionship—that is, to have a child to love and to return love to them.

God created a number of needs in human beings; one of them being our need for companionship. In fact, one of the first things God said about us was, "It is not good for the man to be alone" (Gen. 2:18). A teenager looking for companionship through sex is legitimately lonely. It is a real condition, not something cooked up in his or her head. Loneliness was not part of God's design for us.

Sex cannot eliminate loneliness. It can merely displace it, and only for a very short while. When the spiritual need of companionship is not met in an intelligent, rational way, the only recourse is an irrational attempt. Sex, drugs, alcohol, or anything that affects the five senses and numbs the spirit can become a painkiller for loneliness. That type of escapism leaves us void of the blessing God would bring if we would let him fulfill our need.

When God gives us a need, he also gives a way for that need to be met. To deny the need, mask it, or run away from it is to avoid God's plan for fulfilling it. Such responses are self-defeating, and can only be unfulfilling. When we admit we are lonely and have a relational need that must be fulfilled, we are on the way to fulfilling it. Our next move must be in the direction of God, though, because a God-given desire can be met only in God's way.

SEARCHING FOR AN ESCAPE FROM FEAR OF REJECTION

When young people's lives are based on confidence of acceptance and security in Christ, they are able to have a healthy self-image. Without a healthy self-image, kids need something else to make them feel good about themselves. When the source of good feelings becomes a human relationship, kids may become dependent on it. They feel good and accepted as long as the relationship is going smoothly. They feel afraid and rejected when things get rocky. In such a position, they are open to manipulation and abuse.

Fear is another reason young people get involved in premarital sex. As one young person wrote:

> Some people become sexually active not out of need, but out of fear. There is the fear of physical deterioration and emotional abnormality. There is the fear that time is running out. Another fear may be that of losing a treasured relationship. And there is a common fear in our crowded world—loneliness.

This type of dependency on others is unhealthy and dangerous. If relationships are based on performance, the ones being made to perform are not in a loving bond; they are in a living hell. They never know from one minute to the next if they are keeping up with the other's expectations. They can never feel content and secure. They are never allowed to make a mistake or fail. They can never be themselves.

It is little wonder that young people who need a relationship to bolster their self-image are terrified of rejection. As a result, they will do or be anything to please others, to find acceptance. Some will even sacrifice their moral standards to escape these fears. They become so accustomed to playing the chameleon to make others happy that they lose their own identity in the process. The longer this ambivalence continues, the harder it becomes for them to reestablish a healthy self-image.

Young people in such relationships need to get out immediately. Those who "give sex" out of fear of rejection are trying to buy security with their bodies and self-esteem, a price God never intended anyone to pay. They need to turn to Christ and to his truth to find where real security lies. They need to begin seeing themselves through God's eyes.

The following young woman wrote to tell me how the fear factor had affected her view of sex:

> Being in my late twenties and no longer sexually active, I must reflect on my younger years when I was so promiscuous. When I asked myself about the traps that ensnared me into premarital sex, I was faced with some interesting revelations.
>
> The basic human emotion involved in my sexual explorations was fear—fear of not knowing something (or anything), fear of missing out on the "fun," fear of getting old, and fear of commitment.

So many times, the idea of sex had challenged me. What was it really like? Would I know how to perform with approval? Would I know something about pleasing a man and being pleased? And what if I never knew what sex was like? I mean, I could die and never have "known" a man. What a wasted life! I was afraid, afraid that all the excitement in life was passing by my door, afraid that, should I get married, I would end up getting divorced because I wouldn't know what I was doing in bed. I surely didn't want a divorce!

There was a desire to go along with the crowd so I wouldn't feel left out and strange when the conversation turned to sex. But most of all, at the gut level, there was a desire for intimacy, a desire for marriage, a desire for commitment, a desire for fulfillment, and a desire to hear the words "I accept you." With all of those desires, fears arose. What if none of these needs was met? Frustration set in.

The "what if" rationalization was absorbed into my thinking and decisions. As an attempt to find fulfillment and acceptance, "rolling into and out of bed" became a common pattern for me, a balm to cover my fears. Fulfillment took the scope of a few hours instead of what I had imagined—a lifetime. The fears surfaced again and produced the truth: I had become bored and boring; I didn't find any lasting acceptance of me; I didn't find my ideal mate from bedroom gymnastics.

Teenagers have inherited a world that demands instant satisfaction, a world in which the events of an entire day warrant only thirty minutes of news, three hundred years of history fit into a one week mini-series, and dinner is as uncomplicated as the drive-through window of the local fast-food restaurant. It is a world in which palm computers rescue us from having to think. DVDs rescue us from having to read. Abortionists rescue us from taking responsibility.

The TV says we can have it all. And we want it all. Now. And the TV says if we don't get it now, we're out of step, behind the times, and no fun.

Little wonder, then, that young people are gripped with fear that by postponing sex until marriage they are cheated out of something now. I used to be amazed at how many teenagers say they are terrified of dying a virgin, but I can see where that fear comes from. Their culture deifies sex and scorns those who have not experienced it. They have been conditioned to believe that sex is the ultimate in life and without it they risk dying unfulfilled.

So they have sex—and come away empty, wondering how the ultimate in life could leave them so hollow. Then they have more sex to keep up with everyone else. They get quickie gratification and little else, but they have been told that gratification is enough. Without God and his Word, they don't know any better.

Our culture is one in which people feel powerless. We elect politicians who don't do what we want once they are in office. We work, save our money, and invest; then the economy changes course and leaves us awash. We try to stop wars in other countries, but we're afraid to go outside at night.

We feel overwhelmed and helpless. And in helplessness we resort to mindless pleasure. We may not make it home alive tonight, but we are sure going to feel good right now. Sex, as the writer above so accurately put it, is a balm for covering fears. But it doesn't make the fears go away.

Another reason for premarital sex is the fear of never finding a permanent partner in a world where people and things are always changing. This can lead to a "live for now" or "get it while I can" mentality. Fear of not finding a suitable mate is actually a problem of inner contentment. When people think that by changing their circumstances, such as by getting married, they will find happiness, they are kidding themselves. If they are not at peace in their present state, they will not be at peace when change comes.

Many teenagers think that getting married will magically change them into the person they want to be. Yet married couples stress that when you get married you are the same person. A person who lacks joy and peace in his or her present circumstances will not find instant joy after a wedding ceremony. Inner peace is a reflection of character, not circumstances.

Most young people have a desire to marry someday. God gave that desire to nearly everyone, and marriage is in the normal course of most people's lives. However, the Bible also says that absolute contentment is indeed possible without marriage (read 1 Cor. 7). God alone is able to provide inner peace. Marriage is not necessary.

As a male who did not marry until age thirty-one, I know this from experience. I hate to think how my marriage would have turned out if I had counted on my wife suddenly to provide contentment for me. I would have been placing impossible expectations on her and then would have become frustrated with her whenever she didn't come through. By allowing the Holy Spirit to provide contentment in my life as a single man, I was able to enter my marriage with realistic expectations.

Young people who seek sex now for fear of not having it in marriage are trying to solve the wrong problem. They think the problem is sex and marriage. The real problem is their reaction to their circumstances. If we are to help our kids say no to premarital sex, we must help them conquer their fears, both real and imagined, and begin to accept themselves and circumstances they cannot change.

SEARCHING FOR A SPIRITUAL CONNECTION

The Bible tells us that sex is a spiritual act as well as a physical act. This is probably why some people, including adolescents, attempt to find spiritual oneness through sex. But that's getting it backwards. When two people are committed to God and save sex until marriage, their sexual union is an extension of their spirituality, and God, who is pleased, blesses them. Those who engage in sex attempting to find spirituality will not succeed. They may continue having sex, even after feeling the negative spiritual effects that result from its improper use. They may even deny that sex is the cause.

Oneness of spirit with another person can be legitimate only if it is based on true spiritual oneness with God. People who long for spiritual intimacy with another to the point that they violate biblical standards and their own consciences are totally sabotaging their relationship with God.

God wants people to draw near to each other spiritually. That is why we pray together, encourage each other in our walk with Christ, and discuss spiritual matters. Jesus even tells us he is in our midst when two or three gather on his behalf. But to do something completely opposed to the righteousness of God, with the supposed aim of a greater spiritual good, makes for an impossible juxtaposition of goals—the two are incongruous, even mutually exclusive.

Who has ever felt guilty after prayer? Who has ever felt separation from God after encouraging someone in Christ? Who has ever felt cheap and debased after sharing the gospel with another? No, these activities draw us closer to God, they don't push us further away. But illicit sex produces guilt and estrangement. There are certainly spiritual ramifications to sex, but sex can be a blessing only when it is part of God's plan, when it is an act of love within a marriage. Young people seeking spiritual depth in their lives through sex need to turn to God instead and be firmly rooted in him.

◆ ◆ ◆

There is one more reason kids dabble in premarital sex. It's the miniculture in which they are immersed at this time in their lives. Kids spend a significant amount of time every week in school and—before, after, and during school—in the company of friends. In the next chapter we will explore the impact of friends and school on a young person's willingness to say no to premarital sex.

CHAPTER 9

THE PSYCHOLOGICAL REASONS

EVERYONE IS DOING IT, SO WHY SHOULDN'T WE?

THE FOLLOWING PARAGRAPHS, written by a young woman about to be married, illustrate another powerful reason kids are becoming sexually active before marriage.

He stood alongside the busy highway, walked a few paces, then turned to face the oncoming traffic. With his arm extended, the young man thumbed the sky, hoping a traveler would stop to offer him a ride. Somebody did. A green Volkswagen bug came to a halt. The young man, we shall call him Joe, slid into the front passenger's seat and greeted my fiancé, Herb Coates. Herb was eagerly heading to Indianapolis, Indiana, to join my family and me. The long-awaited hour, our wedding, was just a few days away.

After exchanging this and other general information, Joe's conversation with my future husband took an interesting twist. It sounded something like this:

"So, you're on your way to getting hitched. Is your lady 'good'?"

"Good? Oh, she's the best!" Herb replied.

Not completely sure his inquiry was understood, Joe rephrased the question, "I mean, in bed?"

"Oh!" Herb realized the direction the conversation was taking. "I guess I can't really answer that. We've never 'made love.' In fact, we're both virgins."

"You have got to be kidding! How old are you?"

"I'm twenty-two."

By the time the question-and-answer period had ended, Herb had managed to astonish his passenger. Joe stated he had never met a twenty-two-year-old virgin before. He pulled out a small black book used for recording names of people who had provided him aid. He wanted something descriptive to remember the owner of the green bug. It was a simple task. The note read: "Twenty-two-year-old virgin."

Why was Joe astonished? Because "everyone is doing it." At least that's the perception many people today have of premarital sex. Here's what two other young people had to say on this topic.

Why wait? It's the number-one teen question. My parents are always telling me what to do and what not to do. I hate their nagging. Besides, everyone has done it. Nobody's a virgin.

◆ ◆ ◆

Not only is there direct pressure, but there is also indirect pressure to have sex. After learning the truth that she is the only one who is still a virgin, the "last remaining" girl gives in to worrying and feeling abandoned. She feels awkward and wonders if she should have "done it," too.

One of the greatest pressures on young people today is the pressure not to be left out of the sex derby. Teenagers get the idea that everyone else is doing it, and they don't want to be different. They feel that if they just conform to what all the others are doing, they'll be in the norm and won't be loners.

The idea that everyone is doing it brings up two big questions: (1) Is it really true that everyone else is doing it?; (2) Are all those who are doing it enjoying it? A study commissioned by *Seventeen* magazine addressed those questions:

After interviews of 500 males and 500 females nationwide, ages thirteen to twenty-one, 73 percent of the girls said they would have sex but only because their boyfriends pressure them. Of the 67 percent of the girls who were sexually active, a whopping 81 percent said they were sorry they had "done it." . . . The study also showed that boys are pressured by their peers to have sex and are considered wimps if they don't score. Another startling statistic: One in five people will get a sexually transmitted disease by age twenty-one.[1]

The feeling certain teenagers may have—that they are the last virgins in the country—is based on a myth. True, many teens have been sexually involved. Statistics show the figure to be between 65 and 80 percent, depending on the statistics one chooses. Surprisingly, Christian teenagers are generally only 10 percentage points or so behind the overall figure (i.e., 55 to 70 percent of them have been sexually involved).

From this we learn several things. First, our society is experiencing an almost complete breakdown of moral values and is passing its immorality on to our kids. Second, Christian teenagers are giving in to the world's standards in numbers unparalleled in Western culture. Third, those Christian teens who are not sexually active, rather than being left out, are some of the final holdouts against the tide of immorality. They comprise the group that has dug in its heels and refuses to be overrun. Fourth, as the statistics reveal, out of any 100 teenagers, about twenty-five of them will not be sexually active (about thirty-five, if Christians). It simply can't be said that everyone is doing it. A significant minority of teenagers has not given in.

Teenagers who look around and think they see "everyone doing it" are looking in the wrong places. They have allowed themselves to come under the influence of peers, the mass media, and other elements of our culture that shamelessly promote premarital sex. Billboards, television commercials, locker rooms, slumber parties, and classrooms abound with suggestions and direct commentaries on sex. Bumper stickers say things like "Nurses do it with patience and divers do it deeper."

However, even with all this outside influence, much of how a teenager perceives the world depends on his or her own family. A teenage girl who feels pressured and can look to abstaining siblings is able to make intelligent choices. She can say, "My older brother isn't doing it. My older sister hasn't given in. I don't have to either."

Friends are also of great importance in helping teens make decisions. So peer influences such as church groups provide opportunities to interact with people who may not be sexually active.

And of those the teenager knows who are "doing it," not all are finding sex as romantic as the movies say. Most find a temporary thrill in it, but without marriage it always ends up being unfulfilling. To some girls, sex is a physically painful process they go through for the gratification of someone else. They don't enjoy sex while it's happening, their moral conscience is hurt afterward, they have a weakened self-image that must be bolstered by the other person's approval, and so on. This doesn't happen in every case, but it happens often enough that teenagers feeling left out should note: The pain outweighs any gain.

Teenagers who are not sexually active and feel left out need to view themselves in a new light. Rather than feeling out of touch with their society, they need to realize that their society is out of touch with God. Many of the kids I know are responding to the "everyone's doing it" pressure in a variety of ways:

Well, I'm not everybody, I'm me. Besides, I don't really believe everybody is doing it. I think it's a lot of talk.

◆ ◆ ◆

If everyone's doing it, then you shouldn't have too much trouble finding someone else.

◆ ◆ ◆

Yes, I can see that the pregnancy rate of teenagers is fierce.

◆ ◆ ◆

"Everyone is doing it" is a mighty poor excuse for doing something. That pressure doesn't affect me for the simple reason that I don't want what "everyone" else has. I don't want a sexually transmitted disease, a divorce, a broken home, or children bouncing from one parent to another.

◆ ◆ ◆

The frequency with which something happens does not accurately indicate its value. For example, let's say the majority of people develop cancer—does that mean I should be anxious to have cancer? That's as stupid a response as wanting to have sex because everyone else is.

We need to be realistic. Not many teens will have the courage to offer the above responses to sexual pressure. Think of thirteen- or fourteen-year-olds facing the pain of being rejected. Mostly they just think that they really want this guy or girl to like them. They are looking for ways to conform, fit in, and be accepted. They are not eager to buck the popular trend and be singled out as an oddball.

In God's kingdom, the directive is, "Be holy, for I the Lord your God am holy" (Lev. 19:2, NASB). But our culture tells us, If it feels good, do it. One of these two kingdoms must fall, and we must, by word and action, choose which side we are on. A young woman told me how her boyfriend tried to pressure her into sex by saying everyone was doing it. She looked him in the eye and replied, "Everyone but me."

PRESSURE TO CONFORM

Several kids have written to me over the years about the pressure they feel to go along with those engaging in premarital sex. Their comments provide great insight for all of us.

> We are made to feel inadequate if we don't live up to the standards of our parents and teachers as far as grades go. The pressure from our friends to engage in sex is a lot like the pressure we feel to do well in school. We feel inadequate if we don't live up to our friends' standards where sex is concerned.

◆ ◆ ◆

> Pressure is at a high point in the locker room. The little guy is usually picked on, and eventually rumors are spread about his virginity.

◆ ◆ ◆

> The peer pressure by friends is probably the hardest to face as a virgin because people will tease. "It's fun, you're missing out. Are you chicken or something? It's great. You won't get pregnant."

◆ ◆ ◆

> The most important thing in life is how we are viewed by our closest friends.

The need to conform is a particularly strong force in shaping teen choices. Shoes have to be of the right brand and style, hair must be cut and combed a particular way, and clothing must conform to the swings of fashion and fad. Entertainment and possessions for which the young people spend their money are principally those that are in vogue among their friends. The desire to conform—to shape their words and actions to please a certain group—has a profound influence on youth behavior.

One teen wrote about her friend:

> Karen was a virgin. She was insecure with herself and needed to be popular. She was tantalized by her friends who said, "You won't be in the group unless you have sex with John." She could not afford, so she thought, to lose the friendship she had with these girls. She gave in and had sex with her boyfriend, John. She also gave in to her friends because they told Karen she would have more dates with guys if they knew she would do whatever they wanted her to. Karen realized that those girls were not true friends, and they had led her astray. She also realized the guys thought of her as a slut, not a good date.

Conformity is a familiar part of human nature. Few of us want to be noticeably different from our peers. Whether adolescent or adult, we hate to pay the price of being singled out for ridicule because of our individuality. In most cases conformity may be harmless enough—except when it becomes the determinant of our ethics and behavior.

Peer pressure as it operates among today's teens sometimes becomes a kind of "moral blackmail." The basis for this blackmail is the group's power to accept or reject. And in our permissive society, sexual activity is often seen as an important criterion for admittance into a desired group. Even Christian teens, who have grown up with biblical morality, find themselves discarding or ignoring those values because of their fear of rejection.

It is easy for parents and church leaders to discount this peer blackmail and say to kids, "Be in the world, but not of it." However, we are not in the locker rooms. We are not being ridiculed for our lack of a sexual "track record." We are not feeling the pain of rejection.

Obviously, peer pressure has a strong influence on young people and their sexual behavior, as the following statements reveal:

- A recent teen survey revealed that 13 percent of boys said they got involved in premarital sex because of peer pressure, although only seven percent of girls listed peer pressure as their motivation.[2]
- Sixty-one percent of teens surveyed said the media has provided them with *information* or advice about sex in the past month, 57 percent said their friends have, and 55 percent said their parents have. . . . When asked who or what *influenced* their decisions about sex the most, more teens cited their parents than any other influence (37 percent). In comparison, 30 percent of teens surveyed said that friends influenced their sexual decision making.[3]
- One study showed that the age of sexual debut among girls was hastened by having a "high-risk" female best friend, having older friends, and having "high-risk" boys as friends.[4]
- Having the perception that a majority of peers are sexually active appears to increase the risk of becoming sexually active.[5]

Can you think back to your teen years? The issues were different, but even then groups of adolescents could be very cruel. I remember certain people being singled out for total humiliation. Personally, I remember the pain I suffered because my friends knew I had an alcoholic father.

Young people often assume that their needs for feeling loved, being popular with peers, or being more grown-up can be met by becoming sexually involved. Following the lead of peer pressure, however, is seldom rewarding or satisfying.

One reason peer pressure is so strong is that today's teens spend much more time with people their own age than they do with their parents. As a result, parents influence their children less today than ever before. Values are not being communicated effectively from generation to generation. With parents seldom available to their teens, it is not surprising that the teens are influenced most by the permissive culture of their peers.

Rather than being an integral part of a family and a community, kids are growing up with kids. They have their own subculture. They talk to each other. They grow dependent on each other. Since their friends provide their main source of identity, teens cannot risk alienation. So when the peer group moves in a particular direction, individual kids within the group go along.

Even within church families, young people are in effect segregated from their parents—we segregate people according to age. Adolescents go to the youth group; parents go to various adult activities. What if our churches began offering activities and programs aimed at restoring intergenerational communication? It might help our kids stand up better to peer pressure.

Much of the "don't get involved" pressure of years past resulted from the younger generation perpetuating values from their parents. But now that society is more segregated by age, that doesn't happen much. Without an inherited value system for determining right and wrong, teenagers are largely left to themselves to make choices. Tragically, most teens are totally unprepared. As parents and as youth leaders, we must take the power of negative peer pressure seriously. It is a devastating force for sexual permissiveness.

PRESSURE TO BE POPULAR

Cool is a difficult term to define, yet we all more or less understand it. A cool person is popular, accepted, welcome. You don't even have to be likable to be cool. You just have to be cool. This elusive state of being is foremost in the minds of many teenagers. The desire to be cool is the driving force behind much of adolescent behavior. It is ultimately a desire to be accepted, and since sexual involvement is often a prerequisite for acceptance, having sex becomes cool.

Here's what the kids are saying about it:

> There were no feelings at all, not for each other and not for ourselves. We were basically "doing it" because it was cool.

◆ ◆ ◆

> Someone asked me if I was still a virgin. I wanted to be cool, so I said no. Now that people have that in their heads about me, why should I wait?

Being cool, being in, being faddish is simply going along with others. A person who tags along just because something is cool says, "I don't know who I am; I don't have my own values, so I'll just do what everyone else does."

Rather than demonstrate the maturity of one who has internalized personal values and stands up for them, some kids who are trying to be cool are moral chameleons. They become what others expect them to be instead of who God created them to be. They live according to the behaviors and expectations of those they are trying to impress.

Many girls think the image of a sexually experienced woman is cool. You can almost hear them saying, "Don't tell me you're still a virgin. How uncool." An adolescent girl trying to prove how cool she is by having sex has an inaccurate, unbiblical view of herself. She is saying, "My worth is determined by how I perform and what I can accomplish." This view is just as false a basis for self-worth as outward appearance.

Macho may be considered cool by many guys, so they try to show their macho, manly traits through sex. "You don't want someone to think you're not a man, do you?" they chide each other. But boys trying to be macho through sexual activity are caught in a self-defeating mentality. Their basic view of a real man is one who can drink everyone else under the table and make it with the women. A macho man uses others for his own pleasure and ego gratification, shows little respect for others as human beings, and must continually perform. This means he considers himself of value only as long as he lives up to this warped standard of exploitation and conquest. Such a person does not have a healthy self-image.

Somehow guys have been brainwashed into thinking that if they have sex they are men, and if not, they are wimps. If a guy says to his football team, "I'm a virgin, and I'm going to remain a virgin until I get married," how will his teammates respond? Sure, many—if not all—will ridicule him and accuse him of not being a man. But what in the world does sex have to do with being a man? A twelve-year-old kid can have sex. Does that make him a man? My dog can have sex. Does that make him a man? I can just see it: My German shepherd impregnates another dog, and the dachshund next door exclaims, "Wow, what a man!"

Being sexually active has little to do with being a real man or woman. Adulthood involves overall maturity, responsibility, and being able to form and maintain healthy relationships. Sex no more makes someone a man or woman than standing in the garage makes him or her a car!

How can kids reply to sexual pressure containing such innuendoes? Here are how some kids I heard from respond:

> If I let other people like you tell me what to do, that would show I'm not a man. I'll make up my own mind about what I want to do. That's being a man.

> ◆ ◆ ◆

> Hey, just because I don't want to get sexually involved with my boyfriend doesn't mean that I'm a prude or frigid or that my sexual orientation is in question. Sex isn't all there is to a relationship. In fact, it's not even one of the more important parts.

Girls and guys trying to be cool or macho need to come to an accurate understanding of who they are according to the descriptions given in the Bible. They need to recognize that the worth and dignity of a human being are not based on appearance, performance, or proof of sexual ability. When they begin to recognize that they are special in the eyes of God, they will begin to treat others as being equally special.

PRESSURE FROM A BOYFRIEND OR GIRLFRIEND

Kaysee and Dirk, who had been going together for several months, went to the movies Saturday night as they often did. On the way home, Dirk drove them to a secluded area in the hills where a lot of couples in their town went to "park."

Holding his girlfriend close, Dirk said, "Kaysee, do you really love me?"

Kaysee pecked him on the cheek. "Of course, I love you, Dirk. You know I do."

"Then if you really love me," Dirk went on, "I want you to have sex with me. If you won't do it, then it will prove to me that you don't love me, and we will have to break up."

What could Kaysee do? She knew that sex before marriage was wrong, but she didn't want to lose Dirk. So she gave in.

A week later, Dirk and Kaysee decided to break up. After having sex together in Dirk's car that night, they had lost respect for one another. Kaysee's fear of losing her boyfriend moved her to yield to Dirk's pressure for sex. She not only lost her virginity, she lost the guy she had compromised her morals to keep.

Perhaps the most difficult peer pressure toward premarital sex a young person may receive is from a boyfriend or girlfriend. A recent study revealed that having a steady boyfriend or girlfriend is among the top four risk factors present in teens' lives contributing to a higher probability of becoming sexually active at a young age.[6] In another study of 1,228 parochial school students, over half reported "going steady" as their relationship status when experiencing their first intercourse.[7]

Notice in the survey below how "love" and dating pressure influence sexual activity among adolescents:

WHAT ARE THE REASONS KIDS YOU KNOW HAVE SEX?[8]		
Reason	Girls	Boys
They were curious and wanted to experiment.	80%	76%
They wanted to be more popular or impress their friends.	58%	58%
They were in love.	63%	50%
They were under pressure from those they were dating.	65%	35%

Sexual pressure from a steady is harder to resist because the couple already has a deep, caring relationship. The weaker partner may feel like he or she is obligated to have sex because of the relationship. A girl may reason that her boyfriend has spent a lot of time and money pleasing her, so she owes him what he wants. The pressure is especially intense when the alternative to giving in is breaking up. Here's the sad story of another girl who wrote to me:

> I started going with this real neat guy when I was fourteen. We were each brought up in Christian homes, so I thought he was a Christian. He was fun and nice-looking and very honest. I thought what I was feeling was really love, but it wasn't. I found that out too late.
>
> One Saturday we decided to go to a movie. My father dropped us at the theater and told us he would pick us up at 10 p.m. The movie was over at nine,

so we had an hour to kill. After we left the movies we went out the back, and he said he had something he wanted to show me. When we got there, he started kissing me and then a lot more. It really scared me because it was the first time a guy had ever touched me like that. I told him I was a Christian and thought he was too. He told me if I didn't do what he asked, he would never see me again, and he would tell my parents I had asked him to make love. So I did what he told me.

After that, we didn't speak for about three months. Then he called and said he had changed. He came over to my house for dinner, and when my parents were gone, he said he wanted to see my stereo (which was in my bedroom). Well, he hadn't changed. He did the same thing again. But this time I stopped him. I said I did love him, but I was not about to ruin my life because of premarital sex. After that he did not call again for a long time.

Other young people have had similar painful experiences. Here's what some of them have written:

I was scared. My first concern was to please him so I wouldn't lose him. After the first time (the biggest mistake of my life), the craving for love and intimacy became almost an obsession.

◆ ◆ ◆

How about asking yourself this question when you feel pressured into sex: Why am I doing this anyway? Are you so insecure that you're afraid of losing the relationship if you don't go "all the way"? Let me assure you, if you lost a relationship for that reason, you really didn't have any kind of a strong relationship in the first place. Check your motives.

◆ ◆ ◆

Some of my friends have sex because they are afraid of losing their boyfriend or girlfriend or are afraid of not being asked out for a second date. Also, when a relationship is in jeopardy, some of them will go against their principles to save it— especially if they still love that person.

◆ ◆ ◆

A lot of my friends tell me how their boyfriends want them to do sexual things. When a girl's boyfriend asks her to do these things, she's afraid to say no. She thinks if she doesn't go along with him, he will want to break off the relationship.

◆ ◆ ◆

Deciding not to have sex can mean the end of a relationship, though usually it means the relationship wouldn't have lasted much longer anyway.

Nothing is more condemning and degrading in a relationship than to be put on a performance basis. When one of the partners says, "You have to do certain things or I won't love you," that person no longer has an honest and unconditional love for the other. The one being made to perform will spend the remainder of the relationship jumping through hoops. For now, it may be sex; later, there may be other requirements.

Most of the time, it's the boy manipulating the girl. When a girl allows herself to be pushed around and emotionally abused for the boy's gratification, she is depriving herself of her God-given dignity. She is allowing herself to be robbed of something very precious.

Part of the problem here is the heavy emotional attachment that can come in dating relationships. If a boy threatens to dump a girl because she won't give in, she may be fully aware that she is being manipulated, yet she has become so dependent on him emotionally that she does what he wants. The pressure line is "If you won't have sex with me, then we'll have to break up." Or, "If you don't have sex with me, someone else will." If he really cared about his girlfriend, he would respect her feelings and not pressure her to have sex. Such pressure shows that the relationship isn't a very good one to start with. Most of these couples break up later anyway. Relationships should be based on caring and respect, not on sexual performance.

How should a girl respond to such pressure? Here's how some girls respond:

I just explain I'm not ready for sex by saying, "It's quite easy for you never to call or speak to me again, but I have to live with myself in the morning."

◆ ◆ ◆

Well, if that's the way you feel, I'm going to miss seeing you. But that's the way it's got to be.

◆ ◆ ◆

If all I mean to you is a body to have sex with, maybe we'd better take a closer look at why we see each other. You have no right to use me.

Our culture has come up with a number of definitions for love, one of which is "I give to you in order to get what I want." This kind of "love" allows one partner in a relationship to manipulate and coerce the other into sex—that is hardly the selfless, giving love described in the Bible.

For example, a boy pressures his girlfriend into sex knowing he has a lot of leverage. He knows she wants acceptance. He knows she wants security, companionship, and the emotional boost the relationship gives her. He knows she will give in to his pressure because she wants to keep all of those things. And he does it all in the name of love.

But true love seeks to give and encourage. It shows respect and reaffirms a person's dignity. It does not force another to violate his or her conscience. And perhaps above all else, true love takes into consideration the consequences an action would have for another and acts in light of that person's best interest.

Young people who are aware of their identity in God don't need acceptance by others to feel secure. They recognize the dignity each of them already has, and they will protect the dignity of the other as vigorously as they protect their own.

Many young people try to escape problems they may be having with friends or with their families by having sex. Sex certainly can provide a short-term escape from a troubled adolescent life. In this sense, sex is like a tranquilizer, something to numb the pain. But sex is only temporary, and afterward the participants discover that the problems are not solved.

A guy and girl may feel that their relationship is in trouble. They feel a distance coming between them. One or both of them may think that having sex will give them a feeling of intimacy and renew their closeness. And it may, but only for a short time.

Here's the question kids need to answer for themselves: Is having sex a rational, legitimate way of dealing with my problems? Looking at it this way, it's a no-brainer. Rather than try to numb themselves to their problems through sex, they need to deal with their tough issues. The first step is for kids to acknowledge that problems exist and that they are having a negative effect. Next, they should try to understand why the problems exist. Then they need to seek counsel from someone who can help them deal with the problems intelligently and effectively.

God gives Christian young people three resources for bringing about change in their lives: the Scriptures, the Holy Spirit, and loving relationships within the family and the body of Christ. These resources are free, and they are available in unlimited supplies. We need to help kids utilize these resources as much as we can. Once our young people find God's solutions to their problems, they will not need to escape them through premarital sex or other activities.

PRESSURE OF A DIFFERENT KIND: SCHOOL SEX EDUCATION

A high school freshman shared with me the following story:

> The school nurse was giving a sex education class and was telling us all the different ways to keep from getting pregnant. She finished by saying, "The only method that is 100-percent guaranteed is not to have sex, but of course that isn't very practical."

This little episode illustrates another way our kids are being pressured into premarital sex. It's called sex education as presented in our public schools. The problem is, when sex education is presented without a moral foundation, kids are left with no reasons not to try out what they have been taught. When the material tells a kid that an orgasm feels great, what does he or she want to do? He wants to try it out and see how great it is. After all, it "isn't very practical" to tell him to wait. To paraphrase the old saying, a little knowledge about sex, without any standards to govern sexual activity, can be a dangerous thing—especially knowledge without moral guidelines.

"Values-free" sex education, which has been promoted so strenuously in our nation's schools in past years, is now being called into serious question, even by its founders. Instead of preventing sexual experimentation, sex education sometimes piques curiosity and sparks interest. What values-free educators wrongly assume is a healthy education is for many kids a seductive invitation into sex, drugs, alcohol, and other behaviors.

This is what our young people are up against at school, the institution that influences them for more hours and with more repetition than any other. When school sex education talks only about what the body can do, without teaching the dignity and value of the individual, there is no right-or-wrong context for sex. Kids may learn some basics of anatomy, which only arouses more curiosity. No wonder a 1995 study of 976 junior high students concluded, "Our findings suggest that current school-based efforts to alter teen pregnancy rates and sexual behavior are unlikely to succeed."[9]

Whereas school instruction in sex may be ineffective at delaying sexual experimentation, the school experience itself may be a deterrent for many students. American adolescents stand a better chance of avoiding risky behavior when they experience and express strong connections to their school. In a study that examined all the measures of school environment, only two make a difference for adolescents' mental health: feeling connected to school (positive effect) and believing students at school to be prejudiced (negative effect). Both older and younger students who feel connected to their school report lower levels of emotional distress; they are less likely to think about or attempt suicide. Students who perceive other students to be prejudiced report higher levels of emotional distress.[10]

A feeling of connectedness to school also protects youth from cigarettes, alcohol, and marijuana use. Feeling a high level of connectedness to school also is associated with a delay in first sexual intercourse. Other factors associated with a modest delay in early sexual activity include attending a parochial school and attending a school with high overall average daily attendance.[11]

Measures of classroom size, teacher training, and parent involvement with school appear unrelated to adolescents' health behaviors and emotional well-being. Likewise, school policies appear to have little or no relationship to the behavior of teenagers who attend the school. What seems to matter most for adolescent health is that schools foster an atmosphere in which students feel fairly treated, close to others, and a part of the school. Our adolescent children, both younger and older, stand a better chance of being protected from health risks when they feel connected to their school.[12]

It is understandably difficult for public schools in a pluralistic society to take a stand on moral issues, because for every person they placate, they may offend two others. This is why sex education must begin in families and churches.

It is easy to say that sex education must begin in the home. But it can be quite difficult for parents to overcome their own embarrassment and uncertainty when talking about sex with their kids. This is why the church needs to offer biblically-based sex education as an aid to families. Again, it is easier to say what should be done than to do it. But when individuals who are able to teach reach out to their congregations, kids can learn about the values that accompany sex. They will understand the proper use of sex in God's design along with the biological facts before they even hear what the schools have to say. We will present some practical strategies for effective, home- and church-based sex education in part 4 of this book.

◆ ◆ ◆

In this section (part 2) we have examined six prominent reasons why many of our young people today do not wait until marriage to engage in sexual activity. Are we to simply give up the fight against adolescent premarital sex, since so many kids are participating for so many reasons? Absolutely not! Why not? Because the potential for physical, emotional, relational, and spiritual harm is so great, we must continue to instruct them, encourage them, and even warn them to wait. In part 3 we will discuss in detail the most prominent reasons why our kids should wait.

PART THREE

REASONS KIDS SHOULD WAIT FOR SEX

◆ ◆ ◆

CHAPTER 10

ABSTINENCE

GOD'S PROTECTION AND PROVISION

OFTEN WHEN I SPEAK about saving sex for a loving, committed marriage relationship, I get a response like, "You take sex too seriously." Yes, I do take sex seriously. When you consider the devastation of STDs, unwanted pregnancies, and the emotional trauma our kids experience as a result of adolescent premarital sex, can you blame me? As loving, deeply concerned Christian parents, pastors, youth leaders, and teachers, we must consider the current crisis of adolescent premarital sex an extremely serious issue. Most people take it too lightly, and our kids are experiencing the terrible consequences.

When kids get involved in premarital sex, they are taking an enormous risk. The negative results of premarital sex are not always evident at first. Kids often don't even think about them because a relationship can "feel so right." But how they feel does not diminish the risk or alter the consequences.

The wise author of Proverbs talks a lot about illicit sexual relationships and their sad consequences. For example, Proverbs 9:16-18 pictures the temptation to sexual compromise as a loose-living woman attempting to snare unwitting men: " 'Come home with me,' she urges the simple. To those without good judgment, she says, 'Stolen water is refreshing; food eaten in secret tastes the best!' But the men don't realize that her former guests are now in the grave"(NLT).

Did you notice the tantalizing line she uses to "bait" her victims? Sounds inviting, doesn't it? But did you also notice the potentially fatal risk behind the attractive come-on? This woman reminds me of the black widow spider who lures the male into sex—and then eats him for dinner! That's the way it is with premarital sex. It looks so good at first, but the consequences can be a killer.

In part 2 we looked at the many ways kids are lured into premarital sex. On the surface, these reasons are attractive or at least justifiable to the unsuspecting youth. But the experience often drives kids into a world of hurt. Is the momentary pleasure worth the risk? No way! That's why we must help our kids understand the reasons to wait for sex before they become seduced by all the reasons to get involved. We will explore many of those reasons in this section of the book.

GOD'S VIEWPOINT ON PREMARITAL SEX

Let's enter the world of a college freshman, Dana, as she faces a life-changing decision: to wait or not to wait. Dana lives on campus. She is an honor student, active in student body activities. This year has been especially exciting for her, mainly because of the guy she has been dating, Troy. Troy is good-looking. He is a member of the university debate team and aspires to become a lawyer some day. But best of all, he is crazy about Dana. They have been dating for eight months, and things seem to be getting better and better. Sometimes when they are alone it is hard to control their sexual drives because their feelings are so strong for each other. Dana is beginning to wonder why she should still hold back.

Dana is facing an important moral decision. But she has a number of influences readily available to help her make the decision.

First, Dana can consider the standards of morality her parents established for her. Dana knows that her mom and dad do not approve of premarital sex. But she is away from home and her parents no longer have the influence on her they once had.

She also must consider Troy's view of their physical relationship. He has not so subtly hinted that they go away for a weekend and "take the next step" in their romance. Dana knows exactly what he means: sex.

Dana also gets advice from her friends. Dana's best friend and roommate, Marie, encourages her to go ahead if she really loves Troy and plans to marry him. "As long as you are committed to each other," Marie says, "you might as well enjoy all the benefits of that commitment." A lot of the girls in the dorm say the same thing: Go for it!

Another influence shaping Dana's decision is the media. The message she gets from her favorite magazines, television shows, and music videos suggests, "It's your body, so it's your decision. Do what feels right to you."

Then there are Dana's own moral standards. At first she felt she would be violating her standards by becoming sexually involved with Troy. But as she falls more deeply in love with him, she begins to compromise her views. With all these influences speaking into her life, Dana is not sure which way to go.

There is, however, one viewpoint Dana has not considered yet: God's viewpoint. Dana might respond, "Oh, now you're going to give me a lot of ancient, outdated rules from a book that never made much sense to me anyway. I'm talking about love here, not some pious standard set up by a God who I'm not sure even exists."

I would tell Dana that I am also talking about love—not human love, but superhuman, divine love. I am talking about God's love for her. The God who created the universe also created Dana. In Psalm 139:13, David says of God, "You created my inmost being; you knit me together in my mother's womb." God knows what makes us tick. In Psalm 139:1-2, David marvels at God's knowledge of him: "You have searched me and you know me. You know when I sit and when I rise; you perceive my thoughts from afar."

Not only does God know us intimately, but he also loves us dearly. John 3:16 tells us of the extent to which God loves us: "He gave his one and only Son, that whoever believes in him shall not perish but have eternal life."

I would share with Dana that these verses point out one of the most exciting principles of biblical reality I have ever encountered: Not only does God know her intimately, but he also loves her dearly. Whenever God does something, he does it out of love for us.

"God loves me—yeah, right!" Dana may argue cynically. "That's why the Bible is full of 'Thou shalt not' verses. He's only interested in spoiling my fun. That's not love."

Dana's response is rather common. Perhaps you have heard it from some of your young people. How do you answer the argument that God is just a killjoy, that he is only out to squash our fun and make us miserable?

I want to share with you how I answer this argument. The principles I offer are at the root of all the other reasons for saying no to sex we will discuss in this book. It's where you must start when you instruct, advise, counsel, and encourage young people to wait for sex until marriage.

"THOU SHALT NOT" IS EVIDENCE OF GOD'S LOVE

As we have said, God's motivation behind every command in the Bible is to provide for us and protect us. At first glance the commandments may seem imposing and prohibitive, but there is clear proof that the God who says "thou shalt not" has our best interests at heart.

Please remember this: God deals with his children out of a heart of love. He seeks our well-being at every turn. How can we be sure of his loving intentions? Consider the life of Christ as recorded in the Gospels. His day-to-day ministry consisted of acts of compassion and healing toward the hurting. He demonstrated and taught compassionate acceptance of the sinner, being known as a friend of cheats and outcasts (see Luke 7:34). And he exhibited deep grief over human sin and its consequences on people. Everything he did, from healing the sick and teaching the multitudes to dying on the cross, was a clear picture of God's love in action.

God doesn't just *say* he loves us; he continually *demonstrates* his love for us. We can question his motives all we want, but the only evidence we have is evidence of his love. He does nothing that will bring us any harm. Instead he sets boundaries for our activities, including sex, to keep us from doing ourselves harm. When we read the negative commandments of the Bible in this light, they don't look ominous and threatening anymore. As one young man wrote:

> Let me clear up a misconception you may have. God is pro-sex! He invented it and thinks it's beautiful when enjoyed within the correct framework: lifelong marriage commitment. His rules about sex are not there to deprive us of something fun, but are a sign of his love to protect us from harm.

A Negative Perception of Our Loving God

One serious obstacle to the discussion of the Christian argument against premarital sex is a theological one. Some people have a negative perception of what God wants for us. Even many Christians don't believe that God wants good things for them.

Christians have always been quick to give the *what* about the biblical view of premarital sex: Don't do it. What has been lacking is the *why*, which is just as important. People don't realize how God uses such commands to protect and provide for us. Without an understanding of God's loving nature, we could easily come to view negative commandments as being to our detriment rather than to our benefit. If we don't have a relationship with one who claims to be in authority over us, we won't understand the motives behind his orders, and we won't want to cooperate with them. We must know our position in Christ.

Rules without relationships lead to rebellion. That's how it is in the family. That's how it is in the spiritual realm.

I once saw a study in which some 40 percent of "Christian" and Jewish leaders thought that fornication was all right for today. When those we look to for spiritual guidance tell us the opposite of what the Scriptures tell us, we are confused. If those who supposedly are leading us to God reject his commands, how are the rest of us supposed to feel about God's authority?

We are failing to look at God's commands in light of his character. He loves us so much he sent his Son to suffer on the cross, a punishment that should have been dealt to us. Everything about God's character reflects the deep love and concern he shows for his people. When someone loves a person, he will do two things: He will protect that person, and he will provide for him.

Why do parents give their children new shoes when the old ones wear out? They want to provide for them. Why do parents tell their children not to run into the street? They want to protect them from being hit by a car. Why do the children respond and obey? They have a relationship of trust with their parents. And even if the children disobey, they know they are taking a risk (Mom and Dad must be saying "don't" for a reason), and they know they will be in trouble afterward.

It's easy to see how this principle applies to families, but for some reason we have a rough time admitting that it also applies to our relationship with God. So many of us see him as just a big killjoy, hovering in heaven with a rolled-up magazine, waiting to clobber us as soon as we have a little fun. We ignore the biblical account of his character and we rebel. Then we get mad at him when there are consequences!

Part of the breakdown of our culture has come through certain psychological schools of thought about child rearing. Adherents to these ideas say that any negative injunction is unhealthy. They admonish parents to say only nice, uplifting things to their children, not to put any prohibitions on them, not to forbid anything.

This false (and illogical) philosophy has gained a significant foothold in child rearing; even Christians are buying into it. The Bible says: "Train a child in the way he should go" (Prov. 22:6). Our society says: "Let them do anything they want." And our kids are paying the price.

Young people who have lost sight of God's plan for them—and are sexually active because of that loss—need to reevaluate the trendy philosophical and theological ideas they have absorbed. They need to hear the words of one of their peers who wrote:

> At some level, people often feel that God's commands are there to deprive or hold them down. We need to hear Christ's answer to his own rhetorical questions in the Sermon on the Mount. "Which of you, if his son asks for bread, will give him a stone? Or if he asks for a fish, will give him a snake? If you, then, though you are evil, know how to give good gifts to your children, how much more will your Father in heaven give good gifts to those who ask him!" (Matt. 7:9-11).

GOD GIVES LAWS TO PROTECT US AND PROVIDE FOR US

Think of a swimmer who has trained, competed, and proven herself over the years as a world-class athlete. She is ready to compete in the Olympic Games and go for the gold. When she gets there, she goes to the pool to start her race. Some of the starting platforms are on one end, some are on the other, and some are on the side. Some competitors are on platforms, and some are already in the water. There are no lanes in the pool, only arrows on the bottom pointing in various directions. The competitors dive in at different times heading in different directions, bumping into each other.

Is this how races are set up? Well, you can do it that way in your own pool if you want, but it would never happen at the Olympics. That's not a race; it's a human demolition derby! For a swimming race, the pool must be marked in lanes. There must be someone watching to make sure everything is fair. There must be a specific starting point and time so the competitors can know when to dive in and swim. Without those parameters, no one can win.

The rules, the lanes, the specific starting time and so on provide our swimmer with the opportunity to win; they protect her from anyone else in the race who might hinder her. Similarly, God has established rules to keep us in our lanes and to keep others in their lanes.

With reference to sexual activity, there is one basic rule: Wait until marriage. Of course, a number of subheadings fall under that, such as, "Be holy, for I am holy" (1 Pet. 1:16, NASB); "Control [your] body in a way that is holy and honorable" (1 Thess. 4:4); "Honor God with your body" (1 Cor. 6:20); and so on. Out of his boundless love and wisdom, God has given us boundaries for our protection.

Seeing God's protective boundaries as limitations on our fun is like a goldfish regarding the fishbowl as a limitation on his fun. He sees the exciting world all around him and feels left out. "Why should I be stuck in here and miss all the fun?" he complains. One day he leaps out of the bowl, plops onto the floor, and dies. While in the bowl, he was fed and kept safe from the dangers outside. The bowl was there to provide for him and protect him, but he wouldn't accept it that way. Think how sad his owner was when he found the dead little fish on the floor.

Our loving God says, "For your own safety and well-being, stay within the bounds of my provision and protection." When we transgress those bounds, we get hurt—and when we hurt, he hurts. When we recognize God's loving plan for us—a positive plan for our welfare, not a negative plan to limit us unfairly or frustrate us—our response should be one of loving obedience to him. As Dr. Bill Bright has said:

> If God loved us enough to send his Son to die for us and to provide us with eternal life in heaven and an abundant life now on earth, can we be motivated to do any less than totally obey him? True, we are no longer under the law. But as Peter reminds us in 1 Peter 2:16, "You are not slaves; you are free. But your freedom is not an excuse to do evil. You are free to live as God's slaves" (NLT).[1]

Our Creator is not out to harm us but to provide for us and protect us. But when we want to cross his protective line, including his directives about sex, we tend to twist his love around to make it seem as if he is trying to spoil the fun. He is not. God created the world we live in and the people who live in it, as well as our physical relationships and sex, to be "very good" (Gen. 1:31). Why would he then beat us down for enjoying what he provided within the loving guidelines he has set down?

Sometimes it may appear that God is trying to suck all the fun out of our lives. According to Jeremiah 29:11, nothing could be further from the truth: " 'For I know the plans I have for you,' says the Lord. 'They are plans for good and not for disaster, to give you a future and a hope' " (NLT). Deuteronomy 10:13 instructs us to "obey the Lord's commands and laws . . . *for your own good*" (NLT, emphasis added). He knows that waiting for marriage to experience a sexual relationship is in our best interest.

God's commands are not arbitrary; they have the stated purpose of keeping us safe from harm. They are not random but are targeted to provide for us in specific ways. They are not there to frustrate us but are a reflection of the freedom we have in Christ. The lanes on a swimming pool may appear regimented and stiff, but those lanes can be used for freestyle, breaststroke, backstroke, butterfly, and so on. There is a freedom of style and movement within those limitations, just as with God's limitations.

God's commandments are a reflection of his character. The Bible instructs us to be transformed into the image of Christ: We are to be holy, for he is holy (1 Pet. 1:16); we are to be truthful, for he cannot lie (Titus 1:2), and so on. The picture of what God is like is in the Scriptures. We become like him by obeying his commandments. We were originally created in his image, but even though we fell away, he gives us the provision for turning back to him.

Protection from What?

What is God protecting us from? Is it really that bad outside the fishbowl? What many young people fail to consider in their quest for freedom from rules is that such freedom has a price tag. Actions have consequences. When we live within God's protection and provision, we don't have to worry about those consequences. When we step outside, we are vulnerable.

Imagine an astronaut in space preparing to make his first space walk outside the capsule—except he has decided to go outside without his pressure suit and oxygen. He gets ready to open the air lock when a colleague screams at him. "Are you crazy? Get your pressure suit on. You'll die in a second without it!"

The astronaut replies, "The suit is too bulky. I think the space walk will be more fun without it."

This crazy guy is free to open the air lock if he wants to, of course. But his freedom will be short-lived, because he will not be able to escape the consequences of his choice.

God's negative commandments are there to protect and provide for our young people. Our task in communicating that to our kids is well stated by this young man:

I firmly believe that curiosity is very dangerous in a teenager's mind regarding sexual immorality. Parents need to teach children the "whys" for living their lives pleasing in the sight of the Lord, not just "because I said that's the way it's going to be." There are a hundred "good" worldly reasons to have sex in your life as a teenager. Parents need to have a thousand better reasons for waiting. Most important, each of those reasons must have love behind it.

◆ ◆ ◆

In the chapters ahead I don't offer a thousand reasons kids should wait for sex until marriage. But the reasons I present all spring from the heart of a loving God who, in his undying compassion, desires to provide for our kids and protect them from the painful consequences of premarital sex.

CHAPTER 11

THE PHYSICAL REASONS TO WAIT

OUR YOUNG PEOPLE are paying a huge price for misusing God's gift of sex, reducing it to a form of entertainment. God designed sex to take place in the intimate commitment of marriage. In so doing, he has provided for us an environment in which we can experience true sexual freedom. Sexual freedom means the ability to let down all barriers, to be completely vulnerable to another person, knowing we can trust the other without reservation. It means partners have nothing to fear in any way by participating in sex. All of this is possible in marriage and only in marriage.

The secular view of sexual freedom means the ability to sleep with as many people as one wishes as often as he or she wishes. This automatically excludes intimacy from the relationship. It's impossible for two people to be open and vulnerable when they don't really know each other well. And how can you trust yourself to someone whose sexual history is a mystery or who may walk out of your life next week or next month? This type of sexuality may make the body free to do as it pleases, but it puts the person inside in emotional bondage.

One reason people can't be free in casual sex is the constant, looming threat of taking home a permanent reminder from a temporary tryst. This is a very important reason why kids should wait for sex until marriage. When they do, they avail themselves of God's protection from the ravages of sexually transmitted diseases and complications of unwanted pregnancies. At the same time, young people who decide to wait are candidates for God's provision of a satisfying, guilt-free sexual relationship in their future marriage.

In God's perfect plan, everything about sex is beneficial, edifying, unifying, and pleasurable for both partners. That's why he commands us to wait until marriage for sex. Although it may seem to many adolescents like a negative command on the surface, it is actually a positive command. He has set aside something so valuable and wonderful that he doesn't want them to spoil it through immaturity, impulsiveness, or impatience.

God is good to us. Not only has he provided a means of bringing pleasure and total unity through sex, but he also has given us boundaries in which to enjoy his gift fully. He has told us to wait until marriage because he loves us and wants us to have an abundant life. When we choose to ignore God, we leave ourselves open to the consequences.

Is it any wonder that those informed in the medical profession and other related areas are advocating monogamy? God set sex aside for marriage for the protection and happiness of his human creation. Sex within marriage brings increased unity and an opportunity for each partner to bring pleasure to the other. Sex outside marriage brings a momentary thrill, a release, a way to block out problems, but it brings with it an avalanche of negative consequences.

Simply said, sex within marriage is within God's design and is good; sex outside marriage is outside God's design and cannot ultimately be good. It might feel good for a moment, but sin can never be a good thing.

By reserving sex for marriage, God protects us from emotional hurt, from disease, from damaged relationships, and from the misery that accompanies sin. Sex needs the commitment, trust, and longevity that a marriage can provide.

Just as sex is safe and free within the limits of God's protection, it is also able to reach its fullest and most exciting potential within those limits. There is no fear of rejection, no need to pretend, no need to sneak around, no guilt, and no fear of a baby ruining your life. This is God's provision for sex within marriage.

This spiritual side of sex is often overlooked. Even many Christians are not aware of the profoundly spiritual nature of their sex lives. A person will feel acute spiritual pain and separation from God when engaging in sex outside marriage, but he or she may not realize how spiritually beneficial and unifying sex is within marriage.

A 1993 Voter/Consumer Research poll of 1,000 adults found that the people most apt to report that they are satisfied with their current sex life are married individuals who "strongly" believe sex outside of marriage is wrong.[1] This is just one evidence of the benefits of God's provision and protection within the sanctity of marriage.

SEXUALLY TRANSMITTED DISEASES: THE HEALTH RISK OF PREMARITAL SEX

Our young people should wait for sex until marriage because of the epidemic of sexually transmitted diseases among sexually promiscuous individuals. Despite the growing threat of STDs, despite the explosion of STD cases among those under age twenty, many kids today do not recognize the danger. One study found that, even though girls might be well-informed about sexually transmitted diseases and knew how to avoid infections, this knowledge had little influence on their behavior.[2]

Anyone who has sex outside of marriage is at risk. This year 25 percent of sexually active youth will be infected with a sexually transmitted disease.[3] STDs do not recognize a person's religious or moral beliefs, only his or her actions. Dr. Edward Weismeier, director of the UCLA Student Health Center, warns students, "Even an honest answer to an intimate question is no guarantee that a person is safe. While dormant in one person, an STD can be transmitted to another." He admonishes them that "one chance encounter can infect a person with as many as five different diseases."[4]

What are these diseases from which God wants to protect us? There used to be a handful. Now there are dozens. The major ones will be addressed here in detail because this is a subject that cannot be passed over lightly. STDs are changing the nature of our society, and those who are concerned about showing that the unchanging message of Jesus Christ is relevant to this culture must be informed.

STDs have always been around, but they can be spread only through promiscuity, something our society did not accept until this generation. When two unmarried individuals had sexual intercourse in the 1960s, both were relatively safe as far as STD risk. It was assumed by the majority of people that first-time sexual encounters would occur at the time of marriage. Those who did experience sexual intercourse before marriage usually restricted the number of partners.[5] However, all of that has changed drastically. Today the incidence of premarital and extramarital sex has skyrocketed, and STDs can be passed on through various forms of sexual intercourse—oral, anal, or vaginal—and even through mutual masturbation or "dry sex." Annual numbers of doctor visits for STD treatment reflect that increase.

Until recent years, public-health experts counted barely five types of sexually transmitted diseases. Now, they know that more than twenty-seven exist. "Eight new sexually transmitted pathogens have been identified since 1980, including HIV."[6]

The following chart provides a quick overview of how widespread this epidemic is:

INCIDENCE AND PREVALENCE OF STDS[7]		
STD	Incidence (Estimated number of new cases every year)	Prevalence* (Estimated number of people currently infected)
Chlamydia	3 million	2 million
Gonorrhea	650,000	–NA–
Syphilis	70,000	–NA–
Herpes	1 million	45 million
Human Papillomavirus (HPV)	5.5 million	20 million
Hepatitis B	120,000	417,000
Trichomoniasis	5 million	–NA–
Bacterial Vaginosis**	–NA–	–NA–

*No recent surveys on national prevalence for gonorrhea, syphilis, trichomoniasis, or bacterial vaginosis have been conducted.

**Bacterial vaginosis is a genital infection that is not sexually transmitted but is associated with sexual intercourse.

It has been said that when two individuals engage in sexual intercourse, they are actually having sex with all the other people with whom their partner has had sex. No wonder STDs have reached epidemic proportions. The following chart graphically illustrates how they spread:[8]

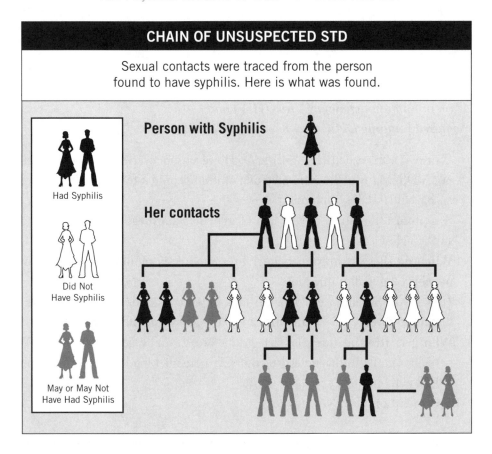

CHAIN OF UNSUSPECTED STD

Sexual contacts were traced from the person found to have syphilis. Here is what was found.

Had Syphilis

Did Not Have Syphilis

May or May Not Have Had Syphilis

Person with Syphilis

Her contacts

Pregnant women with sexually transmitted diseases are more likely to have premature deliveries and newborns with serious abnormalities, according to two studies. The studies, in the *Journal of the American Medical Association*, are among the most definitive to make that link. One study of 534 women, by University of Washington at Seattle researchers, found 19 percent had bacterial vaginitis, a vaginal infection caused by several kinds of bacteria, and 9 percent had chlamydia.

As you look at many of the sexually transmitted diseases plaguing our population in the wake of rampant promiscuity, remember that the consequences of sex outside of marriage are not a minor problem. STDs kill. Of 513,486 persons with AIDS reported in the United States through December 1995, more than 62 percent (319,849) have died. The largest number of deaths related to STDs other than AIDS is caused by cervical and other human papillomavirus-related cancers. A recent study found that more than 150,000 deaths were directly attributed to STDs, including AIDS, from 1973 through 1992 among American women fifteen years of age and older.[9]

Helping our kids wait is a matter of life and death.

Human Immunodeficiency Virus (HIV) and Acquired Immune Deficiency Syndrome (AIDS)

- **Cause:** A virus called HTLV-III/LAV. However, not everyone exposed develops AIDS. Many of the estimated one million people infected by the virus so far have no AIDS symptoms.
- **Symptoms:** Tiredness, fever, loss of appetite, diarrhea, night sweats, and swollen glands.
- **When do these symptoms occur?** From about six months to five years or possibly longer after infection.
- **How is AIDS diagnosed?** Doctors look for certain kinds of infections; they do tests to reveal AIDS antibodies and damaged white blood cells.
- **Who gets it?** The three largest groups are: sexually active gay men, 73 percent of cases; intravenous drug users, 17 percent; blood-transfusion recipients, 2 percent.
- **Treatment or cure:** None as yet.

The acronyms that strike the greatest fear in the hearts of the sexually promiscuous are HIV and AIDS. Acquired immune deficiency syndrome, since first reported in the U.S. in 1981, has doubled its number of new victims each year.

AIDS damages the body's immunity against infection, leaving its victims without a defense against a host of serious diseases. According to officials of the United Nations and the World Health Organization in 1996:

More than 3 million people, mostly under age twenty-five, have become newly infected with the AIDS. . . . The new cases bring to nearly 23 million the total number who are infected. In the fifteen years since the discovery of AIDS, an additional 6.4 million people—5 million adults and 1.4 million children—have died. . . . Of the 8,500 new infections each day, 7,500 are in adults and 1,000 in children. About 42 percent of all those living with HIV, the virus that causes AIDS, are women, and the proportion is growing.[10]

If there is any reason for our kids to say no to premarital sex it would be to take advantage of God's protection from this deadly disease. Here are the hard, cold facts about HIV/AIDS and the general public, based on the latest data available at this writing:

- As of December 1997, an estimated 30.6 million people worldwide were living with HIV/AIDS. Cumulative AIDS-related deaths worldwide as of December 1997 numbered approximately 11.7 million.[11]
- The total number of AIDS cases worldwide has risen to 1,025,973—up 20 percent from a year ago, says the World Health Organization. The largest portion (39 percent) is in the U.S.[12]
- As of November 1996, it was reported that 830,000 children were living with the AIDS virus worldwide; 22.6 million people had AIDS or HIV infection worldwide.[13]
- About 900,000 Americans are infected with HIV.[14]
- As of June 1996, . . . 548,102 had [AIDS]. Seven new HIV infections occur each hour (or 150 to 220 new cases each day), most of those being minority (57 percent black and 20 percent Hispanic) heterosexual women.[15]
- By mid-1997, over 360,000 Americans had died of AIDS.[16]
- The Centers for Disease Control reports that AIDS is the number one cause of death for Americans between the ages of twenty-five and forty-four. Since 1981, more than 400,000 have contracted AIDS and 250,000 people have died. The disease has dramatically increased among heterosexuals.[17]
- According to new federal statistics, AIDS has become the leading cause of death among Americans between the ages of twenty-five and forty-four. Statistics also show that HIV is spreading the fastest in women and minorities.[18]
- The number of new cases of HIV infection is declining in the population with the greatest numbers of infections: men who have sex with other men. However, this is the only group with declining numbers. All others continue to grow, some at the fastest rates in the history of the epidemic.[19]
- HIV is spreading fastest among blacks in America. In fact, in 1996 (for the first time) the number of AIDS cases in blacks (41 percent of the

total) exceeded those diagnosed in whites (38 percent) in spite of the fact that blacks account for a far smaller portion of the national population.[20]

◆ According to a 1998 report in *Archives of Internal Medicine*, four out of every ten HIV-infected people surveyed at two New England hospitals failed to tell sex partners about their disease.[21]

◆ Women in their reproductive years are the fastest growing HIV-infected population in the United States.[22]

◆ STDs that cause sores on the genitals provide an easy entrance for HIV. But even STDs that cause no visible lesions can increase transmission risk because they stimulate an immune response in the genital area that makes infection more likely.[23]

◆ Babies are the most vulnerable victims, and about 6,000 babies are born to HIV-infected women every year.[24]

◆ It is estimated that by the end of 1995, maternal deaths caused by HIV/AIDS will have orphaned 24,600 children, and the number can be expected to escalate during the next few years.[25]

A REPORT BY THE WORLD HEALTH ORGANIZATION (WHO) AND THE UNITED NATIONS GIVES THE FOLLOWING SOMBER HIV/AIDS PROFILE:	
People newly infected with HIV in 1999	5.4 million
Number of people living with HIV/AIDS	34.3 million
AIDS deaths in 1999	2.8 million
Total number of AIDS deaths since the beginning of the epidemic	18.8 million[26]

Even more frightening is the way HIV/AIDS is affecting our adolescent population. One of the fastest-growing AIDS populations in the U.S. is teenage youth. AIDS cases in thirteen- to nineteen-year-olds increased 524 percent in the first six months of 1995, compared with all of 1994. Most of the increase occurred among homosexual teens, although a greater percentage of teens with AIDS are female (35 percent vs. 14 percent of adults with AIDS). Approximately 63 percent of teens with AIDS are African-American or Hispanic, compared to 51 percent of adults; 20 percent were infected through heterosexual contact, as compared to 8 percent of adults.[27]

If the following statistics don't chill you to the bone, I don't know anything that will:

- The adolescent population—persons thirteen to twenty-one years old—has been catastrophically hit with human immunodeficiency virus (HIV) infection and acquired immune deficiency syndrome (AIDS).[28]
- Twenty percent of all AIDS cases are in the sixteen- to twenty-nine-year-old age group, and the rates among eleven- to twenty-four-year-olds double each year. AIDS among teenagers accounts for less than one percent of all cases. However, these cases increased by 51 percent between 1988 and 1989.[29]
- A 1991 study at the University of Texas at Austin found that one in 100 students were HIV infected. Subjects were students who were at the student health center to have blood drawn for various reasons. Some may have been there because they were experiencing symptoms of HIV infection, but others were there just for cholesterol or other routine tests. (No known AIDS patients were included.)[30]
- In 1990, about 25 percent of the 10,000 women who were diagnosed with AIDS were in their twenties, as were about 20 percent of the 100,000 men. This means that many, if not most, of these men and women became infected while they were still in their teens.[31]
- An HIV seroprevalence study done in Washington, D. C., from October 1987 through September 1988, found one in 250 adolescents to be HIV infected. During the period between October 1991 through March 1992, the investigators found the rate to be one in forty-five, a 500 percent increase since 1987.[32]
- One-fourth of all new HIV infections in the U.S. are estimated to occur in those between the ages of thirteen and twenty. In the first six months of 1995, AIDS cases in thirteen- to nineteen-year-olds increased 524 percent compared with all of 1994.[33]
- A report from the Centers for Disease Control and Prevention found that AIDS cases among young people ages thirteen to twenty-five rose 20 percent through sex and drug use between 1990 and 1995.[34]
- Nearly 50 percent of all teenagers infected with AIDS are girls.[35]
- Half of all HIV infection has occurred in people under age twenty-five.

Because it is generally accepted that there is an average ten-year lag between infection with HIV and serious AIDS-related illness, it can be concluded that many of the young adults dying from HIV/AIDS were infected initially as adolescents.[36]

Some people mistakenly believe that contracting another sexually transmitted disease, such as chlamydia, gonorrhea, or HPV, means they cannot get AIDS/HIV. In reality, the presence of most STDs increases the risk of AIDS, and the following studies reveal:

- Those who have both HIV and another sexually transmitted infection are more likely to spread the AIDS virus during sexual contact and are thus more infectious.[37]
- STD infections increase susceptibility to HIV. When infected with a serious STD such as chlamydia or human papillomavirus, the risk of HIV conveyance is increased by as much as 100 times.[38]
- People with an active syphilis, genital herpes, or chancroid infection, or who have chlamydia, gonorrhea, or trichomoniasis are three to five times more likely to contract HIV than other people. More than half (54 percent) of American adults under 65 do not know that STDs increase susceptibility to HIV.[39]
- Herpes infection—along with numerous other STDs—has been shown to increase risk of subsequent HIV infection.[40]
- "Both 'ulcerative' STDs, such as chancroid, syphilis, and genital herpes, and 'inflammatory' STDS, such as gonorrhea, chlamydial infection, and trichomoniasis, increase the risk of HIV infection." Many studies have shown that STDs increase both "infectivity of and susceptibility to HIV." In Tanzania the incidence of HIV infection was 42 percent lower in communities with improved management of STDs. It has been predicted that a 50 percent reduction in STDs in Uganda could decrease HIV transmission by 43 percent.[41]
- A model has been developed by M. C. Boily showing that "HIV infection could not be established in the general U.S. heterosexual population in the absence of chlamydial infection (or other STDs with comparable effects on HIV transmission). In addition, it is estimated that successfully treating or preventing 100 cases of syphilis among

high-risk groups for STDs would prevent 1,200 HIV infections that are ordinarily linked to those 100 syphilis infections during a ten-year period."[42]

The good news in the midst of all this bad news is that the mortality rate for HIV/AIDS has declined in recent years. Age-adjusted death rates from HIV infection in the U.S. declined an unprecedented 47 percent from 1996 to 1997, and HIV infection fell from eighth to fourteenth among leading causes of death in the U.S. over the same time. For those ages twenty-five to forty-four, AIDS dropped from the leading cause of death in 1995 to third leading in 1996 and fifth leading in 1997. The age-adjusted HIV death rate of 5.9 deaths per 100,000 is the lowest rate since 1987, the first year mortality data were available for the disease. The 1997 rate is less than half the 1992 rate (12.6) and almost one-third the rate in 1995, the peak year (15.6).

The data come from a report, Births and Deaths, 1997, prepared by the National Center for Health Statistics, a part of the Centers for Disease Control and Prevention (CDC).

The decline in AIDS deaths is primarily due to the continuing impact of highly active antiretroviral therapy helping people with HIV live longer and healthier lives. At the same time, success in treating those with HIV does not mean the nation can relax its efforts to prevent HIV transmission.[43]

Chlamydia

- **Cause:** The bacterium *chlamydia trachomatis*, spread to adults through sexual contact and to babies of infected mothers during birth.
- **Symptoms:** For men, discharge from the penis or a burning sensation during urination. For women, vaginal itching, chronic abdominal pain, or bleeding between menstrual periods. Up to 80 percent of chlamydia infections in women are asymptomatic compared to 40 percent in men.[44]
- **When do these symptoms occur?** Sometimes two to four weeks after infection. But many men have no symptoms. Four of five women will not notice anything until complications set in. Victims can go for years not knowing they have it.
- **Complications:** In both sexes, possible infertility. In women, pregnancy problems that can kill a fetus and, occasionally, the mother. In babies, infections of the eyes, ears, and lungs, possibly death.

◆ **Diagnosis:** For men and women, a painless test at a doctor's office.
◆ **Cure:** Usually the drug tetracycline or doxycycline. However, experiencing one infection and then being cured does not provide immunity. A woman can become reinfected, and each reinfection increases her chance of infertility.[45] A Pap smear can detect it, and antibiotics can cure it. If not treated, it can cause pelvic inflammatory disease (PID), which can lead to ectopic, or tubal, pregnancy and bring pneumonia and eye diseases in children born to infected mothers.
◆ **Condom effectiveness:** Condoms are only partially protective.[46]

Some have humorously quipped that chlamydia is "faster than a speeding sperm. Able to evade latex like the Road Runner escapes Wily Coyote. More powerful than your favorite spermicide. Yes, it's chlamydia." In reality, it's no laughing matter.

Chlamydia is an infectious organism, classified as a bacterium, although it possesses properties similar to both viruses and bacteria. It is called an "energy parasite" because it cannot make "energy" for itself but rather grows inside a person's cells, where it draws nutrition and protection.[47] Although no cases of chlamydial infections of women's cervix, uterus, and fallopian tubes were reported before 1976, it is now the most common nonviral STD in the U.S.[48]

In 1995, the first year that chlamydia was nationally reportable, the disease led the list of infections reported to the National Notifiable Disease Surveillance System (NNDSS).[49] By 1996, 382,388 cases were reported in the U.S., far outpacing gonorrhea, the next most commonly reported at 298,462. However, as with so many other STDs, reported chlamydia cases are only a small portion of the total number, estimated by the CDC to exceed 4 million.[50]

Studies tell us more about this insidious infection:

◆ More than 600,000 cases were reported to the U.S. Centers for Disease Control and Prevention in 1998 — 1,665 new infections each day.
◆ Five percent of sexually active teens are infected each year.
◆ The *American Journal of Obstetrics and Gynecology* reports that "at least 10 percent of all sexually active teens are infected with chlamydia."[51]
◆ Chlamydia is a leading cause of infertility and pelvic inflammatory disease.

- Chlamydia can cause serious infections to babies born to infected mothers.
- Eighty percent of women and 35 percent of men who do have an infection do not know that they are infected.
- Chlamydia is curable with antibiotics, but some damage cannot be reversed.
- Chlamydia is the most commonly reported infectious disease in the U.S. and may be one of the most dangerous sexually transmitted diseases among women today.[52]
- Seventy-five percent of women and 50 percent of men with chlamydia have no symptoms. The majority of cases therefore go undiagnosed and unreported. The number of reported cases—about 660,000 cases in 1999—is merely the tip of the iceberg.[53]
- An estimated three million people contract chlamydia each year in the United States; 40 percent of cases occur in fifteen- to nineteen-year-olds.[54]
- A woman can carry the disease in her cervix, uterus, fallopian tubes and ovaries for months or years without knowing it.[55]
- A major cause of female infertility, chlamydia accounts for 20 percent to 40 percent of all cases. About 80 percent of infected women and 35 percent of men won't have a clue they were infected until several years later, when they have trouble getting pregnant.[56]
- Almost one in every ten women who contract chlamydia will experience a potentially life-threatening ectopic pregnancy.[57]
- Twenty-seven percent of American women who have undergone in-vitro fertilization were infertile because of past pelvic infection, primarily caused by chlamydia.[58]

Our adolescent population is being ravaged by chlamydia as a result of pre-marital sex. Consider the following facts.

- Although it doesn't get as much attention as AIDS, chlamydia—probably the most common bacterial STD—is potentially a more serious threat to teenagers. Girls fifteen to nineteen years old appear to have the highest infection rates of any age group.[59]
- "Today's most prevalent STD is chlamydia, . . . [infecting] one in seven sexually active girls and about one in ten sexually active boys. . . . [Chlamydia has] infected 38 percent of sexually active teens."[60]

- In some populations, up to one of every four teenagers is infected with chlamydia.[61]
- Nationally, almost seven percent of females fifteen to nineteen years old who were tested at family planning clinics in 1995 were infected with chlamydia. The major risk factors are being young—usually younger than twenty-five—and having sex.[62]
- Up to 69 percent of adolescents with positive cultures are completely symptom free.[63]
- Teenagers are more susceptible to chlamydia because cells lining the cervix of female adolescents and young women are less resistant to infection by certain sexually transmitted organisms.[64]
- Between 8 and 25 percent of sexually active college students, as well as 31 percent of patients examined in STD centers, have chlamydia.[65]
- In New York City, officials say teenagers account for about 40 percent of the 25,000 cases of chlamydia reported each year.[66]
- Chlamydia is more common among teenagers than among adults; in some studies, up to 30 percent of sexually active teenage women and 10 percent of sexually active teenage men tested for STDs were infected with chlamydia.[67]
- The rate of recurrence for previously infected adolescent females is 40 percent within fourteen months.[68]

As with other STDs, the only way to avoid contracting chlamydia is to avoid all sexual contact until marriage and then to faithfully maintain a lifelong, monogamous relationship. We must encourage our kids to wait.

Pelvic Inflammatory Disease (PID)

- **Causes:** A spectrum of female upper genital tract disorders caused mostly by chlamydia and gonorrhea ascending from the cervix and vagina.[69]
- **Symptoms:** Inflammation and abscesses of a woman's fallopian tubes, ovaries, and pelvis.
- **Possible harm:** A woman with PID faces increased risk for chronic pelvic pain, ectopic pregnancy, and infertility.[70] One in seven women with a PID attack becomes infertile. After three attacks, up to 75 percent cannot conceive.
- **Diagnosis:** Examinations of abdomen and pelvis, laboratory tests.

◆ **Cure:** Antibiotics for some cases. Severe cases often require surgery that results in infertility.

One of the most serious threats to the reproductive capability of women is pelvic inflammatory disease (PID). Chlamydia is the most common cause of PID, which in turn is the most common reason, with the exception of pregnancy, that women of reproductive age end up in hospitals. Damage to women's fallopian tubes as a result of PID is the most rapidly increasing cause of infertility in America today.[71] Of the estimated 2.6 million American women with chlamydia, 20 to 40 percent of those with untreated infections will develop PID.[72]

- Women who experience one episode of chlamydial PID have a 25 percent chance of becoming infertile. A second episode brings that percentage rate up to 50 percent.[73]
- Each year more than one million U.S. women experience an episode of PID.[74]
- Among women of reproductive age, 10 to15 percent have had one or more episodes of PID.[75]
- At least 15 percent of all infertile American women are infertile because of tubal damage caused by PID resulting from an STD.[76]

Once again, young people who do not avail themselves of God's provision and protection by waiting for sex are in great danger of harm from this infection.

- A fifteen-year-old is up to ten times more likely to develop the infertility-causing pelvic inflammatory disease (PID) than a twenty-four-year-old with the same type of sexual encounters.[77]
- A teenage girl is at greater risk for PID than an adult just by having sex: A fifteen-year-old has a one in eight chance of developing PID just by having sex. A twenty-four-year-old in the same environment has a one in eighty chance.[78]

One of the greatest dangers caused by PID is ectopic or tubal pregnancies. A partially blocked fallopian tube may allow sperm to ascend to the ovum, but the fertilized egg is too large to descend, so it implants in the tube. In 1992, the estimated number of ectopic pregnancies was 108,800, or one in 50 pregnancies.

Of all women who are infertile because of tubal damage, no more than one-half have previously been diagnosed and treated for acute PID.[79]

According to a 1995 Russian publication, chronic PID complications include:

- disorders of sexual and menstrual functions;
- primary or secondary sterility;
- spontaneous abortions or premature birth;
- fetoplacentar insufficiency;
- intrauterine fetus contamination and other perinatal troubles;
- pain syndrome.[80]

Young women who heed God's directives for sexual purity will be protected from PID.

Gonorrhea

- **Cause:** The bacterium neisseria gonorrhoeae.
- **Symptoms:** For males, a pus-like discharge. From 30 to 80 percent of women with gonorrhea are asymptomatic, while fewer than 5 percent of men are asymptomatic.[81]
- **Complications:** Many, from back pains and urination problems to arthritis and sterility. One bout of gonorrhea PID infection in a woman results in a 12 percent possibility of infertility; a second bout of such infection results in a 25 percent possibility of infertility.[82] Babies of infected mothers may be born blind.
- **Diagnosis:** Cell-culture tests.
- **Cure:** Penicillin works in most cases. A major concern is that strains of gonorrhea resistant to penicillin have been found in all fifty states.[83]
- **Condom effectiveness:** Condoms diminish but do not stop the spread of gonorrhea.

Gonorrhea, which is caused by bacteria that multiply quickly in moist, warm areas of the body, such as the cervix, urethra, mouth, or rectum, is not the most deadly of infections, but it is one of the most prevalent. "It has a long history (the Greeks complained of it and Hippocrates recommended treatments for this disease) and a lot of ugly names (drip, clap) all spelling sexual promiscuity. This infection is received only if one has sex with an infected person, which means that they have had sex with someone other than you, too."[84]

Worldwide, an estimated 250 million people are infected every year. In the United States, 750,000 cases, mostly among teenagers and young adults, are recorded annually. Officials say the real number is closer to three million.[85]

About 80 percent of those infected with gonorrhea are not aware of its presence for varying lengths of time. There is a 40 percent chance of contracting gonorrhea from just one sex act with an infected individual. Teens are especially susceptible to the disease, and the number of teens infected with it is rising alarmingly.[86]

A woman's risk of contracting gonorrhea from one act of unprotected intercourse is as high as 90 percent while the risk to a man is approximately 30 percent.[87] A new class of antibiotics, which health authorities had been counting on to help control this disease, may not be as effective as they hoped.[88]

Further studies on gonorrhea reveal:

- The rate of new infections, twelve times higher among blacks than whites a decade ago, is now thirty-nine times higher.
- Between 1997 and 1999, gonorrhea rates increased by 9 percent (DSTDP, CDC, 2000). . . . Rates of infection remain high among adolescents, young adults, and African-Americans. Gonorrhea remains a major cause of pelvic inflammatory disease (PID) and subsequent infertility and tubal pregnancies in women.[89]
- Studies have shown that gonorrhea can facilitate HIV transmission and may be contributing significantly to the spread of HIV in the South.[90]
- The reported gonorrhea rate in the U.S. remains the highest of any industrialized country and is roughly fifty times that of Sweden and eight times that of Canada.[91]
- A California study found that within three years of being infected with a sexually transmitted disease 12.6 percent of gonorrhea patients and 8.6 percent of chlamydia patients become infected again.[92]

Many statistics underestimate the true risk of STDs among adolescents who are sexually active. The highest incidence of gonorrhea among women is seen in the fifteen- to nineteen-year-old age group, according to 1995 data on gonorrhea rates from the CDC and Cycle IV of the National Survey of Family Growth. When adjusted for history of sexual activity, the rates in fifteen- to nineteen-year-olds are more than double those for any of the older age groups. One-third of gonorrheal infections are asymptomatic in teen women, and the proportion may be higher in males.[93]

The following studies paint a bleak picture of gonorrhea and the adolescent population.

- ◆ Gonorrhea rose 13 percent among teens between 1997 and 1999, with teenage girls having the highest rates of any females.[94]
- ◆ Gonorrhea most dramatically affects teens and young adults. Gonorrhea rates are highest among females between the ages of fifteen and nineteen and males between the ages of twenty and twenty-four. This is true regardless of race or ethnicity.[95]
- ◆ Among adolescents, gonorrhea increased 13 percent between 1997 and 1999, although 1999 rates were slightly lower than those in 1998.[96]
- ◆ A California study found that fifteen- to nineteen-year-olds were three times more likely than people of other ages to become reinfected with chlamydia and 60 percent more likely to become reinfected with gonorrhea. African-Americans were more than twice as likely as Latinos to become reinfected with gonorrhea.[97]

Gonorrhea is the most easily spread STD: When a woman has sex with an infected man, her chances of contracting the disease are one in two, while men have only a 25 percent chance of infection after one encounter with an infected woman. The woman's greater risk holds true for all the STDs studied except genital warts and genital herpes. And yet men are more likely than women to be carrying an infection.[98]

Dr. John Diggs provides the following insights into gonorrhea:

This bacteria has been recognized to cause . . . sexually transmitted diseases (STDs) for thousands of years. There was no reliable cure until the 1940s with the discovery of penicillin. . . . Unfortunately, because so many millions of people around the world have required treatment with penicillin, many gonococcal organisms have developed a resistance to this drug and stronger antibiotics have had to be developed and used.

Gonorrhea likes company. It doesn't always travel alone. Some of those companions are infections that cannot be cured—human papillomavirus, herpes, HIV.

The good news is that for the time being, gonorrhea remains curable. Still, not a good way to end a relationship. "Oh, by the way, baby, you might want to see your doctor."[99]

Genital Herpes (HSV)

- **Cause:** The herpes simplex virus (HSV) is a sexually transmitted disease that is almost always contracted through intercourse or other intimate physical contact. It can be transmitted to sex partners even when no genital ulcers are present and can be transmitted from mother to infant during delivery.
- **Symptoms:** From 50 to 90 percent of people infected with genital herpes do not experience recognizable symptoms and are unaware that they are infected. Symptoms begin with several days of painful itching or burning in the genital area at the site of the infection. Blisters form and then, in a week or so, rupture to form open or "wet" ulcers on the skin. Initial outbreak is sometimes accompanied by swollen glands, headache, or fever. After several days a scab or crust forms over the open sore and the pain decreases. The primary episode may last about three weeks. Later outbreaks are shorter and less severe.
- **Diagnosis:** A physician can identify HSV through laboratory tests or while sores still exist.
- **Cure:** There is no medical cure for herpes and infected individuals may periodically shed the virus. The drug acyclovir reduces severity of flare-ups.
- **Condom effectiveness:** Condoms do very little to prevent the spread of HSV.[100]

There are actually two types of herpes symplex viruses (HSV). HSV-1 is a common cause of oral herpes infections which also can be transmitted sexually. HSV-1 accounts for 20 percent of new genital herpes infections in the United States. It is generally thought that the increase in oral sex practices among young people plays a role in the rise of HSV-1 genital herpes infections. HSV-2 is primarily transmitted through sexual activity and causes the majority (80 percent) of genital herpes in the U.S.[101]

Regarding herpes simplex 2 (genital herpes):

- It is the second most common sexually transmitted disease in the country.
- It is incurable. Medicines only shorten the duration of the flare-ups.
- It can be spread from one person to another even when there is not an active rash.
- Fifty percent of infected people are not aware they are infected.
- Approximately 45 million people in the U.S. are infected, which is one out of six Americans.
- Newborns can be infected at birth by their mothers. This is a deadly serious occurrence.[102]
- A 1997 study of genital herpes showed that one in five Americans over the age of eleven shows evidence of genital herpes infection.[103]
- There has been a 500 percent increase.

Genital herpes is transmitted by sexual contact. This transmission—including skin-to-skin and skin-to-mucous membrane contact—explains why herpes infection can be transmitted by sexual behaviors other than sexual intercourse, including oral sex, anal sex, and mutual masturbation.[104] While scientists have yet to establish a firm link between genital herpes and cancer, women infected with genital herpes are eight times as likely to develop cancer of the cervix as women not infected with genital herpes.[105]

Due to the fact that genital herpes is both incurable and lifelong, it may be passed on to any sexual partner at any time. Even previously infected individuals now involved in a monogamous sexual relationship carry the risk of transmitting herpes to their current partner. Marriages between individuals where one spouse is infected may be significantly affected by feelings of guilt or resentment, thus making herpes an infection that is emotionally difficult to cope with.

From the late 1970s to the early 1990s, herpes prevalence increased 30 percent. Genital herpes continues to increase, spreading across all social, economic, racial, and ethnic boundaries, but most dramatically affecting teens and young adults.[106] Numerous studies have been conducted to ascertain the broad scope of the herpes epidemic. The summary listed below captures the general range of the population affected:

◆ Most researchers estimate that one in every five Americans—20 percent of the population above age twelve—is infected with herpes.[107]

◆ When considering only sexually active persons, the estimate jumps to approximately one in three—30 percent and higher.[108]

◆ The age-adjusted prevalence of genital herpes has risen by 30 percent in the past two years (from 16 percent to 21 percent). Genital herpes prevalence among Americans twelve or older now exceeds 20 percent.[109]

◆ Herpes rates were highest among those with multiple sexual partners throughout life.[110]

◆ Every year between a quarter of a million and one million people are infected with the herpes virus.[111]

◆ Herpes is more common in women than men, infecting approximately one out of four women, versus one out of five men.[112]

◆ It is most common in blacks (45.9 percent), followed by Mexican-Americans (22.3 percent), and whites (17.6 percent).[113]

◆ Other studies indicate that if an individual has herpes (or certain other STDs), he or she is five times more likely to become HIV infected if a subsequent sexual partner has HIV/AIDS.[114]

The third National Health and Nutrition Examination Survey, a statistical sampling of 40,000 people conducted by researchers at the CDC from 1988 to 1994, found that about 90 percent of those who test positive for HSV-2, the genital herpes virus, don't know they have it. HSV-2 can cause severe genital ulcers but often its symptoms are so mild it goes unrecognized, says the CDC's Robert Johnson, a coauthor of the study in *The New England Journal of Medicine*.[115]

Think about it: approximately one in every five people you see every day is infected with the incurable herpes simplex virus. And a majority of them do not even know they are infected, so they continue to infect other sexual partners.

An editorial in *The New England Journal of Medicine*, October 1997, stated, "Since at least one in five people now has HSV-2 [genital herpes] infection, those who have unprotected contact with multiple sexual partners should know that unsuspected exposure to HSV is virtually guaranteed." The effectiveness of condoms in this situation is questionable because genital herpes lesions can occur on any area of the body. In addition, the virus can be transmitted even when there are no lesions present.[116] An individual with only two sexual partners over the course of his or her lifetime faces a 39 percent probability that at least one of them has genital herpes (assuming those sexual partners are chosen at random).[117]

Tens of thousands of uninfected Americans are becoming infected every month through sexual promiscuity. Between 1988 and 1994, only 10 percent of those who tested positive for genital herpes reported a history of the disease.[118]

Fifty percent of people infected will never have another episode, but about 50 percent will have outbreaks from that time on—especially when under stress, following intercourse, or after wearing tight clothes or swimming suits.[119] Nearly all who have experienced a symptomatic *primary* episode of genital herpes will have at least one symptomatic *recurrent* episode. And most will experience periodic recurrences for several years (if not for life) with recurrences becoming somewhat less frequent over time (after eight years, the mean recurrence rate without treatment is still approximately three episodes per year).[120]

Why the dramatic rise now in the incidence of herpes? Sexual freedom is obviously implicated. "With herpes, every new case is added to the pool," says Dr. Yehudi Felman, a New York City venereal disease specialist. "The increase is exponential after a while." Not only are more people indulging in sex, they are also more active—starting younger, marrying later, divorcing more often. The wider acceptance of oral sex also has played a role. Richard Hamilton, a San Francisco family physician and author of *The Herpes Book*, thinks science has wrought the herpes epidemic: penicillin allowed greater sexual contact with little risk, and the pill and other contraceptives largely replaced condoms, which prevented direct contact with sores.

Adolescents have quickly become one of the high-risk groups for contracting genital herpes, as the following studies document:

- ◆ Genital herpes increased fastest among white teens ages twelve to nineteen years old.[121]
- ◆ Between 15 to 20 percent of young men and women become infected with herpes by the time they reach adulthood.[122]
- ◆ Herpes prevalence among white teens ages twelve to nineteen years old in the 1990s was five times greater than the prevalence in the 1970s.[123]
- ◆ A report published by *The New England Journal of Medicine* in October 1997 revealed that genital herpes has quintupled since the late 1970s among white teenagers and doubled among whites in their twenties.[124]
- ◆ There has been a 500 percent increase in genital herpes in white teens

during the past twenty years. In addition, the study reported that 45.9 percent of all African-Americans over the age of eleven show evidence of genital herpes infection.[125]

Tragically, there are very tiny victims of herpes—newborns. Pregnant women with genital herpes can transmit the infection to their infant during the birth process. Even with appropriate treatment, approximately 14 percent of infants with herpes encephalitis and approximately 54 percent with disseminated herpes infection will die. Survivors may experience long-term complications including mental retardation, learning disabilities, and/or blindness.[126]

Due to the huge increase of herpes-infected men and women in their teens and early twenties, a substantial number of women entering their childbearing years are infected with HSV-2 or are at risk of contracting infection because their partners are more likely to be infected.[127]

Part of the pain for herpes patients is the conviction of being damaged goods. George Washington University's Elisabeth Herz reports "intense guilt feelings" among women who get the disease and hears again and again the feeling that they are unclean and dirty. "We're all looking for someone to love," says a New York woman, a freelance artist. "In this world our chances seem so slim anyway. Then you add herpes and you think, 'Why should anyone want me now?'"

The only way to be completely safe from genital herpes, and the most effective way to limit spread of the infection on a public health level, is to avoid all sexual contact before marriage, marry an individual who has done the same, and remain monogamous with marriage.[128]

Genital Warts from Human Papillomavirus (HPV)

* **Cause:** Human papillomavirus (HPV)
* **Symptoms:** Genital warts occur in the vaginal area, on the penis or cervix, and near the anus. As with many STDs, most of these infections are asymptomatic, so that the majority of those with genital HPV are unaware of their infection.[129]
* **Diagnosis:** Some warts appear flat, others look like tiny cauliflowers. Some can only be detected by a physician. It takes a pap smear to detect warts on the cervix. Babies exposed during childbirth may get warts in the throat. Some researchers believe that venereal warts caused by some types of HPVs

increase risk of cancer of the cervix, vulva, penis, and anus. As of 1991, cervical cancers caused by HPV are killing more women than AIDS, about 4,600 per year.[130]

◆ **Cure:** Genital warts are extremely common, but can be treated and cured. Subclinical HPV infection is much more common than genital warts, and there is currently no treatment. The disease can lead to cervical, penile, and anal cancer.[131]

◆ **Condom effectiveness:** The National Institute of Health states: "Condoms provide almost no protection against HPV."[132]

Human papillomavirus is the most common sexually transmitted disease. In one study of female college students, HPV infections were five times more common than all other STDs combined.[133] Most women find they are infected when their doctor reports an abnormal Pap smear. Since this procedure is not done with men, millions of men are infected with HPV and don't know it.[134]

Dr. John R. Diggs, Jr. states, "HPV is remarkably contagious. Statisically, college students will almost certainly be infected after having four sexual partners. You have probably been given a false sense of security that condoms will protect you. Not so. With or without a condom, if you have multiple sexual partners, HPV will find you. No protection. No safe sex. Most school-based educators were trained at a time when the importance of this infection was not recognized."[135]

The virus grows best in moist areas of the body. It is commonly a genital growth that grows better in women than in men, often growing in the vagina or on the cervix of women. The virus is mixed in with the sexual secretions of men and women and can grow on moist skin. That is why it is so easily spread even by genital contact that does not include penetrative sex. That is also why it is not usually contained by condoms. Most experts agree that condoms do little to protect against this, the most common STD.[136]

HPV is very infectious. Its transmission rate with each act of sexual intercourse with an infected partner is 50 percent.[137] Up to 90 percent of sexual partners of infected people also become infected. There are usually no symptoms unless warts get large, causing irritation and/or bleeding.[138]

Although often painless, genital warts can be dangerous and need medical attention. Preventing the spread of genital warts is especially difficult because HPV, the wart virus, can remain in the body even after removal of warts. Sometimes the virus is still contagious even though there is no visible sign of infection.[139]

In a recent Kaiser Family Foundation survey, only 11 percent of teens ages fifteen to seventeen and adults aged eighteen to forty-four could name HPV as an STD, and only 30 percent of them were aware that HPV is incurable.[140]

The prevalence of HPV in our population at the dawn of the twenty-first century is mind-boggling. The most recent studies available at this writing, noted below, are bad enough. But keep in mind that countless numbers of infections are never reported due to shame, embarrassment, denial, or asymptomatic conditions.

- As many as 45 million Americans may already be infected with HPV.[141]
- Another study estimates that 80 million Americans between fifteen and forty-nine years of age have been infected by genital HPV at some point in their lives.[142]
- Between 5 and 5.5 million individuals are newly infected with HPV each year.[143]
- Between 50 and 75 percent of sexually active individuals are now, or have previously been, infected with HPV.[144]
- Only 2 percent of men or women have symptoms of infection.[145]
- [HPV] will kill 5,000 women this year. This is more than the number of women who die from AIDS on a yearly basis.[146]
- [HPV] is the cause of more than 90 percent of all cervical cancer.[147]
- A 1998 report of sexually active women at Rutgers University showed that 60 percent tested positive for human papillomavirus (HPV) at some time during the three-year study.[148]
- HPV causes nearly all cases of cervical cancer. Cervical cancer annually causes the death of approximately 5,000 American women and 250,000 women worldwide.[149]
- Because of their patterns of transmissibility, genital herpes, syphilis, and HPV can all be transmitted by mutual masturbation. In fact, a recent study demonstrates that many individuals with genital warts transmit the HPV virus on their fingertips.[150]

HPV affects both men and women. In men, genital warts almost always announce the presence of human papillomavirus. In one study, reported in *Geni-*

tourinary Medicine in 1991, researchers detected HPV DNA in 85 percent of semen specimens from men attending a clinic for treatment of genital warts. A subgroup of men studied had warts just inside the urethra. In this location the man would not know he had warts, and the woman would have no way of knowing he was infected with warts.

All the semen collected from these men with warts just inside the urethral opening contained HPV organisms. Ninety-five percent of these men also had a second HPV organism present. Therefore, most men who have genital warts will have the wart virus present in their semen. A woman can become infected in those areas of her body which come in contact with his semen.[151]

The Medical Institute of Sexual Health (MISH) estimates that 33 percent of all women are infected with HPV.[152] Among women under the age of twenty-five, studies have found that 28 to 46 percent are typically infected with HPV.[153] An increased risk of HPV infection was found in younger women, as well as those of Hispanic or black race, those with an increased number of vaginal-sex partners and high frequencies of alcohol consumption, and those involved in anal sex.[154]

In a three-year study of college women, the average annual incidence of HPV was 14 percent. Including the 26 percent of women who tested positive for HPV at the beginning of the test period, about 60 percent of the women were infected with HPV at some time during the three-year period.[155]

Once again, our young people are vulnerable to this potentially deadly disease. In one study, genital warts infected 30 percent of sexually active teens.[156] Statistically, college students will almost certainly be infected after having four sexual partners.[157]

The greatest threat of HPV is the potential for cancer, most notably, cervical cancer in women. In his testimony before the House Committee on Commerce, subcommittees on Health and Environment in 1999, Dr. Ronald O. Valdiserri, deputy director of the National Centers for HIV, STD, and TB Prevention, provided this chilling documentation on HPV and cervical cancer:

> Eighty types [of HPV] have been identified. . . . Approximately thirty of these are found primarily in the genital area and are considered "genital HPV. . . . While some of these thirty types are considered "low-risk," primarily causing genital warts and low-grade Pap smear abnormalities, approximately ten of these types

are considered "high-risk" for cancer in that they are found in approximately 95 percent of all tissue specimens from cervical cancer. . . .

Being infected with one of these high-risk HPV types increases the risk of cervical cancer by at least thirty-fold, a level similar to or higher than the risk of lung cancer from smoking. . . . Having HPV seems to be "necessary" for developing cervical cancer. . . . It has been estimated that approximately 5 to 10 percent of women with high-risk types of HPV infection will develop cervical cancer.[158]

Dr. John Diggs states tersely, "Cervical cancer is a sexually transmitted disease."[159] Additional studies provide the following data linking HPV with cancer:

- [HPV] is the cause of most cancer of the vulva, vagina, cervix, and penis. Death rate from HPV is about 4,800 women annually—more women than are killed by AIDS.[160]
- The presence of HPV is much more than a cosmetic problem. Some types are known to cause precancerous and cancerous lesions of the cervix, vagina, vulva, penis, and anal areas.[161]
- Up to 70 percent of female HPV victims will later develop precancerous changes of the cervix. "Almost all abnormal Pap smears indicating precancerous or cancerous cells are a result of infection from HPV. This is the primary reason doctors advise every woman to have a Pap smear every year."[162]
- Cervical cancer is the second most common cancer among women in the United States, the second most common cancer among women worldwide, with more than 450,000 new cases estimated to occur each year.[163]
- HPV-induced cervical cancer occurs in about 13,000 and kills approximately 5,000 American women per year.[164]
- HPV has been linked to over 90 percent of all invasive cervical cancers,[165] which is the number two cause of cancer deaths among women, after breast cancer.[166]
- HPV infection also can lead to vaginal cancer. One study of seventy-one biopsy specimens from women with vaginal intraepithelial neoplasia ("precancer") revealed that all seventy-one specimens showed evidence of infection with HPV.[167]

- HPV infection also precedes cancers that develop in men. Men with HPV infection on the penis are at higher risk to develop penile cancer. About 1,400 American men develop cancer of the penis each year.[168]
- HPV infection of the anus can lead to anal cancer in both men and women. The incidence of this cancer has more than doubled in men and increased by 46 percent in women since 1973.[169]
- Currently, more than 3,000 individuals develop anal cancer each year. At-risk individuals include men who have sex with men, and women who have anal sex. Anal carcinoma in women may also be due to "migration" of the infection from the genital area to the anus.[170]
- Cancer of the oral cavity is another cancer that may be caused by HPV infection. Studies have shown an association between the presence of the HPV virus and the presence of cancers in the mouth.[171] These infections may be transmitted by oral sex.
- One Russian study found that "HPV infections of the uterine cervix are found in 90 percent of women who had surgical operations on pre-invasive and invasive cervix carcinoma." The study also concluded that the risk of cervical cancer is higher among women who engage in sexual relationships at an early age and those who have multiple sex partners.[172]

In light of the above research on the connection between HPV and cancer, what is happening among our college students is horrifying. A study of sexually active female students at Rutgers University revealed that 26 percent of participating women were infected with human papilloma virus (HPV) at the beginning of the study. An additional 43 percent of participants contracted HPV during the three-year study period. Taken together, 60 percent of all women studied were infected (and infectious) at some point during the study.[173]

Health experts across the country agree that there is only one way our young people can avoid contracting and transmitting HPV: abstinence. In one medical test, which included 151 young women aged ten to twenty-five who had never had sexual intercourse, there was absolutely no genital HPV infection. The test concluded that "HPV 16 is sexually transmitted because none of our virginal women harbored this viral type in the vagina" and "human papilloma-virus is rarely present vaginally in virginal women, even with the use of tampons or digital penetration."[174] In a similar test, "None of the fifty-five virginal women had HPV DNA in virginal cells."[175]

Interesting, isn't it, that the following advice mirrors the protection and provision stated in God's Word:

- ◆ The only way for nonmarried individuals to achieve adequate protection from HPV is to be sexually abstinent. . . . With the high prevalence of HPV in our country and the high incidence of new HPV infections, nonmarried sexually active Americans are at substantial risk of HPV infection.[176]
- ◆ You can eliminate your risk of getting genital warts by not having sex with anyone (abstinence) or by having sex only with a noninfected partner who has sex only with you.[177]
- ◆ Condoms give almost no protection against HPV. It is a skin-to-skin disease that has no reliable prevention—except one: abstinence until marriage.[178]
- ◆ The only way for you to avoid HPV, if you don't have it, is to establish a permanent monogamous relationship before you have sex again. It is called "marriage."[179]

Syphilis

- ◆ **Cause:** The bacterium *treponema pallidum,* an organism that can be killed with soap and water.
- ◆ **Symptoms:** Syphilis causes genital ulcers, which increase the likelihood of sexual HIV transmission two to fivefold. They occur in two stages and usually in three weeks. First, a painless pimple, blister, or sore erupts where the germs entered the body. Then a rash, hair loss, and swollen glands may follow.
- ◆ **Diagnosis:** Blood test, microscopic examination.
- ◆ **Complications:** Brain damage, heart disease, paralysis, insanity, death. Babies born to untreated women may be blind, deaf, or crippled by bone disease.
- ◆ **Cure:** Penicillin

Syphilis is an infection that begins primarily through contact and progresses continuously. Approximately half of all syphilis patients do not know they have the disease, either because they show no symptoms or because they believe the painless lesions to be harmless. Yet 50 percent of all women who have intercourse even once with an infected man will themselves become infected with the disease. And those who have syphilis lesions are nine times more likely to become infected with HIV.[180]

Syphilis has been a health problem in the U.S. for many decades. With the introduction of penicillin and the resulting drop in recorded cases of syphilis and gonorrhea, people became optimistic that the battle against these diseases had been won. In fact, the incidence of infectious syphilis in the United States had dropped from a high of more than 100,000 cases in 1947 to a low of 6,516 cases in 1955.

That decline, however, sparked two reactions. First, health care officials relaxed their attempts to control syphilis because it seemed that eradication of it was at hand. Second, sexual promiscuity in the United States increased. By the early 1990s, reported cases were at their highest in forty years.

Although that number has since dropped, syphilis is still the eighth most commonly reported infectious disease in the United States.[181] The Centers for Disease Control and Prevention is pressing to rid the nation of all new cases of syphilis; in 1996 there were 52,995 cases reported.[182] In 1999, 556 cases of congenital syphilis—in infants who acquired infection from their mothers during pregnancy or delivery—were reported.[183]

Trichomoniasis

- **Cause:** The parasite trichomonas vaginalis
- **Symptoms:** For women, a frothy discharge, itching, redness of genitals. Men usually have no symptoms.
- **Diagnosis:** Pap smear or microscopic examination
- **Complications:** None in men, gland infections in women
- **Cure:** Drug metronidazole

An estimated 5 million cases of trichomoniasis occur each year in the U.S.[184] According to a Russian publication, trichomoniasis can coexist with bacteria causing gonorrhea, herpes simplex virus, chlamydia, and other sexually transmitted bacteria.[185] There is evidence that chronic trichomonal infection may predispose the cervix to cancer.

Hepatitis B

According to the Third National Health and Nutrition Examination Survey (NHANES III), about 5 percent of the U.S. population has been infected with hepatitis B, with an estimated 200,000 infections occurring each year (Coleman, 1998). Of these, it is believed that 120,000 infections are acquired through sexual transmission annually, mostly among young adults. An estimated 417,000 people are currently living with chronic sexually acquired HBV infection. An estimated 5,000 to 6,000 deaths occur each year from chronic hepatitis B-related liver disease.[186]

One of those viruses for which there is no known cure is hepatitis B. It is estimated that, in the United States alone, at least 100,000 people are infected with this disease annually as a result of sexual intercourse. Hepatitis B is ten times more infectious than HIV, and is present in approximately 60 to 70 percent of all sexually active homosexual males.[187] Russian doctors V. P. Smetnik and L. G. Tumilovitch, writing in a 1995 article titled "Non-Surgical Gynecology," expressed their concern over hepatitis B's effects on the unborn, who can be infected with the disease even while in the womb.[188]

Cancer

As has been previously noted in this chapter, a number of sexually transmitted diseases are linked with cancer. This is one of the most chilling potential outcomes of premarital and extramarital sex. The following studies further emphasize this sobering reality.

- ◆ In 1999, a reexamination of earlier data led to the conclusion that HPV infection was actually present in over 99 percent of cervical cancers.[189]
- ◆ HPV is the most prevalent viral STD in the United States. In fact, current estimates suggest that 5.5 million Americans acquire the infection each year. Nearly 20 million Americans are currently infected with the virus.[190]
- ◆ Perhaps the most astounding statistic is that 80 million Americans between 15 and 49 years of age have been infected by genital HPV at some point in their lives! This means that approximately 75 percent of

sexually active individuals are now, or have previously been, infected with HPV.[191]

◆ These estimates are supported by numerous scientific reports. In 1998, an article in the *New England Journal of Medicine* reported the number of sexually active females who tested positive for HPV infection during a three-year study at Rutgers University. Twenty-six percent of the women tested were HPV positive at the beginning of the study, and another 43 percent of participants tested positive for HPV at some point during the 36-month follow-up period.[192]

◆ When the researchers included those participants with preexisting infections with those who became infected (or reinfected) during the course of the study, they concluded that 60 percent of the young women tested showed evidence of HPV infection at some point during the study. Other studies confirm that HPV is the most common sexually transmitted infection among adolescent girls.[193]

◆ The earlier a girl begins having intercourse, the higher her risk of developing cervical cancer as an adult.

◆ Hepatitis B virus is a sexually transmitted virus that causes hepatocellular carcinoma (liver cancer), one of the most common forms of cancer. Other sexually transmitted pathogens that are associated with cancers include human T-cell lymphotrophic virus type 1 (HTLV-1), linked to adult T-cell leukemia and lymphoma; human herpes virus type 8 (HHV8), linked to Kaposi's sarcoma; and Epstein-Barr virus (EBV), linked to lymphoma and nasopharyngeal (nasal cavity and pharynx) carcinoma.[194]

Adolescent premarital sex can be deadly. Sexually transmitted diseases, cancer, and other physical dangers may ensnare the unsuspecting youth who violates God's protective command to reserve sex for marriage. It is vital that we help our kids wait.

UNWANTED PREGNANCY

Another reason our young people must say no to premarital sex is the ever-present possibility of unwanted pregnancy, foisting on the immature mother and father the role of parent before they are emotionally ready for it. Many students who write to me have keen insight into this dilemma. Here are some of their comments:

Although precautions can be taken, pregnancy is always a possibility. There is no 100 percent protection. Many think they won't get caught, and they use that as a cop-out. They think, God won't allow me to get pregnant and ruin my life, as though he were in the business of helping us sin. There is a price to pay for sin. Even David was caught, and he was a man after God's own heart. The Bible records the consequences of his actions: His son died and his family was disgraced.

◆ ◆ ◆

The very consequences of sex prove that it is not intended for anyone other than a husband and wife. Creating another life (or engaging in activity with that potential) is an awesome responsibility that cannot be borne by any who are not committed to each other fully. The bond between the parents must be stronger than the bond between parent and child. The couple's relationship must be the foundation for all others, both in and out of the home.

◆ ◆ ◆

I wonder about the pregnant girls I see at school. What are they feeling? What are their desires, hurts, frustrations? What will their lives be like? And aside from the obvious biological aspect, why are they pregnant? If two people don't have the love needed to raise a family (if they did, they would be married), they have no business taking the chance of getting pregnant outside marriage.

◆ ◆ ◆

God made sex not only as the most intimate expression of love for the one you're committed to, but also as the means of reproduction. If you're ready to have sex, are you ready to have kids? Girls, what will you do if you get pregnant? Regardless of your answer, three lives are permanently marred for the sake of a few minutes of self-gratification. Is it worth it? God made sex, among other reasons, so a godly man and woman could share the joy of bringing up children in the admonition of the Lord. Do two selfish teenagers in the backseat of a car live up to that high calling?

We live in a culture that deceives itself daily. We have surrounded ourselves with amazing drugs and technology that should take all responsibility out of casual sex, yet look at us. We have the pill and think we are safe, and as a result the nation is infested with dozens of sexually transmitted diseases. We have, readily available to anyone, creams and foams and gadgets to prevent pregnancies, yet the illegitimate pregnancy rate is going up, not down. We have developed a handful of methods to "terminate" pregnancies (with euphemistic language to accompany them), yet millions of women are wracked with guilt and anguish over having taken the life of their child. The deception goes on.

At the same time, we are becoming callous to the pain we cause ourselves and others. Many people who contract STDs seek revenge on society by deliberately passing on the diseases. Men and boys get girls pregnant and abandon them. Some women and girls genuinely suffer after an abortion; others simply become hardened.

In this strange society, young people are caught in the crossfire of opposing and often nonsensical views on sex. As one young writer above noted, our society is two-faced about sex. If young people aren't sexually active, they are outcasts and prudes. If they are sexually active and suffer some consequence as a result of it, they may find people to be unsympathetic and judgmental.

If society is reluctant to explain the negative aspects of premarital sex, the church must be willing to speak up. Kids must have the knowledge to make intelligent decisions. They must be taught what God says about sex, why he gives commands concerning sex, his provision and protection for those who obey, and the potential consequences for those who don't.

One of the consequences, of course, is the potential for a new life to be created. The pregnant girl has one of four choices: give the baby up for adoption, marry the father of the child, raise the child alone, or have an abortion. Regardless of her choice, she will probably have to make it alone because most of the men who get teenage girls pregnant eventually abandon them. She may not even be able to turn to her family.

Social stigma and family problems aside, the health risks for teenage mothers and their babies are enormous. Girls still in adolescence find the energy they need for their own growing bodies being diverted to the baby, leaving the mother open to a number of health problems. Many pregnant adolescents do not take care of themselves physically, so the problems with babies born to teens are often due to poor health care rather than age.

As the values in our country continue to change, and moral standards once generally accepted are ignored, young people will continue to pay a high price in unwanted pregnancies. I have talked to so many pregnant teenage girls and unwed mothers who were very disillusioned about what had happened to them. The magic of the sexual encounter had long since evaporated, and they were left with the burden of an unwanted pregnancy or a new baby.

Many come to feel very trapped by their parenting role and by the fact that they're missing out on the fun other teenagers are having. To a considerable extent this is often sadly true.

ABORTION

The tragic alternative to parenthood and adoption considered by many is abortion. In the United States an abortion is performed every twenty-two seconds; that is more than 4,000 a day. In 1993 there were 1,330,414 legal abortions in America—334 abortions per 1,000 births.[195] It is currently closer to 1.5 million legal abortions performed in the United States each year.[196] Statistics in Canada are climbing as well. "The number of 'therapeutic' abortions performed in the country rose to 104,403 in 1993, a 2.3 percent increase." The statistics show that the rate of abortions performed in Canada also rose "to 26.9 abortions for every 100 live births."[197]

Abortion is a volatile issue among young people. Here is what a couple of students wrote to me about it:

> Abortion is also a so-called "way out." But do two wrongs make a right? Should murder be added to fornication to make everything OK? Many women who have abortions are later unable to have children; that risk alone should be enough to prevent premarital sex.

> ◆ ◆ ◆

> God did not give us the ability to have sex and then want us to misuse it. He wanted it to be right, so he told us the place for sex, which is marriage. He meant it to be an act of love. If you're not married and you think you're "making love," you run the risk of creating a new life, and I would ask you: Would you kill something that was made in an act of love?

Abortion may seem like the "easy out" for unwanted pregnancies, but the emotional and physical damage to the mother is often underestimated. Recent studies have shown a possible link between abortions and breast cancer, dealing a setback to the "safe and legal" brigade. A study that appeared in the October 1996 *Journal of Epidemiology and Community Health* reported that "women who have abortions are one-third more likely to develop breast cancer." Although there are those who would argue with the findings of this and other studies, those who perform abortions are being urged to "inform their patients fully about what is already known."[198]

In another recent study, "researchers conclude that abortion is a 'significant independent risk factor for breast cancer'—one that raises a woman's lifetime risk by roughly a third and causes 'thousands of excess cases per year.'"[199]

Proponents for abortion campaign fervently on the woman's rights to her own body. But along with the common argument that abortion is a woman's right to choose whether or not to be a mother is another argument that attempts to justify this destructive procedure: that a fetus feels no pain during the abortion. A British panel of medical and scientific experts, appointed by the Royal College of Obstetricians and Gynecologists, disagree, declaring that "fetuses may sense pain as early as twenty-six weeks." As a result, the panel has advised British doctors to administer anesthesia to fetuses in late-term abortions and for various diagnostic tests.

Dr. Mark I. Evans, vice chairman of obstetrics and gynecology at Wayne State University in Detroit, argues that this is unnecessary. "Third-trimester abortions are hardly ever done. . . . And when they are, medicine is usually used to stop the heartbeat" so the fetus is already dead when aborted.[200] This statement is a lie. Any doctor or nurse who has ever watched the heinous partial-birth abortion performed on a squirming, 90-percent-delivered baby knows that is not the case.

In addition, the Elliott Institute reports that approximately 40 percent of all abortion cases involve coercion, usually from boyfriends.[201] The emotional damage to the women involved in abortions can be devastating. Vincent M. Rue, codirector of the Institute for Pregnancy Loss, says that "10 to 50 percent of women experience postabortion psychological harm."[202]

The answer to the problems of teenage pregnancy is not to make contraceptives more available. It is not to promise food and housing for life to single mothers. It is not to take the life of an innocent child for the sake of convenience. The answer is to take God at his infallible Word and realize that his wise commands are there for our own good.

He has provided sex so married couples can have children and raise them in the ways of the Lord. The book of Proverbs says children are a blessing, and in a committed and loving marriage, that's just what they are. As the father of four children, I know the reality of this truth.

God's commands are also there for our protection. He doesn't want anyone ever to have to make gut-wrenching decisions about unwanted pregnancies, so he tells us to wait to have sex until marriage. He gives a solution that is so simple it confounds the modern mentality.

The Bible promises that God can work all things to the good for his believers (see Rom. 8:28). He can even take something as disastrous as premarital pregnancy and make something good come of it. But knowing this is no excuse for continued premarital sex. The life-changing pain of such pregnancies is immeasurable.

◆ ◆ ◆

The real and present dangers of STDs, pregnancy, and abortion that accompany adolescent premarital sex are only the beginning. These grave physical consequences cannot be separated from the equally painful emotional consequences of promiscuity. In the next chapter, we will consider a number of emotional reasons young people should wait until marriage for sex, and we will explore God's generous protection and provision to kids who do.

CHAPTER 12

THE EMOTIONAL REASONS TO WAIT

SEX THERAPIST MARY ANN MAYO says the couples most apt to succeed in marriage are those who bring the least amount of sexual baggage into the relationship.[1] As we saw in the previous chapter, that baggage can be the physical consequences of sex outside of marriage: infection, pregnancy, cancer, ongoing medical needs, etc. But perhaps the most damaging sexual baggage from promiscuity is emotional. Long after a sexually transmitted disease is treated and maybe even cured, emotional scars can remain. Long after the physical pain of an abortion has subsided, guilt or shame may fester like an open sore.

Our kids don't need this kind of baggage. Another reason we must urge them to wait for sex until marriage is to avoid the emotional pain that results from premarital sex. We must encourage them to accept God's protection from emotional distress and his provision for a rich, guilt-free marriage relationship.

But some might ask, "Don't premarital sexual experiences in these and other relationships increase the quality of later marital sexual relationships through practice and experience?" Though on the surface this might appear to be a valid argument, the limited data available doesn't support this. In fact, in the case of young teenagers who have negative premarital experiences, the adverse effect on a later marriage relationship might be quite significant.

We have no way of quantifying the damaging effect of premarital sex on the immature mind of a teenager. Getting involved in the *physical* aspect of sex before the *emotional* aspects of trust, security, and mutual respect have been developed can cripple a possibly lasting, loving relationship.

Emotional damage is a virtually unavoidable consequence of premarital sex, since an act of such spiritual intensity, an act so expressly forbidden by God, entails rejecting the established spiritual order of things. It flies in the face of what is beneficial to us. When this emotional damage goes unchecked, the problems can last for life.

God wants to protect our young people from the psychological and emotional trauma they inflict on themselves through premarital sex.

PROTECTION FROM THE EMOTIONAL PITFALLS OF PREMARITAL SEX

Part of what God wants to protect our kids from by limiting sex to marriage is the devastating emotional consequences that premarital sex can bring. Those effects may be immediate or they may not show up for some time. The person may find that through prayer and the support of friends the emotional distress can be dealt with and put in the past, or it may drag on for years. Regardless of how each individual may be affected, God doesn't want that kind of distress to happen in the first place.

There are all kinds of emotional baggage that a young person may have to carry into his or her future marriage from promiscuous sexual relationships. Here are a number of them from which God will protect our kids if they remain sexually pure.

Protection from Guilt

Guilt is one consequence of premarital sex that may haunt a person longer than any other. It is a nagging, gnawing feeling that seems to surface at the least appropriate times. If not dealt with, it can be a great hindrance to spiritual growth and emotional well-being.

Premarital sex produces guilt, because God has wired us together in such a way that we know we've violated his intentions. The Bible says, "Marriage should be honored by all, and the marriage bed kept pure, for God will judge the adulterer and all the sexually immoral" (Heb. 13:4). Whether the offenders acknowledge God's laws or not, they feel guilty because they are guilty before a holy God. It often has been said that there is no prophylactic for the conscience.

When sex is entered into casually and without commitment, no concern is shown for the other person. People get hurt physically and emotionally. Sex without meaning damages the self-image of those taking part. Ironically, many young men and women get involved in sex as an expression of their freedom. In reality, they have forfeited their freedom from a guilty conscience.

Guilt is the awareness of having transgressed a standard of right and wrong or the lingering awareness that perhaps an act was wrong. Our society is plagued by those two kinds of guilt. The first is a moral guilt, one that Christians are subject to, which tells us specifically when we have stepped outside God's boundaries. It is a conscious awareness of specific transgressions.

The other kind of guilt can be called a floating sense of guilt. This floating guilt comes from a relativistic society, a society that says there is no right and wrong. Rather than being free, people in such a society are constantly questioning: "Are these things I'm doing right or wrong? How do I decide?" Regardless of whether they are aware of those questions within themselves, the questions are there. Such people have no form to their lives, no standards by which to measure actions. They have a feeling of being adrift, they continually have a floating sense of guilt about doing things wrong—yet they are not able to pinpoint the reasons for their guilt.

Christians have the Bible, which, in addition to revealing the character of God, his redemptive plan for man, and our ability to have a relationship with him, also gives us a basis for determining right and wrong. It tells us which actions are pleasing to God and which are not. It doesn't leave things open to debate. In this way, Christians have form to their lives, a framework for understanding good and evil and making decisions accordingly.

A friend of mine once asked a farmer if it was better to raise cattle on open grazing land, in a pasture, or in a corral. The farmer said, "Well, on open grazing land they are always subject to attack from wild animals, or they could wander off for good. In a corral they are safe, but somebody has to take care of them. In a fenced pasture they have everything they need. They are protected, yet they have the freedom to graze."

The Bible defines our pasture. God has put intelligent boundaries around us to keep us "home" and to keep away those who would prey on us, yet within those boundaries we have freedom to make a variety of choices. Persons without God's boundaries are wandering aimlessly and feel lost. Persons in a legalistic system of beliefs are in a corral where they are fed and hosed off but are unable to move.

For example, God has provided marriage as the place for sex, and persons moving within God's limits are free to marry or not marry. Should they decide to marry, they are able to enjoy intimacy in a context where no one can be hurt. The husband and wife won't catch diseases from each other. They won't use each other and then run off to the next sex partner. Since sex is an open and un-abashed part of their lives, they are free to discuss their sex life. They can plan ahead for their family, should they decide not to have children for the time being. If they do have children, the children become part of a family, not reminders of a grave mistake.

There is no guilt in any of this. God protects us from destructive, shattering guilt by reserving sex for marriage.

Protection from Performance-based Sex

Sexually active people suffer from comparison and a performance syndrome. In our sex-oriented society, intimacy, genuine personal involvement, courtship, romance, and love are regarded as less important than how well your partner can please you sexually. When people are judged on performance (which means they are accepted only when they act or do something the way another person expects), the value and dignity given to them by God are lost. They are not considered important because of who they are, but rather are deemed acceptable because of what they do. How degrading and dehumanizing that is, yet it is characteristic of the "free sex" in our society.

Without the committed bonds of marriage, sex is inherently a selfish act done for personal gain. For the relationship to go on, the sex partners must continuously please each other. As soon as one partner no longer lives up to what the other wants, the relationship is in trouble. The partners are kept in a state of perpetual insecurity, a state that symbolizes much of what true love is not. Couples in this circumstance experience an unspoken element of fear: the fear of rejection. Such a relationship is totally contrary to God's plan for us. God protects us from being valued only for our performance by reserving sex for the commitment of marriage.

One young couple went for counseling because of sexual difficulties. The wife had been a victim of incest as a child, but she hadn't told her husband that until it came out in counseling. Her background had caused her to be very inhibited sexually, which in turn caused her husband to feel rejected.

After the problem came to the surface in counseling, they could look forward to beginning a normal sex life. The husband was able to encourage his wife in the freedom of her sexuality. In the process of wanting to help her, however, he went out and bought the book *The Joy of Sex*. His wife went back to the counselor and said, "I appreciate what he is trying to do, but this book just makes me feel more inhibited. All it deals with is physical positions and things two bodies can do to each other. After I looked through it, I felt like a piece of meat, something to be used for another person's pleasure."

Although the husband's intentions may have been good, his purchase was way off base. A book that primarily deals with sex on a physical level (as most books on sex do) can make a person feel that only performance counts, even if that is not the intention. Fear of inadequate sexual performance is the major cause of sexual dysfunction. What needs to happen is an edification of the partners, a mutual building and encouraging that lets both know they are free to fail, to make mistakes. They need to know they are on solid ground emotionally, intellectually, and spiritually, so that the physical expression of their love can be free.

That, of course, is possible only within the commitment of marriage, and even married couples need to work continually at edifying each other. God has provided marriage as the lifelong training ground for sex. It is a school in which a person cannot fail, because the only criterion is to reach out in love to the other.

Protection from Misleading Feelings about Sex and Love

One of the reasons I hear most often for sexual involvement taking place is the confusion between sex and love. Premarital sex can take a person who may actually have had a legitimate understanding of love and confuse him or her terribly. Sex outside of marriage masquerades as lasting intimacy, but it's only an illusion. The kind that makes a marriage survives.

Sex before marriage is outside God's will, so it shouldn't exist in the first place. When it does, it turns relationships upside down and mixes emotions to the point where a person can misinterpret feelings. You can sense this in the words of the girl who wrote the following:

> I remember when the "love" I had been waiting for came along. Three months after we started dating, we began having sex. Suddenly we avoided friends and social activities as much as possible in order to be alone, but our goal was only to satisfy our physical hunger. Ironically, we actually referred to this misplaced passion as love!

When we mix sex and love, we have confused the simple concepts of giving and taking. Love always gives and always seeks the best interests of the other person. Premarital sex takes. Each individual has his or her own goal in having sex before marriage, but each is in it for personal reasons. The problem is, the taking can sometimes look like giving. This is where the water gets muddy.

A girl may "give her boyfriend what he wants," thus making it look as though she is giving to him in love, but she does it from a personal motive. She may want the security he provides. She may want to achieve popularity by being his girlfriend. She may have one of a dozen other reasons, but her "giving" is actually a form of taking. She is manipulating him for her own ends. It takes maturity and understanding to realize this, something a girl who behaves like that does not have. She is misled by her emotions.

Not only are these mixed-up feelings destructive in a dating relationship, but they also can have tragic consequences if the relationship continues on to marriage.

Studies show that a relationship based on physical attraction may hold itself together for three to five years. During that length of time two people are fooled into thinking, "Well, we've been going together for so long, surely we can make it for a lifetime. This must be love." On the other side of marriage, they wake up to see they had little in common and no basis for a quality relationship.

Premarital sex can fool an individual into marrying the wrong person: A strong bond is created through sex, fooling the couple into believing their relationship is deeper than it really is, that they know each other much better than they really do. By restricting sex to marriage, God protects us from the devastating effects these confused emotions can have.

Our goal as Christians is to grow in agape love, the kind of love God has for us, the kind that gives with no expectations of getting something in return. As sinful people, we will always fall short. Consciously or unconsciously, we will put some conditions on our love, meaning we give in hope of getting something in return. But as we grow in Christ and continue to mature, we should get closer and closer to agape love. We will never be sinless, but as we grow we will sin less.

Love is a series of choices. It is an emotion expressed by acts of the will. The description of love in 1 Corinthians 13 does not describe emotional feelings but rather acts of the will. And even though love is primarily an act of the will, it has tremendous emotional overtones because it has to do with how we relate to people. Our actions of love—the choices we make in dealing with people—are deeply tied to our emotions because relationships automatically have emotional bonds.

Likewise, sex has a powerful emotional aspect, because although sex is a physical act, God meant for it to be a joining of the soul and mind and moral conscience and all the other intangibles about two people. That's why premarital sex can leave us feeling good for a moment, and not just physically. It gives us an emotional rush. But when the wave of good emotional feeling is over (however long that may take), bad emotions set in. When we deal in the moral realm, we are faced with moral consequences.

Even though sex and love both have strong emotional components, those components are not the same. Rather, they are parallel; they cannot be one until two people have been made one through the commitment of marriage. In that context, sex and love can be expressions of the same emotions. Marital sex becomes a model of God's provision and selfless giving, drawing us closer to each other and to him.

Protection from Addiction to Sex

Another emotional pain kids experience from promiscuity is an addiction to sex. Once they have experienced the thrills of sexual activity, the craving for sex grows. It becomes a strong drive that can control the relationship. They become hooked on sex, and it becomes increasingly more difficult—sometimes even impossible—to leave sex out of the relationship. Here are how a few students described it to me:

> The more sexually involved I became, the more I thirsted for this "ultimate experience." Looking back on that part of my life, I feel I really was addicted to sex. I never found a balance; I never found real love; and the more I searched, the more miserable I became. I also got into other vices because of my sexual involvement.

◆ ◆ ◆

> I began to notice that the more I had, the more I wanted. I had always heard the excuse that having sex was the way to get rid of sexual tension, but the opposite was true. Having sex increased the desire. It was like a drug. I couldn't stop myself, yet at the same time I wasn't satisfied at all. The people I knew who were outright promiscuous were even worse than I was—it was all they ever talked about and evidently all they ever thought about. It controlled them; they never controlled it. Sex was an all-consuming fire that never burned out, but instead burned them out.

◆ ◆ ◆

> Sex is like drugs. You keep wanting bigger highs. In fact, I think it made me do more drugs too.

Many modern views of man maintain we are nothing more than primates in tennis shoes, beings whose physiology is no different from any other mammal. Science books often equate our sexuality with animalistic instincts, and this is where the concept of the "sex drive" comes in. Sex is seen as a primitive force required for survival, just as food, water, and shelter are required. If human beings are only smart monkeys and our sexuality a primal urge we cannot control, sex could legitimately be considered a drive.

Such a view robs us of dignity and the value of life. As Christians, we know that God desires to give us the dignity of choice. His desire is motivated by love; he wants to both protect us from hurt and provide for us in abundance.

We are far more than primates. We are created in the image of God, and we have the capacity to know God personally. Our temporal needs are for food, water, and shelter, but we have both a temporal and eternal need for a relationship with God also. When any one of those needs is not met, our survival is threatened, and we go after what we need. In the United States, food, water, and shelter are generally available. But when it comes to seeking God, many of us get caught. In order to establish that relationship, we have to admit our failings and acknowledge our need for God, something that most people refuse to do. So instead of having that basic need met, they look for fulfillment in other ways.

Many people, including adolescents, look for fulfillment in physical relationships. They take the spiritual need they sense within themselves and confuse it with a physical need. Once they proclaim sex as a basic desire, they allow themselves the freedom to fulfill it as often and with as many people as they wish.

The result? They come up empty time after time, because they are trying to fill a spiritual vacuum with physical pleasure. Rather than change their actions, they become swallowed up in their sexual pursuits. The sexuality that had started out as a desire now becomes the master, demanding to be sated. As the young person above stated, sex becomes an all-consuming fire that never burns out. Instead, it burns people out.

Premarital sex is inherently unfulfilling since it is outside God's will. It is sin, and it has consequences, many of them unpleasant and costly. But when two people continue in an illicit sexual relationship, they will find it increasingly more difficult to say no. They may intend to stop their sinful behavior at some point in the future, but every sexual encounter only takes them further from realizing that intention.

One of the greatest dangers of intimate physical contact in a dating relationship is that it very easily becomes the pattern for every date. Other aspects of the dating relationship suffer; the couple only go through the formalities, waiting for the make-out session at the end of the evening.

God, in his love, gives us his command to avoid sexual immorality to protect us from the destructive, self-defeating cycle of sexual addiction. When we are obedient to his wise edicts, we are spared the frustrating habit of seeking temporary and illegitimate physical highs.

God's provision for dealing with sex in the manner he prescribed is sexual fulfillment in a marriage relationship. This does not mean that sex will be continually available, nor does it mean that each lovemaking session necessarily will be great. It means that the couple is able to have the proper attitude about sex. Rather than see each other as objects to be used for a personal high, they see each other as God sees them: unique creations of the Master who have an inherent dignity and who deserve being ministered to.

Only in marriage is it possible for the sexual relationship to reaffirm the dignity and uniqueness of each partner. Sex strengthens the marriage bond. It brings pleasure to one's spouse. It can create a new life that is welcome in the family. It brings personal pleasure. It displays patience, maturity, and understanding. Sex, as God intended it to be, makes you want to give to your mate, not take. That's an addiction you can live with.

Protection from the Hardships of Breaking Up

Sexual desire drives many couples apart, yet it makes others stay together. The problem is, they are together for the wrong reason. One student wrote:

> Although having sex does hurt a relationship, it also makes it harder for a couple to break up. Breaking up when you've had sex together can be a terribly tearing experience emotionally. Sex creates an emotional bond so powerful it must be reserved for marriage.

While secular researchers may try to ignore the spiritual ramifications of our sexuality, they are forced to acknowledge that something more than a physical act takes place during sex. They see the emotional consequences of premarital sex as clearly as we do. It's impossible for two people to have sex without getting involved at a level deeper than the physical. That's just the way God wired us. Sex connects people emotionally and spiritually as well as physically. And something of those deeper connections remains with the participants for life. No wonder some sexually active couples cannot seem to break off a relationship even when they are at odds most of the time. And when they finally do break up, the heartache can be deep and lasting.

A person with a moral conscience who is caught in the trap of premarital sex may find ways to justify the relationship. If it is a young woman who thinks she has found her future husband, she will continue to give in to her partner in the hope that all of the wrong they have done might still turn out all right, since they are getting married. She knows it won't actually be right; she just hopes it won't be as wrong as sleeping together and then breaking up would be. So she holds on to the relationship.

So many people who were involved in premarital or extramarital sex have said to me, "When I walked away from that relationship, I left a part of myself behind." Sex forms an emotional bond that can exist no matter what happens in the relationship. Even if communication has broken down and emotions are strained, sex forms an almost unexplainable bond. It locks people into relationships. The longer it goes on, the harder it is to break it off. As one girl said, "After you've done it, you're really attached to that guy. It's as if he's your life; you feel really vulnerable."

But for the problems in the relationship to be resolved, the couple must break up. They may be able to start over after they have cooled off, or they may not. In any case, they are better off spiritually, emotionally, mentally, and possibly even physically after they break up. Trying to stop the sexual aspect while continuing the relationship is nearly impossible. Once a couple has gone all the way, it is no small task to go back to holding hands.

The following letter is an example of how sex can hurt a relationship:

> I went with a guy for four years, and we really loved each other. All through the four years we were sleeping together. During that time, I was a Christian and knew it was wrong.
>
> Then we had a falling out. The breakup hurt so bad I knew I could only get rid of it by turning to God. We then got back together and my strength as a Christian has helped, except for not having enough faith to say no to sex. Since we've gotten back together, sex has been an uphill battle for me. My boyfriend is a Christian, too, but he sees no wrong in us making love as long as we love each other.

Another thing is, I'm not sure if I love him. But I feel we need to stay together, because it says in the Bible that when two people make love they become
one in God's eyes. Does that mean if I am to do God's will I should stay with him?

I know the logical answer to my question about sex is to have more faith. But
how can I get that through my boyfriend's head? And how can we pull together
and fight this urge? We have talked about it a million times and it never helps.

As you can see by this example, sex has confused this girl. The answer, however, is not "more faith." The logical answer—at least the practical answer—is
for her to break up. The pull of sex, particularly when it has long been a normal
part of their relationship, would be extremely difficult to resist, even if they both
agreed it was wrong.

Another common emotional effect of premarital sex is resentment, which
can lead to bitterness. A guy or girl becomes bitter and resentful toward the person who "caused" him or her to violate his or her moral standards, even though
he or she participated willingly. Such feelings work against the development of
a deep and lasting emotional relationship.

In reserving sex for marriage, God protects us from these emotional traps.
He knows how easily we can fall into a rut of sin and not see a way out, so he
gives us guidelines to keep us out in the first place. God's provision for us is this:
once we are married, that same sexual bond strengthens the marriage and
makes the partners want to stay together.

Protection from Poor Self-Image

Our decision making is significantly influenced by the way we perceive ourselves. People who see themselves the way God sees them—as unique creations
of the Master, made in his image, endowed with talents and personality traits
that set them apart from everyone else, valuable and significant to God—are
free to be themselves. They have a healthy self-image, one that lets them stand
tall on who they are in Christ, not needing to depend on another person in order
to feel good about themselves.

Without a healthy self-image, people are insecure. Poor self-image is one of
the leading psychological problems in our culture. People who do not believe
they are lovable often have difficulty liking others and fitting in with society.
These people will seek some kind of boost, some kind of infusion of self-esteem
from another person in order to feel right about themselves.

Sex is a common tool used in the effort to bolster a weak self-image. An insecure guy may try to be macho and prove to himself and others how masculine and attractive he is. An insecure girl may try either to hold a guy's affections by giving him sex, thus making her feel secure, or to be sexually appealing to a lot of guys, thereby proving to herself she has value in their eyes.

The problem is, those strategies backfire, as echoed in these sad notes from students:

> I finally got a girl into bed (actually it was in a car) when I was 17. I thought I was the hottest thing there was, but then she started saying she loved me and getting clingy. I figured out that there had probably been a dozen guys before me who thought they had "conquered" her, but who were really just objects of her need for security. That realization took all the wind out of my sails.
>
> Worse yet, I couldn't respect someone who gave in as easy as she did. I was amazed to find that after four weeks of having sex as often as I wanted, I was tired of her. I didn't see any point in continuing the relationship. I finally dumped her, which made me feel even worse, because even I could see she was hurting. At least one of her parents was an alcoholic (maybe both were), her home life was a disaster, and just when she thought she could hold on to someone, I ditched her. I didn't feel very cool after that. I felt pretty low.
>
> ◆ ◆ ◆
>
> I think my heart became hardened. After a while, I didn't care whether or not I loved the guy. I didn't like doing it that much, and I didn't even care who I did it with. My self-concept went way down. I quit caring about myself.

Sex, as it should be in marriage, is based on security. In God's plan and provision for sex, there is total love, trust, companionship, and freedom in giving sexually. The marriage is designed to be a permanent commitment in which the partners are completely secure in the relationship. There is no need to prove anything, no need for ego boosts, no cause whatsoever for insecurity. Yet even though God has provided that perfect arrangement, people think their plans are better. They think they can buck the system, play by their own rules, and somehow come out ahead.

Young people place terrific expectations on sex. They think sex in itself can work miracles, giving them a better view of themselves, making them look better in another person's eyes. One of the greatest expectations kids place on sex is that of establishing intimacy. Many people have low self-esteem because they feel unable to establish intimacy with another. They feel unlovable and in- capable of truly loving anyone. They hope that through physical intimacy they can find emotional intimacy and thus feel better about themselves. But it doesn't make them more capable of intimacy.

When God commands us to reserve sex for marriage, he does it to protect us. He knows that a person's self-image will be damaged in the long run through pre- marital sex. He knows that the artificial "high" that people feel about themselves after physical intimacy will wear off, leaving no sense of emotional intimacy, and that they will crash hard when they realize how empty their "freedom" is. So he protects us by establishing boundaries within which sex is good and edifying and brings lasting pleasure.

As our young people grow nearer to God in a personal relationship with Jesus Christ, they will understand that they don't need the temporary, fickle ac- ceptance of others to have a healthy self-image. They will realize that they are complete in Christ and are accepted by God just as they are, free to be their own persons. They are free to give to people and don't have to take from them. They are free to minister without having to manipulate. They are free to say no to what is not within God's plan for their lives.

For a more complete explanation of the concept of healthy self-image, see my book *See Yourself As God Sees You,* published by Tyndale House Publishers.

PROVISION FOR EMOTIONAL WHOLENESS IN FUTURE MARRIAGE

God not only seeks to protect our young people from the emotional suffering brought about by sexual immorality, he also wants to provide for them the emo- tional and psychological wholeness that results from saving sex for marriage. A couple of young people share their insight into this truth:

My celibacy—which was not always my preference—has played an important role in the success I enjoy today. I've been able to start a career without the problems and worries encountered by Christians and non-Christians who couldn't wait any longer: the bouncing baby who is really a bundle of tragedy; the loss of respect for another when the relationship is revealed as infatuation or a one-night stand, and the sense of being used that accompanies it; the emotional responsibility of maintaining a predominantly physical relationship; dealing with a person's true feelings once the new wears off and it's time to move on; explaining ourselves to those who look to us as examples; AIDS, herpes, and all the rest.

◆ ◆ ◆

What it comes down to is a matter of choice. Gratification of the immediate says, "Sleep with him!" After all, most anyone else would. But looking beyond that to what I would have to live with keeps me saying no. I would be paying a much higher emotional price for that sex than it would be worth. I choose, instead, to invest in loving, caring relationships that don't include sex but do include the kind of emotional support, gratification, and challenge that keep me going in life. Sex alone just can't do that.

Such an approach to sex opens the door to God's abundant provision for emotional wholeness. Let's consider several facets of God's provision.

Provision of Maturity

One of the primary benefits of waiting for sex until marriage is the development of maturity. Here is how a couple of students expressed it:

People should wait until marriage to engage in sex, because waiting gives your mind and body the time they need to mature.

◆ ◆ ◆

A patient couple who realize they are in God's will and want to achieve God's purposes together can experience a fulfilling sex life in its proper setting: marriage. Sex can unify a couple, be a time of ecstasy and pleasure, and result in a child who is loved. Because I didn't have those three functions of lovemaking in mind before marriage, I couldn't experience everything God intended for sexual relations. Only those who are united for God's purpose, who realize they are united by God, and who are willing to accept the responsibility of a child can experience healthy sex.

One of the marks of maturity is the ability to delay immediate gratification. But we live in a "do it now" society, a culture that insists on instant pleasure and a fast fix. In other words, our society is immature as a whole, and it encourages teenagers to live in the same way.

If you give a small child a pack of gum with five sticks and say, "One is for now, the others are for later," you can be fairly sure that when you come back a few minutes later the child will have a huge wad of gum in his cheek and five empty wrappers. Because children are not mature, they do not display the characteristics of maturity. They are seldom able to wait for anything.

Life is a process, and developing maturity is part of that process. It doesn't happen overnight. Just as God wants to protect us from the consequences of immature sexual behavior—the demand for immediate gratification—he also provides for us in the process of waiting until marriage. He builds character and maturity in our lives as we display self-control and obedience.

Physical gratification is fleeting. Maturity is a quality of character that can never be taken away.

Provision of Genuine Love

Waiting for sex until marriage gives genuine love an opportunity to develop in a relationship, as the following student so aptly explains:

> Physically expressing your love for one another may seem acceptable now, but what is your rush? If you are counting on marrying him and you will be spending the rest of your lives together, why does sex need to enter the relationship at this point? Marriage is an institution in which a man and woman share in every facet of each other's lives, and it is only when they are united in the legal and social sense that they may be united legitimately in the physical sense. If you are really in love, you will recognize this.

Love always, in every case, with no exception, seeks the best interest of the loved one. Its motivation is *always* to protect and to provide. That is why we can be secure in God's love. He will never do or say anything that is not in our best interest. When he says, "Wait until marriage for sex," he does it to provide a solid basis for our relationship: genuine love.

One passage of Scripture, 1 Corinthians 13, always comes up when Christians start talking about love. There is a reason. Its brief lines about love encapsulate many of the qualities of an emotion people often find hard to define. Instead of just saying, "Well, it feels like love, so it must be," this passage gives us something we can sink our teeth into, a standard by which we can measure our actions and feelings. Consider these verses:

> *Love is patient,*
> *love is kind,*
> *and is not jealous;*
> *love does not brag*

and is not arrogant,
does not act unbecomingly;
it does not seek its own,
is not provoked,
does not take into account a wrong suffered,
does not rejoice in unrighteousness,
but rejoices with the truth;
bears all things,
believes all things,
hopes all things,
endures all things.

1 COR. 13:4-7, NASB

Here's a good way for young people to see if what they feel in a romantic relationship is really love. Have them substitute their name for the word love in this passage. Are their actions and thoughts directed for the benefit of the other? Do they put the other person's happiness and well-being on a plane equal to or higher than their own? If not, they need time for genuine love to develop.

And if they are in a dating relationship, have them substitute their partner's name in place of love. How accurate is the description? If they are in a premarital sexual relationship, this list won't fit them or their partner very well.

Provision of Respect for One's Body
Our bodies are described in the Bible as temples of the Holy Spirit (see 1 Cor. 6:19-20). How can a person claim to love someone while causing that person to misuse his or her body, the tabernacle of the Holy Spirit, through premarital sex? One of God's provisions for those who save sex for marriage is a healthy respect for their own bodies, God's temple. One student commented:

> Your body is something you should save for your mate for life, not some one-night stand. If you think you've found the one you really love and he says he loves you, he will wait. Don't fall for the old line, "If you love me, you'll do it." If he tries that, just say, "If you love me, you'll wait."

When premarital sex is equated with love, things once considered black and white start turning gray. If young people wonder if their dating relationships demonstrate love and respect for each other's body as a temple of the Holy Spirit, encourage them to study 1 Corinthians 6:19-20. God has provided us with clear guidance in his Word to keep us from allowing momentary emotions from overriding his unchanging truth.

Provision of Dignity

The Bible clearly declares in numerous passages the inherent dignity and value in each person. In Genesis 1:27 we find that we are created in his image. What a dignified beginning! In Romans 12:3 we are challenged to view ourselves with sound judgment because God has allotted to each of us a measure of faith. And in 2 Corinthians 5:17-20, we are called new creations to whom God has given the vital ministry of being his ambassadors in the world.

We are valuable because we are handmade by God in his image. We are not chemical accidents. We are not monkeys who have learned to use tools. We are living sculptures, the finest handiwork of the Master.

The essence of God is love. He doesn't just show love; he *is* love. The nature of his love requires an object; it has to give. But God does not need us. He can completely satisfy his expression of love within the Godhead (Father, Son, and Holy Spirit). In his sovereignty it pleased God to create us so that he might love us and that we might have fellowship, a relationship, with him. He did not need us; he wanted us.

Because God created us in his image, we have worth in God's creative plan. He provides us with redemption, with salvation—and that has nothing to do with any human merit. Rather, it is the result of God's divine sovereignty.

When we come to realize these truths, we will not think more highly of ourselves than we ought to. We will accept our looks and talents and brains for what they are: gifts of the Master, added in just the right measure for our benefit and to his glory. We will not be conceited, but at the same time we will not be self-effacing. We will think of ourselves correctly, knowing we are unique and of great value in God's eyes.

Those of us who have recognized the truth of Christ's words, accepted his forgiveness, and given our lives to him, have an added measure of dignity. We are royal envoys, ambassadors of the King of kings, called to live in a manner worthy of our high office.

Human sexuality is a reflection of the dignity God has given to us, a dignity that, in the right time and place, can be expressed in sex. It is precisely this dignity which our sinful nature destroys. When we are impatient for sex, when we fill our minds with pornographic garbage and dwell on it until we are moved to action, when we act immaturely and demand instant gratification, we degrade ourselves and the calling we have been given.

As an example of that dignity being tried and tested, consider the experience of the following young woman:

> I was very naive about sex (the only information I was able to get was from booklets and listening to friends). I had the usual crushes on boys who didn't notice me. My ninth grade year, though, I found out what it's like to stand up for your morals. The first kiss was not all that enjoyable and the hands up the shirt shocked me. The next time we were alone, the boy tried to go all the way. After I said no and explained my position, he took me home in complete silence. I was hurt when he no longer wanted to see me, but I was confident I had done the right thing.

This brave girl held to her standards and did not let herself be degraded by someone trying to use her for his lust.

Provision for Only One "First Time"

After hearing me speak at a "Why True Love Waits" rally, a seventeen-year-old girl wrote to me:

> You gave me courage when I heard you say why God wants us to wait and how beautiful he intended sex to be. So Tuesday I had lunch at school with my friends who have always joked about my virginity and made fun of me. I finally said, "Look, I don't want any more jokes about my virginity, because each of you needs to realize that any day I want to I can become like you, but you can never again become like me."

In the true physical sense, there is only one first time for sex. And unless a young person has a memory loss or was extremely drunk, that first time will be indelibly stamped in his or her memory. And students do think about it, as reflected in the following comments:

> If you jump into sex for the first time before marriage, you will remember that time for the rest of your life, regardless of whether you remember it as good or bad. Sex after marriage will be extra special to me because it will be new and ex-

citing, and the result of our love. We won't have to worry about listening for foot-steps of returning parents, tattletale brothers and sisters, or uneasy feelings around the house.

◆ ◆ ◆

Why wait? Because you're playing with fire. The consequences are for life—there's no turning back. Once you give away your virginity, you can never, ever get it back.

◆ ◆ ◆

If you decide, that night, to be "with" this person even though you are not mar-ried, you are essentially saying, "My will be done." You're taking a very precious part of yourself and giving it to someone (who is more than willing to take it) who, for all practical purposes, is not committed to you or the relationship. This gift, once given, can never be taken back, even though you will realize you have made a mistake.

◆ ◆ ◆

Emotional scars often accompany premarital sex. There is only one first time to have sex. If you share it with someone other than your partner for life, it could turn into something you want to forget.

◆ ◆ ◆

The idea of virginity as a lost gift can apply even to those who end up marrying their original sex partners. One who gives away virginity in a relationship without the commitment of marriage gives a gift which implies far more love and commitment than either person is prepared to deal with. A once-in-a-lifetime blessing, which echoes the very relationship between Christ and his church, is thus squandered.

A 1994 survey of 500 women conducted by EDK Associates and *Redbook* magazine found that roughly two-thirds (64 percent of the 500 women sur-veyed) "would want to be a virgin if they were getting married today."[2]

YM magazine did an on-line poll of 15,000 girls ages thirteen to twenty in February 1999 and found the following:

- Seventy-three percent of the respondents said they were virgins.
- Of those, 59 percent plan to keep on waiting to have sex until their wedding nights.
- Of the respondents who said they were not virgins, only 29 percent described their sexual experiences as "romantic."[3]

What a joy it is to be able to share that first time with the one who is committed to you for life! God's provision for marriage is that first-time bond, the memory of an act of love that made the relationship complete. Even if the wedding night is awkward, rushed, or maybe a little painful, the memory of having first made love with one's lifelong partner often overrides it all.

God instructs us to restrict sex to marriage in order to provide freedom from memories of past sexual activity. He knows the power that the "first time" has in influencing our view of sex and its relationship to the past.

If someone has had sex but is not yet married, he or she can't technically be a virgin again. But the forgiveness and regeneration of being a new creation in Christ make it possible for a sense of innocence to be restored. God always meets us right where we are—no matter where we are—and offers us a fresh start. He can instill forgiveness where there is guilt; self-control where there is none; a healthy appreciation of sex where there is either obsession or aversion. We will talk more about forgiveness in chapter 21.

If an unmarried couple is sexually active, they may feel that since neither of them is a virgin anymore, they may as well continue right up until marriage. God, however, can work in a person's life at any time. If the couple stops sleeping together, they can begin to reestablish their self-control and their appreciation and respect for themselves and each other, aspects of their relationship which they have ignored. They can show one another they are capable of submitting to God and of controlling themselves, each for the sake of the other.

Many people have thanked me for encouraging them to cool their relationship for a while—maybe even break up—in order to stop the sexual activity that was controlling them. Almost 100 percent of those couples who went on to get married have written or called to thank me. They were able to use the waiting period to build their commitment to each other and regain the trust they had forfeited through sex. They were able to approach their wedding night as a new "first time."

After listening to their jokes about her virginity, one seventeen-year-old lovingly replied, "Anytime I want to I can become like you; but you can never again become like me." Needless to say, they never joked about her virginity again.

God provides us with a fresh start if we are willing to obey him.

Provision for Intimacy

True intimacy between a man and woman is another one of God's provisions for young people who say no to premarital sex. Emotional intimacy comes through recognizing and understanding our own emotions and then sharing those feelings openly with another person in order to strengthen that relationship. It means taking the risk of opening up to someone, not just unloading pent-up feelings or getting physically involved. It means letting our true self be visible, which holds the danger that our true self may not be found acceptable in the other person's eyes.

So to be able to be transparent with someone, we first have to be secure in ourselves. Then we must have a sense of security in the relationship that tells us our openness will not be abused. As fallible beings, our security ultimately can be found only in the Lord. When our self-image is firmly rooted in a relationship with Jesus Christ, we are able to see in ourselves and others the dignity and worth God has given us.

If I am aware of my position in Christ and of the dignity God has bestowed on someone close to me, I am able to open up to that person, and he can open up to me. He can tell me anything going on in his emotions, just as I don't have to hold back from him. We won't reject each other. We won't blackmail each other with the information shared. We won't condemn each other. Rather, we are there to strengthen one another and build our relationship. We are achieving emotional intimacy with each other.

One young person expressed it this way:

> As I review my relationship with my fiancée, Jane, our most special times are when we have excellent conversations. Kissing is great enjoyment, but we have found intimacy through conversations, talking about intimate things as well as working through problems. It sounds dull but it's not.

Without the security of knowing my position in Christ, without an understanding of the value and dignity of another person, I will be incapable of this intimacy. And even though I have a God-given desire for emotional closeness, I will close down my feelings rather than seek to open them up. If I am unable to open up to another and allow another to open up to me freely, I am forced to resort to a substitute for intimacy. Since I can't go to my soul, I go to my body and my five senses. I turn to sensory closeness and become involved sexually.

The problem is that this false intimacy doesn't last. It proves itself to be shallow. People who discover this often fail to recognize what is happening, and instead of giving up the futile search for intimacy in bed, they intensify it. Time after time they achieve a type of closeness, and then watch it quickly fade. If this cycle is not broken, they will become numb to the idea of finding true intimacy. They settle for the cheap substitute.

Intimacy is built as a result of trust. Premarital sex easily breaks down that trust factor. Trust is built over time with a lot of communication as you work through problems. You see that the other person isn't going to "dump" you. You know that he or she is committed to you. Trust is established, and trust leads to vulnerability, and that leads to transparency, and that results in intimacy—a closeness to another person.

Intimacy, then, is twofold. First, having faith in Jesus Christ, we must be aware of our position in him. When we know we are loved, accepted, and deemed important by God no matter what, we have security and can develop a healthy sense of self-worth.

Second, we must have love and acceptance from some person in our life, in order to see this tangible expression of God's love for us. We must see that it is possible for someone to accept us no matter what, that we in turn may be loving and accepting toward others. We must learn to love.

A healthy self-image arising from our relationship with God, combined with an experiential knowledge of how loving relationships work, makes us capable of emotional intimacy. It is God's design. When we achieve that intimacy in a dating relationship, we don't have to look to physical closeness. We know that it can wait until the relationship has been sealed.

◆ ◆ ◆

God's protection and provision for our kids extends beyond their physical health and emotional wholeness. In the next chapter we will explore the relational reasons our young people should wait for sex until marriage.

CHAPTER 13

THE RELATIONAL
REASONS TO WAIT

MANY ADOLESCENTS CHARGE HEADLONG into sex thinking the relationship with a boyfriend or girlfriend will only get better as a result of their physical intimacy. And many times, at the outset, they feel closer and more connected to each other. But as married couples know, there is more to building intimacy and fulfillment in a relationship than sex. And when kids lack the maturity and commitment that comes with marriage, sex can often do more harm than good for a relationship.

This is another area where God's protection and provision come into play. God wants our kids to enjoy intimacy in relationships, both now and when they marry. He has reserved physical intimacy for marriage, and when young people fail to wait, they experience the consequences of relational pain and they forfeit a degree of intimacy God reserved for them in marriage. Let's explore how adolescent premarital sex disconnects kids from God's protection and provision in their relationships.

PROTECTION FROM UNHEALTHY RELATIONSHIPS

Another reason our young people should wait for sex until marriage is to avoid the relational problems that result from promiscuity. God desires to protect our kids from these relational pains, and that's why he says no to premarital sex.

Protection from Communication Breakdown

Hunger for an intimate relationship is built into each of us. We all want to love and be loved. We all want to relate to and communicate with others at a deep level. Sex is merely the physical expression of that intimate love we seek, not the source of it. That is why premature sex will shortcut an immature relationship. It tries to express something that isn't there yet.

When young people delay physical involvement until its proper time, they allow the relationship to grow and mature. Then, once that relationship has developed into a lifelong marriage commitment, sex can become meaningful, constructive, and beneficial to the relationship. Until that commitment is sealed, however, the couple needs to spend time discovering each other, finding out what it is that makes the other unique and attractive. This forms the friendship that lays the foundation for love, which leads to the personal intimacy each seeks.

It is a building process, and cutting it short by getting into sex before marriage may make it impossible to put the process back on course. Communication breaks down, as the following students discovered:

> Like many others, I have learned that if there is too much touching in a relationship, it can cause uneasy feelings that lead to lack of communication. This will lead to fighting, boredom, and eventually to a breakup.
>
> ◆ ◆ ◆
>
> Another situation to consider—communication. You are getting to know and enjoy a person, their likes and dislikes. You appreciate it when they let down their walls and allow you to see them as they really are. But when sexual activity starts, the lines of communication break down.
>
> ◆ ◆ ◆
>
> Premarital sex can inhibit communication, especially when each person's view of the other is lessened. He figures, *"Who else has she slept with? She's not worth much."* She thinks the same about him, and wonders, *"How do I compare with his other women? Does he tell anyone how I perform in bed?"* Each then becomes less willing to talk, and communication is destroyed.

Waiting until marriage to have sex requires that the couple develop some basic qualities. A commitment to obey Christ and his Word will mean exercising self-control, discipline, and patience. Those same qualities are necessary to form a lasting, intimate relationship. Our society is facing a crisis in the ability of its members to form intimate relationships, a crisis caused by disregard for commitment and faithfulness, the cornerstones of intimacy. A commitment to be faithful to Christ's commands regarding sex lays the groundwork for building intimacy.

Still, many couples who are committed to each other cannot enjoy true satisfaction in sexual relations because they have not learned self-control, discipline, and patience. They have weakened the communication that had made them strong in the first place. God's provision for those who obey is the opportunity to develop these basic qualities that are valuable not only in forming solid friendships now, but invaluable in marriage in the future. As one young man said:

> By obeying God and waiting to have sex until marriage, a couple can discover other ways to communicate that will facilitate a healthy relationship. The patient couple can really get to know each other and start to discover God's purpose for their marriage before they ever sleep together.

Protection from Difficult Courtships

One of the gifts God allows us to give another person is a demonstration of self-control. When we establish a relationship, self-control must be evident for trust to be built, and trust is the foundation for any continued growth in the relationship.

Premarital sex undermines such trust by proving that a person is not in control of his or her desires, but instead is controlled by them. When two young people are controlled by their desires, sex controls their relationship. When they become victims of their own inability to put off gratification, the relationship suffers and may end. I'm convinced that illicit sex has damaged more relationships than it has enriched. More engagements are broken by couples who have had intercourse than by those who have not, and the more frequent the intercourse, the more likely the rings will be returned.

Once the physical aspect takes root, it quickly takes over. The people lose the ability to communicate and learn about each other. They don't develop the social, intellectual, moral, and emotional aspects of the relationship. Instead of growing stronger, they grow weaker. So, rather than being the culmination of a mounting intimacy between two people, marriage (if it happens) becomes a permanent seal on an incomplete relationship.

God's commandments against sex before marriage are there to protect young people from hurting their relationships. If couples are sexually active, they may find themselves hooked into a relationship; the wise move, regardless of how close they may be to marriage, is to break it off and reestablish the self-control so vital to a marriage. If couples are able to get back together without sexual involvement and continue on to marriage, they have achieved a major accomplishment that will strengthen rather than weaken their marriage. The sooner they can break it off, the better.

It is difficult to end a steady relationship, more difficult to end an engagement, even more difficult to end a marriage, and terribly painful to end a marriage with children. The further you go, the harder it gets, and the more pain results. That is why God commands us to "flee immorality." He knows we need to run from a bad situation as soon as possible.

God's admonition to wait does not guarantee a smooth courtship, but waiting allows the opportunity for developing an ultimately healthy courtship. When issues are not clouded by sex, people are better able to understand each other and can know with certainty if they are making the right move in getting married. I discovered this when I dated a young woman for three and a half years. Even after all that time, we were able to understand that marriage was not right for us. We are still friends to this day. By being obedient to God's commands concerning sex before marriage, we were under God's protection and able to partake of his provision.

Protection from Comparison

Sexual involvement before marriage is a force a young person may have to deal with for years afterward, especially in marriage. I have had people in counseling who can describe a number of sexual encounters and remember in detail exactly what happened, yet they don't even remember their sex partners' names. Such is the influence sex has on our emotions and memories. Abraham Maslow describes sex as the peak human experience.

Why do memories and comparisons of past sexual experiences haunt people so mercilessly? Simple. God created the sexual experience to give us the most unforgettable, vivid, and often-recalled memories we will ever have. Let's look at how memory works and why this is true.

There are two basic approaches to understanding human memory: (1) the neurobiological approach, which studies the molecular brain processes (like studying the circuits of a computer); and (2) the practical approach, which examines the functions and principles of memory (like studying the software for a computer). We will look at the practical approach, as it is more applicable to our purpose.

Scientists have discovered a number of principles that help us understand why sexual memories are so intense and permanent. One principle involves what is called "consolidation" of memories; that is, how short-term memories become long-term memories that can be recalled in the future. There are at least two important factors involved in creating a long-term memory: (1) the intensity of the experience; and (2) how much we rehearse or review the experience in our mind. Sex is likely to involve both of these, as it is by any measure intense, and we are likely to rehearse the experience often because of the emotions involved. Our sexual experiences seem to be written in indelible ink in our memories, never to be erased.

Another memory principle that applies to sexual experiences is that people tend to learn and remember more clearly when they are alert and stimulated, when their bodies have large amounts of adrenaline in them, and when emotions are involved. It is difficult to imagine any experience that involves as many of these factors as sex does. Few experiences leave us with memories that are as vivid.

Our five senses are involved also in learning and remembering. Specifically, the more different senses we involve in an experience, the more likely we are to recall it later. One highly effective Scripture memory method illustrates this. The method includes reading the verses out loud three times from the text; writing them three times; reading the verses out loud three times from what you just wrote; and saying them three times as you now remember them. This method involves three senses: sight (as you read), hearing (as you speak), and touch (as you write). These same three senses can be involved in an even stronger way in sex, and the other senses can be as well.

In addition, memories are called to mind by association. Something from within us (thoughts, feelings, actions) or from without (through our five senses) reminds us of something similar from our past. Think of what can be associated with sex: anything from any of the five senses; any of the automatically strong positive, negative, or ambivalent emotions involved in sex; anything related at all to the person one was with at the time; anything about the location or the time of day, and the list goes on.

In considering these various principles, we realize that a young person who has had premarital sexual encounters probably will have the same feelings in subsequent encounters, such as in marriage. This is especially true if the earlier occurrences involved hurt, exploitation, mistrust, or guilt. (That is one reason rape and incest can devastate people's lives—permanent scars are left.) When past experiences are transferred into marriage, there is trouble.

We can see that the most important sex organ God gave us is our mind. In reality, that's good news! Since God created sexual experience in such a way that we automatically have the most unforgettable, vivid, and often-recalled memories, think of what happens when two people learn about sex from their first time—together—within marriage. Indelible, extremely positive memories are formed that can bind those two people together in a loving, trusting unity, without any interference from the past.

But when a person brings previous sexual experiences—along with vivid memories—into a marriage relationship, problems are virtually guaranteed. The spouses are automatically in competition with the other unseen partners. Fears and concerns often develop about how one matches up or compares to a previous lover. In quarrels or fights, unfortunate comments or comparisons can be made that will be detrimental to the marriage.

God has given us his commands to postpone sex until marriage in order to protect us from these unfair comparisons. When we are disobedient and shun his protection, our sexual experiences start to condition us mentally. One man who discovered this was a worker in a Christian organization. He offered to drive me to the airport after a conference.

On the way there, he said, "I need your help. I am married to one of the most wonderful women I've ever met. I love her. I would do anything for her. But before I became a Christian, I was very active sexually, to the point where my sexual adventures became distorted and rather depraved." At that point he began crying. "I would do anything—*anything*—to forget the sexual experiences I had before I met my wife. When we have intercourse, the pictures of the past and the other women go through my head, and it's killing any intimacy. I'm to the point where I don't want to have sex because I can't stand those memories. The truth is, I have been married to this wonderful woman for eight years, and I have never been 'alone' in the bedroom with her."

Hebrews 13:4 instructs that the marriage bed is to be kept pure. "Pure" means to be void of any foreign substance. Premarital or extramarital sexual relationships defile the marriage bed. They so affect our minds that we carry a foreign element, the memory of those past relationships, into the marriage bed with us. One woman, relating the effects of her previous sexual relationships on her marriage, referred to the "ghosts" of relationships past. Another referred to the negative "reruns in the theater of the mind." The foreign element had entered each of these women's marriage bed and it was no longer pure.

A young person may give back the ring, return the pictures, and throw away the mementos, but he or she cannot give back the mental pictures or the memories. They remain in the mind throughout life. The mind is the number one sexual force to be reckoned with. God has given us his wise and loving commands to protect our minds, not to frustrate us or ruin our fun.

Another young man approached me one time and said, "I used to be sexually involved and look at a lot of pornographic magazines, and it has messed up my marriage. I got so hooked on being turned on by those pictures that I still have to have them. When I go to bed with my wife and have sex with her, I can't even have an orgasm without a foldout next to her head on the pillow."

Some weeks later I was approached by a woman who told me her self-image had been shattered. I asked her why. She said, "Every time my husband has sex with me, he has to have a pornographic foldout on the bed next to me. He can't even come to a climax without it."

This young woman's self-image was destroyed. Her husband was having sex with her but was making love with the woman in the picture. Like the man who took me to the airport, he had filled his mind with so much junk and so many salacious memories that he was paying the price years later in his marriage. Neither of those men wanted it that way. But they were reaping the consequences of their earlier disobedience.

When one partner fears comparison to the spouse's previous lovers, he or she begins to seek assurance that he or she is actually good enough to compete. That kind of unhealthy need for affirmation certainly does not allow freedom and self-expression in the bedroom. It creates insecurity, which comes from a feeling of being threatened. Further, fear of an outside threat can lead to jealousy—a strange kind of jealousy that pits a person against "competition" that has not been around for years. It is not so simple as an attractive person at the office making a pass. It is a memory that enters the bedroom with the spouse.

Although most adolescents think and even fantasize about sex (boys more than girls), they fail to see the power of their thoughts on their sexual activity, and the power of their sexual activity on their thoughts. They don't realize that the way they live their lives now has a direct bearing on how they will live later. If they remain in line with God's instructions and keep themselves pure, they will reap the reward in marriage of being able to concentrate fully on their spouse when making love. If they are sexually active beforehand, they are setting themselves up for future mental battles. This is not mere hypothesis. It is a reality played out every day in the fear and insecurity found in countless marriages.

God provides a way to freedom for those who have been sexually active and are haunted by it. Since he commands us to be transformed by the renewing of our minds (Rom. 12:2), it must be possible for our minds to be renewed. In specific instances in my own life I have prayed for a certain memory to be blotted out. It's hard to imagine that such a thing is possible, but it is. I remember being needled by something out of my past, something I knew intellectually God had forgiven but I was unable to shake. I remember praying that God would relieve me of the burden of that memory. Incredibly, I became aware at some point after praying that a burden had been lifted. I didn't recall exactly what it was, but I wasn't supposed to remember. All I knew was that another area of my thoughts was transformed and renewed, no longer weighed down and haunted.

So many of us need to be brainwashed. We need to have our brains washed by God. We need to bring our memories and past experiences under the lordship of Jesus Christ and allow him to repair the damage. We need to begin today building relationships that will leave good memories, relationships we can look back on with appreciation as we see personal and spiritual growth rather than relationships we look back on with regret and self-disgust. God always meets us right where we are and offers us a fresh start.

The Father knows what is best for our minds and has set up boundaries around sex to protect and provide for our minds. One young bride who found this out wrote:

> The first benefit I am experiencing as a result of obedience is freedom from the jealousies I would be experiencing had my husband been with another woman before me. I would be haunted by the possibility that sex was better, more exciting with her. I could never be fully assured that he is as satisfied and fulfilled in our physical love. The second benefit is, I have no guilt to deal with, no conviction by the Holy Spirit for having been disobedient.

Protection from Sex-dominated Relationships

A young woman wrote to tell me her sad story of sexual activity and love lost:

> My boyfriend was the only one I ever had sex with. I loved him and needed him. I wanted to keep him, but it didn't work. Our communication broke down. Pretty soon we were fighting a lot. He tried to patch things up by having sex, and I gave in because I wanted him to love me. We both got really selfish. We stayed together, but all the love was gone from the relationship.

The very nature of a male-female relationship is that of companionship, friendship, and intimacy. When the relationship is dominated by sexual activity, the results can be disastrous. The marriage relationship is supposed to last a lifetime, and to make that possible, people get to know one another in the period leading up to the marriage. They are not committed to one another legally, morally, or otherwise. They do not live together and do not have mutual responsibilities. They are free to spend time together and learn what makes each other tick, free to question and discuss and debate. They are able to make clearheaded choices about spending their lives together. When the growing intimacy between them leads to the altar, they know what they are getting. After the wedding, they are free to seal the relationship as only a husband and wife can do.

The above process comprises the foundation for building a lifelong relationship. When sex enters the scene too soon, the foundation is weakened and frequently collapses completely. Sex takes over dating relationships like wildfire. It consumes everything built to that point.

When young people reveal their character to each other by having sex before marriage, there is distrust on both sides. Each knows the other is incapable of controlling physical desires. What will happen if they should be apart for a while? What is to keep each from seeking out other opportunities for gratification? Frequently, nothing. Whether they say it out loud or not, they know it.

One by one, the vital mutual concerns needed to build a lasting intimate relationship are consumed by sex. Sex displaces and then destroys love.

God's provision for a couple committed for life is a relationship that grows with the years, not one that falters under pressure. Sex is only one of many, many bonds that hold together a permanent relationship. It is not the focal point. Too many couples have discovered that sex doesn't make their mortgage payments go away. It doesn't resolve the crises that are normal in the course of a lifetime. Premarital sex prevents development of those aspects of a relationship that must be present for a marriage to work.

Although the physical is the most direct route of communication and the easiest to learn, it is only the tip of the iceberg of a good relationship. Anybody can kiss, but not everyone can carry on a meaningful conversation. Often a relationship begun on a plane of physical attraction is never able to reach the deeper intimacy of mind and spirit.

God's protection, seen in his command to restrict sex to marriage, is designed to keep young people from hurting themselves and those they care about by ruining their relationships. A young couple making cow-eyes at each other may not see the terrible pain that can come from a relationship that dries up because of sex. The Father knows how nearsighted we can be, so he tells us which road to take. He takes the guesswork out of relationships by giving us clear instructions about the place of sex. If we stay within his boundaries, we are protected. If we leave his protection, we are open to whatever consequences may lie outside.

Protection from Damaged Family Relationships

One of the things God protects by reserving sex for marriage is the trust and assurance of fidelity that a proper sexual relationship brings. That assurance provides peace of mind for both spouses when they are apart (for whatever reason). Both know they are deserving of trust. Both know the other is deserving of trust. Why? Because, in the period before their marriage, they have proven their character, their maturity, and their self-control.

When a man says, "I do," remember that he is answering a question. The question is "Do you take this woman to be your wife?" When he says yes, he means he takes this woman, not some future ideal, not an improved version of her he has pictured in his mind. He is saying, "I take her and accept her just as she is, and I know what I'm getting." The same holds true for the woman's answer of "I do."

That's why premarital sexual activity can be such a source of distrust in a marriage. A person is generally not changed by marriage; rather, one's personality traits are intensified. People who can't control themselves before marriage will have a hard time controlling themselves after. People who have become involved in premarital sex are more likely to become involved in extramarital sex than those who have saved sex until marriage.

Our society has taken its nonchalant attitude about sex to such extremes that some people actually enter marriage agreeing that both are free to have affairs. They want commitment as long as it is not a bother. They offer love and security in portions designed only to please themselves. Instead of the true view of marriage, which is designed for each to give 100 percent without expecting a return, or even the cheaper but widely accepted view of "I'll give 50 percent if you'll give 50 percent," these couples have reduced marriage to an opportunity for taking 100 percent of the time and giving only when they feel like it. This approach can only damage a couple's relationship. God wants to protect our young people from such damage.

To a great extent, the desire to pursue sex before marriage comes not from a physical yearning for continued sexual release, but from the established habit of trying to solve problems with sex. When a couple becomes physically involved before marriage, sex can easily become a panacea, a way to feel good instantly when problems arise. It becomes a mask, a glow that makes the problems go away for the moment.

The same mind-set carries over into marriage. When the responsibilities of children and mortgage payments pile on top of rough points in the marriage, a person who has learned to look to sex for an answer will do it again. When sex with the spouse leaves the problems unresolved, tension in the marriage mounts. The couple begins to back off from each other physically and emotionally, and one or both may go looking for the "good feeling" somewhere else.

People who look to this escape and allow the affair to become serious—to the point of changing their lives to accommodate it—find themselves in for a rude awakening. I have seen it happen many times, when people find a sexual release outside marriage to be just the medicine they thought they needed: no demands, no responsibilities, no entanglements. They then become enamored with the situation, divorce their spouses, marry their sex partners—and suddenly find themselves back in a relationship with demands and expectations. When tension returns, they go looking again.

By insisting that we wait until marriage for sex, God protects us from these destructive relationships. He wants a couple's sex life to be a point of strength and unity in the marriage relationship, not a point of division. His wisdom supersedes all our rationalizations and excuses.

Premarital sex also can damage relationships with the children conceived by that union. One of God's provisions for sex within marriage is the blessing of children. A married couple is complete without children, of course, but as the father of four, I know the great joy children add to a marriage.

This blessing can be tarnished when the children are conceived outside marriage. While such a couple must deal with the guilt, financial stress, and other problems brought about by a premarital pregnancy, the child can also pay a heavy price.

When an unmarried couple conceives a child, they have a number of options. First, and one often taken by Christian couples, is the "shotgun wedding," the marriage that takes place quickly out of a sense of responsibility (and usually under a fair amount of pressure from the families). These marriages are not necessarily doomed to failure, but instead of beginning in joy and anticipation, they begin in guilt and stress. Such marriages cause two people to begin a family when often they are really too immature to handle the responsibility.

The child, rather than being a symbol of the self-perpetuating love in the marriage, becomes a reminder of a big mistake. There may be a subtle though subconscious resentment toward the child, as though the child was the one who forced the marriage. If such resentment is present, the child grows up with it and is aware of a kink in the parent-child relationship, even when the parents are not.

A second option is giving the baby up for adoption. Although we see it being done less in our culture, it is often the most loving thing to do, especially when the couple (and the mother in particular) is too immature to raise a child. With so many childless couples desperate to adopt, it is a tragedy that so many young people are raising children they may not even want, and who are often the victims of child abuse.

A third option is single parenthood. If the mother is a teenager, chances are she is still living at home. She will eventually move out and be on her own, but according to statistics, her chances of remaining below the poverty line for life are very high. Immature mothers who insist on raising a child without a husband often do so in an attempt to establish a loving relationship. They want the baby as an object for their love, and they want to be loved and accepted by the child. As the baby grows, the mother may find that the child does not fulfill her requirements of love and affection, and the child becomes a victim of the mother's immaturity.

A fourth option is abortion. Taking the life of the child may be the quickest way out, but it also may have the most damaging repercussions physically, emotionally, and morally. What it does to the mother is so extensive and complex that we cannot deal with it here. But the abortion of one child can have an effect even on future children. In some instances, the presence of a child in a marriage becomes a continual reminder of the sibling the mother aborted. She is constantly aware that the family is one person short, and the psychological battles she endures are felt by her living children. Again, the children become victims of the parents' premarital sex.

God can work all things for good in the lives of those who believe in him. He can take the most embarrassing, destructive situation, such as an unwanted pregnancy, and somehow make things turn out right (Rom. 8:28). That does not make premarital sex right, nor will it make the child magically go away. But God does respond to the repentance and prayers of his people. His amazing grace is greater than our worst mistakes.

By instructing us to reserve sex for marriage, God protects young people from even getting into these situations. By limiting sex to marriage, he protects everyone involved, including those not yet born.

Premarital sex also can damage the relationship between the young person and his or her parents. Frequently an adolescent will become promiscuous in an attempt to find the love he or she lacks at home. In so doing, he or she often makes the parent-child relationship worse, especially if an unwanted pregnancy is the result.

When the parents are Christians endeavoring to raise their children to follow God's principles for morality, they are going to be hurt if their children knowingly violate those principles. This hurt may be experienced in different ways. Parents may hurt for themselves through embarrassment, taking the child's disobedience to God as a personal blow. Or parents may genuinely hurt for the child, since they want the best for their child at all times. They know that straying from biblical principles will bring their child pain. Parents may also feel personal hurt because of what the unplanned pregnancy takes away from their expectations or desires.

Young people who desire to please their parents by avoiding sexual immorality are under the protection of God's blessing. But there is something better. When young people have established a personal relationship with God and keep his commandments as a willing response to his love, they have internalized God's values. They are showing maturity and independence, and they are free to become the unique persons God created them to be.

God's provision for seeking to maintain his standards is described in the words of this young woman:

> When I lay down next to my husband on our wedding night, I did not need to sneak away before dawn. My parents knew where we were. We had their blessing. Friends and family had sent gifts and cards of congratulations. It was right in "my crowd's" eyes as well as my Lord's. I had waited long for my wedding day, and I have been enjoying the relationship ever since.

Protection from the Pitfalls of Cohabitation

Living together before marriage has become a common practice in today's society. In the 1950s, approximately nine out of ten women got married without first living with their partners, compared with one in three by the early 1990s.[1]

Over half of all first marriages are preceded by cohabitation today, compared with virtually none earlier in the century. Since 1960, the number of cohabiting couples has increased by nearly 1,000 percent. Today 4 million couples cohabit, compared to fewer than 500,000 in 1960. Approximately half of women between the ages of twenty-five and thirty-nine have lived together with an unmarried partner.[2]

Cohabitation is on the rise while marriage is on the decline, as documented in a recent study:

◆ The report . . . by Rutgers University's National Marriage Project . . . found that the nation's marriage rate has dipped by 43 percent in the past four decades—from 87.5 marriages per 1,000 unmarried women in 1960 to 49.7 in 1996—bringing it to its lowest point in recorded history.

◆ The percentage of married people who reported being "very happy" in their marriages fell from 53.5 in 1973–1976 to 37.8 in 1996.

◆ In the immediate post-World War II generation, 80 percent of children grew up in a family with two biological parents. That number has dipped to 60 percent.

◆ The National Marriage Project report blames the declining marriage rate on people postponing marriage until later in life and on more couples deciding to live together outside of marriage. According to the report, nearly half of people ages twenty-five to forty have at some point set up a joint household with a member of the opposite sex outside of marriage.

◆ Whereas 90 percent of women born between 1933 and 1942 were either virgins when they married or had premarital sex only with their eventual husbands, now more than half of girls have sexual intercourse by age seventeen, and on average they are sexually active for about eight years before getting married.

◆ The percentage of teenage girls who said having a child out of wedlock is a "worthwhile lifestyle" increased from 33 percent to 53 percent in the past two decades.[3]

◆ Sixty-two percent say it is okay for a woman to have a child alone if she lacks a soul mate, according to a Gallup poll sponsored by Rutgers University.[4]

◆ How men and women in their twenties feel about living together:

Sixty-two percent say living together before marriage is a good way to avoid divorce; 43 percent would only marry someone if that person agreed to live together first.[5]

A study by Rutgers University's National Marriage Project and David Popenoe, who cowrote the study "The State of Our Unions: The Social Health of Marriage in America" with Barbara Dafoe Whitehead, found that the number of marriages per 1,000 unmarried women aged fifteen or older dropped to about 49.7 in 1996 versus 87.5 in 1960. At the same time, the number of unmarried couples living with each other rose to 4.2 million in 1998 versus 439,000 in 1960.[6]

Cohabitation is emerging as a significant experience for young adults. It is now replacing marriage as the first living-together union. It is estimated that a quarter of unmarried women between the ages of twenty-five and thirty-nine are currently living with a partner, and about half have lived at some time with an unmarried partner.[7] A growing percentage of cohabiting unions include children. For unmarried couples in the twenty-five to thirty-four age group, the percentage with children approaches half of all such households.[8]

University of Chicago sociologist Linda J. Waite finds that cohabitation involves a different "bargain" than marriage. Compared to married couples, cohabiters expect less mutuality and sharing of resources, friends, leisure activities, and goals.[9] They are less likely than married couples to "specialize" in their living-together unions and thus to achieve higher levels of productivity. In many respects, cohabiting couples behave like roommates, sharing a residence and some household expenses but remaining separate in many of their social and economic pursuits.[10]

Some people see cohabitation as a part of their courtship. They claim it provides a couple the opportunity to really get to know each other and thus be able to decide if they're compatible. Their assumption is that living together is a good sample of what married life will be like and that, if a couple gets along well while cohabiting, they will have a good and long-lasting marriage. On the surface, this seems to make sense.

However, what a couple learns during cohabitation does not particularly work for or against success in a marriage. Some evidence suggests that cohabitation may in fact have a negative effect on the quality of a subsequent marriage. Here are some insights into the difficulties of cohabiting couples:

◆ A 1991 study published in the *Journal of Marriage and the Family* discovered that those people who have lived together have much less stable unions than those unions that begin as marriages.[11]

◆ Forty percent of people who cohabit dissolve their union before marriage. Marriages that started out as cohabiting unions have a 50 percent higher divorce rate than those that did not.[12]

◆ A Wisconsin study of over 13,000 adults conducted in 1992 found that when people create a union outside of marriages there is more conflict and poorer communication.[13]

Let's look at several areas where cohabiting couples seem to struggle. These are difficulties from which God desires to protect young people who wait until marriage to move in together.

Cohabiting couples often struggle with communication.
Apparently, live-together couples usually do not adequately communicate their deeply held beliefs, ideas, or fears. They are so intent on making the live-in relationship work that individuals keep important aspects of their true selves hidden from one another.

It appears that couples who are living together are afraid to look closely at issues, fearing that their differences will hurt their relationship. Their partner just might move out if significant differences arise, since living-together arrangements are much easier to dissolve than marriages. You don't have to go through the hassle and expense of getting a divorce. You can just walk out.

Cohabiting couples often skirt vital decision making.
Live-together situations also allow a couple to avoid dealing with some of the joint decisions that married couples have to make. For example, money and property tend to be either his or hers, not theirs. Consequently, it isn't all that important how he or she spends his or her money. However, if they marry, they know they will have to decide jointly how they are going to spend their money, when to save it, and how to invest it.

In-laws are rarely a factor in a live-in arrangement; they often disapprove and stay aloof from the couple. Only after marriage do in-laws intrude and cause disagreements, tears, and divided loyalties. And then some joint decisions must be made by the couple as to how to handle this.

Nor does a live-in arrangement usually have to adapt to children, who require adjustments and sacrifices that some relationships cannot accommodate. Married couples have to resolve these issues.

Cohabiting couples often split because of sexual dissatisfaction.
If there are sexual adjustment problems, one member of the couple in a live-to-gether arrangement easily can seek sex outside the relationship. In fact, the cohabiting couple is under no real pressure to try to work out their sexual problems together. As a result, one of the leading causes for the breakup of cohabiting couples is sexual problems or dissatisfaction.

A recent study reported, "Research shows that only 4 percent of married women have a 'secondary' sex partner. (Contrast this with the 20 percent of cohabiting women and 18 percent of dating women who admit to having 'secondary' sex partners.)" The same study noted, "Married couples have more frequent sexual activity and higher levels of sexual satisfaction than couples in any other type of sexual relationship."[14]

My close friend Jacob Aranza is a youth speaker and author. He helped to clarify the issue about the perceived need for sexual experimentation before marriage as a prelude to sexual enjoyment in marriage or as a means of resolving sexual problems before entering into marriage when he shared with me:

But what if we don't get along sexually? Wouldn't it be better to make sure before we decided if we are "right" for each other?

The answer is quite simple. The bodies of men and women are made to join together. There is no way that they couldn't be "right" for each other.

The question I'm really being asked is, What if my partner likes sex one way and I like it another way?

Sex, like any other part of marriage, is something you grow into. It's a learning experience for both people, a giving and taking. When you really love your husband/wife, you want to do what pleases them, and vice versa. You learn to tell each other what you do and don't like. It's not like the passion they show on TV where it looks like every couple is in ecstasy!

It's much better than that. You're getting to know each other intimately and can have a lot of fun in the process!

With the proper emotional and spiritual bonding from the beginning, sex can *become* ecstasy for most married couples. Let's just say practice makes perfect.

People make a mistake when they equate sex with love. Many couples may hit it off sexually, but being sexually compatible doesn't mean that two people truly love each other. A successful marriage involves both sexual compatibility and a loving relationship apart from sex.

Millions of people have been fooled by physical attraction or a "romantic relationship." Couples engaging in sex in the hope of helping their future marriage may find sex actually to be a barrier to the relationship. They may have a false sense of feeling good about each other because of a favorable sexual experience. They may overlook other weak spots in the relationship that can lead to trouble after (or, more likely, even before) marriage.

Cohabiting couples are no more or no less compatible than married couples.
"I wouldn't dream of marrying someone I hadn't lived with," some young people say today. "That's like buying a pair of shoes you haven't tried on."

Sounds logical, doesn't it? Couples have a trial period of cohabitation. If they find they are compatible, they get married. If not, they go their separate ways. They find out before they marry whether they'll get along. That should cut down on the divorce rate. Right?

Wrong, say sociologists Jeffrey Jacques and Karen Chason of Florida A&M University, who studied two groups of students married for at least thirteen months. In one group, the couples had lived together before their marriage; in the other, they had not. The researchers say they could find few differences between the couples. Satisfaction with the marriage was no higher or lower if the couples had lived together first. Neither was dissatisfaction. As many couples in one group as in the other seemed headed for conflict or divorce. However, both groups reported that they still found their partners sexually attractive and rated their sex lives as highly satisfactory.

Furthermore, several studies have determined that cohabiting couples are generally less well off than married couples:

- A 1991 study found that cohabitating unions are much less stable than [unions] that begin as marriages.[15]
- A 1992 study found that couples who lived together before marriage

reported greater marital conflict and poorer communication than couples who did not live together before marriage.[16]

◆ A 1992 review of ten cohabitation studies reported, "Those who cohabit prior to marriage have been shown to be significantly lower on measures of marital quality and to have a significantly higher risk of marital dissolution at any given marital duration."[17]

◆ Most cohabiting couples either break up or marry within two years, and after five years, only 10 percent of cohabiting couples are still together.[18]

◆ Married couples report more frequent sexual activity and higher levels of sexual satisfaction than couples in any other type of sexual relationship.[19]

Cohabiting increases the risk of domestic violence for women. The risk of physical and sexual abuse for children is twenty times more likely if biological partners are cohabiting and thirty-three times more likely if the male is not the natural father.[20]

Why doesn't a trial period of living together benefit the marriage experience? For one thing, both people know that it's a trial. The man knows the woman doesn't have to put up with him if he mistreats her; the woman knows the man doesn't have to put up with a moody mate. So they both tend to be on their best behavior. Since it is a trial, each may be willing to put up with traits in the other that would be intolerable if a shared lifetime loomed ahead.

Cohabiting couples tend to focus on personal gain.
When people try to get the benefits of marriage without the commitment of marriage, it can be only for personal gain, such as companionship, sexual gratification, or economic gain. All are self-directed. They have nothing to do with giving to another or strengthening a relationship. This focus opens the door to fights over possessions, relationships, and expectations about commitment.

Cohabiting couples are no more likely to find Mr. or Ms. Right.
Finally, this research shows that living together will not help someone find the right person to marry. It all comes down to the basis for establishing a marriage.

If people want to find the right sex partner for marriage, they are going about it backward by living with someone. They could itemize qualities they desired in a mate, sexual prowess being among them, and begin to hunt, eventually settling for the person who best fulfills their "shopping list." But that person must continually live up to the expectations or be considered insufficient. That's no way to start a marriage, although it is done every day.

The secret to a lasting marriage is for each person to focus on improving himself or herself and the quality of his or her character. In that way, one can become the right person for someone else to find. There's no shopping involved.

This effort to be the right person for marriage must start early. Adolescents, rather than resenting their youth and its limitations, should be glad for the opportunity it presents. They have complete freedom to strengthen their character and begin to instill positive traits in themselves so that when the time comes to consider marriage, they don't have to go shopping. They don't have to practice sex. They don't have to worry about the quality of the relationship they are entering, because each of them already will have become a high-quality person.

PROVISION FOR A UNIQUE RELATIONSHIP IN MARRIAGE

You would never wish the following scenario to be true for your children. Neither would God. He has provided a much better relationship for those who say no to premarital sex:

> I never realized that I felt cheated until my wedding night when we got to our hotel room. As I was getting ready for the most romantic evening of my life, I looked in the mirror and realized I had already done this. What a letdown. What was there to be excited about? This was nothing new. It was as if all the life had been drained out of me.
>
> As months went on, we got frustrated and uptight. Sex used to be so much fun before we got married. What happened? Sex had been just a game before. Now, when it should have been the ultimate expression of love between a husband and wife, it had no meaning.
>
> We struggled with this for almost a year. It was about to destroy us when we finally went to some close friends and received counseling, prayer, and forgiveness from the Lord. Now things are as they should be.

Have you ever searched around the house to find a present with your name on it and peeked in to see what it was? There was a sense of daring and espionage about it, but when it came time to open the present in front of everyone, you had to fake surprise. The gift itself was still just as valuable, but the most important part—the giving and receiving—was tarnished.

God does not want a young person's wedding night to be just another occasion for sex. He wants it to be the beginning of a very special physical relationship between two persons who have followed his timing for sex. His instructions provide the opportunity for a groom and his bride to learn the ways of sexual pleasure with the one he or she will spend a lifetime enjoying and pleasing. This learning process forms one of the strongest bonds in the marriage.

The special nature of sex within marriage is clearly seen when we remember what marriage is: a lifelong opportunity to minister to another person. Sex within this context of giving and meeting the needs of the other then becomes a matter of emotional, spiritual, and psychological oneness as well as of physical oneness.

Provision of Virginity

Lisa shared her words with regret shadowing her face:

> I'm not a virgin, and now that I've found the man I want to spend the rest of my life with, I wish I were. He's a virgin, so we've talked about it and he accepts that I'm not. We've decided not to have sex until after we're married and are comfortable with that decision.

Virginity can be lost only once, and many (possibly even most) people feel some degree of regret when they squander it prior to the wedding night. This is especially true with girls, since they are more likely than boys to regret that the relationship with their first sex partner did not improve after intercourse. Regret is a terrible thing to have to live with day after day. The value people place on virginity, even people without biblical beliefs, makes us know it has inherent importance. No wonder God desires to bless every couple with this beautiful gift. Part of God's provision is the new attitude we are able to have about virginity: It is not something we lose in marriage—it is something we are free to give.

Cindy, twenty-four, is a high school swimming coach from the southwestern part of the United States. She lost her virginity to a man she didn't know or care about "just for the heck of it." She has drifted in and out of love affairs and one-night stands ever since, not really sold on intercourse as a casual activity, but figuring you don't miss a slice from a cut loaf. "I wish I were still a virgin," she says, echoing a common sentiment. "It would be nice if I could marry someone and we could grow in all ways together as whole people, to have nothing bad to look back on. But I guess I had to get where I am now to know that."

Part of God's provision for sex within the marriage is the openness, honesty, and freedom the permanent relationship brings to physical sharing. This is the gift he offers for every young person. Yet when kids are sexually involved before marriage, they can't bring it into the marriage.

When people forgo God's provision and seek sex outside its intended bounds, they not only open themselves and their sex partners to hurt, they hurt their future spouse, possibly someone they haven't even met yet. They may even forget this is a person with feelings, someone who will one day be hurt by the present promiscuity.

Sex in marriage is designed to be a loving act of giving, not an act of taking. Virginity is a beautiful symbol of the giving relationship. God wants us to be able to say, "I have something to give you that I have given to no one else, a gift that is ours alone for life."

Yes, lost virginity can never be recovered. But God can take even the worst situation and make it good. He is able to heal any wound, no matter how deep. However, his number one plan is that our kids never have to deal with the resentment or disappointment of lost virginity. When kids wait for sex until marriage, they will enjoy the full measure of that provision.

Provision of a Bond of Love and Trust

What would you give to hear the following statements from your children or the young people in your church, youth group, or class?

◆ ◆ ◆

As a Christian, I feel I am going to love the man I marry more than anyone else in the world. If that isn't the case, I shouldn't marry him. Because of this, abstaining from sex before marriage is one way to show my future mate how much I love him. Abstinence shows that my marriage is so important to me I am willing to practice faithfulness to my mate even before we meet. A romantic view? Perhaps. But I want my marriage to be romantic.

◆ ◆ ◆

I want to save myself and my virginity for my wedding night. I believe it is a wedding present and a sign of love for my spouse.

◆ ◆ ◆

Last July, God gave me the most wonderful man in the world to be my husband. I had asked for Prince Charming, and the Lord gave me much more than that. He gave me someone I can share my deepest feelings with, someone I can talk to God with, someone I know will always love me and be faithful to me, someone I am glad I waited for.

On our wedding night, I experienced sex for the first time, and it was with my husband. I wouldn't have wanted to share my first time with anyone else. I had no riches or jewels to offer my husband, but he asked for none. All he wanted was me, and that is just what I had to give him—all of me, untouched, his alone. That meant a great deal, and we both knew it. This was a good enough reason for me to wait.

As these young people have shown, God has provided a powerful way for his human creation to demonstrate love to their marriage partners. When we wait until the wedding night to have sex, we establish a bond of trust and love that has no equal. The following studies bear this out.

A 1992 University of Chicago survey of 3,432 Americans between the ages of eighteen and fifty-nine found that monogamous married couples register the highest levels of sexual satisfaction. According to the survey, 87 percent of all monogamous marrieds report that they are "extremely" or "very" physically satisfied by their sexual relationship and 85 percent report that they are "extremely" or "very" emotionally satisfied. Those who are least satisfied sexually (both physically and emotionally) are those singles and marrieds who have multiple partners.[21]

A 1991 review of longitudinal research by the National Center for Health Statistics and the University of Maryland found that women who save sex for marriage face a considerably lower risk of divorce than those who are sexually active prior to marriage. This finding holds true even after differences in maternal education, parents' marital status, religion, and other measures of family background are taken into account.[22]

Those who try to create that bond outside of marriage fail miserably. It is a self-defeating process. Those who desire to show love strive for what is to the greatest benefit of the one loved. They will seek to see his or her social life stimulated, intellect challenged, emotions and spiritual life strengthened, and health protected. None of this is possible in a sexual relationship outside marriage, so any attempt (or supposed attempt) to show love by premarital sex is defeated from the start.

God's command is to limit sex to marriage, a command that protects our young people from hurting or endangering each other and provides a setting in which they can express love through sex.

♦ ♦ ♦

The physical, emotional, and relational consequences of adolescent premarital sex are serious and significant. But there is also a spiritual downside to promiscuity. In the next chapter we will consider the spiritual reasons for postponing sex until marriage and identify God's loving protection and provision in this area.

CHAPTER 14

THE SPIRITUAL REASONS TO WAIT

SINCE IT IS GOD who commands us to reserve sex until marriage, there are serious repercussions to our relationship with God and our spiritual life if we ignore his commands.

PROTECTION FROM SPIRITUAL DECLINE

Our young people must understand the negative spiritual consequences of promiscuity and embrace God's protection and provision for their spiritual life and growth.

Protection from a Sin against the Body

The Bible declares that sex before marriage is a sin against the body. First Corinthians 6:18 admonishes us, "Flee from sexual immorality. All other sins a man commits are outside his body, but he who sins sexually sins against his own body." In other words, premarital sex is a sin against God's purpose of purity for the human body. Saying no to sex protects a young person from committing this grave sin.

Here is how a few young people view the "sin against the body":

Obviously, God gives us a choice. He says everything is permissible, but not everything is beneficial. None of us likes to do anything not beneficial for us and our bodies. After all, we exercise and try to go easy on high-calorie foods in order to take care of our bodies, so why shouldn't we guard them from harm in the area of sex, too? God says that when we get caught up in sexual immorality, we are committing a sin against our own body. Why do something that obviously causes harm to our very own bodies, to what the Bible refers to as the "temple of the Holy Spirit"? It is just not worth it to be so diligent in every other aspect in taking care of our bodies if we do this. We flee from impurities such as fattening foods, why not flee from the impurity of misused sex? If we do flee, we will be obeying God and the results will be totally pleasing. You know why? Because obedience brings blessing.

◆ ◆ ◆

Sinning against your own body means that you lose respect for your body, as well as for the body of the one you're involved with. Once you lose respect for your body, it becomes increasingly easy to indulge in promiscuous sex. Your attitude toward this divine gift becomes practically as casual as a handshake.

Losing respect leads to a warped view of love and centers your definition of love around the physical. You get caught in a deceitful illusion of seeking love in a sexual relationship. The needs of security, commitment, and oneness then reach paramount heights because those needs cannot be met by the world's definition of love.

God created these emotional needs. The felt need of wanting someone to hold you was put in you by God, but God's gift of sex cannot be enjoyed ultimately until it is placed in the framework of marriage.

God created each person as a total being, and therefore he is interested in each of us as total beings. Most important, he wants to see us grow close to him spiritually. He also wants to see our minds challenged. He wants to see us emotionally and physically healthy. He is interested in our moral conscience, desires, speech, social relationships, and plans for the future. He is no less interested in our physical well-being and how we treat our bodies. The body is the vehicle for all the rest.

The owner's manual for a car I bought was entitled *The Proper Care and Maintenance of Your Vehicle*. If car manufacturers, who already have my money, are so interested in how I care for my vehicle that they print a sixty-page booklet about it, how much more is God concerned about how we care for the "vehicles" he has placed us in?

We don't put gas in the radiator or water in the engine. Why? Because we know it will ruin everything. Even people who know very little about cars know that much. And even if they don't know such things, all they have to do is check the manual to find out. Yet even though we see the awful damage premarital sex continues to cause in lives all around us, millions of people engage in it none-theless. They may even glance through the manual and claim a knowledge of the subject, yet they continue to take part in sex out of the context God estab-lished. If God tells us sex is wrong because it harms our bodies, he knows what he is talking about. Remember, this vehicle is his design.

God wants us to be good caretakers of what he has given us. That goes for money, possessions, talents, spiritual gifts, our bodies—everything entrusted to us.

Just as true love displays love for the whole person, counterfeit love in the form of premarital sex is detrimental to the whole person (perhaps to a greater degree than anything else). Sexual immorality harms the emotions. It clouds both the intellect and our ability to make godly decisions. It causes social uneas-iness. It wreaks spiritual havoc. It can have permanent, damaging repercussions physically. Nothing is safe from the damage it can do.

If we want our cars to keep going, we check the oil and radiator and rotate the tires now and then. It's all spelled out in the manual. If we want to keep bad things from happening to our bodies, we avoid overeating, we exercise, and we stay away from sexual wrongdoing. It's all spelled out in the manual, God's Word. Kids who wait for sex until marriage are free from the grievous sin against God's purpose for their bodies.

Protection from God's Judgment
We read in Hebrews 13:4: "Marriage should be honored by all, and the mar-riage bed kept pure, for God will judge the adulterer and all the sexually im-moral." If God has committed to judge those who defile marriage through adultery, we can assume that he reserves a similar judgment for those who defile the marriage bed by practicing premarital sex. As one student wrote:

> If we choose to ignore what God says, we are placing ourselves under his judg-ment, and we are subject to the natural consequences of living outside the limits he has set for his children. Because of our corrupt society, most find it difficult to wait to experience sex. From everything I've heard and read, sex sounds great. That's why I believe it is worth waiting for!

The Bible paints a clear portrait of God as being just. As a just God, he must act when his unarguable laws are broken. If he allowed his people to flaunt unrigh-teousness, doing damage to themselves and others, he would not be a fair judge.

Please remember that God's discipline comes out of his love for us—just as parents, out of love, discipline their children for playing with matches after being told not to. God created us with dignity and value and the freedom to make choices, but he hasn't set us adrift. He has given us a framework, a value system within which we are to make our choices. A spiritual law of cause and effect is at work, so that choices made within God's value structure bring blessing, and those that transgress his boundaries bring negative consequences.

When we see evil in the world, however, we may sometimes wonder where God's justice is. We read the papers and we think that crime really does pay. But there is always justice in the spiritual realm. Civil laws are often arbitrarily established and can be circumvented with tricky legal maneuvers, but God is not impressed with clever arguments. His laws are an expression of his righteousness, protection, and provision for us. They are not arbitrary, not designed to benefit one person over another. Although he understands our frailty, he doesn't listen to excuses, and he can't be bought off. Sooner or later, those who transgress his holy statutes will pay the price.

God isn't out to make your young people suffer as a result of their sexual misadventures. He wants only one thing: sincere repentance and obedience. One young person wrote the following in a letter in hopes of convincing a friend to turn from sin to avoid God's judgment:

> I hope that God has truly spoken to you through this letter. He desires the very best for you. He designed you and he loves you so much. But he is also a righteous and just God. He will not tolerate sin. The sexual freedom you desire brings with it a high price tag. I sincerely pray that you consider the facts and turn to your Father. He is waiting. He earnestly seeks to restore to you the newness and purity you once possessed. His promise to you: "Therefore if any man is in Christ, he is a new creature; the old things passed away; behold, new things have come" (2 Cor. 5:17, NASB).

Protection from Interrupted Fellowship

Whenever we exercise an act of our will that goes against the will of God, it will affect our walk with him. Sin drives a wedge between us and God. Isaiah 59:2 says, "Your iniquities have made a separation between you and your God, and your sins have hidden His face from you" (NASB). Since the Bible is adamant about reserving sex for marriage, a young person who chooses to have sex outside marriage will experience conflict with God, thus damaging his or her relationship with God. One young person expressed it this way:

> Believe me, there are repercussions from willful disobedience. I went through a lot of unnecessary, gut-wrenching pain and heartbreak when I separated myself from the Lord. I should have heeded the Word of the Lord. I discovered that, as true children of God, everything in Scripture is absolutely vital to us.

Prolonged sin, such as unrepentant premarital sex, not only clouds the relationship with God, it also leads to a downward spiral in a young person's spiritual life. One youth told me that his sexual activity made him "uncomfortable" in the presence of God. When kids are uncomfortable with God, they will begin to avoid him. This cooling of feelings, if not reversed, will lead to indifference.

Sexual sin will cause a person to lose his desire for spiritual things. Jesus said, "Everyone who does evil hates the light, and does not come to the light, lest his deeds should be exposed" (John 3:20, NASB). Everything that has to do with God, such as prayer, Bible study, witnessing, and strong Spirit-filled preaching exposes our sins and brings guilt, and so we begin to shun such things. And after a while, even though we know that what we are doing is wrong, we don't care. We have become enslaved to our passions (see 2 Pet. 2:18-19). At this point, apart from the grace of God it is impossible to repent and come back to him.

When a young Christian becomes involved in an improper sexual relationship, he or she begins to feel "uncomfortable" with God. This initial discomfort eventually will lead to unbelief and to a cold, calloused relationship with the Creator.

As young people begin this downward spiral, they are more apt to fall into other types of ungodly behavior. I have frequently seen how young Christians who are sexually active are more likely to cheat in school, drink, and become involved in drugs. They are less likely to attend church, pray, seek out fellowship, and read the Scriptures. When sex becomes more important than God, priorities in general will change. You can see these changes in what the following students wrote:

> I couldn't help crying when you told me that since you and Jay started sleeping together your relationship with God has deteriorated. You even told me how helpless you feel, knowing that sin looms between you and your Maker. I think you'd

agree with me when I say the biggest problem I see with premarital sex is not wondering if you'll get caught, catch something, or even get pregnant. The tragedy is the feeling of separation from fellowship with God. You have discovered that, like any other sin you engage in for any length of time, you become a slave to it.

◆ ◆ ◆

If you are a Christian, the Holy Spirit dwells within you. If you try to mix worldly lusts with the Spirit of God, you will fail. My friend Sally had a sexual relationship while she was backslidden. She said, "It destroys your relationship and fellowship with God. I knew he still loved me, but he seemed very far away."

◆ ◆ ◆

Julie and her boyfriend were both brought up in Christian homes where they learned they should wait for marriage to have sex. They had heard from the "old folks" that they would get carried away if they let their emotions get the best of them, but they both felt they could control their urges.

After eight months of dating, they began to have sexual contact with each other, and a couple of years later they finally had intercourse.

At one time they had both been very close to God and had good relationships with him, but their indulgence interfered terribly with that relationship. The feelings of guilt have been there since they started going too far, and are still there.

God wants to protect our kids from that. After all, every Christian was at one time lost and separated from God but then made a decision to respond to Christ's calling and enter the kingdom. There is safety in God—safety from the repercussions of sin, safety from an evil world charging ahead with no direction, and safety from the uncertainty and fear of being adrift in a society that knows no right and wrong. When God calls us to righteousness and a daily walk with him, he is doing it for our benefit.

Even when kids are living in sin, God never completely breaks off the relationship. He allows the wanderers to come back to him at any moment. His patience in the midst of his anger is a remarkable thing; his willingness to forgive even our foulest sins is even more remarkable. He is the one who, by his grace, seeks to restore our damaged relationship with him.

Protection from Being a Negative Influence on Other Christians

A basic principle of the Bible is that we should not cause others to violate their moral consciences or do things detrimental to themselves. If a Christian young person's promiscuity is made known, other Christian kids may be negatively influenced to engage in similar behavior. Premarital sex by one believer can cause other believers to stumble in their walk with the Lord in at least three ways.

First, a more mature Christian who becomes sexually involved with a younger Christian will hinder the younger believer's spiritual development. When one Christian fouls up the maturing process in another through sexual involvement, God's handiwork in that young believer's life is damaged and the body of Christ is weakened.

Second, a Christian who persuades a more mature Christian to do something they both know is wrong has violated that person's moral conscience. The offending Christian will have to account for a deliberate sin, and once again the body of Christ is weakened.

The purpose of a Christian dating relationship should be to build each other up in the Lord. To determine whether a relationship is good or not, each must ask, "Am I growing in my walk with the Lord through this? Is the other person growing closer to the Lord?" If the answer is no, the relationship is not edifying, and the people are not ministering to each other. It may be that the relationship is based on manipulation, which is "giving in order to get."

Third, a Christian can cause another to stumble by his or her example. For instance, Paul has been a Christian for a long time, but he also has been sexually active for some time. Steve, who has never dated before, has just started going with a girl in his youth group and is very happy about it. While talking to Steve, Paul reveals his sexual activity. Because Paul seems to have his act together, Steve begins to wonder if it would be all right for him to have sex with his new girlfriend.

Paul needs to realize that he is not in a right relationship with God. He is not growing consistently, and he cannot be filled with the Spirit. Unrepented sin short-circuits growth and the Spirit-filled life. In addition, Paul may even be causing his Christian brother to stumble, which would be further evidence of how far out of God's will he is.

Paul may have hurts or needs in his life, such as family problems or a poor self-image, and he may be endeavoring to deal with those through sex. However, he needs to know that this is an irrational attempt to mask his problems through physical release, and he is hardly a desirable role model for Steve.

On the other hand, rather than follow Paul's example, Steve should encourage Paul to walk according to God's principles. Depending on Steve's level of spiritual maturity, he may be able to motivate Paul to study the Scriptures concerning sex and to be in prayer about living righteously. Such opportunities to build up a brother in Christ and turn him from a pattern of sin can be key in strengthening the body of believers.

But if Paul continues to live in bold contradiction to God's commands, there comes a time when Steve must decide if Paul is to remain an influence in his life. The longer Paul is sexually active and talking about it, the more likely Steve is to feel the influence of it and be tempted to sin.

If Steve continues a relationship with Paul without speaking up, he is intentionally putting himself under a bad influence.

God protects us from the bad influences of others when he admonishes his followers not to cause one another to stumble. He knows we may be swayed when a fellow Christian is involved in a sin, since we then can more easily rationalize the sin in our own lives.

Protection from Being a Negative Influence on Non-Christians

One student had these wise words of advice regarding a Christian's ministry to the world:

> As Christians, we are a witness to non-Christians during our lifetime. As we go through life we need to remember that our actions will always speak louder than our words. Premarital sex is a very "loud" action; therefore it would not be good for our testimony as Christians.

A life of contradiction and inconsistency in words and actions is a poor testimony for Christ. This person may verbally proclaim Jesus as Lord, yet when his or her actions conform to the world, the verbal witness loses its effectiveness.

When we live contrary to the principles of God, there are serious consequences. We send mixed signals to those who are observing our faith. Perhaps there is no more tragic consequence to the sexual sin of Christians than its effect on non-Christians. Nathan said to David in the wake of the king's sexual sin, "By doing this you have made the enemies of the Lord show utter contempt" (2 Sam. 12:14).

The damage is done when non-Christians become aware of a Christian's consistent sin. This can be in a relationship between Christians, or between a Christian and a non-Christian. I have known many young people who got involved with unbelievers in the hope of bringing them to Christ but instead wound up in sexual relationships with them. On one hand, they were trying to witness; on the other hand, they were conforming to the non-Christian's lifestyle.

This creates conflict first within the Christian, who more than anyone else is aware of the inconsistency involved. It also creates conflict within the non-Christian, who receives a double message. The Christian seems to be saying, "Jesus Christ has cleansed me of my sin, so in return I'm going to sin some more."

God knows that young people are in a fallen and tempting world, but he calls them to a consistent witness and provides the means by which to maintain their convictions: the Scriptures, the Holy Spirit, and the body of Christ.

PROVISION FOR SPIRITUAL BLESSING FOR SEXUAL PURITY

"It is God's will that you should be sanctified: that you should avoid sexual immorality; that each of you should learn to control his own body in a way that is holy and honorable, not in passionate lust like the heathen" (1 Thess. 4:3-5). God's Word is clear. He forbids any type of sex outside the marriage relationship. Sexual purity is one specific way young people can show people their respect for others and affirm their dignity and value as human beings. When they maintain sexual purity, they become useful channels of God's love. They can accurately represent him to others.

Sexual purity protects us from the awful consequences of abusing the sacredness of sex. It protects us from misusing our bodies, the dwelling place of the Holy Spirit. It protects us from making a mockery of our position as ambassadors of Christ, allowing us to represent him in truth. It protects us from the pain Solomon described in Proverbs 6:27-28, when warning his son not to lust after an immoral woman: "Can a man scoop fire into his lap without his clothes being burned? Can a man walk on hot coals without his feet being scorched?"

By remaining sexually pure, young people enjoy the provision and the promise of God's blessings, both in their future sex lives in marriage as well as many other areas in life.

Provision of the Blessing of Patience

The exercise of waiting patiently for something builds excitement. The longer you wait and dream of it, the greater your response will be when it finally arrives.

That's why birthdays are so great for most of us. All year long we wait for that special day. We don't know exactly what will take place, but we know that it is a day set aside for us. Waiting patiently all year adds energy to the events of the day.

Patience is one of the fruits of the Spirit. Galatians 5:22-23 reads: "The fruit of the Spirit is love, joy, peace, patience, kindness, goodness, faithfulness, gentleness and self-control. Against such things there is no law." When young people consciously postpone sexual activity until marriage, they are candidates for the blessing of patience and self-control and other character qualities that the Holy Spirit develops in them. Here's what a couple of young people wrote to me about patience and self-control:

> A godly character is the result of patience and perseverance in times of trial. Had I been patient and waited to consummate my marriage at the proper time, my character would have been developed and my self-esteem could have been built up. I would have anxiously anticipated my wedding date instead of dreading it. Fortunately, God can use even my mistakes to conform me to Christ's image, but that's no excuse for exhibiting impatience as I did.

◆ ◆ ◆

> On the positive side, waiting will help one to subject his or her physical drives to the lordship of Christ and thereby develop self-control, which is an important fruit of the Holy Spirit.

Patience is indeed a characteristic of one empowered by the Holy Spirit. So when Christians are involved in sexual activity before marriage, they should realize, in addition to everything else, that they are not living in the power of the Holy Spirit. The fruit of the Spirit is the visible evidence of God at work in someone's life. If that person deliberately chooses to rebel against God, the Spirit is unable to work fully in that person's life and will be hampered as long as the sin is unresolved.

The Spirit and the traits he works into our lives show God's provision for us. When we have self-control, we will have goodness and peace; when we exhibit patience, we will have love and joy. In fact, each time one element of the fruit of the Spirit is evident in us, other elements surface. When the Spirit is at work in our lives, God blesses us in such abundance that we can hardly take it all in.

At the same time, the workings of the Spirit are there to protect us. God keeps us out of trouble when we keep our minds on him, and we have to be thinking about him when we are living in the Spirit.

In other words, the fruit of the Spirit goes against everything our sinful nature would automatically stand for. As fallen people, our immediate reaction is irritation and impatience when things don't go our way. For kindness, gentleness, patience, and the other fruit to be evident, we have to make a conscious choice to react as God would have us react. So when something hits me, rather than fly apart I can say to myself, "Patience. Keep calm. Measure your words carefully. Don't say anything that's not edifying. Remember, you are a witness for Christ in this situation too." That makes me think about God all the time. And the more my mind is on him, the less I stray from him. In this way the working of the Holy Spirit in my life protects me from hurting myself or others.

Young people who are continually striving to be filled with the Spirit will find premarital sex to be less of a temptation. When they are in a position to act out an impatient urge for sex—such as on a date, at an unsupervised party, etc.—they won't have to fight the urge, because patience will be an integral part of their lives. Self-control will be evident in the choices they make. They will have joy and peace, knowing their patience is not only paying off now, but that it also will pay off in the future, and in an even more significant way.

In chapter 17 you will find helpful steps for encouraging your young people in their relationship with Christ, including drawing on the power of the Holy Spirit in their lives.

Provision of the Blessing of Trust
God knows that marriages need to be built on a basic trust factor. Suspicion of a spouse's potential infidelity undermines that trust. Here's what a number of young adults wrote about the element of trust in a relationship:

> I know how difficult it is to stop having sex once it becomes part of your relationship. There is pressure from friends to continue, and society endorses it. But I've already seen how my sexual involvement with my former boyfriend affects my present dating relationship with Scott. Scott feels as if I have betrayed him and he doesn't have as much trust in me as he would like to. Just think—I betrayed God too! For a long time I felt guilty for what I had done, but I finally asked the Lord to forgive me and help me live the way he wants me to.

◆ ◆ ◆

> God introduced me to Mr. Right and we struggled through a fourteen-month engagement to refrain from premarital sex. And at the age of twenty-three, after

three years of marriage, I have never regretted the no's or the reasons for the no's. I firmly believe that waiting until after the "I do's" to experience sex can only enhance the marital relationship. Our doing that established a trust that cannot be equaled. We both loved the Lord and each other so much (even before meeting) that we wanted our first time to be with our partner for life.

◆ ◆ ◆

If you have sexual relations before marriage, you are involved with someone's spouse-to-be. And what if you think you will marry this person? Does that make it all right? No. In 1 Thessalonians 4:3-4, it says: "It is God's will that you should be sanctified: that you should avoid sexual immorality; that each of you should learn to control his own body in a way that is holy and honorable." No matter how much your spouse loves you, we are all human, and lurking somewhere in the back of her mind you will probably find the question, "Was I the first, or has he given in before?"

How can you base a marriage on that kind of doubt? It might never show up until someday it comes out in the middle of an argument. Suddenly there is a great big hole in the relationship.

God's command that we reserve sex for marriage is an expression of his love for us. He wants to protect us from the damaging effect that distrust or suspicion has on a marriage. At the same time he wants to provide us with the most fulfilling sex life possible.

Marriage counselors, therapists, and psychologists tell us that a key factor in producing a fulfilling love, marriage, and sexual relationship is trust. Trust becomes the fertile ground for vulnerability and transparency to develop in the relationship, and these lead to intimacy. Suspicion or distrust works against, or undercuts, intimacy and vulnerability in relationships.

Sexual involvement almost always, and often very subtly, wipes out trust in a relationship. Sex, the way God intended it, calls for 100 percent abandonment to your mate. It doesn't take a genius to realize how distrust prohibits such abandonment. This is what God wants to protect us from.

One person who felt the emptiness of a lack of trust was Gretchen Kurz. A student at San Jose State University, Gretchen talked very candidly in *Mademoiselle* magazine. She entered school, she said, ready for the "decadent life."

◆ ◆ ◆

There I was, well equipped with my No. 2 pencil, student service card, and an adequate supply of birth control pills. But somehow, I missed the boat on the pleasure cruise to carefree, guilt-free sex. Actually, I now believe it's all a myth perpetuated by a lot of disappointed students too afraid to tell the truth. But then again, how are you supposed to admit it's all a crock after you couldn't wait to get out and break all the rules?

Gretchen never doubted that when she got to San Jose State she'd "share" sex. But she discovered "sharing" wasn't all she expected it to be.

◆ ◆ ◆

To put it mildly, "share" was a gross misnomer. My first encounter with Mr. Variety-Is-the-Spice-of-Life left me utterly confused by a number of things. Do I leave now or spend the night? What will I say in the morning? Is it kosher to borrow his bathrobe? Was I any good? He wasn't. Does this mean we've started something somehow permanent? [She discovered it didn't.] To say that I was overcome by guilt would be a lie, but the experience was far from euphoric. The most positive description I could use to label the exchange would be "dull." It was void of emotion, or perhaps any trace of emotion was deftly disguised as avant-garde nonchalance. I soon found this cool and detached approach characteristic of any future encounters.

This lack of emotion not only baffled me, but it also infuriated me. I wanted to know why it existed and why it was so instrumental in the sexual liberation of my college friends. Obviously, it was the all too common basis for an active sex life.

Disturbed, Gretchen began to ask the many men in her life why this detached unemotionalism existed. What was their view of sex? The answers were similar. Sex is "fun and games," "a natural reaction," and "consenting adults and a good time."

"Words like love, share and happy never entered the conversation," she admitted.

She decided to return to her "celibate, but happy, style of life." Some time after making this decision, she talked to a close male friend who was airing his gripes about the free and easy college sex circuit. In describing what he felt was the thinking of a majority of college males, he said:

Most of the times I found myself in bed with someone, I usually wished it never had gotten that far. After I reached a point where I knew I would wind up spending the night with her, it was all downhill. I just went through the motions. There were times when all I wanted was to hurry up and get it over with. I finally stopped messing around when I realized sex is no good unless there is true trust and love involved. Without it, it's just not worth the hassle.

Gretchen concluded her article with these words:

Now, with all this fuss about sexual freedom, it's a little hard to stand up and admit it's not what everyone imagines, especially to an anxious world that refuses to let the subject die. Consequently, here we sit, tight-lipped, and too embarrassed to say we couldn't find it. We can't admit it to the world or, worse yet, to ourselves. Perhaps we could all begin to set the record straight—by saying that without love and trust, "it's just not worth the hassle."[1]

When I was single, I never dreamed how powerfully my dating life years ago would affect my marriage right now. Many people have found painful, negative consequences of premarital sex, which must be dealt with in marriage. Because I waited, I found something great and positive: the blessing of God's provision through trust.

I dated a young woman named Paula when I was in graduate school. We dated for three and a half years and almost got married. Even though we were very compatible and enjoyed and respected each other immensely, the fullness of a love given by God was missing. We finally broke up and continued to be the closest of friends.

Three years later I met Dottie. Not long after she and I were married, Dottie met Paula. They became good friends and started spending a lot of time together. Eventually Paula moved close to our home in California, where her parents and sister also live. We practically became neighbors.

One morning I arrived home from a trip, and Dottie wasn't there. When she returned, she told me she had spent the morning with Paula. She came over, put her arms around me and said, "Honey, I'm sure glad you behaved yourself for three and a half years."

I took a deep breath and asked hesitantly, "Why?"

Dottie responded, "Paula told me this morning that she was so in love with you that there were times she would have done anything, but you never once took advantage of her." Needless to say, there was a big sigh of relief from me. I was profoundly glad I had never pushed Paula in the area of the physical.

Can you imagine what that conversation with Paula meant to my wife? It affirmed, "I can trust my husband!" In an interview Dottie shared this:

> You must build your relationship on trust. I trust Josh to be a good provider for my children. I trust him to be faithful to me. I trust him to be our spiritual leader and to have his own relationship with Christ. And I trust him as the person who is going to take care of our finances.
>
> He can trust me to be a good mother while he's gone. He can trust me with feeding the children properly and nutritiously. As he travels he can trust me not to be spending lots of money or having wild parties. Everything you do, every step you take in a relationship together, has to be built on trust. It is the foundation for your marriage. It is easy to abandon yourself to someone when you trust him.
>
> The reason I totally trust Josh is because he has a trustworthy track record.

Trust is built by consistency and commitment backed up by sacrifice, a sacrifice demonstrated by a desire to meet the needs of the other person, not merely to get our own needs met. It is built by showing love in action. We can trust God because we not only have the spoken message of his love, but we also have tangible evidence of it in his actions. We know he seeks what is best for us. Marriage relationships, as mirrors of spiritual realities, are built in the same way.

As one young writer said:

> The command to wait until marriage to become sexually involved not only protects a person from destroying himself by linking harmful emotions to the sex act, fracturing his inner self, but it also presents him as a gift to his marriage partner. It promotes the greatest fulfillment in sex by paving the way for trust, emotional satisfaction, joy, and passion unthreatened by mental battles. How good and intelligent the Creator is.

Premarital sex lays a foundation of distrust and lack of respect. In stark contrast is mature love, which radiates trust. Don't you yearn for your young people to approach marriage embracing the blessing of trust? It is worth our time and effort to help them say no to premarital sex.

Provision of Jesus to Fill the Void

Many young people get into sex because they feel empty inside. Whether they realize it or not, promiscuous students are looking to their sex partner(s) to fill that void. But it doesn't happen, because God did not design sex to meet a person's deep, inner longings. Jesus does that. And those young people who commit to obey God's Word and wait for sex open themselves to the blessing of Christ's presence filling their emptiness. Here is what one young woman wrote after making that discovery:

> Since becoming a Christian, I have realized that the spiritual emptiness I thought could be filled only by another person could actually be filled only by Jesus Christ. I can feel deep, intimate love without sex. I also see that because the sexual union is so sacred and you do become one with the person, God has reserved it for the sanctity of marriage. Sex is the greatest display of love possible other than dying for someone. It is to be shared only by those who have made the commitment to love each other for better or worse for the rest of their lives. I am very grateful to be forgiven and released from my guilt, and to have a new beginning by being a virgin again in God's eyes. I am grateful for the opportunity to wait this time and share that intimacy only with my husband.

A lifelong marriage relationship between a man and a woman is something to be held in awe. When two people overcome all forces that would drive them apart and devote themselves to mutual edification and giving for life, something very powerful is at work. This relationship, in effect, goes against all that our flesh would have us selfishly pursue. It is a bond of love that defies an egocentric and uncaring world.

But there is a bond of love even greater than that. Most people are not aware of it, either because of ignorance or because of refusal to take part in it. And even many of those who enter this bond do not enjoy it to its fullest.

It is the love that exists when a person repents of his sins, turns to Jesus Christ, and accepts a relationship with him. God calls each person to this relationship. He extends love. The only thing people have to do is respond. They don't have to initiate the relationship.

Once the relationship is established, only we can break the fellowship. God never turns his back on anyone or acts selfishly. He never does anything to harm those he loves—something that can't be said for even the best human relationships.

As young people move into that part of life in which relationships with the opposite sex become important, they may come to feel that those relationships will bring the greatest feeling, the greatest fulfillment, the greatest joy they will ever find. When that turns out not to be true, they may try to increase their search for joy and fulfillment through sex.

But they always come up empty—they always experience a void. They are looking for intimacy in relationships that lack the cornerstone of building intimacy: commitment.

Each person can be fulfilled only by a right relationship with God. We are then loved and accepted as complete persons, faults and all, which gives us security. We don't have to earn God's love. We are free to do what we were created for: to glorify God by doing the work of the Father in ministering to others. This gives us significance. We know we are loved because of who we are, not because of what we do.

Such a knowledge inspires obedience to God's authority, which in turn strengthens our relationship with him. It is a synergistic, growing love, a relationship in which we are complete and fulfilled. God may, of course, provide a mate to love and love us in return. But marriage is not meant to be the goal of a Christian's life. It is icing on the cake.

To understand why a Christian is truly complete in God, we need to take a look at the nature of God and his relationship to man. "God is love," say the Scriptures, but for love to exist, it must have an object. It must love someone. Not even God's love is possible without a recipient. But what is beautiful is the uniqueness of the Trinity. God's need to love someone is satisfied within the Trinity: the Father, Son, and Holy Spirit.

So God did not have to create man in order to love. Instead, he created man so that man could have the blessings of God's love. In other words, he didn't create us in order to receive; he created us in order to give to us. God didn't need us; he wanted us. Let's personalize it. God doesn't need you, but he sure does want you.

Not only did he proclaim his love for his creation, a people who stubbornly turned away from his offer of love, but he also proved his love by sending Christ to redeem us. It was the greatest price that could be paid on behalf of another. It means that each person is of infinite value to God. Each person is worth the life of Jesus. When we realize that, and make it a part of our lives, we live as people of great value. We become aware of being accepted, aware of having security, and aware of our enormous significance in God's eyes.

Adam was complete in his relationship with God. He had all he would ever need. But God gave him icing on the cake because he wanted him to be happier still. Each Christian, having established a personal relationship with the same God whom Adam knew personally, is just as complete as Adam. Every need is met in Christ. So we find our security in a relationship with him. We find our significance in doing all that we do, whether it is mundane or earthshaking, to the glory of God—in carrying out the work of the Father, which is to minister to others.

Why should our young people wait until marriage for sex? Because premarital sex won't bring the fulfillment they are looking for. That fulfillment is in Christ. It is in ministering to others on his behalf that kids will become aware of their significance, of the honor they have of representing the King of kings on earth.

Ultimately, marriage is meant to be a ministry to another person, a one-on-one relationship of commitment and love for the edification of each other to the glory of God, in sickness and in health, "till death do us part." It is worth waiting for. And it is worth the time it takes for us as parents, pastors, or youth leaders to teach, train, and model to our young people God's biblical mandate for sex.

The Blessing of God-ordained Sex

In our "sexually saturated" culture, where worship of "self" has replaced worship of God, the rise in sexual activity among our youth shouldn't surprise us, although it certainly should alarm us. Our current culture bombards our children with antibiblical thinking, proclaiming these self-promoting lies as truths:

- There is nothing more important than the individual. As an individual, I have the right to pursue anything I desire or perceive as beneficial to myself.
- My greatest goal should be my own personal pleasure and satisfaction. No one has the right to take that from me.
- I must constantly guard against others trying to come in and deprive me of my rights to have my needs and desires met.
- I must first love and serve myself if I am to fulfill myself in any meaningful way.
- More is better.
- Instant gratification is my right, regardless of consequences to myself or others.

◆ My physical appearance, comfort, satisfaction, beauty, and health are of primary importance.[2]

If we are to effectively combat this worldly thinking in our children, we must be willing to take a stand for God's truth about sex. Yet as Christians who claim to believe that sex is a gift from God, we seldom discuss the subject openly. When we do, we are often visibly uncomfortable. As a result, our children receive little or no training in biblically based sex education, leaving them wide open to the world's indoctrination on the subject.

The current culture gives our children the message that illicit sex is positive, desirable, and wonderful, but the church, through failure to adequately address the subject, often gives them the message that sex is negative, undesirable, and shameful. If those two contrasting messages are combined with an adolescent's raging hormones, which message is going to be more appealing and believable to a young, impressionable mind? Where is a child most likely to turn to have his or her questions about sex answered? If we believe what we say we believe about the beauty and sanctity of God-ordained, married sex, we must be willing to clearly and practically impart that truth to our children. To effectively do that, we must:

◆ Emphasize God as Creator, helping our children understand that God has a specific plan and purpose for each of our lives.

◆ Teach our children that because God created us, we belong to him; therefore, we are responsible to fulfill his requirements and purposes for our lives.

◆ Help our children understand that sin is both physical and spiritual; that it is not only what we do but who we are.

◆ Model through our own words and actions that everything we do is an act of worship, either toward God or toward someone or something else; that which we worship will set the agenda for every area of our lives.

◆ Teach our children that however hard it may seem at the time, there is only one right choice, and that is to do things God's way rather than our own.

◆ Enable our children to grasp the truth that our ultimate goal is to conform to God's will, to yield our agenda to his, even at the cost of personal pleasure.

◆ Impress upon our children that salvation through Jesus is more than escaping hell; it is the freedom from following our own destructive, sinful natures so that we may live under the control of the Holy Spirit.[3]

Teaching and modeling to our children that only Jesus can fill the void in our lives is both time- and energy-consuming. But planting and cultivating the seeds of moral purity in their young lives is the only way to protect them from the onslaught of the world's perverted view of sex and all of the destructive ramifications that go with it.

◆ ◆ ◆

There is one more reason our young people need to consider for saying no to premarital sex. It is the devastatingly injurious lie of safe sex being foisted on them through the media and even the educational system. In the next chapter we will investigate God's protection from "safe sex"—which is at best only "safer sex"—and the security of his provision of abstinence.

CHAPTER 15

WHY "SAFE SEX" ISN'T SAFE

AMY STEPHENS WRITES, "A doctor friend of mine called last week. He shared with me that his day consisted of telling four women they had an incurable sexually transmitted disease. His next comments hit me: 'I spend hours in surgery treating incurable STDs and they want me to throw a piece of latex at my seventeen-year-old and say "it's safe"?'"[1]

Another physician, Dr. John R. Diggs, serves as medical consultant to the Family Research Council. In his article, "Why the Sex Experts Are Wrong," Dr. Diggs presents a hypothetical case to illustrate the fallout from one of the great lies being perpetrated on our culture—that "safe sex" is really safe.

❖ ❖ ❖

Jenny, a sixteen-year-old girl, follows her doctor's, her teacher's, and her parents' advice and uses condoms. She contracts chlamydia, HSV, and HPV. In most Western countries, at any given time, 10 percent of all fifteen- to nineteen-year-olds have chlamydia. In America, 20 percent of adults are seropositive for HSV type 2, and there are an estimated 40 million cases of HPV.

What will happen to Jenny? There is an 80 percent chance that she will not know that she has chlamydia. She may have it for decades. It will damage her reproductive system, possibly rendering her sterile. Maybe she will develop pelvic inflammatory disease and require hospitalization. Maybe she will experience an ectopic pregnancy resulting in the child's death and the loss of one fallopian tube, or severe hemorrhaging and possibly her own death if she does not seek prompt medical care.

The herpes may cause painful flare-ups that cause her to miss school or work, or require medicine that costs $150 for each treatment, which could be as often as every month. If the chlamydia has not rendered her sterile, there is a one to four percent chance that she will pass the infection to her newborn during childbirth, placing the child's life in danger. Furthermore, Jenny will be contagious for the rest of her life.

Jenny may consider herself lucky if she gets only genital warts from HPV. Some HPV patients get abnormal changes on their cervixes, sometimes picked up by Pap smears. Up to 40 percent of Pap tests are reported as "normal," even when cancerous or precancerous changes are present. If the changes are discovered early, she will be subject only to painful biopsies, then surgical procedures or laser burning to destroy the cancerous cells. If the changes are found late, she may suffer a hysterectomy. Otherwise, she may be one of the 300,000 women who die each year from cervical cancer.

A healthy young woman obediently followed unhealthy advice from the people she trusted most. Teens want truth, but the prestigious "safe sex" advocates—including the American Medical Association, SIECUS (the Sexuality Information and Education Council of the United States), and Planned Parenthood—are offering sugarcoated toxic messages instead.

Nobody can guarantee that someone who follows all the rules in life is going to have a good outcome. But doctors have a responsibility to inform patients of what they do know, and of what is reasonably foreseeable. They do know that condom-centered "safe sex" is bad advice. HSV, HPV, and chlamydia laugh at latex.

If someone had told Jenny the truth, known even before the invention of the microscope, antibiotics, or the condom: "Jenny, your body is not designed to be shared with any willing condom carrier. Sex within the context of marriage with your spouse, who also waited for you, is the only 'safe sex.'"[2]

Diggs's story may be hypothetical, but sadly it is based on fact. The "safe sex" message of our culture encourages a false sense of security in our young people. They rationalize, "I want to have sex, but I don't want to get pregnant or catch a disease. So I will do what my health class teacher recommends. I will practice safe sex by using a condom."

The only problem is this: Safe sex isn't safe. At best, safe sex is only "safer sex." And yet condoms are often recommended in schools, even distributed in some. Physicians warn their patients, "If you're going to have premarital sex, at least protect yourself with a condom." Even agencies such as the Public Health Service state: "Although refraining from intercourse with infected persons remains the most effective strategy for preventing human immunodeficiency virus (HIV) infection and other sexually transmitted diseases (STDs), the Public Health Service also has recommended condom use as part of its strategy."[3]

These warnings make about as much sense to me as any of the following warnings:

- Russian roulette is potentially fatal, so you should never play it. But if you just have to play, we recommend that you only put one bullet in the cylinder.
- Driving the wrong way on a busy freeway can get you killed, so it's best to stay on the right side of the road. But if you just have to try it, we recommend that you flash your lights and sound your horn.
- Jumping off a fifty-story building can be hazardous to your health, so don't do it. But when you just can't fight off the urge, we recommend that you at least flap your arms on the way down to slow your fall.

These warnings are meant to be totally ridiculous, of course, to illustrate the point. When condom use is peddled among our youth under the heading of safe sex, they tend to believe condoms can keep them totally safe from pregnancy and disease. The recommendation of condoms comes across to many of them as approval of premarital sex and safety from harm. As we shall see, leaving out one little "r"—the difference between *safe* sex and *safer* sex—can spell disaster for some of our kids.

Our young people should wait for sex until marriage because "safe sex" won't keep all of them safe from pregnancy or disease. God desires to protect our kids from this potentially damaging sense of false security and provide for them ironclad sexual safety and security in his design for abstinence.

THE DANGERS OF CONDOM FAILURE

The concept of "safe sex" isn't new. It dates back about half a century when the birth control pill was introduced. Men and women everywhere sensed a freedom to enjoy their sexual relationships without the nagging fear of getting pregnant.

The medical experts never dreamed that the freedom the pill would provide also would usher in a devastating epidemic of sexually transmitted diseases. In addition, many sexually active adolescents and adults don't realize that, although contraceptives such as sterilization or the pill can protect against pregnancy, they do nothing to prevent STDs. Condoms, the only method of birth control that also helps prevent STDs, are certainly not foolproof. Even when used correctly and consistently (which is seldom the case, particularly with adolescents), they succeed only in cutting the risks, not eliminating them. Condoms may also give a false sense of security by discouraging once-infected men and women from changing their lifestyle in order to prevent reinfection.

One of the problems with the "safe sex" programs currently taught in our schools is that they give a false sense of security regarding the prevention of pregnancy and STDs. Many experts agree that condoms in particular are a dangerous way to practice "safe sex." Why? Because they are not foolproof. They leak. They rupture. And some viruses are so microscopically tiny that they can find their way through the pores in condom material.

Dr. Susan Weller, associate professor of Preventative Medicine and Community Health at the University of Texas, states: "The public at-large may not understand the difference between 'condoms may reduce risk of' and 'condoms will prevent' HIV infection. It is a disservice to encourage the belief that condoms will prevent sexual transmission of HIV."[4]

A lot of people believe that a condom is a safe shield against AIDS. That belief is not grounded in fact. In 1993, Dr. Weller examined the results of ten studies involving the effectiveness of condoms in preventing the spread of HIV/AIDS. She found an average failure rate of 31 percent.[5]

Consider the following data on the effectiveness—or more correctly, the *ineffectiveness*—of condoms:

- According to a 1993 report from the Medical Institute for Sexual Health, "A more complete review of the scientific data [regarding condom failure rate] shows condom failure to range between 0 percent and 31 percent. . . . Condoms only reduced HIV transmission by 69 percent. . . . The resultant 31 percent failure in prevention means many HIV infections, all resulting in premature death. . . . Medical studies confirm that condoms do not offer much, if any, protection in the transmission of chlamydia and human papillomavirus."[6]
- A March 1991 edition of the *American College of Obstetricians and Gynecologists Newsletter* referred to condoms as "an antiquated system of birth control," going on to say, "Condoms often do not prevent sexu-

ally transmitted disease. Each year 25 percent of women whose partners use condoms for contraception get pregnant. . . . The FDA allows
condom manufacturers to market condoms that have three or fewer
holes per 1000 condoms. . . . Condoms rupture about 7 percent of the
time during use."[7]

◆ "[Condom] effectiveness may be as low as 45 percent or as high as 82
percent," said Susan Weller, Ph.D., author of the report and associate
professor of Preventative Medicine and Community Health at University
of Texas Medical Branch at Galveston (UTMB). Dr. Weller's report,
published in the June 1993 (No. 36-12) issue of *Social Science and
Medicine,* is an analysis of data from eleven studies, published prior to
July 1990 and involving a total of 593 partners of HIV infected people.[8]

◆ Approximately 40 out of 100 couples purchasing a condom in the U.S.
would experience a condom failure due to leakage or rupture. . . . *In vivo*
tests, though, report much higher rates due to rupture and slippage.[9]

◆ Even Planned Parenthood acknowledges that analysis of data from the
1988 National Survey of Family Growth—corrected for the under-
reporting of abortion—reveals that contraceptive failure during the first
year of use remains a serious problem in the United States.[10]

◆ One hundred fifty per 1,000 couples actually using condoms apparently experience an unplanned pregnancy during the first twelve
months of use.[11]

◆ Planned Parenthood studies show condom failure of 18 percent among
young people for preventing pregnancy, and upwards of 30 percent
failure among certain minorities. Pregnancy can only occur during a
few days per month, and HIV and other STD infections can happen
anytime, so condoms offer even less protection against HIV and other
STDs.[12]

◆ According to Dr. Henry J. Redd, a pediatrician, "Condoms have an
annual 18 percent failure rate for all teens, and the failure rate jumps
to 36 percent annually among young, unmarried minority women.
The annual failure rates of condoms extended through high school
means that a promiscuous fourteen-year-old girl has an 87 percent
chance of becoming pregnant before she graduates. . . . Yet, the center-
piece of the 'safe sex' message is condom use. Clearly, 'safe sex' is a
myth."[13]

- The failure rate for the condom in preventing AIDS is as high as 31 percent with a disease that is 100 percent deadly. That is a long way from being safe![14]
- Approximately 40 out of 100 couples purchasing a condom in the U.S. would experience a condom failure due to leakage or rupture.[15]
- A woman has a 20 percent chance per year of becoming pregnant and an almost 100 percent chance over a period of years of developing an STD infection even if she uses condoms.[16]
- A draft government report says there's insufficient evidence that condoms guard against sexually transmitted diseases other than HIV and gonorrhea. . . . The National Institutes of Health report says "research published so far is too flimsy to draw definite conclusions about the effectiveness of the latex male condom in reducing the spread of chlamydia, trichomoniasis, and human papillomavirus, which is linked to cervical cancer."[17]
- Condoms will not protect your child from HPV.[18]

Notice that the failure rate for condoms in these studies hovers at around 30 percent. Let's put this in human terms. For every ten students who believe the safe-sex message and have sex using a condom, three of them will experience condom failure. The condom will break or fall off during intercourse. So for three students out of ten, the sexual episode is not safe — or even safer; they are open and vulnerable to pregnancy and infection. These kids would have a better chance of surviving Russian roulette with one bullet in a six-shot revolver — only a 17 percent "failure" rate.

The combination of condoms and medication is purported to prevent or cure sexually transmitted disease. The current epidemic of sexually transmitted diseases proves this assumption to be untrue.

Contrary to this assertion, modern science finds that there are several serious diseases for which condoms provide no protection, and others for which condoms provide markedly limited protection, which is insufficient to qualify them as "safe." Furthermore, a series of diseases has arisen for which there is no cure. The only way to prevent incurable disease is to avoid the disease. The only effective avoidance is to refrain from sex until marriage and marry someone who has done likewise — practiced abstinence.

Dr. John Diggs, medical consultant for the Family Research Council, outlines these findings on the issue.

◆ ◆ ◆

Multiple investigators find that condoms do not reliably accomplish their chief goal in teenagers. In the first year of use, between four and six in a class of twenty-five women will become pregnant! Hardly the number for safety. Even their secondary use, STD prevention, is a failure. Condoms are the cornerstone of the 'safe sex' approach. The truth is that the three most common sexually transmitted diseases are transmitted from one person to another at about the same rate as if no condoms were used.

The most prominent sources of sexual information, Planned Parenthood and the Centers for Disease Control and Prevention, have decided that it is better to hide these flaws from teens. Dr. Diggs continues:

There is a significant reduction in the transmission of HIV and gonorrhea when condoms are used for every single act of intercourse. First, consistent and proper use is the exception, not the rule. Second, even then, tragically, some will still be infected. In the case of gonorrhea, this is just inconvenient. On the other hand, HIV is a uniformly fatal disease. Although death can take years, death will surely come. In the meantime, the infected person can infect untold others. So even a small percentage of transmission of a fatal disease is disastrous.

Genital herpes (HSV), human papillomavirus (HPV), and chlamydia infect millions of Americans each year. The first two are incurable. HSV is a lifelong disease which is periodically painful. A mother can infect her newborn child, causing devastating neurologic complications, and possibly death. HPV causes cervical abnormalities which require surgical procedures on tens of thousands of women every year in the United States alone. Worldwide, the death rate is towering because of less preventative health care availability.

The irony is that this is all the result of people treating sex like trading cards—exchange with whoever's got something you like. These problems are totally preventable when sex is limited to committed marital relationships.

Naturally, one wonders why organizations which are charged with protecting our health have chosen not to make teens aware of the failings of condoms. The answer, I believe, is because they fear petitioning the public for the "hard" answer—change in behavior. Condoms are the easy answer. They are cheap, available, and portable. Those characteristics don't overcome the fact that they don't work. A paradigm shift is necessary, recognition that what God says about sex is really true—it should be reserved for married persons. The hard answer is for public health sources to recommend the development of real character and the making of better choices to curtail this epidemic.[19]

It is not completely clear why HSV, HPV, and chlamydia so effectively breech the barrier provided by condoms. In part, this is due to the fact that HSV and HPV are spread through skin-to-skin contact, in areas that are not covered by condoms. Then the organisms can migrate to other areas where they do their damage.

It cannot be overstated: the transmission rate for these diseases is as if condoms were not used at all. Condom promoters will suggest that they rarely fail by saying, "Well, they aren't perfect." Just the opposite is true: They are perfect—perfectly useless for these three diseases.

Even for HIV and gonorrhea, the failure rate among teens is too high to recommend their use. Teens don't even regularly make up their beds. Why expect perfect condom use? When the stakes are this high, parents are not doing their kids any favors by stocking their drawers with condoms. This strategy has historically produced a rise in pregnancies and STDs.

Flawed "Protection"

Here is the straight story in a nutshell: Condoms provide only limited protection against sexually transmitted diseases. Though they may be commended to us and our children as implements of safe sex, they are not totally safe.

A prospective study using two brands of condoms found that of 405 condoms used for intercourse, 7.9 percent either broke during intercourse or withdrawal or slipped off during intercourse; none of these events were related to condom brand, past condom use, or use of additional lubricant. Of the remaining condoms, 7.2 percent slipped off during withdrawal; slippage was not related to condom brand or past use of condoms, but it was significantly higher when additional lubricant was used.[20]

C. Michael Roland, editor of *Rubber Chemistry and Technology*, stated:

> There exists direct evidence of voids in the rubber comprising condoms. Electron micrographs reveal voids 5 microns in size (50 times larger than the [HIV] virus),

while fracture mechanics analyses, sensitive to the largest flaws present, suggest inherent flaws as large as the 50 microns (500 times the size of the virus). When recourse is made to condoms for the prevention of HIV infection, my personal recommendation is that at least two be worn during sexual activity.[21]

The pictures below graphically illustrate the relative size difference between human sperm and several sexually transmitted viruses. Can you see how a microscopic flaw in one condom could allow passage of one or more of these viruses?

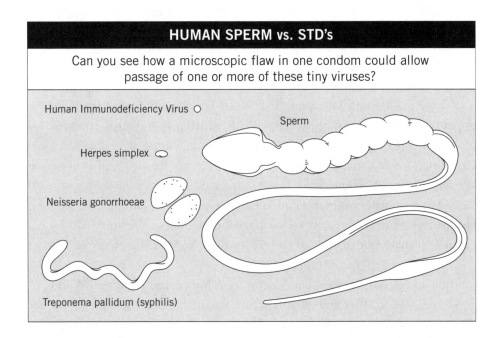

Condoms provide little protection against bacterial vaginosis and HPV (the most common STD)."[22] Likewise, Michael Campion, director of gynecologic endoscopy, Graduate Hospital, Philadelphia, said, "Condoms are useless in preventing HPV transmission because the virus is spread by cells that are shed onto the scrotum, which then come in contact with vulvar skin." Published studies have failed to demonstrate that the male latex condom protects women from HPV infection.[23] A 1995 study showed that "of 162 women who had sex with HIV positive men, thirty-one developed HIV in spite of the fact that they always used condoms."[24]

The Health Risks

The following paragraphs were taken from an on-line article entitled "Do Condoms and Seat Belts Promote Risk Taking?"

◆ ◆ ◆

Seat belts and condoms are two safety measures promoted to reduce risk and save lives. But in Saturday's issue of *The Lancet,* three British researchers pose an interesting question: Is it possible that some people using these safety devices take new risks, such as driving faster or having sex with more partners, to compensate for an increased feeling of safety?

In addition, the researchers suggest that such behavioral compensation parallels the increased degree to which men and women who choose to use condoms may also choose to engage in sex with more partners, or take part in risky behavior with regards to the transmission of sexually transmitted diseases (STDs).[25]

These researchers have a point. The safe-sex concept has received greater impetus among our young people with the distribution of free condoms by schools, health agencies, clinics, and physicians. Along with the condoms comes step-by-step, graphic instruction on how to use them. I heard about one Western university where the freshman mixer at the start of the school year included a game where students had to practice putting a condom on a banana. Health officials and educators are saying to kids in effect, "We know you are going to be sexually active. At least protect yourself. And to make sure you do, take these condoms with our compliments."

But studies have shown that condom distribution has backfired. With condoms so easy to obtain, some sexually active students are becoming even more active, increasing the frequency of sex and/or engaging more partners. And kids who previously had not been sexually active are emboldened to experiment. A study of adolescents taking part in a three-year condom promotion experiment in Switzerland showed that the proportion of girls under the age of seventeen engaging in sexual activity increased by almost two-thirds—from 36 to 57 percent.[26]

Dr. Brian Morris reported in the *Canadian Family Physician:* "Condoms are widely promoted for preventing sexually transmitted diseases, with an implicit message that a properly used condom will ensure that you are safe from STDs. A literature review shows that little solid evidence supports this belief."[27] The availability of condoms and hands-on training lulls our kids into a false sense of security and bravado. Consider the following report documenting the outcome of condom availability programs in high schools located in San Francisco, St. Paul, and Dallas:

> San Francisco: Even though students were exposed to "graphic demonstrations" of proper condom use, the Balboa High School condom availability program turned out to be a colossal failure. The percentage of sexually active students using condoms almost doubled, but, despite that supposedly positive change in student sexual behavior, the school's overall pregnancy rate increased by one-fourth.
>
> Before the condom experiment began, 37 percent of the school's female students were sexually active, and the annual pregnancy rate was 5.9 percent per year. . . . When the experiment ended two years later, 46 percent of the school's female students were sexually active, and the annual pregnancy rate among these girls was 16 percent, so the school's overall pregnancy rate was 7.4 percent per year.
>
> With an increase in pregnancy, it can be assumed that there was a similar increase in student exposure to HIV infection and other sexually transmitted diseases.
>
> St. Paul and Dallas: In two school-based programs that dispensed condoms . . . the results were even worse than those in San Francisco. Specifically, a St. Paul program that was supposed to reduce annual teenage births actually caused them to spiral upward by one-third (from 22 per 1,000 to 29 per 1,000). An inner-city Dallas school that distributed condoms ended up with an 11.2 percent overall pregnancy rate, 47 percent higher than the 7.6 percent overall pregnancy rate found in an almost identical Dallas school that did not implement such a program.
>
> At the end of the two-year experiment, 80 percent of the girls in the school that dispensed condoms were sexually active, and the annual pregnancy rate was 11.2 percent per year. . . . By contrast, only 76 percent of the girls in the school that did not dispense condoms had ever engaged in sex, and the annual pregnancy rate among these girls was only 10 percent, so the school's overall pregnancy rate was only 7.6 percent per year.
>
> It is folly to believe that dispensing condoms to teenagers might work better if accompanied by expert counseling on how to use condoms without mishap. . . . Efforts to bring about effective condom use through intensive counseling have proved uniformly unsuccessful, even when the persons being counseled are adult females.[28]

It bears repeating: The only true "safe sex" is abstinence until marriage.

DOES VIRGINITY EQUAL ABSTINENCE?

A 1998 study by the Centers for Disease Control and Prevention discovered that "nearly 52 percent of high school students are virgins."[29] Some young people may believe they are abstinent because they are virgins. However, one 1996 study reported in the *American Journal of Public Health* found a discrepancy in the definition of these terms.

The study found that 47 percent of "adolescents were virgins (42 percent of male adolescents and 53 percent of female adolescents). Of those who were virgins, 29 percent and 31 percent reported that during the prior year they had engaged in heterosexual masturbation of a partner and masturbation by a partner, respectively. The corresponding rates for heterosexual fellatio with ejaculation, cunnilingus, and anal intercourse were nine percent, ten percent, and one percent. . . . Few high school-aged virgins engaged in anal intercourse, but many engaged in other genital sexual activities." The study concluded that "we must avoid the tendency to think of adolescents as sexually active or not sexually active based on their virginity status alone."[30]

One of the reasons it is so important to clarify and teach the meaning of true abstinence is that virgins can contract STDs. It is possible to be a virgin and yet, by not practicing true abstinence, still contract a sexually transmitted disease.

These sorts of consequences and studies reaffirm the importance of stressing the total-abstinence-until-marriage message, showing it to be the only way to fully ensure protection against STDs. In addition, the abstinence message is needed because it works and because, apart from sex within marriage, it is God's plan for all humanity. Emphasizing God's moral standards to our young people is the only responsible thing we can do. Without those standards, they are easily susceptible to all the destructive and devastating consequences of premarital sex.

If the whole story [about sex] were told, teens would hear about the ineffectiveness of condoms in protecting against AIDS (up to a 31 percent failure rate). Telling the whole story from beginning to end would also require educating teens about the emotional effects of premarital sex. It cannot be overemphasized that there is no condom for the heart.[31]

TRULY SAFE SEX

The only safe sex today is a monogamous relationship between two faithfully monogamous individuals. In virtually every survey ever taken, it has been proven that "only true abstinence (abstinence chosen as a lifestyle which avoids penetrative sex, genital contact, or outercourse) is 100 percent effective against both pregnancy and sexually transmitted disease."[32] "True abstinence, as defined by the Medical Institute for Sexual Health, is a lifestyle of commitment to save sex for a single, special, lifelong relationship. This lifestyle does not have a failure rate of contraception and condoms."[33]

Clearly the healthiest sexual behavior for adolescents is sexual abstinence. Abstinence until marriage when coupled with sexual fidelity within marriage eliminates—not merely reduces—the risk of nonmarital pregnancy and sexually transmitted infection.

The Medical Institute defines sexual abstinence as "the calculated decision and deliberate action to refrain from sexual activity." Sexual activity is "any activity that involves intentional contact for the purpose of sexual arousal." Sexual activity, then, includes sexual intercourse, oral sex, mutual masturbation, and other purposeful sexual touching.

Recent increases in the numbers of young people who are virginal indicate that sexual abstinence is not just healthy—it is achievable. Abstaining from sexual activity is more than a moral or religious issue—it is an issue of personal and public health.[34]

Provision of Virginity

Although in the past younger Americans have had more permissive attitudes about premarital sex than the general population, that discrepancy is lessening as the abstinence message becomes more widely accepted. In Atlanta, Georgia, a local nonprofit agency called Families First has placed signs on billboards along the interstates proclaiming, "Virgin: Teach your kid it's not a dirty word." They are also running similar commercials on television during shows popular with children ages nine to thirteen.[35]

Many believe that messages like these are beginning to have an impact across the nation. Here are several more indications:

- The results of a 1994 poll, asking more than 1,200 teens and adults what they thought of "several high profile athletes [who] are saying in public that they have abstained from sex before marriage and are telling teens to do the same," showed that 72 percent of the twelve- to seventeen-year-olds and 78 percent of the adults said they agreed with the message. In addition, 44 percent of those under eighteen said that teens need to hear more about abstinence. In fact, of 143,000 adolescents surveyed, 82 percent wanted to know how to say "no" and still keep a friend.[36]

◆ Sixty-eight percent of the 983 adults included in a 1991 survey believed that premarital sex among teens (fourteen to sixteen years) is "always wrong."[37]

◆ According to a 1992 review of several sex surveys, the proportion of young adults (eighteen to twenty-five years) who believe that premarital sex is "always wrong" has risen six percent since the mid-1970s.[38]

◆ Sixty-seven percent of the 585 married people included in a 1994 survey said they believe "being a virgin when you get married is a good idea."[39]

◆ When asked by a 1991 Gallup poll to assess some "changes that took place in the '60s and '70s," 56 percent said that "more acceptance of premarital sex" had been a "bad thing."[40]

Furthermore, a 1995 study of more than 500 high schoolers showed that 62 percent of sexually experienced girls and 54 percent of all teens who had experienced sex at least once said they "should have waited."[41] An earlier survey in 1994 had similar results, finding that of the teens who have had sex, more than half wish they had waited. The survey also found that "teen sexual activity is declining—36 percent of high schoolers report having had intercourse compared to 54 percent of the same age group in a 1990 study."[42] A 1996 report found that even among those teens who had previously had sex, 25 percent were currently abstinent.[43]

Based on five school-based surveys, the Centers for Disease Control and Prevention found:

◆ Fifty percent of teenagers reported ever having sex in 1999, down from 54 percent in 1991.

◆ Sixteen percent said they'd had four or more partners, down from 19 percent.

◆ Eight percent had sex before age thirteen, down from 10 percent.[44]

According to two 1996 studies, more teens are now remaining virgins:

Males (15-19)[45]		Females (15-19)[46]	
1990	38.6 percent	1990	45 percent
1995	45 percent	1995	50 percent

Abstinence until marriage, followed by mutual monogamy within marriage, is God's perfect plan for safe sex. It is his loving provision for us and our children. It may not be popular in many circles, but it works, as illustrated by the following story shared with me by a friend:

A local school board invited parents of their high school students in to discuss their sex education program. One of the couples commented after the initial presentation, "There isn't enough emphasis on abstinence."

The speaker made fun of them and everyone else there laughed.

A few moments later, there was a break for rolls and coffee. This couple sensed they would not be welcome to mix with the rest of those present, so they stayed in their places.

Following the break, the leader said, "Please look on the back of your name tags. One of them has a flower."

The person with the flower raised his hand.

Then the leader said, "Will those who shook hands with this man please stand?" Half did.

Then he asked, "Will those who shook hands with those standing please stand?" Nearly everyone else did . . . everyone except the couple who advocated teaching abstinence.

Then the leader said, "The person with the flower on his name tag represented someone with a sexually transmitted disease. Now, all of you have the same sexually transmitted disease. That's how swiftly it can spread."

The couple who advocated abstinence said, "We didn't have a relationship with the rest of you. We don't have the sexually transmitted disease in your illustration. We advocate abstinence. We accept your illustration and rest our case."[47]

◆ ◆ ◆

In this section we have considered a number of reasons why young people should say no to premarital sex. In many ways, abstinence for our kids is a matter of life and death. But it's one thing to agree to that and quite another to convince our kids. In the final section of this book we will explore several positive strategies to encourage our young people to make the vital commitment to wait for sex until marriage and to help them keep that commitment.

PART FOUR

HOW TO HELP OUR KIDS WAIT FOR SEX

◆ ◆ ◆

CHAPTER 16

DEVELOP A NURTURING RELATIONSHIP WITH KIDS

HOW CAN WE HELP our young people resist the cultural riptide that would pull them into premarital sex? In this section we will consider several practical strategies. But it all starts at home. And I couldn't put it better than two students who expressed their concern to me in writing:

> I think it's time kids get the love they need at home, instead of in the backseat of an old Chevy.

◆ ◆ ◆

> Parents need to wake up to the fact that if they don't show love to their kids, their kids will find love somewhere else—which might lead into premarital sex.

The first critical step in safeguarding your kids against involvement in sex is a strong love bond in the home, both between Dad and Mom and between parent and child. The prototype of the love God offers us should be found in the family. God established the family as a way of representing his image. Yet when families fight or break up and children feel a lack of love at home, the image and understanding of God's love grows weaker. God desires the family to point a child to the source of perfect love, God himself.

A Christian's relationship with God is based on trust; a child needs to grow up knowing nothing but trust in his or her parents. A Christian has security in a relationship with the Father; a child finds his or her security in the home. Just as with a child of God, children love their parents in response to the love the parents first have for them.

That is how it should be. When the image of God in the family breaks down, there is a tremendous price to be paid. For example, consider Dakota, a sixteen-year-old girl whose parents are caught up in their careers and activities. Day-to-day life is hectic and harried. Mom and Dad spend little time nurturing their marriage or investing themselves in their daughter's life and activities. Dakota feels left out, ignored, and alone. So when Bjorn, a twenty-year-old clerk at the local market asks her out, Dakota is bowled over by the attention. It's not long before Bjorn gets what he wants—sex—and leaves the girl pregnant.

Dakota now faces the great pain and disadvantages of becoming a teenage mom. And her baby also faces many potential risks. One extensive study found that "males born to teen mothers (defined as seventeen and younger) grow up to be 2.7 times more likely to commit crimes than the sons of women who wait until age twenty to have their first child."[1] Michael Dye, director of counseling programs at Bethel House and Santa Barbara Rescue Mission, believes much of the reason for those findings is that "teenage mothers are more likely to be single, dysfunctional, and addicted. They don't have the ability to give and receive love. We learn nurturing from our mothers, but teenage mothers haven't learned to love themselves."

Dakota's child likely will grow up without a father, which becomes another complication. Dye also noted that fathers instill in children "a sense of identity, purpose and goals."[2] Without mothers capable of showing love or fathers present to give a needed sense of identity, purpose, and goals, it's easy to see why sons of unmarried teenage mothers are more likely to drift into a life of crime. In most cases, the heartache could be avoided if the parents provided a strong love bond at home.

The positive impact of a loving home on a child's sexual behavior has been well documented:

- ◆ An ADD Health Study . . . found that higher grades, the presence of religious identity, and a sense of connectedness with his or her school and parents were all associated with increased rates of sexual abstinence.[3]
- ◆ Research demonstrates the importance of the parent-child relationship in influencing choices young people make about sexual activity. When

adolescents feel that they have a good relationship with their parent or parents, they are more likely to remain abstinent and/or delay the onset of sexual debut. In addition, if adolescents engage in sexual activity, they are more likely to have fewer sexual partners and less frequent intercourse. Studies also show that many parental factors contribute to help teens make healthy choices, such as: strong parent-child relationships, attachment to parents, and parental support.[4]

◆ "We know from studies that close relationships between parents and their children over many years reduce sexual risks," said Sarah Brown, director of the Washington, D.C., National Campaign to Prevent Teen Pregnancy.[5]

As parents, we need to spend more time with our children, no matter the cost. Perhaps we should consider the time spent away from our children when we choose the location for our next home. Perhaps a shorter drive to work is worth more to your children than a more comfortable house. Perhaps a promotion that requires a parent to be away frequently from his or her family may not be worth accepting. If you have a teen or preteen at home, is that second income really needed? Those are tough questions, but it is time we parents begin giving high priority to our relationships with our children. Be aware that

◆ if our kids can't talk to us, they will talk to their peers.
◆ if we don't spend time with them, they will spend more time with their peers.
◆ if they don't have intimacy at home, they will seek it among their peers.
◆ if they don't get hugs from dad, they will get hugs from their peers.
◆ if we won't listen to them, their peers will.
◆ teens respond to relationships. That is why they are so responsive to their peers.

A PARENT AND CHILD CONNECTION EQUALS REDUCED SEXUAL INVOLVEMENT

Danny was a bright Christian teenager who had come to me for counseling. "Sometimes I feel so alone, like no one cares. My folks live in their own world and I live in mine." He looked up and gazed past me as he spoke more slowly. "It didn't always seem to be this way. I know it sounds crazy, but I want them to leave me alone, and yet, I want to be part of their lives. Most of the time, they do leave me alone and it gets pretty lonely."[6]

It is this sense of feeling alienated from family, a lack of relationship, that makes young people extremely susceptible to sexual involvement. Yet I'm convinced it is not sex they are seeking.

If I were asked to name the number-one contributing factor to the adolescent sexuality crisis, at the top of my list would be adolescent alienation brought on by parent inattentiveness. If you want to insulate your child from the many sexual pressures, develop a close, open relationship of mutual respect and love. Establishing sexual prohibitions and rules with a relationship often leads to rebellion. But rules within the context of a loving parent-child relationship generally lead to a positive response. The thesis is: As parents provide the proper emotional, spiritual, and psychological stability for their child in a loving relationship, closeness will increase and temptation to seek intimacy through sexual involvement will decrease.

There are five elements that I would like to share that may help you develop a closer, healthier parent-child relationship. Applying these relational building blocks goes a long way toward avoiding adolescent alienation.

Communicate Your Acceptance.

A child needs to be convinced that no matter what happens, no matter what he or she does, our acceptance and love will never waver. This acceptance will give our children the sense of security which they so desperately need, especially in today's world.

Sometimes parents offer performance-based or conditional acceptance. As long as the kids perform as their parents require, they will accept them. But if the children fail, the parents' love and acceptance is temporarily withdrawn.

One way to communicate unconditional acceptance is to praise *effort* more than *success*. The crucial question is not did your child win a sporting event? earn an A in school? or receive a standing ovation for a dramatic performance? Rather, did your child do the best he or she could do? When our son, Sean, was in soccer as a boy, I would take him out for ice cream after every hard-played game, whether he scored a goal or not. When I praised him for his play, I talked more about his effort than I did the number of goals he scored. In this way I hoped to demonstrate that I accepted him on the basis of who he is, not what he accomplished.

Lavish Them with Appreciation.

Expressing appreciation for who your young person is gives him or her a sense of significance. Kids need to know that their parents appreciate them for who they are. Yet many adolescents, especially the kids I talk to, feel that their parents are always finding fault with them, pointing out what they do wrong, bugging them to clean up their rooms, take out the trash, and so forth. As our kids were growing up, Dottie and I made a conscious effort to find things our children did that were worthy of praise. We had to work at making this a habit. Our motto was: Try to catch them doing something good. Look for the good things your child is doing, and when you find something, be quick to express appreciation.

Be honest with your appreciation. Most kids can detect insincerity in a heartbeat. Don't fake appreciation just because you feel you have to find something to praise. If you look closely, you should be able to find plenty of good things your kids are saying and doing for which you can express genuine appreciation.

Be Available to Your Kids.

When you make yourself available to your kids, it gives them a sense of importance and worth. Simply put, if you spend time with your children, they will feel important because they perceive themselves as a priority in your life. And a child yearns to know that this is the case. Being available to your young person will also bring you rewards in the future. As my wise wife says, "If we spend time with our kids now, they will spend time with us later. If we show an interest in them now, they will show an interest in us later."

As parents, we have many demands on our time, and the kids seem to be going in twenty different directions at once. It is largely out of this concern that the concept of "quality time" developed. The idea is that you don't have to spend a lot of time with your child (quantity) in order to be a good parent, as long as the time you do spend is "quality" time. While I agree that we need to spend quality time with our kids, I also am convinced that there simply is no substitute for spending quantity time with our kids. Making ourselves available will communicate to them that they are important to us—a key ingredient to avoiding adolescent alienation.

Here are just a few ideas for making and spending time with your young people. Allow them to stay up an hour later than usual every so often and spend that time with them with no distractions. Take the phone off the hook. Talk, play games, wrestle on the floor, watch a TV program or video together, or whatever. The idea is that this is a special occasion, and they have your undivided attention.

Ask your young person to go with you when you need to run errands, and leave the car radio off. This is a good time to talk, and it's also an opportunity for you to model the attitudes and behavior you want to develop in your youth.

You are probably familiar with progressive dinners, where you go to a different house for each course of a meal. How about a progressive dinner with your young person at different fast-food restaurants? Or try going to the mall together, sitting on a bench in a busy area, and watching the shoppers go by. Pick out the funniest people, the happiest, the saddest, the weirdest-dressed, the best-dressed, and so on. Not only does this provide conversation, but it also will give you tremendous insight into your child's perspective—what he or she thinks is funny, happy, sad, or weird.

Availability means more than carving out time for special occasions with your kids. It means that they are more important than anything we may be doing when we're not with them, and so they are free to interrupt. When I would be writing in my study at home, for example, my kids knew they were always welcome to come in and talk with me. I would gladly set aside my work for a few minutes with them. I realized back then that I will always have deadlines from publishers and crises to solve. But I won't always have a child coming in and wanting to ask me a question, seek my advice, want a hug, or need to be comforted. So I made a commitment to the Lord that by his strength I would never allow projects or things to become more important to me than people, especially my own family.

Display Your Affection.

Showing affection to your young people will give them a sense of lovability. That is, if a child feels confident, *Hey, Mom and Dad really love me*, then he or she is also able to think, *Other people will be able to love me, too*. And that confidence is essential to a child's self-image and ability to have good relationships outside the family.

Kids can't get too much affection, even in their teenage years. They need lots of verbal love; they need to hear "I love you" over and over. They also need lots of physical love such as hugs, kisses, shoulder pats and rubs, and head strokes. Naturally, it's easier to do this with older children if you started when they were younger, but it's never too late to start. Kids drink in affection like a desert soaks in rain.

Another part of affection is just having fun with your kids. When they see that you are having fun and are glad to be with them, it reassures them of your love. Once when we were on a family vacation, we had taken along a friend of Kelly, our eldest daughter. One day while we were there, the two girls said they would like to have some fun styling my hair. I couldn't imagine it, but I figured, why not? However, I said I would go along only if they would go out to dinner with me that night—and sit with me. They had a great time doing up my hair in a sort of a Mohawk. And that night we went out for dinner, but I had to wear dark glasses!

Some kids may shrink back from physical affection and complain a little as they approach adolescence. But even then they still need it, especially in private and particularly if you have been affectionate to them for years.

A study showed that 61 percent of mothers will give verbal affection each day to their five-year-olds. By the time a child is nine, only 37 percent of mothers do it every day. For fathers, 40 percent express verbal affection to five-year-olds each day, and only 24 percent do it to nine-year-olds. Physical affection is more common than verbal affection. Eighty-three percent of the mothers gave a hug or a kiss to their five-year-olds each day, and 49 percent gave it to their nine-year-olds. Sixty-four percent of the fathers demonstrated physical affection to five-year-olds each day, and 33 percent to nine-year-olds.

It scares me to think how little affection children of fifteen are getting, when they actually need more. The trend to give less and less affection to our children needs to be reversed since we live in a very emotion-oriented society. It's the affection you give kids that will nurture lovability in them.

Establish Accountability with Your Kids.
Establishing accountability into your relationship with your children will give them a sense of responsibility. I'm not talking here only about letting your children be responsible to you. That's only half the story. It is also good to make yourself accountable to them. I have asked my children to help me be the best parent I can be by pointing out areas where I can improve. I also ask them to point out those times when I say or do things that are contrary to what I've tried to teach them.

Several years ago, we were all going out to a fast-food place for dinner. Everybody except Kelly wanted to go to the same place. And in her frustration she made some disparaging remarks about the place where everyone else wanted to eat. I corrected her for her attitude and language.

We compromised on the choice of restaurants by agreeing that those who wanted to go to the one place would be dropped off there, and Dottie and I would take Kelly to the place she liked. As we pulled up to the first restaurant, I said, "Everyone out for the gag bag." As we pulled away, Kelly promptly and firmly pointed out to me that I had just done what I had reprimanded her for. She was right. I swallowed hard and thanked her for showing me my inconsistency. She not only helped me be a more responsible person, but I also was given the opportunity to set a proper example of how she should respond when called into account for her own attitudes and actions.

On another occasion, I asked my children to write down five ways they wanted others to treat them. The number one thing they listed was kindness. Building on that and applying Matthew 7:12 (the Golden Rule) to it, I said that if they wanted others to treat them with kindness, they should start by being kind to others themselves. I pointed out that we needed to be especially kind to each other in the family.

Numerous times since then, when I have noticed one of my children being unkind to someone else, all I have had to say is, "Remember when we listed how we wanted others to treat us?" And that's been enough to make them aware of their attitudes and actions.

I also have tried to help my children understand the matter of accountability and how we treat others in terms of our relationship with God. One day I was in the car with Sean and we pulled into the parking lot of a busy shopping center. Somehow I found two empty spaces side by side near the entrance of the store where I wanted to shop. When I first pulled in, I didn't do a very good job of it, taking up part of both empty spaces and making it impossible for another car to park next to mine. I was tempted to leave the car that way and go on in, but it occurred to me that this was not a loving thing to do, and that it was a good opportunity to teach Sean a lesson from 1 Corinthians 13:4-7.

I backed the car out and reparked properly, staying within the lines of one space. "Sean," I said, "do you know why I bothered to do that? If I took up both of those parking spaces, someone else who wants to go to this store would have to park a long way away, and that wouldn't be very loving of me, would it?"

I found that little lessons like this really stuck in my kids' minds, helping them see that I am accountable to God for how I treat others as well as how I treat them. It teaches them responsibility in the process.

BUILDING YOUR CHILD'S SELF-IMAGE EQUALS REDUCED SEXUAL INVOLVEMENT

These five elements—acceptance, appreciation, availability, affection, and accountability—built into your relationship with your young people will make it a strong and healthy one. The relationship we have with our kids is the most important key to helping them say no to sexual involvement. If the relationship is good, if we really connect with them lovingly, our kids are far more likely to understand, respect, and obey our rules.[7]

One of the primary reasons adolescents get involved in premarital sex is that they have an unhealthy self-image, which can prompt sexual activity. Some young people use sex as a way to increase their self-esteem, as the following comments from two young men illustrate:

> I used premarital sex to deal with my lack of self-esteem. Each time it proved to me that I was a man and equipped me with good stories for the locker room. I looked to premarital sex to bolster my self-image.
>
> ◆   ◆   ◆
>
> I looked to female attention for proof of my worth as a male. The attention I received from a young lady became the gauge for my own worth. As I got more physically involved, I found it more difficult to stop at necking and petting and my life became increasingly filled with guilt.

Although both of these statements are from young men, young women with low self-esteem tell similar stories. They become involved sexually to "prove" their worth, to "prove" they can please another person, to "prove" they are attractive to the opposite sex, and to bolster their self-esteem by having experiences to describe to their sexually active peers.

Other young people, however, become sexually active as a way of reinforcing their low view of themselves. They are simply acting out what they believe to be true about themselves. We tend to act in harmony with how we see ourselves. Our self-image is like a set of lenses through which we view all of life. Based on what we see through those lenses, we make choices about what to think and how to act.

If an adolescent girl, for example, has low self-esteem and is feeling pressured to become sexually involved, it is easy for her to think, when she looks through her distorted lenses, *I'm not worth much anyway, so what difference does it make? This is what bad people do.* Soon such a young person is acting out her low opinion of herself.

While building your child's self-image doesn't directly address the issue of sexuality, it is nonetheless one of the most vital ways for you to help prepare your child to say no to sexual pressures.

The Right Perspective of Themselves

A healthy self-image is seeing yourself as God sees you, no more and no less. In others words, a healthy self-image is a realistic view of yourself from God's perspective. I add the phrase "No more and no less" to the definition because some people do have an inflated view of themselves, and that's pride. But others have a self-deprecating view of themselves, and that's *false* humility.

In Romans 12:3, Paul says, "I say to every man among you not to think more highly of himself than he ought to think; but to think so as to have sound judgment" (NASB). We ought to think according to sound judgment. That is the truest thing about us. True humility, which all people with a healthy self-image have, isn't saying, "I'm nothing." Rather, true humility is knowing who you are from God's perspective, accepting yourself as you are, and giving God the glory for it. A healthy self-image includes neither pride nor false humility.

That definition also makes us examine the biblical perspective. If the goal is to see ourselves realistically from God's perspective, we need to know what his perspective is. This is the perspective we must also engender in our young people.

First, the Bible tells us that God made man and woman the high point of his creation. Of everything he made, only we were made in his image (see Gen. 1:27). By itself, this fact of being made in God's image gives each of us great worth. We are very special to him, much more so than any other part of this universe that he made.

Second, the biblical picture of how much God values us doesn't end with our being made in his image. You are of great value and worth to God. And the simplest and most logical way to tell how much something is worth is to find out how much someone is willing to pay for it. And the great God of the universe considers you and your children to be of such value, even though you are sinners, that he was willing to pay the price of his Son's life to redeem you from the penalty of your sin. Would God have paid that price for a nobody, a worm? No, but he gladly paid it for me, for you, and for your young people.

Third, each of us is unique. God created only you to be you, and no one can be *you* better. Each of us and each of our children is unique and priceless. As a parent you should get in touch with the uniqueness of each of your children and accept each child just as is. Understanding and appreciating a person's uniqueness will let him or her know that he or she is somebody special.

Finally, the biblical perspective on how we should view ourselves says that we are loved and accepted by God. God tells us, "I have loved you with an everlasting love" (Jer. 31:3), and he accepts us just the way we are. The moment someone puts his or her trust in Jesus Christ as Savior and Lord, the Holy Spirit baptizes that person into the body of Christ. We are accepted into God's family. We belong.

Building a healthy self-image within your young people involves three principal elements. It can be likened to a three-legged stool. If you take away or shorten any one of those legs, the stool won't stand upright. Let's look at each of these three "legs" and what you as a parent, pastor, youth leader, or teacher can do to make the "chair" of each young person strong.

They belong.
The first leg to developing a healthy self-image within is a sense of belonging or a *feeling of being loved.* We looked at this earlier in the chapter, but our emphasis there was on how a child needs to sense your acceptance. A child also needs to understand that your acceptance means that he or she belongs. It's the knowledge that someone "really cares for me." Belonging is what I feel when I know I am loved unconditionally, just as I am.

They are worthy.
The second leg on the stool of healthy self-image is to *feel worthiness.* Whereas belonging means believing others love you unconditionally, worthiness means feeling whole and good about yourself on the inside—a sense that you deserve the love and acceptance of others. There's a clear connection between belonging and a sense of worthiness. Some children can verbalize these feelings at a surprisingly early age. Others, however, never do understand why they feel unworthy to receive love, and yet they spend a lifetime trying to earn it.

Besides being available to your child, as discussed earlier in the chapter, how do you instill a sense of worthiness? One of the most important things is to be careful how you discipline. When you must discipline your child, be sure to distinguish between the behavior, which may be offensive, and the child himself or herself, for whom you must reinforce your love. Kids who grow up with a good self-image are usually disciplined as often as kids with a poor self-image. But those with a healthy self-image are disciplined for displaying unacceptable *behavior*, whereas those with a poor self-image are disciplined for being "bad children."

We all have to discipline our children. But when we do, we should take great care to make this distinction between behavior and personhood. When I caught my son, Sean, lying, for example, the worst thing I could have done was to say something like this: "Son, you are a liar, and we don't tolerate liars around here. Liars are bad, and we punish them. God said liars will never get to heaven either." Do you see what that approach will do to a child's sense of being worthy to receive love?

Instead, I should say something like this: "Sean, you are my son, and I love you, but you lied to me. Now, your mother and I are not pleased with lying because it dishonors God, it is wrong, and it will ruin your reputation. So because we love you, you're going to have to be disciplined." This time I focused on his behavior, and at the same time I reaffirmed my love for him and the fact that my discipline grows out of love, not hatred or anger. It's a crucial difference. I've said nothing to suggest he is unworthy of love. In fact, in the midst of the discipline I have reinforced my love for him.

They are competent.
The third leg on the chair of healthy self-image is having a *feeling of competence*. As children grow and go through life, they need the confidence that they can meet new tasks and challenges successfully. They need the optimism that sees each new day as a fresh set of opportunities to be explored. Children lacking this sense of competence fear what a new day will bring and what the world will do to them next. Rather than seeing themselves as active in shaping their world and their destiny, they feel inadequate to cope with the world and the problems they face.

I would like to suggest three ways you can help your young person develop a sense of confidence.

First, help your child find at least one area of special competence. If a child can feel especially good about his or her ability in a particular area, it will largely compensate for inability in other areas. A kid who is poor in math, for example, may shine at languages. A child who lacks athletic skills may turn out to be an excellent actor. A child who can't play a musical instrument may have a strong aptitude for business. The key here is to help your child find at least one area of competence, then encourage and foster the development of that area.

Suppose a girl struggles with school, with music lessons, and with every sport she has ever tried. This is a girl who will have a hard time feeling competent. But then one day she picks up a tennis racquet and hits a few balls with some friends. She enjoys it and discovers that she has a natural aptitude for the game. The wise parent will see this discovery as a tremendous opportunity to help the girl develop a sense of competence and, with it, a healthy self-image. The parent will praise her accomplishments, buy her a good racquet and shoes, find some way to get her good instruction, and make sure she has access to courts for practice time and a way to get there.

Second, help your child develop a sense of competence by encouraging him or her aspire to great things and pursue big dreams, especially when these involve helping others. I am convinced that those who most enjoy life and have the healthiest self-image are those who have a dream of what they want to be and do and have dedicated their lives to the pursuit of that dream.

If you have a daughter, for example, who wants to be a lawyer in order to help people, teach her about the various types of work lawyers do, the skills that are most important to a good lawyer, and the kinds of study that would best prepare her for law school. Encourage her to visualize herself doing well, and gently guide her in working to make the dream a reality.

It is much easier for children to pursue worthwhile goals if their parents are cheering them on and assuring them they can do it. Persistence can overcome many obstacles, including lack of natural talent. It is young people with a strong sense of competence who will stay with a dream and make it happen. And they need parents to reinforce the fact that they can be competent.

Helping your child find areas of competence not only will develop a confidence in his or her competence but will give him or her a sense of control. A person who feels securely in control of one area—the area of his or her competence—can begin to generalize that sense of control to other areas as well. *If I can do this well in one area*, a child understands intuitively, *maybe I can exercise some control over other areas of my life, too.*

Third, each person is a special and unique creation of God, the object of his personal attention and indescribable love. The Lord has declared your child to be of incredible worth, so much so that he gave the life of his Son to redeem your child's soul. If you can convey that reality to your child and build on that foundation the three legs of the chair of self-image, then you will have done much to equip your child to make the choice to live a morally pure life.

FOSTERING OPEN COMMUNICATION WITH YOUR CHILD EQUALS REDUCED SEXUAL INVOLVEMENT

An indispensable skill in the process of nurturing a loving relationship with your child and building his or her self-image is communication. If you can't talk to your young person—and more critically, if he or she can't talk with you—you will have difficulty developing a close relationship and contributing to his or her self-image. Furthermore, without a good foundation of open, healthy communication, how will you be able to talk about sex when the opportunity arises?

In the next few pages I want to share with you some time-honored principles for communicating with your young people. I am very grateful to my friends Dave and Neta Jackson for assisting me with this section of the book.

The Skill of Listening

"Do you know what I am?" a teenager once asked. "I'm a comma."

"What do you mean?" the listener replied.

"Well, whenever I talk to my dad, he stops talking and makes a 'comma.' But when I'm finished, he starts right up again as if I hadn't said a thing. I'm just a comma in the middle of his speeches."

Many of our young people are crying out for a real conversation with a parent—one that involves not only the exchange of thoughts, but also of feelings. A conversation that includes both a listener and a speaker throughout .

Adolescents are very sensitive to rejection or ridicule. If they feel ignored, or experience being "put down" when they speak up, or get an argument every time, they will hesitate to share their real feelings or opinions. Who wants to feel ridiculed or rejected? And though they may try, what kids can hope to win an argument with an adult?

Some parents think that communication consists of stating the rules loud and clear; what those parents don't realize is that rules without relationships lead to rebellion. If you don't have a good relationship with your children, the rules will elicit rebellion instead of response. Adolescents respond to relationships. The relationship necessary for good communication with your young people is built on mutual respect. If you respect your children, they will respect you.

Where does respect begin? With listening. If you feel that someone is listening to you, you feel respected. So do your children. The biggest problem with listening is we usually just don't want to take the time. But when we are too busy to listen to our children, we are too busy. Jesus was not too busy. To the contrary, he was very interested in them. One day, right in the middle of his public ministry, some children were brought to him. The disciples tried to turn them away, claiming the Savior was too busy for them. But Jesus said, "Let the little children come to me, and do not hinder them, for the kingdom of heaven belongs to such as these" (Matt. 19:14).

Even when we do listen, we often can get hung up on the words we hear and miss the message. For example, your child comes into the house after school, slamming the door behind her. "I hate Katie McDaniel, and I'm never going to speak to her again!" The real message may well be: "I feel really rejected because Katie went off with Tanya and didn't bother to tell me." It takes practice, but parents need to listen for the feelings behind the words. This is possible if we're not too quick to jump in and respond but give time for the real feelings to emerge.

We can pick up some clues to young people's feelings if we remember that part of good communication is listening with our eyes as well as our ears. Look for physical and nonverbal communication: the way your kids use their eyes, the gestures they make, the body language. Are they anxious? excited? indifferent? depressed? If you watch for these nonverbal signs, you'll catch a great deal more of the communication.

Eleven Principles for Good Communication

Communication is vital to showing love to our young people. It is also true that communication with our young people is essential in helping them determine their approach to their own sexuality. Some research suggests that good communication between parents and children may reduce irresponsible sexual behavior.

Some parents are quite ready to listen, but their kids won't talk. All they get is a grunt on the way through the kitchen to the telephone. Or the parents are thoroughly bewildered when the kids do talk because the parents don't understand the world they live in or the language they use.

How can you encourage your kids to open up? How can you become a better communicator with your adolescents? The following eleven principles have helped me a good deal over the years as I have worked at becoming a better communicator with my wife. And I have discovered that what works for adult-to-adult communication also works with adult-to-adolescent communication. Learning to apply the following principles will greatly reduce the complaint, "You never listen to me!"

1. Work at it.

Doing what comes naturally may be the motto for many in our culture, but becoming a good communicator does not just happen naturally. All of us are tainted by self-centeredness, so we need to make a lot of effort to communicate better with our kids.

Some parents plan for occasional meals out (just a dad and his daughter, for instance) to help create an opportunity for communication. Sometimes the talk is low-key; other times, deeper issues are raised, or feelings surface that might not otherwise come up in the everyday world at home. One father and his teenage son go away for a hunting weekend each fall. Besides doing something together that they enjoy, the long ride in the car and the evenings camping out help them get to know each other better.

Other suggestions include:

- swimming together, jogging, cooking, attending an evening class or a concert, etc.;
- planning topics for discussion at dinner or during rides to and from school or church;
- inviting your young person into your bedroom to talk, or asking to come into his or hers from time to time;
- asking their opinions and respecting those opinions.

2. Seek to understand.

A little placard I've frequently seen posted on office walls reads: "I know you believe you understand what you think I said, but I am not sure you realize that what you heard is not what I meant." One of the keys to communication and developing intimacy is to convey to the other person that you are not only trying to understand, but you truly care. That kind of empathy will cause both individuals to be more open in the relationship.

On the other hand, if a child senses that a parent doesn't want to listen, or is not trying to understand, it affects the child's self-esteem. He or she soon begins to withdraw, feeling that what he or she has to say is not viewed as being important.

Parents need to enter their children's world enough so that they are speaking the same language. You need to get your children's perspective. It's difficult for me to think back to junior high and recall exactly what I was going through. Still, I'm constantly trying to see my children's viewpoints. I want to know their world, and I must know it if I am going to communicate with them. I need to listen to their music, read what they read, know their friends, and laugh at their jokes.

I also need to consider how what I say will affect them. They may not take things the same way an adult would, so I need to look at my statements to them from their perspective. If a light-hearted statement (by me) gets a big negative reaction (from them), that's a clue that I need to develop more understanding of their perspective. When I do that, it expresses my love more clearly to them.

3. Give a response to show you're listening.
Concentrating on what your child is saying can be difficult sometimes. For every 100 words spoken, our minds could have received and understood 500, so it's easy for the mind to wander. A parent may seem to be listening but mentally may be making out the grocery list or thinking about a gardening project. We move the conversation along with a few well-spaced "Uh-huh's" and "I see's." But it helps to ask yourself, *Can I repeat back to my child what he or she is saying?* Taking the time to hear, between the words, the feelings that are being communicated helps me concentrate.

If there is one thing that always encourages sharing, it is giving either verbal or body-language feedback. Here are some helpful suggestions to show that you are absorbing what your child is saying:

React physically. Turn toward your child. Lean forward. Nod your head in response. Keep looking into his or her eyes. Nothing shows greater interest than eye contact.

Request more information. Ask a question that seeks clarification or additional details: "What did you mean by that?" Or "Why is that important to you?" In asking questions you are saying, "Tell me more—I'm interested."

Reflect on what has been said with a leading statement: "You seem quite excited by meeting him" or "That must have been rough on you." Reflective listening pays off in more intimate sharing.

Repeat or rephrase statements with feeling. "Your history class might go to Washington, D.C.? That is exciting." Echoing the meaning or feeling of a statement both clarifies that statement and encourages further communication.

Remain silent when your child is telling a story. Don't interrupt, and don't finish sentences for him or her. This is a hard one for me. I have to keep telling myself, "Don't interrupt, don't interrupt." Also, don't rush to fill a pause in the conversation simply to avoid the silence—you may cut off something important your child was preparing to share.

Refrain from concentrating on your answer while your child is still talking; it makes you impatient to speak. When you are constantly constructing a rebuttal or a way to justify something you've said, you are merely building up a defense mechanism. As a result, you are not truly listening.

Express your encouragement and appreciation for what your child has been sharing. Both of these enhance healthy communication. Wise Solomon stated, "Kind words are like honey—sweet to the soul and healthy for the body" (Prov. 16:24, NLT). Say, "I really appreciate you sharing that with me, honey. I didn't know you felt that way" or "What you said makes a lot of sense. I want to give it some thought."

These techniques are just a few ways to respond actively to your kids when they try to talk to you. Remember that your open ears can open the door to their heart.

4. Affirm your child's worth, dignity, and value.
Every person has a deep need to be heard, to be listened to. The very act of listening communicates a sense of value, esteem, love, and dignity. It makes your child feel important.

An adolescent with low or unhealthy self-esteem will fear transparency because of possible rejection. I can't stress strongly enough how important the parent's role is in helping the child develop a healthy self-image. A parent who belittles his son or daughter's opinions ("That's stupid! You don't know what you're talking about"), teases about physical characteristics he or she is sensitive about (weight, pimples, height), expresses contempt for choices he or she makes about clothes or friends, or fails to express confidence in him or her ("You're so lazy; you'll never amount to anything"), will soon discover a thick wall around the child that blocks out all real communication.

On the other hand, a parent who makes a point of expressing unconditional love, affirms the importance of the child making his or her own choices in certain areas, respects a child's feelings, refuses to embarrass him or her in front of others, allows room for him or her to make mistakes, and in other ways affirms the personhood of his son or daughter will find a foundation being built not only for a good relationship but also for communication. And don't assume your kids know you love them; tell them, every day:

- "I love you."
- "I'm proud of you."
- "You make me so proud."
- "You are special to me."
- "I'm so proud to be your dad/mom."

5. Be positive and encouraging.

Being positive is a real plus factor in communication. It promotes openness with your children, whereas criticism tends to hinder healthy communication.

During a three-day lecture series at the University of Tennessee, I was in a meeting with some Campus Crusade staff people and several key students. One of the students walked in and said, "I'm not going to hand out any more fliers. Everybody's negative about the meetings. All I've heard are negative reports this morning."

I immediately asked, "How many people have given you a hard time? Twenty-five?"

"No."

"Ten?"

"No."

"Five?" I asked.

"No."

We discovered that only two people had reacted negatively to the 200 to 300 fliers she had handed out. Everyone in the room, including her, realized that she had accentuated the negative.

In our communication, we tend to notice and remember only the negative statements about ourselves. Ten positive statements and one negative one may be made, but we remember the negative one. Thus the ratio of praise to criticism in a conversation with your kids needs to be 90/10 — 90 percent praise for every 10 percent criticism.

Touching and hugging is another key to reaching children in a positive way, even after they become teenagers. Hug them when they hurt; hug them when they're joyful; hug them just for the fun of it!

6. Keep their secrets.
Recently two mothers were commiserating about child rearing. Later that day, however, one called the other and apologized for having revealed something of a very private nature about her child. She said, "If she knew I had told anyone, she would be extremely embarrassed." She was right; there was no reason for the other parent to know. Respect for the child's confidence was the real issue. We need to talk about our children with the same kind of respect we do other human beings and not embarrass them unnecessarily.

When your young people know that you are able to keep things to yourself, they automatically feel a greater willingness to be open with you. In speaking, I regularly use personal illustrations to amplify my points, but I must be very careful of what I say about my relationship with my kids. If I were to speak too openly about their struggles, they would become cautious and defensive.

Many kids hate to be talked about in front of others. One mother thought her preteen's remark was clever; but when she mentioned it to a friend over the phone in the child's hearing, the child was very upset. Another emerging adolescent was totally embarrassed whenever her parents referred to her bedtime in front of her peers. Parents need to learn to be sensitive to the level of trust and confidence that each child expects. If you blow it, apologize — but remember next time.

7. Wait for the right time.
Proverbs 15:23 declares, "It is wonderful to say the right thing at the right time" (NLT). In any relationship, dialogue will be enhanced if the timing is right. Love must be your guide as to when and where you share bad news or discuss a difficult subject with your kids.

One of the hardest places to apply "gracious speech" is with your own children. One parent described the following incident:

> One morning recently my oldest got off to a bad start. As he was grabbing his books and his lunch, I noticed that his bed wasn't made, the dog wasn't fed, and his laundry hadn't been put away. "Don't plan on doing anything with your friends when you get home from school today," I fumed at him as he went out the door. "We've got to get a few things straight around here. You can count on some adverse consequences!" He threw me a frustrated look and ran belatedly for the bus.
>
> The moment the door closed, I wanted to bite my tongue. What a way to send a kid off to school. He was already late and frustrated. He might miss the bus and get marked tardy. Yes, we did need to get a few things straight about his morning preparation. But was when he was going out the door the right time to stick it to him?

The timing of a correction or criticism can make it a building experience or one that tears a child down. There are three especially crucial times when parents should choose their words carefully: (1) when your child is going out the door (what words do I send him off with); (2) when your child first comes home from school (what words is she greeted with at the end of the day); and (3) when your child is ready to go to bed (what words do I leave my child to sleep on).

8. *Share your feelings.*

Learn to say how you feel in conversation with your kids, as well as what you think. If they experience your willingness to be vulnerable too, they may be more willing to be open about what they are feeling. Do they know that you sometimes feel lonely? afraid? unsure of yourself? That can be a real revelation to an adolescent!

Sometimes parents suppress their feelings to avoid conflict, but holding in your gripes diminishes real communication with your kids and usually creates pressures that will cause the feelings to come out in other ways. Rather than stating clearly, "I'm feeling very angry right now," a parent may stuff down feelings that come out in an explosion a few hours or days later over some minor provocation.

Some parents misuse their feelings as a way to manipulate their children:

"You don't care how I feel!" or "Yes, I'm depressed, and it's all your fault!" or "You make me so mad!" That kind of venting of feelings will indeed make children feel guilty, but it usually also makes them withdraw.

Psychologists and family counselors encourage us to use "I messages" when we express our feelings to another person. "I am feeling angry"—not "You make me so angry!" "I feel ignored"—not "You never listen to me!" Adopting a first-person style is hard (especially when we feel that our kids really do "make us mad"). But, though our children need to be responsible for their actions, we cannot make them responsible for our feelings.

9. Don't make assumptions.
Warning: Don't take it for granted that your child understands your gestures, tone of voice, or body language. It becomes very frustrating in a relationship when each person assumes that the other knows what he or she is thinking and feeling and wants to do. Mind reading never works. You can't hold your child responsible for knowing that loud music gives you a headache, that you want wet towels hung up, that you like homemade cards on your birthday, or that you're tired and need extra help with supper. Speak up.

One mother was frustrated by her son's habit of watching TV before supper, just when she could use extra help. "You never offer to help!" she fumed.

He said sincerely, "All you need to do is ask."

Kids can seem really dense. They aren't; actually they can be very sensitive. But what they consider important at any one moment and what you consider important at that same moment may be as far apart as night and day. They are worried about whether they will have a date for homecoming; you wish they wouldn't run up the phone bill. Expectations need to be communicated clearly; rules need to be specific: "Come in at eleven"—not "Don't be too late." When they are thoughtless and hurt your feelings, you need to say so. Don't just assume or hope that your kids will figure it out and come to you first. Every relationship would become more harmonious and more intimate if we would just stop assuming, and start communicating our feelings.

10. Learn to compromise.
A healthy relationship with your growing adolescents is a give-and-take situation. While it may have been appropriate to "lay down the rules" when they were younger, kids want more say in the things that affect their lives. They are

becoming their own persons, and family life needs to adjust to give them more responsibility for decisions (freedom to try their wings and make mistakes) and to take their needs into account in the family schedule.

If your kids decide you are inflexible, they simply will give up and not talk to you about rules and expectations that are causing tension between you. They will be frustrated, sullen, or angry, or they will devise ways around the rules behind your back. But if you are willing to discuss issues, negotiate, or compromise, your kids will be much more willing to talk.

This doesn't mean a parent has to be wishy-washy about rules or expectations. But as one family counselor cautions, "You need to choose your battles." In other words, not every issue is of equal importance. You may decide that family rules about curfew and use of drugs or alcohol are nonnegotiable; but expectations for use of the car, chores, dress, and how many meals the family eats together may be open for discussion and mutual agreement.

If adolescents are behaving responsibly, it may be necessary and appropriate to renegotiate and increase their privileges more often, possibly even every four to six months. At certain stages of their development, they actually may mature at that rate. It's sometimes hard for us to keep up with how fast we're "losing little Johnny," but it is important to avoid engendering resentment over rules more suited to someone younger.

11. Be honest.
The apostle Paul saw the issue clearly when he admonished us to be "speaking the truth in love" (Eph. 4:15). To speak the truth in love means to take into consideration the other person's feelings. A truly skillful and loving communicator is sensitive to the consequences of his words and actions.

The barriers to being honest are numerous. When we feel we need to be honest in something that could hurt another, we not only need to review the style in which we deliver the message, but we also need to examine our motives. Many cruel things have been said by parents to kids in the name of honesty. Is our motive to accuse, to tear down? Or is it to reconcile, to build up?

Another barrier is that honesty can become nitpicky. No young person is going to reveal weaknesses and imperfections if he or she suspects that a complete record of every personal flaw is on file. Honest communication, spoken in love and heard in love, does not keep score. If you need to speak honestly with your kids about a problem, don't drag out any other sins or failures, past or present.

Speaking the truth in love requires care not to exaggerate. *Always* and *never* are loaded words. Keep your communication simple, direct, and on the subject.

Part of being honest is your willingness to ask your kids for forgiveness when you blow it. Some parents think they shouldn't say "I'm sorry" to their children; they might lose their children's respect. The opposite is actually true. Our kids already know we make mistakes. They know when we've acted in haste or been unfair. If we're unwilling to admit it, their trust in us erodes. But if we can admit our mistakes, the damage can be mended; trust is reestablished, and confidence in us grows stronger.

Begin Today
As in learning a foreign language, learning to communicate skillfully with your young people takes time, dedication, focus, and practice. Some families may be better at it than others, so patience with ourselves—and with our kids—is necessary.

Look back over the eleven principles above. Are there one or two that you especially need to work on? Being an effective communicator doesn't happen overnight, but you can start today. Every effort goes a long way toward telling your kids that they are important. Good communication will help build the foundation for a lifelong family relationship and eventually will help your children cope with sexual pressure.

◆ ◆ ◆

Nurturing a positive relationship with your young person is important, but there is another relationship that will be even more influential over his or her decisions about sex. In the next chapter we will discuss the importance of your child's relationship with Christ.

CHAPTER 17

ENCOURAGE AN INTIMATE RELATIONSHIP WITH CHRIST

PERHAPS ONE OF THE GREATEST REASONS for adolescent sexual activity is found in a young person's need for intimacy. The human need for intimate, fulfilling relationships is a valid one. Psychologists tell us that the greatest human need is to love and be loved. We long to share ourselves totally with another person. That's what true intimacy is: sharing every part of our life with someone else. We all desire someone who will love and accept us for who we are, someone whom we can trust and open up to without fear of rejection. We desire love and intimacy, but we don't know how to find it. This is true for adolescents as well as for adults.

Because our kids don't instinctively know where to find true intimacy, they often pursue the illusion of "instant intimacy." Of course, the quickest, easiest, most convenient way to become seemingly intimate with someone is through sex. But the problem with instant intimacy is that it creates an illusion of love that is no more than skin-deep, which ultimately leads to frustration.

Sexual intimacy alone can never fulfill a young person's deep need for intimacy. There is, however, a source of lasting love, acceptance, and intimacy that does meet our core needs. The source of this intimacy is a personal relationship with Jesus Christ. He is the only one who loves constantly and consistently with a perfect, unconditional love.

As a parent, pastor, youth worker, or teacher, one significant way you can help your kids say no to premarital sex is to encourage them toward an intimate, growing, personal relationship with Jesus Christ. As their intimacy with Christ develops and matures, your young people will be less likely to seek sexual intimacy. In this chapter I want to equip you for the important ministry of encouraging kids toward intimacy with Christ through God's Holy Spirit. I will share this information with you just as I share it with young people wherever I go. You have my permission to share it with your young people as you have opportunity.

ESTABLISHING A RELATIONSHIP WITH CHRIST

Here are four points that can change your life:

1. God loves you perfectly and he desires to give you the best in all areas of your life, including your relationships—and, in its proper context, your sex life.
2. We all have a basic attitude problem of rebelliousness and self-centeredness that leads us to push the limits of God's commands (not only in regard to sex but in other areas also). The Bible calls this attitude sin and says that there are penalties for sin: separation from God and the inability to experience all he wants to give us. The Bible also says that there is no way we can bridge this separation on our own.
3. God has solved the problem of separation by sending his Son, Jesus, to die for us, thereby paying the penalty for our sin. Then Jesus was raised from the dead to give us a new life, opening up the way to God so that we can experience his intimate love for us.
4. We each have a personal choice to make. We can choose to accept or reject the provision that God already has made for us. If we reject it, we can continue searching unsuccessfully for true intimacy on our own. If we accept it, God will fulfill our needs for love and intimacy as we experience his perfect love and plan for our lives.

What I'm talking about here is not a religion but a relationship with the person of Jesus Christ. If you would like to enter into this intimate relationship with God through his Son, Jesus, I invite you to pray the following prayer, keeping in mind that it is not the words you say that are important but the attitude of your heart.

Dear Jesus, I need you. Thank you for dying on the cross to pay the penalty for my sins. I desire at this moment to begin a close relationship with you. Please come into my life as my Savior and fill my heart with your love. Thank you for forgiving my sins and giving me eternal life. Help me to live for you from now on, and make me the kind of person you want me to be.

Once you begin a relationship with Jesus, you need to build that relationship continually. Whether you are a brand-new believer or have enjoyed a relationship with Christ for many years, in order to be able to say no to sex, you need to develop and maintain a close, intimate walk with God. Here is what some other kids say about this vital relationship:

We are only human. We need to be loved and to have the feeling of being accepted. The love needs to be given to us at home, but if it is not given to you there, go to your church and get it. Do not let the empty space in your heart leave you vulnerable and open to sin. Fill your heart with the Lord. He gives us love overflowing forever and ever. We will never need to depend on anyone else so long as we keep him near. If our peers do not accept us, who cares? We know what we want out of life and we do not compromise it. There is someplace else to turn besides just to our friends. Turn to God.

◆ ◆ ◆

Even sex at its height cannot erase the loneliness of the innermost heart. There exists only One source to fill that need. Jesus Christ is the only One who can satisfy those deepest longings of your heart.

◆ ◆ ◆

It's important to stay in a close relationship with Jesus. My boyfriend and I have discovered that if we start drifting away from Jesus, we are more vulnerable to our sexual feelings. If your relationship with God is not right, then no other relationship can be right either. If both of you are right with God, it is so much easier to go to him when you need assistance.

Developing an intimate walk with Christ will do at least three important things for you:

1. Your need for intimacy will begin to be fulfilled. Your relationship with God is comparable to the growing process of a love affair. Your loneliness

will be eased, so there will no longer be a need to fill that void in your life through sexual activity.

2. As you develop a closer relationship with God, there will come a natural desire to please him. Out of love for God you will want to do what he commands, which includes abstaining from sexual involvement before marriage.

3. You will have the power of God available to you to resist temptation. First Corinthians 10:13 assures us, "No temptation has overtaken you but such as is common to man; and God is faithful, who will not allow you to be tempted beyond what you are able, but with the temptation will provide the way of escape also, that you may be able to endure it" (NASB).

Handling Temptation

We like to pretend that we are able to handle anything. It takes humility to admit we have a problem with something. Yet when we pretend we can resist any kind of sexual temptation on our own, we are just setting ourselves up for failure. A couple of young people shared with me:

> No one is immune from the possibility of falling into sexual immorality. Scripture says that pride comes before a fall. In the same way, our pride in thinking, *I don't have any problem controlling my sexual desires* is often the warning sign that we are getting ready to tumble.

◆ ◆ ◆

> Young people often find themselves in situations they can't say no to. So many times we say, "Oh, I can handle it if I'm ever in that situation." We don't decide before going in. Instead we try to stop in the middle. It's like reading a good book; once you've started, it's hard to put it down. Sex is the same way. Once you've begun, it's hard to stop.

So don't venture to the edge of your sexual control feeling too confident in yourself. You will probably find out that you are not as strong as you thought. If you insist on placing yourself in compromising situations, sooner or later you're going to find yourself yielding. The first step in avoiding immorality is to admit to yourself and to God that you are weak and vulnerable. When you acknowledge your weakness, you give yourself motivation for consciously avoiding tempting situations and relying on God's strength through the Holy Spirit rather than your own.

Keep your focus on the Lord, realizing that where you are weak, he is strong, and his strength will never fail. One student phrased it this way:

Temptation will surely come. Jesus himself was tempted. The only thing we should fear is that we might think ourselves so great and independent that we take our eyes off of Jesus. How quickly we give in to wrong. But Jesus never designed us to live this life apart from him, and he has promised to bring us victory.

Meditating on God's Word

The best way to keep your mind off tempting thoughts is to keep your mind concentrating on God's Word. Psalm 119:9 says, "How can a young person stay pure? By obeying your word and following its rules" (NLT). It is very important to your sexual purity to immerse yourself in the Bible by reading it, meditating on it, memorizing it, and sharing it. Spend some time interacting with God's Word every day. It will be like a protective shield for you when temptations come.

We live in a world that is constantly exposing us to a variety of images and sounds. If they are negative, they detract from the principles that God has for us. If they are positive, they reinforce his principles. Therefore, it is important to meditate on God's principles as a means of avoiding and controlling sexual temptation.

Basically, whatever we focus our thoughts on will eventually direct our behavior. World-class athletes are a good example of this. When the time comes to perform, they visualize their goal in their minds before going for it. Whether pole-vaulting or high-jumping, the champion athlete visualizes an ideal vault or jump and then tries to do what he or she has visualized. If the visualization is faulty, so is the performance. A poor mental image will usually be followed by failure.

Every temptation begins with something we see or hear, and that stimulus produces a thought. As the mind continues to entertain that thought by meditating on it, a determination to act on that thought is formed. If that determination is not changed, the action eventually takes place. The equation might look like this:

Stimulus + Thought + Meditation + Determination = Action

The way to break this cycle when it's going the wrong direction is to discipline your mind. Our culture is saturated with sexual messages through the media, so you cannot completely avoid exposure to sexual stimuli unless you live the rest of your life in a remote cave. Otherwise you will be assaulted by sexual images and sounds.

Be aware, however, that sexual thoughts and feelings are not sinful. What counts is how you respond to those thoughts and feelings. As the old saying goes, "You can't keep the birds from flying over your head, but you can keep them from making a nest in your hair." When temptation comes, you must deal with it immediately. Don't let it settle down in your mind and take up residence. Brush it away and replace it with something you *do* want to act on: God's Word.

One obvious way to discipline the mind is to choose what goes into it. For example, it's much easier to squelch sexual temptation when one is reading the Bible than when one is looking at a pornographic magazine or video. One student wrote about this discovery:

> Now, I am not the disciplined type at all, but I read the Bible every night—no matter how tired I am or how late it is. Sometimes I'll read for an hour, sometimes for just ten minutes. I also make sure that I spend time in prayer at my bedside before getting in. You know, after having made this decision in my life—and it's been close to a year now—I am absolutely amazed at how God's wonderful grace has protected me.
>
> "Let this mind be in you which was also in Christ Jesus" (Phil. 2:5, NKJV).

It is difficult, if not impossible, to entertain a negative, lustful, or impure thought when your mind is focused on Jesus. One reason is that Jesus was never lustful or impure. So if you want to say no to sexual temptation, you should saturate your mind with God's Word and focus your attention on Jesus Christ.

Proverbs 7:1-5 offers similar advice: "My son, keep my words, and treasure my commandments within you. Keep my commandments and live, and my teaching as the apple of your eye. Bind them on your fingers; write them on the tablet of your heart. Say to wisdom, 'You are my sister,' and call understanding your intimate friend; that they may keep you from an adulteress, from the foreigner who flatters with her words" (NASB). Other helpful verses include: 1 Corinthians 10:13; Philippians 4:8; and Colossians 3:2.

Pleasing Christ

Scripture tells us that we cannot serve two masters (see Matt. 6:24). This is especially true in the sexual area of our life. We cannot follow both the desires of our bodies and the Holy Spirit, who calls us to sexual purity. Our sexual desires tell us to please ourselves, to do what feels good at the moment. God's Spirit calls us to please him, to deny the cravings of our body when those cravings cannot be satisfied in a manner pleasing to him. In this battle between flesh and spirit we must consciously choose to please the Lord rather than ourselves. Two students wrote:

> When you are in your teen years, your only concern should be pleasing the Lord, not your peers. Your friends could, and probably will, turn on you, get mad at you, or even hate you, but the Lord will never leave you or forsake you.

◆ ◆ ◆

> For the sake of love (love for God, love for your future mate, love for yourself), WAIT! If you love that person you are dating, if you love the person you are going to marry, if you love God, you will wait because "love is patient, love is never selfish, . . . it does not demand its own way" (1 Cor. 13:4-5). Why wait until marriage to engage in sex? For the sake of love. That's why.

Saying no to premarital sex in order to please God builds strong Christian character in your life. As you meditate on God's Word and seek to please him, you will develop important Christlike qualities of character: "love, joy, peace, patience, kindness, goodness, faithfulness, gentleness and self-control" (Gal. 5:22-23).

Christ Accepts You Just As You Are

A personal relationship with Christ not only fills your deep need for intimacy, it also meets your need for total acceptance. True acceptance comes only from God. His grace toward us, the love he showers on us—even though we are completely undeserving of it—is the ultimate demonstration of total and unconditional acceptance.

God didn't create you because he *needed* you; he created you because he *wanted* you. God is complete in himself. He is pleased when we respond to him, but it is not something he needs, it is something he desires. We, on the other hand, definitely need God. In him we live and have abundant life, both now and in eternity. Without him, we are tossed about and separated from him, both now and in eternity. It is we who benefit from a relationship with God.

When we realize that, we come to understand how valuable we are in God's eyes. Everything he does, he does for us. God calls you to fellowship with him for *your* benefit, as well as for his.

Because of God's acceptance, our security is in him. He loves us without conditions and apart from our performance. We can respond to his love by loving him back, but we don't have to keep pleasing him out of fear of rejection. God doesn't like our shortcomings, but he loves us in spite of them, and we feel accepted. We are accepted; we have security.

Every person has individual significance in God's eyes. God considers us all so important that he sent his Son, Jesus Christ, to pay the total price for our sins and to open the door to our relationship with him. In so doing, he said we are each so valuable that each of us is worth the life of his Son. All we have to do is respond to his offer of love. With a love so accepting and complete, how can we refuse?

When you are completely accepted in a relationship, you have the freedom to be yourself, to let your guard down. You don't have to pretend. When you have security despite your faults, when you don't have to measure up to some standard to be accepted, you feel significant as a person. You are free to develop your God-given abilities because you want to, not because you have to in order to be accepted. You choose to do good work, to do the work of the Father, out of appreciation for him and his love, mercy, and grace. You choose to live by faith. You know who loves you and who has demonstrated his love by his actions. You are loved for who you are, not for what you do.

This is why true acceptance, security, and significance can come only from God. All persons need the healthy sense of worth that God intended them to have—something defined in Romans 12:3 where Paul says, "Do not think of yourself more highly than you ought, but rather think of yourself with sober judgment, in accordance with the measure of faith God has given you."

This verse tells us how God views us, which of course is how we should view ourselves. We are created in the image of God; we have talents and abilities given to us by God; we have been given the privilege of knowing him personally. Each of us is handcrafted and dearly regarded by the Creator. Yet we should not think more highly of ourselves than we ought. When we keep in mind that all we have and are able to do are gifts from God, we realize that our looks, musical talents, athletic abilities, powers of reasoning—everything—comes from God.

LIVING IN THE POWER OF THE HOLY SPIRIT

Another vital element to saying no to sexual temptation is the ministry of the Holy Spirit in our lives. The following article, written by my friend and colleague Chuck Klein, explains the ministry of God's Spirit clearly and concisely. I can't say it any better than this. Chuck is international director of Student Venture International, the student discipling and evangelism movement of Campus Crusade for Christ.[1]

Has anyone ever told you that you need more self-control when it comes to your sex life? I'll bet you tried. Any luck?

The reason a lot of God's kids today (and a whole lot of adults) have trouble in the sexual area is that living a good, clean sex life, the kind that God asks us to live, is just plain tough. In fact, to a lot of folks it seems hopeless. The pressures and desires are just too great. A friend of mine once said, "A good Christian sex life isn't hard to live—it's impossible!"

One of the most important things in learning to say no to premarital sex is learning to say yes to the Holy Spirit's leadership in our lives. Only one person has ever lived a perfect Christian life, and that is Jesus Christ. Now, by his Spirit, he wants to live that life through us.

God's design for sex is an A-1, award-winning, top-of-the-line blueprint. What's best, he designed it for our protection and pleasure. But let's be honest. His plan is beyond our power. We can't make it alone by tightening our belt buckle or gritting our teeth.

However, if there is one thing we soon learn about God, it is this: God never asks something of us without giving us the resources to do it. That's what knowing God is all about. Christianity is not a self-improvement program; rather, it is letting God improve us (or should I say, change us?) his way, with his power. How does God do this?

The definition of the word *Christian* gives us the answer. A Christian is someone who has Christ in him. That is the phenomenon that makes Christians unique people. We can tackle big issues like sex because Jesus Christ, by his Spirit, God's Spirit (Rom. 8:9), actually lives inside us.

In the Bible, 1 Corinthians 3:16 asks us, "Don't you know that you yourselves are God's temple and that God's Spirit lives in you?" If you have received Christ, God's Spirit (the Holy Spirit) lives in you right now. What a mind-staggering thought!

But the Holy Spirit doesn't just live within you. If you allow him, he will give you more power than you could ever dream of or imagine. Here's the kind of power we are talking about: "And if the *Spirit* of him who *raised Jesus from the dead* is *living in you*, he who raised Christ from the dead will also *give life* to your mortal bodies through his Spirit, who lives in you" (Rom. 8:11, italics added). Awesome, death-defying power! The Holy Spirit makes us new people in Christ. Then he offers us the resources to live a new kind of life. He gives us the tools to deal with serious pressures and problems, like the big issue of sex!

How does the Holy Spirit do all this? He does it with a lot of cooperation on our part. You see, the Holy Spirit is a person, the same as God our Father is a person, and because of that, the Holy Spirit is very personal and sensitive with each one of us. He knows us intimately and loves us unconditionally, but he also gives us a lot of "space."

As God's kids, however, we want to make sure we aren't taking advantage of that space to express all the desires of our sinful nature—those desires that can produce some gross behavior, especially in the area of sex. Instead, God wants us to exercise our free will by responding to his Spirit, letting him give us his power to tackle our sexual problems.

In Galatians 5:22-23 the apostle Paul tells us that one of the qualities God's Spirit wants to develop in us is self-control (not a bad quality to have when it comes to sex). In addition, he wants to develop love, patience, and kindness, qualities that produce great relationships with the opposite sex, the kind of relationships that fill our lives with satisfaction, not with the empty feelings and stains of premarital sex.

Where the Holy Spirit is producing his qualities in us, we have freedom to experience God's kind of relationships. There is power to say no and to wait. How can we give the Holy Spirit the green light in our lives?

Confess Sin

The Holy Spirit cannot fill us with his power if we choose to live independent of God. We can't do things our own way and expect the Holy Spirit to produce his qualities in our lives at the same time. So we need to begin with confession. As has been said, confession means to "agree with" God concerning what he already knows about our sin, attitudes, and behavior.

God has a perfect verse of Scripture to help us: "If we confess our sins, he is faithful and just and will forgive us our sins and purify us from all unrighteousness"

(1 John 1:9). Confession clears the air with God and restores our intimacy with him. You see, he hasn't withdrawn from us, but we have withdrawn from him.

What are some symptoms that tell us we need to confess? Here are a few: bad relationships, a lot of jealousy, diminishing faith, critical attitudes, apathy, misuse of sex. If your desire is to make things right with God, take time right now, privately, and list the things you know you should confess. Agree with God about those things through prayer. Then thank God for his forgiveness, which he has already given you.

Once you have confessed your sins, God expects you to forget them—not to dwell on them or to feel guilty. Agree with him on what you have done: you have sinned. Agree with him on what he has done: He has forgiven you. If you don't accept what he has done for you, you are denying the sufficiency of his grace— and that, I suspect, brings greater grief to him than your original act of sin did.

Recognize God's Will
What lies ahead? God wants you to be filled (led and empowered) by his Spirit. Ephesians 5:18 says, "Don't be drunk with wine, because that will ruin your life. Instead, let the Holy Spirit fill and control you" (NLT). This verse of Scripture tells us not to rely on the synthetic influence of things like alcohol, drugs, or anything else we might be using to find satisfaction. Rather, we are to allow the Holy Spirit to fill us and let him begin to "grow" his qualities in us. That's real living, and it is God's will and command.

If God's will is for us to be Spirit-filled, what should we do next? First John 5:14-15 tells us, "This is the confidence we have in approaching God: that if we ask anything according to his will, he hears us. And if we know that he hears us—whatever we ask—we know that we have what we asked of him." Talk about promises from God! This verse of Scripture is one of the dearest and most exciting in all the Bible. When we ask God for something that he intends for us to have, he is going to give it to us. Does God want us to be filled with his Spirit? Does he want to "grow" his fruitful qualities in our lives? Does he want to give us power in our sexual lives? You can count on it. Does God stick to his promises? You can lay your life on his faithfulness.

Ask for His Filling
God wants us to come to him humbly and sincerely and ask him, by faith, to fill us with his Spirit; to begin to produce his love in place of our fear and jealousy;

to give us his patience in place of our anger; to fill us with his self-control in place of our being controlled by our sexual desires.

Let's face it, when it comes to our sexual lives, we can't afford not to be under the loving influence of God's Spirit. This is what living the Christian life is all about.

If that is your desire, then ask God's Spirit to take over right now. If you didn't do it earlier, take some time first to confess (agree with God concerning areas of your life that have been under your own control). Remember God's command (Eph. 5:18) and his promise (1 John 5:14-15). Trust him to fill your life with his Spirit.

You may or may not feel different when God's Spirit takes control. Feelings are not consistent and we should never use them as indicators of God's work in our lives. *Remember, God works in our lives because we put our faith in the facts of his Word.*

Follow His Leading

Being filled and led by God's Spirit is both an event and a process. In other words, there are specific times in our Christian lives when we realize that God is not in charge, and we give the controls to him. Those are important events. But the other side of the Holy Spirit's work in our lives is a process.

Fruit on a tree is not produced instantly. It takes an entire season for it to grow from a green bud to a ripe piece of fruit. The Spirit's fruitful qualities in our lives are like that. Self-control, for example, may not be overwhelming when we first learn how to allow God's Spirit to fill us. But as we grow in our faith and spend day after day trusting his Spirit to lead us, that fruit of self-control will grow and mature. The lustful desires of our flesh never go away, but the strength of God's self-control becomes a greater and greater force in our lives.

But beware. You must always be cooperating with God's Spirit. You have to make the decision to give the Holy Spirit leadership in your life. He won't control someone who chooses to control his or her own circumstances. There will be times when you again will need to confess particular sins and ask God again to fill you with his Spirit. When you stumble, let God pick you up.

There will be other times when you just need to turn and run from something that is tempting you, whether it is a magazine, movie, television program, or when you are alone with someone in the backseat of a car. That is why Paul told Timothy, "Flee the evil desires of youth. . . ." But he didn't leave Timothy hanging with nothing to turn to, "and pursue righteousness, faith, love and peace. . . . Call on the Lord" (2 Tim. 2:22).

We have to make choices and turn from the things that damage our sexual lives, our personalities, and our relationship with Christ. If we are willing to turn, God's Spirit bursts through with his power and helps us make those critical choices. Let him fill you. Learn to walk with him today.

Let's review. To be filled and led by the Holy Spirit you need to

- Confess your sin;
- Remember God's will for you: to be filled with the Holy Spirit;
- Ask God, by faith, to fill you—he promises to answer;
- Keep cooperating with the Holy Spirit. Learn to make right choices, and God will keep producing his powerful qualities in your life.

Where the Spirit is in control, we find power and liberty.

◆ ◆ ◆

Relationships are key to helping your young people say no to premarital sex. They will benefit greatly from a loving, supportive relationship with parents and other adults, and an intimate relationship with Christ and his Spirit is vital. Now let's talk about the home in broader terms. In the next chapter we will explore some practical ways parents can strengthen their kids' resolve to remain pure.

CHAPTER 18

TEACH AND MODEL MORAL VALUES AT HOME

ONE OF THE GREATEST DETERRENTS to young people becoming sexually involved is parents who love them and whose lifestyle and marriage they respect and desire to emulate. If my own kids answer yes to three specific questions, then regardless of the moral issues involved, they will comply with my wishes. For example, if my kids come to me with a moral issue—what is right, what is wrong—and I feel they are contemplating doing something they shouldn't, I will ask them three questions:

1. Do you know that I love you?
2. Do you know that I love your mother?
3. When you get married and have love and sex and children, do you want with your future family what we have in our family? (This question is crucial.)

If they can answer yes to all these questions, then I have the perfect platform to influence their thoughts, their behavior, and their attitudes. This is one of God's designs for parents to be able to impact and influence their children's ethical and moral development. Our kids need all the help they can get to cope with the sexual pressure facing them in today's sex-saturated society. The more help we give them, particularly in the example we display in the marriage relationship, the more capable they will be of making right choices.

HOW TO MODEL A CONTEXT FOR SEX IN YOUR MARRIAGE

I have heard the following from adolescents,[1] and it makes me sad:

> I never want to get married because I never want to go through what my parents
> have gone through, and I don't want my kids to go through what I've gone through.

◆ ◆ ◆

> I am determined to have a great marriage and not be like my parents.

I hurt the most for adolescents who have given up on the committed relationship of marriage because, as it turns out, they have good reason to feel that marriage doesn't work. It usually means they haven't encountered a positive, successful marriage that has affected their lives in a constructive way. To them, all the talk about commitment and marital happiness is bogus. They have yet to see it.

Apart from seeing a working model, kids have no means of understanding commitment. To them, a relationship is worthwhile only as long as the feelings are good and personal satisfaction results. As soon as conflict arises, they abandon the relationship. They have learned to do this by watching others. These kids won't be helped with a trite lecture or quickie answers. They need live, working models of what a marriage should be. They could read a library full of books on the joys of commitment and marriage, but until they see it, it will remain a theory without credibility.

When adolescents settle for sex as a substitute for committed relationships, they are acting on their emotions regarding relationships. Those who have given up on relationships are caught between what God says to be true and what they have seen to be true.

The relationship we have with our children is their first line of defense in trying to help them say no to the pressures to engage in premarital sex. And right up there in importance with it is the relationship we have with each other as their mother and father. It takes secure children to say no to pressure, and a great deal of that security comes from knowing that the relationship between Mom and Dad is secure.

Since that's true, one of the greatest things I can do for my kids is to love their mother. If kids don't have the confidence that Mom and Dad love each other and will always be together, they have to worry about the permanence of every relationship, including their own future marriages. And if you can't count on marriage to meet your human need for love and intimacy forever, why wait for marriage to enjoy sex?

It is significant that the verse we parents like to quote to our children— "Children, obey your parents in the Lord, for this is right" (Eph. 6:1, NKJV) comes immediately after Ephesians 5:33 where Paul tells each husband to "so love his own wife as himself, and let the wife see that she respects her husband" (NKJV). A secure home that comes from a husband and wife loving each other and modeling love, obedience, and respect in responding to each other is one basis for obedience in the children. Ephesians 6:4 says, "Fathers, do not provoke your children to wrath, but bring them up in the training and admonition of the Lord" (NKJV). One way we can provoke our children to wrath is to fail to provide a model for them of a family relationship in which the father loves the mother.

The Need to Model Love
Most young people who get involved in premarital sex aren't really looking for sex per se. They want intimacy—communication, dialogue, to know and be known, to love and give love, to understand and be understood. This intimacy used to be found in the family. Kids received the love and security they needed from Mom and Dad and brothers and sisters. Today, however, with families falling apart all around us, such intimacy is often missing in homes.

We learn to love from seeing our parents love each other. We learn it as we see modeled the giving and receiving of love between Mom and Dad. But so many kids today are seeing exactly the opposite modeled in their families and in the families of their friends. Too often the American home is no longer a place of intimacy and expression of love between a husband and wife.

My wife Dottie has pointed out an important difference she discovered when reading Ephesians 5:33: "Nevertheless let each one of you in particular so love his own wife as himself, and let the wife see that she respects her husband" (NKJV). The difference is that while the primary need of a woman is love, the primary need of a man is respect. Both men and women equally need love and respect, but it seems women desire a deep, loving relationship. Love motivates a woman and meets her deepest need. Men, on the other hand, seem to long to be respected as the provider and protector of the home. Thus, when I talk about showing love, I'm talking primarily to husbands. When I talk about showing respect, I'm talking primarily to wives.

Dottie says that for a man to feel respected by his wife, he needs to know that she supports him, she admires him and will stand behind him, and she believes in him and will defend him. He needs the assurance that she will encourage him and that she is his greatest fan.

Fathers need to model love, and mothers need to model respect to their children so that they will feel secure, have their intimacy needs met, and learn how to give and receive love and respect. But practically speaking, how do we model love and respect?

Mainly, love and respect need to be verbalized. Children need to hear Mom and Dad tell each other, "I love you" and "I believe in you." Don't be shy about saying something like this to your spouse in front of your children. They need to hear it.

I frequently give verbal reassurance of my love and respect for my wife to my kids also. I will say to them, "You know, your mother is the most fantastic woman in the world. I can't believe how lucky I am to be married to her! I sure do love her." This verbalizing of love can come in a negative context as well. During our oldest child's preteen stage, there were times when my wife and daughter found themselves clashing in an occasional tug-of-war. And during this time, Kelly got into the habit of sassing her mother, usually while I was out of town.

Because Dottie was there every day and Kelly's sassing had gradually become more common, she didn't fully realize the disrespect Kelly was showing. Dottie therefore tolerated her behavior. One time, however, Kelly sassed Dottie while I was home, and I overheard it.

I sat Kelly down in a chair. Then I got down on one knee and looked her squarely in the eye. "Young lady," I said, "you might talk to your mother that way, but I'll never let you talk to my wife that way! I love that woman."

Believe it or not, that one stern message broke Kelly of the sassing habit. Just a few months later she started to sass Dottie in my presence again. Suddenly she caught herself, turned to me, and said, "Oh, Daddy, I can't do that to your wife, can I?"

Another way I verbalize my love and respect for Dottie in front of our children is by leaving lots of little love messages for Dottie to find and the kids to see. Around Valentine's Day, stores have mushy cards and stickers, and I'll buy a bunch of them to use all year long. Then before I leave on a trip, I'll hide these all over the house for her, and I'll often ask the kids to suggest where I should put them. They've left them on the milk jug in the refrigerator, on the shower door, in her bathrobe, on her pillow, in a dresser drawer—just about anywhere.

Dottie really enjoys these reminders of my love, and the children have a blast watching her find them. And all that time, they are learning how to give and receive love.

Another suggestion is to involve your kids in helping plan special events for your spouse. Several years ago when our kids were younger, I got the idea of asking them to help me plan my anniversary celebration with Dottie. I got them together and said, "Now look, I'm going to take your mom away for a couple of days. What can I do to really express to your mother that I love her?" The children and I had a lot of fun planning that anniversary, and I've tried to make it a practice ever since to consult them for gift ideas, party ideas, and minivacation ideas for their mother.

To help me know better how to love my wife, not only have I asked her for insights on what demonstrates my love for her, but I have asked many wives what communicates to them that their husbands love them. The list has not only been eye-opening for me, but it is quite long. I share it with you because it might guide you in loving your wife as it has me.

How My Husband Models Love

- He initiates family devotions.
- He initiates conversation on a deeper level.
- He gives me tasteful public displays of affection—winks, pats, eye contact.
- He verbalizes to the family that "my wife is a special person."
- He does something with me that I like to do that he doesn't like to do.
- He verbalizes his love for me to others by bragging on me.
- He is quick to forgive. He shows unconditional love and acceptance.
- He makes sure that I have time for myself and for the Lord.
- He holds me accountable.
- He gives me special surprises and gifts.
- He remembers special days.
- He listens with eye contact, silence, and remembers what I said.
- He values my feelings even if they are not rational or logical.
- He shares his feelings with me and demonstrates trust.

- He loves our children and notices the little things they do.
- He notices the way I look and dress.
- He compliments me on the special things and notices when I work hard at something.
- He helps me with routine tasks like cleaning off the table.
- He babies me when I am sick.
- He initiates and takes care of an entire date.
- He has love for and interest in my family.
- He is sensitive to my moods and, when I am down, encourages me and says something kind.
- He is disciplined and sets goals.

Here is a list for wives similar to the one above for husbands.

How My Wife Models Respect

- She verbally confirms her trust in me.
- She honors, supports, and praises me in public and in front of our children.
- She makes time for me and offers her time to do my interests.
- She seeks my advice.
- She encourages me to be all I can be.
- She never criticizes me in public.
- She listens attentively.
- She believes in me and knows I will do the right thing.
- She trusts and supports my decisions.
- She verbalizes that she loves and respects me.
- She affirms me by suggesting that others seek me out for advice or counsel.
- She gives me freedom and respects my private time.
- She does not flirt with other men.
- She holds a high opinion of who I am, what I do, and what I say.
- She prepares my favorite meals.
- She allows me to dream and set goals and helps me to achieve those dreams.

My wife and I often display appropriate, genuine physical affection for each other in front of our children. I'm convinced that such displays are healthy. Taking that a step further, our children know that Dottie and I have sex together and that we really enjoy it. Of course, we are modest and discreet about it.

It is interesting that many children, even as adults, have trouble imagining that their parents enjoy God's gift of sex. It is a natural and beautiful part of the marriage relationship, and children need to know that. When they see Mom and Dad modeling affection in the proper context (the marriage relationship), they learn that this is the right place for it. They learn that sexual intimacy is a good thing. And they learn it is still possible to have a relationship that will satisfy all their needs and honor God, too, even in today's world.

The Challenges of a Single Parent

If you are a single parent, you don't need me to tell you that you face an especially tough job. Whether it's through death or divorce, you don't have a spouse with whom you can model a strong, loving relationship. If you're married but your relationship with your spouse is cold, at least you have hope that through love, work, counseling, and prayer, your marriage can become what it ought to be. The single parent, however, doesn't have that hope. What do you do?

Unfortunately, there is no easy answer. Other people can be brought into your child's life to help make up for the absence of a father or mother. We will consider that in a moment. And as long as there is no threat of violence, abduction, or moral harm, it's best if both parents, even though divorced, stay active in a child's life.

Still, if you are a single parent, there is no way you can model a loving marriage relationship for your child. There are only three things I can suggest.

First, even more than the married parent, you need to "overdose" your children with love. You need to spend time with them and be creative in planning activities and discussion. As much as possible, you should supply your children's need for parental love by yourself. I know it takes energy and enthusiasm, two things most single parents don't have much of because they live under greater-than-normal pressures due to work and household responsibilities. But it is what your children desperately need. Aggressively loving your children takes a firm commitment on your part.

Second, even if you are divorced, you should talk to your kids realistically but positively about what marriage can be. You can paint for your children a word picture of what married love is all about. You can instill the hope that a lasting, satisfying marriage is a very real possibility. Don't be afraid to admit any mistakes you might have made.

Third, you should demonstrate by your actions as well as by your words that marriage is the only proper setting for a sexual relationship. In other words, as a single parent, you yourself have to resist all the pressures of our society to engage in premarital sex.

HOW TO REINFORCE POSITIVE VALUES
When asked who influenced their decisions about sex the most, more teens cited their parents than any other influences (37 percent).[2] In comparison, 30 percent of teens said that friends influenced their sexual decision making the most. An equal percentage (11 percent) of teens identified the media and their religious communities as the most influential.[3]

Your relationship with your kids and the relationship they see in you as Mom and Dad are powerful and necessary. But unless your family lives alone on a tiny, uncharted island in the ocean, your kids are exposed to many other influences, and some of those influences may not be as positive on their lives as yours. Have you ever thought about how little time you and your spouse actually get to spend with your school-age kids in a typical week? Much of each day from Monday through Friday, your child is in school. More time is used as your child walks, drives, rides a bike, or takes a bus to and from school.

Before school, of course, everyone in the family is running around trying to get ready for the day. After school, your child may be involved in extracurricular activities, sports, a job, or social activities. If you are a single parent, or both you and your spouse work outside the home, you may not see your child before dinner even if he or she does come straight home after classes. On weekends, if you have an adolescent in the family, he or she is probably busy much of the time with friends, work, or dating.

When we stop to tally the time, we probably have only a few minutes or hours at best during the week when we can have much direct input into our kids' lives. Who are the other people who spend time with our children and undoubtedly exert a significant influence on them?

In years past, a child was influenced not only by his or her parents but by grandparents, aunts, and uncles who were living in the same house or nearby. But the mobility and urbanization of our society have made the extended family living in proximity to each other largely a thing of the past. I don't mean to romanticize our pasts, but it is true that children had more influence from other family members when we were a more rural and less mobile society. Today, as parents, we are pretty much on our own. We need to see to it that when our children are not under our influence, the influences they *are* under will help support rather than undermine our values.

Encourage Positive Peer Pressure

Peer pressure is usually thought of as a negative influence, and it often is. But if we help our children find good peer groups, it actually can be a very positive thing. For example, my son, Sean, was part of several soccer teams as he was growing up. These teams provided peer pressure as good as I could hope for. The kids on these teams were a great influence on him. It helped that some of the coaches were Christian men, but this was not essential for good peer influence. We should seek out this kind of experience for our children whenever possible.

Other places where your kids might find positive peer pressure are in Boy Scouts or Girl Scouts, the YMCA or YWCA, Boys and Girls Clubs, 4-H, a church youth group, or some after-school activity, such as sports, drama, band, ballet, or the school newspaper.

Don't assume, however, that just because your children are involved in a good activity they are necessarily under good influence. Take the time to get to know their coaches, advisers, and group leaders, as well as the other kids in the group. You might even invite them over to dinner to become better acquainted with them. I'm not suggesting that you should give them the third degree or immediately withdraw your children from a group if the others involved are not Christians. But you should know what input your kids are receiving and how to counter any negative influence if necessary.

It is also important, of course, that you continually talk to your children about their activities and friends. If you have established a loving connection with them as we discussed in chapter 16, you should have the quality of communication that lets you know pretty well how things are going.

Get Involved with School and Teachers

In addition to peers, a young person's teachers certainly rank near the top of the list of influential people in his or her life. We will want to take advantage of opportunities like parent-teacher conferences, PTA meetings, and parent auxiliaries at school to know our children's teachers. If there are any problems at any time, don't hesitate to call a teacher and arrange a meeting.

Most teachers are caring professionals who want to do a good job. However, you may come across teachers who don't share your Christian values. Remember that, intentionally or not, all teachers, by example if nothing else, promote their values to their students.

Look carefully, also, at the content of textbooks and courses. We need to know what ideas and values are being formally presented to our children. Although some professional educators want to argue this point, the fact remains that our children's education is primarily *our* concern and *our* responsibility, not the teachers'. As parents, we have a right not to have our values undercut by what the school is teaching. So don't be afraid to object if you find offensive material in what your children are being taught.

Latchkey Kids and Single Parenting

The phenomenon of the latchkey kid is growing steadily in this country, and it presents another parenting challenge. If your young person is going to be home for several hours without adult supervision, who or what will be exerting the influence over her or him during that time? Will it be peers, soap operas, videos, MTV, or something else?

You should also know that whereas the backseat of a car used to be the most popular place for adolescent sexual activity, that is no longer the case. Today the most common place is at home, in the afternoon from three to five, when the kids are home from school and Mom and Dad are still at work.

What are your options? You can try to get your child involved in an activity, such as sports, drama, clubs, or an after-school job. Or perhaps you can find a nearby relative, neighbor, or friend who is home and to whose house your child can go after classes, a place where he or she will be supervised by a good adult role model.

If you are a single parent, you can help your child by finding some "para-parents" to get involved with him or her. These people should be a stable and loving married couple who can spend time with your young person and exert a good influence. Among other things, they can show your child what a solid and loving marriage looks like. A good place to look for such people is in your church; your pastor might be able to suggest a couple.

Even if your own marriage is solid, if you live a distance from grandparents, you might want to find some "adoptive" grandparents for your child. These should be people who can spend time with your child, model a strong marriage, and share the wisdom of their years. Such people also can be a tremendous blessing to the single parent.

The Power of Books

While you must seek to provide your child with a healthy circle of contacts, you must also realize that you can influence his or her thinking through good reading material. Try to develop in your child a love for great books, including the Bible. Most young children love to read, and that's a love you should continually encourage. Great books can occupy a child, including an adolescent, for hours at a time. And they can serve to teach and reinforce the Christian values you want your children to make their own too.

I would particularly suggest you introduce your older child to biographies and journals of some of the marvelous saints of the past: Hudson Taylor, D. L. Moody, Jonathan Edwards, Henrietta Mears, Jim Elliot, George Whitefield, Dawson Trotman, Augustine, Billy Sunday, Eric Liddell, John Bunyan, Mother Teresa, and C. S. Lewis, to name just a few. Reading about these spiritual giants, their mistakes as well as their accomplishments, can be a tremendous example and inspiration to your young person. Also, biographies of Christian sports figures and music artists can be extremely helpful.

Guidelines for Helping Kids Navigate Cyberspace

As we discussed earlier in the book, the home computer with its easy Internet access opens the door to potentially damaging influences coming right into our homes. Here are a number of helpful tips for protecting your kids from pornography and other negative influences on the Internet.

- Establish on-line rules and an agreement with your child about Internet use away from home (i.e., at a friend's house, at school, or at the library).
- Become more computer literate and develop Internet savvy so that you can keep up-to-date on products, news, and opinions surrounding the issues of children's safety on the Internet.

- Spend time on-line alongside your child, and establish an atmosphere of trust regarding computer usage and on-line activities.
- Place your computer in an area of your home where you can easily monitor your child's Internet activity.
- Regularly ask your child about his or her on-line friends and activities.
- Implement software tools to protect your family from the intrusion of inappropriate content or activity.
- Supervise your child's chat-room activity, and only allow him or her in monitored chat rooms.
- Block instant/personal messages from people you and your child don't know.
- Do not permit your child to have an on-line profile. With this restriction, he or she will not be listed in directories and is less likely to be approached in chat rooms where pedophiles often search for prey. (Some on-line service providers such as America Online offer subscribers on-line profiles.)
- Many Internet sites allow children to set up free home pages. Discuss with your child what information he or she can have on the page. For example, interests and hobbies are probably okay, but a home phone number is not!
- Check with your child's school to see if kids' projects, artwork, or photos (where material is identified by name) are being put on school home pages. Schools often want to post school newsletters or sports scores, but every time a full name is displayed, there is vulnerability. Schools need to be reminded of the risk.
- Monitor the amount of time your child spends on the Internet, and at what times of day. Excessive time on-line, especially at night, may indicate a problem.
- Watch for changes in your child's behavior (mention of adults you don't know, secretiveness, inappropriate sexual knowledge, sleeping problems, etc.).[4]

Being a parent today isn't easy, not in our postmodern culture, and not when we really have very little time with a school-age child. But with some thought, planning, and effort, we can surround our kids with a healthy circle of contacts who will reinforce the Christian values we are carefully teaching.

HOW TO COMMUNICATE GOD'S PERSPECTIVE ABOUT SEX

It is healthy for young people to study the Scriptures and gain a thorough understanding of God's perspective about sex. Such an understanding is essential for anyone who wants to say no to premarital sex.

God designed and created sex. It is not dirty or evil, and God is not down on sex. It is a carefully planned aspect of our humanness, intended for our benefit and God's glory. The Song of Solomon is not only a beautiful love story, it is also a wholesome sex manual. And the apostle Paul in the New Testament not only approves of sex between marriage partners, he also recommends it often. Anyone who questions whether sex is good is actually questioning God's goodness.

The best place for young people to learn God's perspective about sex is at home. Here are a few key elements about sex you should be sharing with your kids.

In the Beginning Was Sex

To put sex into God's perspective, we need to go back to the beginning. "And the Lord God formed man of the dust of the ground, and breathed into his nostrils the breath of life; and man became a living soul" (Gen. 2:7, KJV). Adam was the culmination of God's creative plan. "God saw every thing that he had made, and, behold, it was very good" (Gen. 1:31, KJV).

Yet after the creation of man, God observed that something was not good. "And the Lord God said, It is not good that the man should be alone" (Gen. 2:18, KJV). God's creation, although good, was incomplete. God had "created man in his own image" (Gen. 1:27, KJV). This made man a social being, because God is a social being. Anyone created in God's image has the God-given ability to relate to others—to God and to other human beings. As good and perfect as God's creation was, it was not good that Adam was alone.

It is interesting to note that God didn't solve Adam's loneliness problem by creating more men. Instead, he created woman. With the debut of the second sex, God's creation was now complete.

It is important for young people to feel good about being male and female and to accept their sexuality as a gift from God. The psalmist says, "I praise you because I am fearfully and wonderfully made" (Ps. 139:14). The creation of the human body, with its sex drives and organs, is something to thank him for. There are no reasons to be ashamed. From the beginning, human sexuality is seen as a reflection of the character of God, and its existence is described as "very good."

As you study God's perspective on sex, three things become apparent:

1. God is pro-sex. He created sex, and he wants us to enjoy it to the fullest. If anyone has any doubts, read the Song of Solomon.
2. Sexual intercourse is intended for oneness. There is no expression of unity between a man and a woman that is more intimate than this. Oneness is one of the primary purposes of sex.
3. God designed sex for marriage—it is meant to take place between a husband and wife. Since oneness is the primary purpose for sexual intercourse, it is evident why God has restricted it to the context of marriage.

Sex is designed to be enjoyable and fulfilling.
God intended for sex to be enjoyable for a husband and wife. You can see that clearly in Proverbs 5:18-19: "Let your wife be a fountain of blessing for you. Rejoice in the wife of your youth. She is a loving doe, a graceful deer. Let her breasts satisfy you always. May you always be captivated by her love" (NLT). People ask me, "Do you take the Bible literally?" I sure like to here! Does this passage of Scripture make sex sound awful, dirty, nasty, not to be enjoyed? No. This is the way God says that a husband should enjoy sex with the wife of his youth, and vice versa.

Sex is something beautiful; it is something that is righteous and holy and enjoyable between a husband and wife. This is how God designed sex, within the context of marriage. But it is not fulfilling when husband and wife engage in it with a selfish attitude. Instead of approaching marriage with the attitude What can you do for me? couples must adopt the attitude What can I do for you?

Sex is oneness.
Eve not only provided companionship for Adam, but her arrival made possible a special kind of male-female unity or oneness—physically, psychologically, and spiritually. "For this reason a man will leave his father and mother and be united to his wife, and they will become one flesh" (Gen. 2:24).

This means not just the blending of bodies, but also the merging of minds, the assimilation of souls. Genesis 2, the last account of a world without sin, ends gloriously with two sexual beings, unclothed and unashamed, free to enjoy sex. God looks on their nakedness and their sexual union with the smile of complete approval.

Marriage, in God's plan, is the permanent bonding of two people. Paul uses the analogy of Christ and the church to provide a deeper understanding of that union (Eph. 5:31, 32). Based on that relationship, divorce is not an option for two believers. To a culture that lives for the moment and marries for the moment, the Christian concept of lifelong commitment to one person stands out in sharp contrast.

God's Specific Plan for Sex

It helps young people say no if they realize that God has a special purpose for their lives and a specific plan for their sexuality, within the context of marriage. One student passed along this simple word of encouragement for other young people about God's plan for sex:

> Know that there is a God in heaven who cares for you very much. He has designed you and your sexuality for a specific plan in your life—to take place in the context of marriage.

There are three basic reasons for sex in marriage: procreation, identification, and recreation.

- *Procreation*: for the purpose of having children and creating a family
- *Identification*: for the purpose of developing "oneness" between a husband and a wife in three important dimensions—the physical, psychological, and spiritual
- *Recreation*: for the purpose of pleasure and enjoyment

The pleasure that sex provides—the very reason it is so appealing even outside of marriage—is God's creation. When, according to God's plan, sex is experienced within the context of marriage, the pleasure is maximized. In the commitment of marriage—without guilt and without any sense of "lustful taking"—the act of intercourse becomes indescribably enjoyable and beautiful. One young person aptly summarized:

> Think of the beautiful compositions of Mozart or Beethoven—it is incredible the number of rules these composers strictly adhered to regarding intervals, rhythms, chord progressions, and so on. Yet their music is far more lovely, harmonious, and

free than the discord that results when no rules are followed. Rules, and especially God's rules, are good discipline that yield greater peace and joy in our lives than we could ever imagine!

HOW TO TEACH SEX AT HOME

Occasionally, when Dottie is busy, my secretary will pick me up at the airport after one of my trips.[5] One time she brought two of my kids along, so I decided to sit in the backseat with Kelly, who was ten at the time, and Sean, who was eight. During the ride home, as often happens with kids, they got into a little argument. In the middle of their spat, my angelic eight-year-old Sean said to his sister, "F___ you!"

My secretary immediately and visibly tensed up and began glancing in the rearview mirror, eager to see how I would respond. How would most parents respond in that situation? When I ask that question in high school and college assemblies, the kids quickly answer that their parents would say things like, "Shut up!" or "That's nasty" or "I'm going to wash your mouth out with soap if you ever say that again." Maybe you would have a similar response.

But I saw Sean's words as a golden opportunity to teach. Sean obviously didn't know what the f-word meant. If I had jumped all over him and told him how dirty the word was, he would have learned not only that the word was bad, but he also would have had a negative impression about the sex act itself when he learned what it was.

So instead I said, "Son, where did you learn that word?"

"On the school bus," he answered.

"Do you know what it means?" I asked.

"No," he said.

"Can I explain it to you then?" I said.

"Yeah!" he answered. "What is it?" He was dying to know. And for the next forty minutes, I had a fabulous opportunity to teach my son and daughter about the sanctity, beauty, and purpose of sex. I shared with him that the f-word degraded God's beautiful gift. It was an opportunity for which I am extremely grateful, an experience I'll never forget—nor, I suspect, will they.

This story illustrates several points. First, and most important, proper sex education, or what I prefer to call "life education," is vital and ought to come from parents before it comes from anyone else. Teaching our kids about sex is part of our overall responsibility and thrilling privilege as parents to prepare them for life and the proper enjoyment of God's gifts.

Second, the first time a parent teaches a child about sex should not be in a formal setting as the child approaches puberty—the "big talk"—but natural opportunities to tell children what they are ready to hear. If you have given your child a good sex education when he or she is growing up, the "big talk" will not be necessary.

Third, it is unfortunate that sex education is ignored by most parents, both Christian and non-Christian, out of discomfort, ignorance, or indifference. According to surveys, most adolescents report they have *never* been given *any* advice about sex by either parent. In another study, "Only about one-third of the adolescents surveyed reported that they had 'good talks with my parents about sex.'" One young person wrote to me:

> Parents need to be more active in the process of their child's developing sexual maturity. Lines of communication need to be opened with the child about his understanding of sex and the feelings swirling around inside him or her, as the door to the sexual world is opened. The parent should be there to offer guidance and point the child in the right direction. Letting a child get into a situation that he or she is not emotionally ready to handle can very easily lead to devastation. In a young adolescent, the mind is often not as mature as the body. Parents need to be involved in each stage of the child's changing sexuality.

As you will see, the following suggestions assume that some or all of your children are still very young. But even if you have older children and adolescents, it is never too late to start teaching your kids about sex.

Where to Begin

The sex education of our children needs to begin at a very early age—in one sense, virtually from birth. Through their very early years, we need to let our children know that the body is a wonderful gift from God, and all bodily functions and parts are normal and nothing to be ashamed of. When children touch their genitals in play during bath time, for example, as they will do, they should not have their hands slapped and told that they are doing something dirty. In the proper context, sex is a natural and healthy part of life, and that's the impression we ought to give to our children—not that sex is some mysterious and somehow ugly thing.

Actual discussion and verbal teaching about sex needs to begin as early as three or four years of age. In our sex-saturated society, kids are being exposed to sexual information from other sources. The question is not whether our children will receive some kind of sex education in their earliest years. They will. The only thing to be decided is whether they will learn first from us or from our culture.

Where do our young people get their information about sex? One study ranked the primary sources of sex information gained by teenagers:

- 61 percent from peers
- 44 percent from sex-education classes
- 40 percent from TV and movies
- 39 percent from teen magazines
- 32 percent from parents.[6]

As a parent, you should be the primary source for molding your child's perception of sex, not someone or something else. Don't let anyone or anything rob you of the joy of shaping your child's perception of sex in a healthy, biblical, and God-honoring way. However, we also need our pastors, youth pastors, and other Christian educators and leaders to support us and reinforce what we share with our kids.

Also remember that children want to learn from their parents. The younger they are, the more they want Mom and Dad to teach them about life and everything in it. Take advantage of your child's desire. Bear in mind, too, that it's always more difficult to correct wrong thinking than to prevent it. If we begin to teach our children the proper perspective early, we can save both us and our children a lot of grief later.

What to Say

The operative principle in teaching about sex is this: Little questions deserve little answers; big questions deserve big answers; and frank questions deserve frank answers. In other words, tailor what you teach to the age and actual question of the child. Loading down a child with too much information too soon can cause confusion and anxiety.

When you talk about sex, use the proper terms. Call a penis a penis and a vagina a vagina; don't use any cute little terms. Your kids will hear all those terms anyway, so teach them the proper terms so they will know what the slang terms refer to. Respect for sex is conveyed by the use of proper language, not the slang or vulgarity kids will pick up if left to themselves. If you are embarrassed to use the proper terms, your kids will pick up your feelings and also be embarrassed to speak frankly and reverently about sex.

Regarding the biological facts of sex and reproduction, you may feel inadequate for lack of knowledge. If so, don't be embarrassed, just go get the facts from a bookstore, library, or your family physician. Remember that you are on a mission to fulfill your obligation to educate your children. Other people who recognize how important that is will be glad to help you.

As your kids grow older, you should also teach them about the consequences of their words and actions in the area of sex. Our society constantly urges us to seek instant gratification of every desire, including sex. So you must constantly teach your children about the potential consequences of such irresponsible actions. They need to know that giving in to sex outside of marriage can lead to pregnancy, life-threatening diseases, and emotional scars that can last a lifetime.

Next, you need to teach your children that character is judged by what people say and do. And the quality of a person's love life — not just sex, but the whole relationship including marriage — is just a reflection of his or her overall character. Thus, when people use foul language with sexual connotations to degrade someone, they are revealing that they have a very low opinion of sex and certainly don't respect it the way God intended. A person's language reveals his or her opinion about sex. We need to urge our children to think carefully about their own use of language. Their alert ears take in a lot of profanity and vulgarity, and it's easy for young people to fall into the habit of speaking the same way if they don't stop to think about what they're saying and what it says about their character.

Always teach sex education in the context of values, never as mere biology. We should remind our children that sex is a gift from God for the committed bond of marriage. What we do sexually involves our relationship with God. Premarital sex violates his commands. On the positive side, his commands are all for our good. He knows and wants only what is best for us, not a cheap substitute.

How to Say It

How do we say to our kids what we need to say about sex? Very simply, you should take advantage of the many little, natural opportunities that come along. First, of course, your kids will ask many questions. Seize these chances; don't see them as crises or embarrassments. Don't be surprised, however, if questions come up at embarrassing moments, such as the night the pastor is over for dinner or when you are in the middle of the grocery store. Kids seem to have a weird sense of timing about speaking their minds.

You can also look for natural opportunities to teach when your child has not asked a question. On a visit to the zoo, for example, talk about the bear cub and how he got there. When you and your child see an obviously pregnant woman, talk about that. The opportunities are all around you. All you have to do is take advantage of them.

Once, when roller skating with Kelly and Sean, who were still ten and eight, we happened upon a wall sprayed with vulgar graffiti. Their eyes bugged out at the obscene pictures and four-letter words in big letters. So I stopped and bought them soft drinks, and we sat in front of the wall for several minutes while I explained all the words and symbols. The kids were all eyes and ears. I used the opportunity to explain to them how these words distorted and cheapened one of the most beautiful gifts God has given to a husband and wife.

Kelly and Sean never forgot that day. About three years later, Kelly and I were in a frozen yogurt shop when some high school kids walked in. Their language was full of sexual four-letter words. Kelly, who was then twelve, turned to me and said, "Daddy, that's not right, is it?"

I said, "No, but why isn't it?"

She then related to me our conversation about the graffiti from three years earlier. The lesson had really stuck. And you can do the same kind of teaching if you just look for the opportunities. Let the explanations and understanding come from you as a parent. You can put sex in the right perspective. You can share God's purpose for sex, its beauty, and the ways many people today are very distant from God's original design.

Bear in mind as you teach that each child is unique. Some kids will be able to understand more at an earlier age than others. Some will ask more questions. Some will just think a little differently. Be sensitive to your child's ability to understand, to his or her level of interest, and to the most effective ways for him or her to learn. Don't make the mistake of trying to push every child into the same mold.

HOW TO INSTILL CHRISTIAN VALUES ABOUT SEX

Teaching Christian values about sex is at least as important as teaching the biology of sex.[7] This was emphasized to me by a young man I will call Ron.

"I grew up in a neighborhood which consisted of about twelve guys, all one to three years older than me," he said. "Every weekend we'd get together to play sports, work on our cars, or talk about girls. Every weekend my mind was bombarded with the same general presuppositions about manhood: real men must be having sex with anyone and everyone. As I continued to listen to the older guys brag about their conquests, I began to fantasize about what it would be like for me."

Lacking objective values that said premarital sex is always wrong and not realizing the truth that everyone is *not* having sex, Ron soon became sexually active himself. And a few years later, he found himself waiting in his car outside the community hospital while his girlfriend was inside being tested for pregnancy. It had been two and a half months since her last period, and they both feared the worst.

"I was terrified," Ron said. "My mind was going crazy with all kinds of things. What if someone she knows sees her getting a pregnancy checkup? Gossip will spread like wildfire. What if she *is* pregnant? I don't believe in abortion, but getting rid of the evidence is sure better than suffering the embarrassment of having to get married!

"Married? Do I really love this girl enough to get married? She's the best thing that's ever happened to me, but I'm not ready to spend the rest of my life with her.

"What about my parents? They worked so hard to develop a good reputation in the community. They'll be crushed. Then there are my neighbors and the people at church. All this time they thought I was such a fine, upstanding young man."

Fortunately, the girlfriend wasn't pregnant, but she and Ron continued to have sex for another year until he became a Christian. Apparently, though, he was going to church all the time he was sexually active before his conversion. And what does Ron think of his premarital sexual activity now?

"As I reflect on this terrifying experience, I have come to realize my whole life could have been ruined, all because I chose to respond to some false thinking I picked up from other guys way back in junior high."

Ron grew up assuming that "real men must be having sex with anyone and everyone." The media bombards you and your children with the same message. And if your kids grow up with the same presuppositions about manhood that Ron had, they will either act in such a way as to be a "real man" or "real woman" or they will have a poor self-image because they assume they are not fulfilling their ideal of a "real man" or "real woman." They may also live a life of frustration because they can't (or feel they shouldn't) do what a "real man" or "real woman" would do.

The Christian Perspective of Relationships

The solution rests with our children internalizing a Christian perspective instead of accepting the world's presuppositions. Instilling this Christian perspective in our children is one of the most important legacies we can leave them and a significant factor in helping them to say no to premarital sex. Just talking about sex with children is not enough; parents must make a definite effort to convey their values and expectations about sexual activity to adolescents and to "connect" with them. Communicating values and expectations and "connecting" involve more than just one or two discussions. Rather, this communication will require modeling by the parent(s) and frequent repetition.[8]

Let's consider four specific ways, all having to do with relationships, in which the Christian perspective or agenda ought to be different from the world's agenda. Looking at them in this way will identify some of the values we need to instill in our children.

1. The Christian believes that each person is special and of great worth because each one is made in the image of God.
This means that every individual deserves dignity, respect, and consideration. In practical terms, a boy who lives with a Christian agenda will give dignity, respect, and consideration to his girlfriend.

2. The Christian believes that we should not manipulate people to please ourselves or to get our needs met at their expense.
To use people cheapens them. It implies that we think we are better than they are, that they don't deserve any better treatment from us. We should teach our children this value so that when they are tempted to use someone, or when someone else tries to manipulate them, alarm bells will go off and they will realize what's happening. For example, when a girl hears her boyfriend say, "If you

really love me, you will have sex with me," she should recognize that he is trying to use her. She will know that not only does he not love her, but he doesn't think much of her either.

3. *The Christian believes that we should treat others with the love and respect God gives us.*

This is the same appreciation we would like to receive from others, as described in 1 Corinthians 13:4-8: "Love is patient, love is kind. It does not envy, it does not boast, it is not proud. It is not rude, it is not self-seeking, it is not easily angered, it keeps no record of wrongs. Love does not delight in evil but rejoices with the truth. It always protects, always trusts, always hopes, always perseveres. Love never fails."

This passage pretty well describes the way God loves us, and that is the kind of love we want to receive from others. A Christian therefore gives to others the same quality of love (see Matt. 7:12).

4. *The Christian believes in the value of waiting.*

"Love is patient," 1 Corinthians 13:4 states. In God's perfect plan for us, there is a proper time and place for everything, including sex. Today not much value is placed on patience, on waiting for anything. The world says, "Are you lonely? Do you feel a need for intimacy? Are you curious about sex? No problem. There is no need to wait until marriage."

There is a time and place for sexual intimacy and pleasure, a time and place that God honors and which is best for us. That time and place is the marriage bed.

Teach Values Naturally and Casually

How can you instill biblical values about sex in your young people? The first is the most important way we instill anything in our kids: by example. The behavior, speech, and attitudes we *model* are the ones we will see most often in them. So we must begin by examining ourselves daily to see what attitudes, speech, and behavior we are displaying before our children. Actions speak louder than words—so much so that the words in most cases are a waste of breath if they are inconsistent with our actions.

But it is not enough to model Christian values. There is a need for deliberate, systematic teaching of them as well. Making the time to explain the values by which we live and why we think they will serve our children's best interests is time well spent. This kind of teaching takes place most easily in casual, relaxed settings. For example, mealtimes offer excellent opportunities to teach. When my kids were still in school, I often took them out for breakfast on the way to school. I would read a biblical passage, explain briefly what it said, and then ask my kids hypothetical questions that applied the principles.

Dinnertime at home can offer an equally good opportunity for discussion. But whenever you teach, you have to plan ahead. Good teaching and discussion don't happen automatically. You practice advance planning in your job, church, and community responsibilities. How much more important is your assignment to instill Christian values in your children.

As you instill values through this kind of informal teaching, you will want your kids to begin using Christian values to evaluate everything they see and hear. These values should become a sort of filter through which our children see the world. To help your child get into that habit, do some things together and then discuss them in light of the Christian perspective. Watch television together, read the same books, go to an occasional movie together, or listen to popular music. Ask, "What perspective is being presented here? How does it compare to our Christian values?"

Younger children will love spending this kind of time with you, but adolescents may be more difficult. They will appreciate the attention, especially if you are consistent in giving it. But it may seem awkward when you first try to do it. Stay with it. You and your kids will get used to it and end up having some great times together.

Parents, then, must assume the responsibility of educating their kids and regulating what the kids are exposed to. It doesn't mean the kids should be sheltered; rather, it means that kids should not be repeatedly exposed to false views of sex or allowed to have their curiosity aroused inappropriately. Sex needs to be discussed in the home.

Prohibition often leads to rebellion, and it certainly leads to curiosity. If parents say, "You can't watch this, and don't argue with me," the kids may sneak out and watch it at a friend's house just to see why. Their curiosity, rather than being toned down, intensifies when a subject is considered hush-hush.

Another way to satisfy this curiosity is to let kids know that their parents enjoy sex. It would be difficult for parents who have rarely or never discussed sex suddenly to be candid with their children, but it is possible. Such honesty and openness is better when started early. It will help take the mystique away from sex and will keep the children from feeling that they are being robbed by their parents of something they should have.

Kids need to understand that sex is so beautiful that it is worth waiting for. Its beauty is worth protecting by keeping it within the commitment of a loving marriage. Our goal as parents, therefore, is not to keep sex among adolescents unknown, just unexplored.

◆ ◆ ◆

Modeling a healthy sexual relationship in your marriage and instilling the facts and values about sex to your children are vital to convincing them to wait for sex. But they will not always be under the direct influence of your example and teaching. At some point they need to establish their own convictions about premarital sex and standards for relating to the opposite sex, so when they are on their own—out on a date, spending a week at summer camp, or away at college—they are ably equipped to deal with sexual pressures and temptations. In the next chapter we will talk about helping kids take such a stand.

CHAPTER 19

HELP KIDS DEVELOP THE STRENGTH TO SAY NO

"ALYSON, I REALLY LOVE YOU."

"I love you too, Brett."

"No, I mean I really love you, Alyson, more than I have loved anyone."

"I know what you mean. I feel that way too."

"Then we should celebrate."

"Celebrate? What do you mean, Brett?"

"You know, the way most people celebrate when they are deeply in love."

"Are you talking about sex?"

"Of course. We love each other. Sex is what people in love do. It's what I want us to do."

"Brett, I love you . . . I do. But love doesn't mean sex to me, at least not yet. I have decided to remain a virgin until I get married—until we get married, if we ever do."

"That's kind of old-fashioned, isn't it? Hey, it's the twenty-first century. Love means sex, sex means love."

"No, Brett, I won't have sex until my wedding night. And if you can't wait until then, maybe you aren't the one I'm waiting for."

"But Alyson, can't we talk about this?"

"No, Brett, because I made up my mind two years ago. I feel deeply about you, but my answer is still the same. The answer is no."

Where did Alyson get the fortitude to hold her ground? Why was her resolve unwavering, even in a moment of passion and deep feelings? It has everything to do with convictions, conscience, and commitment. She had made up her mind about sex; she was determined to wait. Too bad Brett. End of story.

From where does this kind of strength come, the strength to say no to sex even when it may be something a young person wants? It is a process that your young people can experience. It begins with developing convictions and conscience about sex.

ENCOURAGE THE DEVELOPMENT OF CONVICTIONS

People with strong convictions are willing to risk nonconformity with their peers because of their convictions about themselves—"That's not the kind of person I want to be"—and their convictions about values—"I don't think that's right, and I'm not going to do it!" Developing positive convictions can help a young person face negative peer pressure without giving in. A person without convictions will generally follow the lead of whatever group of people he or she happens to be with. However, someone who can stand up and say, "Hey, I've got my reasons," will usually have the strength to act independently of other people.

Consider the insights about convictions shared with me by young people:

It is difficult to wait, to be self-controlled, and not give in when "everybody else is doing it," but convictions and strong character are great benefits for any of us to possess.

◆　◆　◆

How are young persons to answer the unchecked invitations to be sexually indulgent? If an individual does not already possess the inner convictions to delay such "gratification" until after marriage, where will he draw his strength?

◆　◆　◆

Living on a college campus, I am free to live my life as I want—even my mother offered to buy me birth-control pills. I have to live by my own personal convictions.

◆　◆　◆

The decision to have or not have sex before marriage has to be a personal decision, made in one's own heart. If you wait until the pressure is on, chances are you'll be left with a broken heart because of your own failure to make a firm decision.

The Word of God is our only basis for strong convictions. The Bible is clear about sexual activities to be avoided for our own good, such as premarital and extramarital sex.

Flee from sexual immorality. All other sins a man commits are outside his body, but he who sins sexually sins against his own body. Do you not know that your body is a temple of the Holy Spirit, who is in you, whom you have received from God? You are not your own; you were bought at a price. Therefore honor God with your body. (1 Cor. 6:18-20)

◆ ◆ ◆

For this is the will of God, your sanctification; that is, that you abstain from sexual immorality; that each of you know how to possess his own vessel in sanctification and honor, not in lustful passion, like the Gentiles who do not know God. (1 Thess. 4:3-5, NASB)

Passages like these are clear about the quality of sexual behavior expected of Christians. The Bible teaches us to refrain from sex outside marriage, and later to enjoy sex within marriage. But it is not enough for our young people to know only passages dealing specifically with sexual behavior. It is insufficient to know only God's moral standards and principles. Kids also need to have a basis for answering such questions as: Who am I? Why am I here? Where am I going? Who is God? How does he see me? What is unconditional love? They need a total Christian worldview. What is a Christian worldview?

We each have a worldview. We may not be able to articulate it or explain it, but we all have one. It is not some vague, philosophical concept, but rather a personal perspective on the totality of life, a controlling force in each of our lives. Our worldview is the sum total of everything recorded within our minds. Rooted deep down in our psyche, our worldview affects all aspects of behavior, including one's sexual relationships and moral behavior.

Most young people today have worldviews not based entirely on God's truth (if at all). They have been programmed with views about sexuality that are contrary to God's views.

A Need for Transformation

During the Korean War more than half a century ago, a number of captured American servicemen were subjected by the enemy to experiences that were intended to "program" their minds and thus control or change their behavior. This mind-altering process has come to be known as "brainwashing." Interestingly, the apostle Paul was concerned about a related process when he wrote his epistle to the Romans: "Don't copy the behavior and customs of this world" (Rom. 12:2, NLT).

Most young people today in one sense have been brainwashed. The media, parents, and peers have an impact on them. Kids learn to copy the world that they see around them, forming their worldview.

In psychological terminology, young people have been "scripted" by their education, the media, and also by their life experiences, particularly with their families. This scripting, which can be either negative or positive, has a significant effect on their personal identity, self-worth, and sense of well-being. As a result, they may be seriously handicapped in their ability to develop the foundational convictions needed to say no to premarital sexual pressures.

The convictions people have about love and sexuality really begin with the role modeling of their parents. Convictions are built as children watch the actions of their parents and hear explanations about why they act as they do. That's why God gave us the family—to be the environment in which children learn and develop their own convictions about love, sex, and marriage. Regrettably, that critical learning process often malfunctions.

For one thing, many of the parents of today's young people have little or no convictions themselves about sexual values or morals. It is difficult for a child who grows up with people who have no strong convictions to develop any personal convictions of his or her own, particularly in an area as tempting as the sexual. Because of this, a process of transformation is necessary for both the teens and their parents. Romans 12:2 continues: "but let God transform you into a new person by changing the way you think" (NLT).

The transformation process involves three essential factors: God's truth, God's Spirit, and God's people. First, we need to teach the key biblical principles (truth) that relate to sexual morality. Second, we need the Holy Spirit to be the facilitator of the transformation process. Third, God's people—parents, youth leaders, pastors, teachers—need to be models of the convictions we want our youth to develop.

If we are going to help provide young people with convictions for directing their own sex lives, we need to help them find an environment in which the transformation of their minds can begin. That is the only way our young people can erase or overcome the results of copying the flawed patterns around them.

When we work with children from homes where the family has failed, the body of Christ must try to provide an environment in which God can transform their minds. We must become a "parafamily" to them. As Christian brothers and sisters, or even "para-parents," we must become the role models these young people never had. It is not enough to communicate data, no matter how doctrinally correct our words may be. Only in the context of loving relationships can truth be internalized and made a living part of one's life.

Transformed by God's Truth

As we mentioned earlier, young people need to know the whole truth, not merely the truth about sexual behavior. They need to know that

- they are created in God's image, with the ability to have relationships with God and with other human beings;
- they have value and worth because of the price that the Father paid for them: the death of his Son;
- God loves them with unconditional love and desires a relationship with them;
- God's love and acceptance are the basis for their own security;
- the way to express their love to God is to serve others; through serving others they can gain a sense of significance and identity.

An understanding of these truths, learned not by rote but in the context of loving relationships, is the Christian's basis for all behavior and all relationships, including the sexual.

Without this basis, sex is reduced to a matter of hormones and ultimately becomes nothing more than lust. But when sexual relationships are seen from the perspective of a Christian worldview, sex is elevated to its proper place alongside marriage and love. A young person with these convictions will have a much easier time controlling his or her hormones because true love will be the motivating force rather than lust. Remember: Lust can't wait to get, whereas love can't wait to give.

A young person's convictions ultimately must come from his or her own experiences and study of God's Word, not from another person. They must not merely be "head knowledge." They must be internalized deep within the psyche. The young person must "own" his or her convictions. Only then will those convictions be respected by others. One student expressed this insight:

A simple "I believe sex belongs only in marriage" will be respected, but you have to be decided and firm in your conviction, or you will not convince anyone else about your sincerity.

As we mentioned, the role of the Holy Spirit is a key factor in transforming our minds. We cannot live out our convictions apart from the indwelling power of the Holy Spirit. One aspect of the fruit of the Spirit is self-control. Other aspects are gentleness, kindness, and goodness.

How do we help young people develop strong convictions? We don't do it by superimposing our views on them. We can't force people to accept our convictions with a "believe this—or else!"

Let's look at the model of Jesus. When Jesus called his disciples, he didn't say, "First of all, you have to subscribe to my ethical convictions, my doctrines." He simply said, "Follow me." Then in the context of a loving relationship, in which Jesus accepted them and encouraged them, those men became willing to be accountable to their Lord. They grew in their understanding of the doctrines and truths of the faith, and they developed convictions that enabled many of them to face martyrs' deaths. It began, not with subscribing only to the doctrinal convictions of Jesus, but with making a commitment to a loving, accepting person.

One young man recognized the importance of preparing for this commitment:

When I realize a sexual opportunity, I will react either according to the environmental stimuli or according to a predetermined strategy. If I have no convictions, I will surely find myself in a compromising situation and will be overcome by passion. As a Christian, it was and is enough for me that God has said in the Bible that Christians should not have sex outside marriage. Anyone who claims to believe in the Bible and knows what it commands about this issue can have no other view. God has our ultimate good in mind when he gives us principles to live by. It is ironic that the very thing sought by sexually active singles eludes their grasp because of the action they take.

When you help your kids firm up their convictions by providing guidelines for their behavior, they are helped in three major ways:

1. They have an "out."
Caught in a tough situation, the teenager with restrictions always has an out: "Sorry, my parents won't let me"; or "I can't; my parents say no." When a young

person has been kept from undesirable situations, his character can develop with fewer unwanted influences.

2. They can exercise decisiveness.
When teenagers are told, "You can do whatever you want within these parameters," their field of options is narrowed and they are better able to make decisions, to know why they have made them, and to stand by them.

3. They can demonstrate self-control.
When young people follow guidelines, they learn to obey, and when they learn to obey, they learn self-control. It has been said wisely that if you don't have enough willpower to submit to someone else, you'll never have the willpower to submit to yourself. Self-control and decisiveness are two important elements of maturity. These two powerful tools will help young people deal with sexual temptations that surround them.

Mary Aguilera, director of Carson's Community Pregnancy Center in Nevada, says, "They can talk about statistics and numbers, but these are real people's lives. This is something girls are really going through. When government gets involved in things, it seems there's always a lot of red tape. . . . It's in the family that things have to happen. . . . It's about getting back to the fact that there's nothing wrong with teaching right and wrong. Anything else is a Band-Aid. We have to get to the problem."[1]

Standing up for convictions will result in conflict, not conformity. Young people must be aware that they are going to run into conflict with their friends as they develop and act on their convictions. Yet by developing convictions they will be rewarded with self-respect and maturity.

ENCOURAGE A CHRISTIAN CONSCIENCE
God has equipped each of us with a kind of moral compass or prompter that we call the conscience. Our conscience monitors our behavior and reminds us to do the "right thing." We may argue with it, disagree with it, or even try to silence it, but it continues to nag us about any behavior that conflicts with our worldview—how we see the world. If we see the world according to God's principles, our conscience will reflect that viewpoint. If we see our world from a nonbiblical viewpoint, our conscience will be effectively disabled in the area of moral guidance.

I was interested in how young people viewed the conscience in relation to their sexual temptations:

> If my girlfriend and I did not feel bothered by our consciences, perhaps it was because we hadn't fully developed a Christian conscience.

◆ ◆ ◆

> My sweeping passions would doubtless have led me into the grief of lost virginity, but for God's presence in my conscience.

The conscience is created in such a way that we can determine how and how much it works. It can be sensitized or desensitized by the response we make to it. The kinds of people we admire and spend time with, the ideas we entertain, the media we see and hear—all have a part in shaping our consciences. Squelching its promptings can silence it. One young woman wrote:

> I was raised in a good Christian home. I was always taught that sex before marriage was wrong. When my boyfriend and I began to get involved sexually, I felt guilty at first. Before long, I couldn't understand why I ever felt bad at all.

God has given us the freedom to participate in the shaping of our conscience. It can be shrunk or enlarged, dulled or sensitized, depending on how we respond to it. If I, as a Christian, listen to my conscience, I can become more sensitive to the Holy Spirit's voice as he seeks to guide my behavior through it.

How sensitive is your young person's conscience? Has it been weakened by a post-Christian or nonbiblical worldview? Has it been disabled by being constantly ignored? Here are some questions for kids to ask themselves as they evaluate the condition of their consciences in the area of sexuality. You may want to share this list of questions as you talk to them about their convictions:

- ◆ Are you doing things now that you once said you would never do?
- ◆ Was there ever a time when you looked down on others for doing what you are now doing?
- ◆ Are you doing things now, without feeling guilt, that once bothered you?
- ◆ Have you allowed a boyfriend or girlfriend to dull your conscience by going further and further sexually?

If any of the answers is yes, your child is in the process of desensitizing his or her conscience. Unless it is restored to its normal function, the conscience soon will be useless to protect him or her against sexual pressure.

How can the conscience be restored? First, your young person must stop ignoring it and begin listening to it. What people put into their minds directly affects their consciences. A friend of mine told me how shocked he had been the first time he saw sexual intercourse portrayed on a movie screen. Then he admitted that he isn't bothered at all by those scenes today. Repeated exposure to certain kinds of movies, television programming, books, music, and magazines can dull our consciences.

How can we develop a Christian conscience? By developing a Christian worldview. Again, this is done through God's truth, with the empowering of his Spirit, and with the help of his people. Remember that Paul said to Timothy, "The goal of our instruction is love from a pure heart and a good conscience and a sincere faith" (1 Tim. 1:5, NASB).

Here are some simple suggestions you can use to help your young people develop a working Christian conscience:

◆ Ask the Holy Spirit's help to cleanse and restore your conscience.
◆ Flood your mind with God's principles about life, love, and values.
◆ Limit your relationships to mature Christians who already have developed a Christian conscience.

ENCOURAGE A COMMITMENT TO ABSTINENCE

In addition to helping your child fortify his or her convictions and conscience, it is helpful to encourage him or her to make a commitment to wait until marriage for sex. When adolescents report that they have taken a pledge to remain a virgin until marriage, they are more likely to delay intercourse.[2] Abstinence is the only safe sex, so encouraging our kids to make a pledge to remain virgins until marriage is well worth the investment.

A tremendous amount of time, money, and effort has been spent trying to "educate" adolescents about some of the dangers and consequences of premarital and "unsafe" sex. Has it worked? "A study performed by Louis Harris and Associates for Planned Parenthood showed that teenagers who have had comprehensive sex education at school were 54 percent more likely to have had sex than teenagers who have had no sex education. . . . Not a single peer review research study has shown that comprehensive sex education appreciably reduces teen pregnancy."[3]

In contrast, abstinence-only messages seem to be having some positive effects.

- The growth of the abstinence-only message coincides with the [slight decline in the early 1990s] improvement in the data reflecting adolescent behavior.
- Scientific research demonstrates that abstinence programs are effective.
- Between 1982 and 1987 a community abstinence message implemented in Denmark, S.C., reduced teen pregnancy by 59 percent.
- Inner city students in the Best Friends program in Washington, D.C., were reported to have a pregnancy rate of only 1.1 percent compared to an overall city pregnancy rate among high school aged females of 26 percent.
- A recent study in *The Journal of the American Medical Association* entitled "Add Health" reported that the factor most associated with a delay in early sexual onset was a pledge of virginity. The virginity pledge is a foundational aspect of the True Love Waits abstinence program.[4]

Participation in the True Love Waits campaign—those who have turned in pledge cards promising to wait for sex until they are married—is increasing annually. The True Love Waits campaign started small in 1993 with its first meeting in Nashville, Tennessee. The following year, the campaign displayed more than 100,000 signed virginity pledge cards at the Southern Baptist Convention, and 210,000 cards on the National Mall in front of the United States Capitol. In 1996, True Love Waits visited the Atlanta Georgia Dome, where they stacked 340,000 commitment cards to the roof and beyond. In 1997, the campaign hit college campuses, where more than 500,000 commitment cards were distributed. And in 1999, True Love Waits conducted its "Crossing Bridges With Purity" display, where 100,000 signed commitment cards were carried across San Francisco's Golden Gate Bridge.[5]

These numbers represent young people who have categorically decided to wait for marriage before engaging in sexual activity. And statistics have shown that the virginity pledge is not an empty promise. In overwhelming numbers, the pledge has been a pivotal factor in helping young people wait for sex.

Some abstinence-based programs, however, are seeing some marked results. Best Friends, a program that promotes abstinence and includes pairing participants with adult mentors, found that "teenagers involved in Best Friends from grades five through twelve had a 1.1 percent pregnancy rate while teen peers not participating in the program had a pregnancy rate of 26 percent."[6]

A study reported in *The Journal of the American Medical Association* found a strong correlation between abstinence teaching and "delaying the initiation of sexual intercourse," as shown in the following quotes:

- "Significant family factors associated with delaying sexual debut included high levels of parent-family connectedness, parental disapproval of their adolescent's being sexually active and parental disapproval of their adolescent's using contraception."
- "Adolescents who reported having taken a pledge to remain a virgin were at significantly lower risk of early age sexual debut. Nearly 16 percent of females and 10 percent of males reported making such pledges."
- "A higher level of importance ascribed to religion and prayer was also associated with a somewhat later age of sexual debut."[7]

The study also found that "among sexually experienced females aged fifteen years and older, 19.8 percent reported having ever been pregnant. A greater number of shared activities with parents and perceived parental disapproval of adolescent contraceptive use were protective factors against a history of pregnancy."[8]

The study concluded:

With notable consistency across the domains of risk, the role of parents and family in shaping the health of adolescents is evident. While not surprising, the protective role that perceived parental expectations play regarding adolescents' school attainment emerges as an important recurring correlate of health and healthy behavior. Likewise, while physical presence of the parent in the home at key times reduces risk, it is consistently less significant than parental connectedness (e.g., feelings of warmth, love, and caring from parents). The home environment also plays a role in shaping negative health outcomes.[9]

In response to this article, Dr. Jonathan D. Klein said in an accompanying editorial: "The authors also appropriately question the ways that some current social and economic policies threaten family connectedness; one can only hope that federal, state, and local government, including local school boards, will heed this call to develop policies that support families rather than those that try to impose particular values."[10]

Religious Values and Abstinence

An abstinence-only message seems to be an effective preventive measure in protecting young people from becoming involved in premarital sex. A young person's religious convictions are an important element in pledging to remain a virgin. According to teens surveyed by the Kaiser Family Foundation and *YM* magazine, 78 percent identify religion as at least somewhat important to them, while 43 percent say it is *very* important. "The more importance a teen boy or girl places on religion, the more likely he or she is to name this as their reason for delaying intercourse instead of reasons such as 'worried about pregnancy or STDs' or 'haven't met the right person yet.'"[11]

IMPORTANCE OF RELIGION					
	Total	**Very**	**Somewhat**	**Not too**	**Not at all**
Made a conscious decision to wait					
Total	44%	55%	40%	36%	18%
Boys	39%	51%	38%	31%	17%
Girls	49%	59%	41%	45%	21%
Have had sexual intercourse					
Total	31%	24%	36%	35%	41%
Boys	36%	26%	39%	43%	51%
Girls	26%	21%	33%	23%	18%
Have had multiple partners					
Total	15%	14%	16%	15%	20%
Boys	19%	17%	20%	19%	26%
Girls	11%	10%	13%	9%	6%

Without a biblical point of reference, kids feel confused and empty, which leaves them powerless to resist sexual pressures. This in turn leads to insecurity and the need to hold on to something or someone; that is, it drives kids to search for intimacy with another person.

But intimacy requires giving of one's self, and in a culture that is self-centered, young people quickly give up hoping to find lasting intimacy. Instead, they settle for temporary physical closeness. Without guidelines, kids don't recognize right and wrong. They know only that they have found a closeness that makes them feel good for the moment. They have submitted to society's relativism.

HOW FAR IS TOO FAR?

After having established with teens that sex before marriage is forbidden by God and that it's not "smart" for them to be involved sexually, we need to be prepared to answer a difficult question: How far can I go? Or even better, How far *should* I go?

At first glance it may seem that the Bible isn't very helpful in answering that question. It's true there is no list of specific do's and don'ts. You won't find a passage that states, "It's all right to hold hands, but not all right to kiss for longer than one minute." The Bible does not give specific black-and-white answers in every area of sexual behavior. Yet the Bible does give some clear guidelines for avoiding sexual immorality, guidelines that can be used to set personal limits to "necking" and "petting."

The lack of explicit direction, however, has given rise to a number of misconceptions, and we want to look at them here.

Everything But

One common misconception is what I call the "everything but—" philosophy. According to this view, since the Bible offers no express prohibition against anything except actual intercourse, a person can meet biblical standards for chastity as long as they stop short of actual penetration. But does this "technical virginity" really meet God's standards for sexual purity?

In actuality, such an outlook is a kind of reverse legalism. We're all familiar with the kind of legalism that sets up an artificial list of rules and regulations for Christian behavior based on human standards. Yet there is a reverse legalism that sets up a specific list of don'ts and then proclaims that all unspecified actions are acceptable behavior. R. C. Sproul calls this "legal loophole-ism."[12]

This kind of legalism searches for loopholes to get around the laws of God. Somehow one manages to keep the letter of the law but totally disregards the spirit underlying the law.

True godliness results not only in obedience to the letter of the law but also in obedience to its spirit. Doing "everything but—" certainly disregards the spirit of God's commandment to "flee fornication." If we sincerely want to please God, we cannot base our sexual behavioral limits on "everything but —"!

Sexual Brinkmanship

"Sexual brinkmanship" is also an unacceptable approach to the question, How far can I go? It is human nature to test the limits, to go as close to the brink of disaster as we can without getting hurt. While we don't want to go too far, we do want to go as far as possible—because we're afraid of cheating ourselves out of anything that might be pleasurable or exciting. So we go right up to the edge. We push ourselves to the limits of our sexual control. It's like driving a car along a steep cliff and asking, How close can I get to the edge?

The problem is that if we lose control and go further than intended—and the odds are that anyone playing "sexual brinkmanship" will—we end up hurting ourselves and other people. You see, most people who play sexual brinkmanship end up disobeying not only the spirit of the law but also its letter.

Many young couples don't understand that sex is a progressive activity that culminates in intercourse. They think they can just start downhill and then slam on the brakes when they reach the brink of intercourse. However, this is a misunderstanding of how we were created. Once arousal begins it is unnatural to stop short of full expression.

Sexual stimulation was designed by God to prepare marriage partners for intercourse, not as a pleasant activity that can be easily interrupted. Stimulation, or foreplay, is intended for one thing only: precipitating a married couple into a complete expression of their sexuality. Not only is the interruption of sexual foreplay almost impossible, but it is also highly frustrating. When sexually frustrated, our bodies don't care about Christian convictions.

Lust has an insatiable appetite. The more we feed it, the hungrier it gets. With each progressive step of sexual intimacy we take, desire is increased, never decreased. That's why allowing ourselves "minor" compromises of ever-increasing sexual intimacy ultimately violates the spirit of the law and leads us to commit sexual sin.

Measuring How Far

What guidelines *does* Scripture offer to help young people obey both the spirit and the letter of the law regarding sexual purity? Here is one insight that will help kids answer the question, How far is too far? Explaining how believers can live a God-pleasing life, the apostle Paul wrote: "This is the will of God, your sanctification; that is, that you abstain from sexual immorality; that each of you know how to possess his own vessel in sanctification and honor, not in lustful passion, like the Gentiles who do not know God; and that no man transgress and defraud his brother" (1 Thess. 4:3-6, NASB).

The word *transgress* means "to sin by going beyond a limit or boundary." The word *defraud* means "to take advantage of." In this passage, transgress and defraud can mean "to arouse sexually outside the bounds of God's limits." What are God's limits for sex? Marriage, and marriage only.

You have transgressed and defrauded a brother or sister when you have gone beyond the limits and aroused him or her to the point where that arousal cannot be fulfilled in a way that would be pleasing to God. Within the boundaries of a loving marriage, arousal is not defrauding, because our sexual fulfillment is pleasing to God. However, in a dating relationship, arousal is defrauding, because there is no way to fulfill that arousal without displeasing God.

Now the exact point of defrauding may vary for different individuals. Not everyone has the same "turn-on point." Some get turned on by just holding hands. Others are able to go further without being aroused. Of course, some arousal is normal and should not be worried about too much. But if it becomes so strong that it rules your actions, then it is sin. When a young person's hormones replace good judgment in controlling his or her sexual behavior, he or she is in danger of going too far.

If your actions cause your partner to want to go all the way, even though you may not have reached that point, you have gone too far.

Some adolescents do not actually understand what "turns on" members of the opposite sex. Arousal can be the result of your words, actions, activities in which you participate, what you read and look at, and even the way you dress. A good rule of thumb to remember: Guys are primarily stimulated by sight; girls are stimulated by touch. Also, there are erogenous zones, primary areas of sexual sensitivity in the body. Obviously, it is wise to "stay far away" from these sensitive areas before marriage.

To avoid defrauding a brother or sister, each person must first determine that precise point at which one loses control to his or her hormones. Then that point must become an absolute personal limit, never to be crossed. We recommend that young people in premarriage relationships avoid reaching those limits.

Limited Freedom?

How far is too far? When you get sexually aroused, your body doesn't know if you are married or not. You've gone too far when you are no longer able to make intelligent, responsible decisions and act them out immediately. Once your hormones have been aroused, you begin to limit your freedom, that is, your ability to make right choices.

Many situations rob young people of their freedom to say no. First, sensually stimulating activities and situations, such as certain types of music, dances, parties, and so on, appeal to physical passions and arouse sexual desires. Young people should be warned about the inherent danger that comes with repeated exposure to these stimuli.

Second, necking and petting—making out—are "turn-ons" which prepare the body for sexual intercourse. When one is sexually aroused, it becomes extremely difficult to make right decisions. The pleasurable sensations that come from the caressing of sensual areas of your body, whether inside or outside clothes, can cause your feelings to overpower your mind.

Third, drugs and alcohol affect the mind. They give a false sense of security and well-being, weakening the brain's decision-making ability. This euphoria permits feelings to make irrational decisions. Despite the obvious problems with drinking and drugs, these substances rob young people of the freedom to choose wisely to wait for sex.

The Holy Spirit can help young people know when they are going too far. He works through their conscience to convict of sin and help them find a way out. If they resist the Spirit's leading, they may become callous to God's voice, making it increasingly easier to resist. It is important to help our young people stay pliable and responsive to God's Spirit.

Practical Suggestions for Drawing the Line

It is important for young people to be concerned about the other person. The Scriptures are explicit about not violating the conscience of another person. Don't light the fires of sexual passion in another person outside marriage. Remember that sexual involvement is progressive. Even extended kissing begins that arousal process. That's why it makes good sense to draw the line somewhere in the early stages of that progression.

An important guideline—particularly for young men: Don't light a fire that you can't put out! Never overestimate your or your partner's ability to resist sexual temptation. If you have any reason to believe that a specific situation could end up out-of-control, don't be afraid to make a strategic retreat.

Of course the best way to keep from going too far is never to start. Instead of asking how far one can go without suffering the consequences, it is best to avoid precarious situations altogether. How do young people set their limits? Here are a couple of examples given by students:

My suggestions: no extended periods of kissing, not lying down while kissing, no wandering hands, no revealing clothing. I would also recommend spending time in groups. Plan activities where there won't be much free time to get into trouble.

◆　◆　◆

Do not lie down together anywhere. Undressing can also lead to problems. Being scantily clad, like in your bathing suit or other summer clothes, can have the potential for problems if you aren't careful of where you are and who you are with.

Remember that kids often face strong sexual desires with neither the experience nor the know-how to control what they may have set in motion. Paul said to young Timothy, "Flee from youthful lusts" (2 Tim. 2:22, NASB). We must help our teens to be aware of their vulnerability.

When young people are considering where to set their limits, questions like these are helpful:

- ◆ What is my motivation?
- ◆ Do I really want to honor and serve the Lord?
- ◆ How far would I go if I could see that Jesus was physically in the room?
- ◆ Is this action spiritually beneficial to me and my date?
- ◆ Is this action feeding the temptation for further physical involvement?
- ◆ Am I giving *physical* signals that exaggerate my *emotional* commitment to this person?
- ◆ If we break up, will we still respect each other?

When young people are considering where to set their limits, questions like these are helpful: What is my motivation? Do I really want to honor and serve the Lord?

When young people ask the question, How far can we go? they are coming at the whole dating issue from the wrong perspective. Instead they should ask, What can I do to help my dating partner and myself grow closer to Christ? An ideal verse to use as a motto for a young person's date life is this: "Whatever you do, do it all for the glory of God" (1 Cor. 10:31).

STRATEGIES FOR KEEPING SEXUAL STANDARDS

A young person can—and should—communicate moral convictions clearly through his or her lifestyle. Conversation, body language, and even manner of dress are ways of saying no to sexual permissiveness. One young man mentioned how much he appreciated this quality in a girl:

> I dated a girl for seven months who never played on my emotions or told me things to lead me on. She knew that by just saying certain things, she might arouse me physically. It's far better not to lead each other on physically and play a big game with one another. She knew what it meant to be truthful and honest in our relationship.

The secret is for a young person to be secure in his or her self-identity. If kids know who they are in Christ, they can stand beside their peers without taking a holier-than-thou attitude and say no to premarital sex. If they are confident in their identity, they will be free to be themselves and to accept others as they are, without conforming to their expectations or condoning their behavior.

The person who accepts others just as they are is usually accepted and well liked even if he or she observes a different lifestyle. It's amazing how often this kind of person will become a leader (and even a role model) for his peers, Christian or otherwise.

Keep the Mind Pure

In order to act out their moral standards, young people must keep their minds free of thoughts that tempt them to compromise their convictions. Scripture tells us to take "every thought captive to the obedience of Christ" (2 Cor. 10:5, NASB). We are to be in complete control of our thought life. We may not have much control over thoughts that just seem to pop into our minds, but we can control whether we let our minds dwell and linger on those thoughts.

What we feed into our minds determines what we think about, so it is important to be selective. Proverbs 23:7 warns that "as [a man] thinks within himself, so he is" (NASB). In other words, what is hidden on the inside will be seen on the outside. Many Christian young people recognize this truth.

> It's important to realize that lust and sexual desires are products of the mind first. If you nurture and cultivate sinful thoughts, they'll continue to flourish, eventually overpowering you. With God's help you will learn not to entertain lustful thoughts, but meditate on things that are lovely, pure, and holy.
>
> ◆ ◆ ◆
>
> If we are constantly feeding our minds with pornography, tasteless jokes, or trashy romance novels, our actions will demonstrate this.
>
> ◆ ◆ ◆
>
> Wrong action starts with wrong thoughts.

How can young people succeed at taking their thoughts captive to the obedience of Christ? The same way we do as adults. We must share with our kids the steps we also practice.

First, we need a correct knowledge of the character of God. We need to understand that God is righteous, with high standards of morality. He is truthful. He will not deceive us. God's character is just and loving. As we understand his character, we will want to respond to him by attempting to please him and do his will.

The second step is to discover the will of God. Knowledge of it comes from a study of the Scriptures and from listening to godly people in the body of Christ. God's Word, for example, speaks in several places about the importance of maintaining purity of thought.

The third step is to place ourselves in an environment of encouragement and accountability. This means that we will share our struggle to control impure thinking with mature Christians, asking them to pray for us, to help us plan a specific strategy to overcome the problem, and to check up on us to see how we are doing in this area. Accountability will eventually lead to self-discipline, and in time we will be able to self-monitor our areas of weakness.

Other strategies include asking the Lord to set a shield around our minds so that each time an impure thought enters we immediately surrender that thought to the Lord, asking him to cleanse our minds, and asking him to help us deliberately think about something else. We avoid conversation and written or visual material that would stimulate wrong thoughts.

Another effective tool is Scripture memorization. Psalm 119:11 says, "I have hidden your word in my heart that I might not sin against you."

Finally, remember that God always gives us the strength and ability to do what he commands. In Philippians 4:8 Paul says, "Whatever is true, whatever is honorable, whatever is right, whatever is pure, whatever is lovely, whatever is of good repute, if there is any excellence and if anything worthy of praise, let your mind dwell on these things" (NASB).

The sexually oriented media is perhaps the greatest enemy to pure thoughts in both us and our young people. The following students have good advice to share with us in this regard, and we must pass this advice along to our own kids.

> Stay away from pornography, magazines, movies, TV, or anything else that stimulates you sexually. Don't buy into the Hollywood line that life is a constant romance seeking sexual satisfaction.
>
> ◆ ◆ ◆
>
> Stay away from the dirt on television and at the theater. Avoid books that emphasize premarital sex. Most of all, don't be misled by what the majority of the world thinks. Instead look to God for direction.
>
> ◆ ◆ ◆
>
> I'm learning that, with the Holy Spirit within me, I can resist temptation. However, I find that if I've been filling my mind with ungodly things (e.g., certain movies, books, magazines, etc.), then my defense is weak, and I fall so easily to temptation.

Remember that the standards portrayed in most media today are falsely alluring. God's standard is based on his provision and protection. I'm not saying don't ever go to the movies, watch TV, or read books. Scripture does not teach that the media in and of themselves are sinful. We must distinguish between the form of the medium and the content of the medium.

Encourage your young people to be discerning about what they watch, read, and/or listen to. Once an image is imprinted on their impressionable minds, it's there to stay. It becomes a part of them. One part of our minds is like a computer, in that it stores information. But unlike the computer, much of what the mind remembers is accompanied by great emotion. So be selective about what you let in. The more we have conformed to the world's values, the more challenging is the process of transforming our mind into the thoughts, ideas, and values of God.

Glorify God with Your Body

In 1 Timothy 2:9, Paul says, "I want women to adorn themselves with proper clothing, modestly and discreetly" (NASB). In blatant contrast, the dress of many girls and women screams of sensuality. From Barbie doll fashions to the covers of trendy magazines, a lot of women's clothing is seductively attention getting. Influenced by this, most adolescent girls, including Christians, think nothing of wearing the latest provocative fashions.

A young girl may not realize that a guy does not look on her dress in the same way she does. She may be quite confused and angered when her parents and other adults react to her "showiness." In her eyes, she has done nothing wrong. This is an area where parents, especially mothers, need to educate their daughters to understand the effect their dress can have on men.

Modesty in dress is important because guys are turned on by what they see. Since girls are stimulated more by touch than by sight, many of them don't realize this difference. Being modest doesn't mean a girl has to look frumpy. Christian men and women should have the most beautifully kept bodies, faces, hair, and clothing of all people. They are not called to deny or destroy their masculinity or femininity but to use it in a manner that is glorifying to God and will not cause others to stumble.

How does one find the balance between being provocative and frumpy? One teenage girl gives this excellent advice: "On a date (really, all the time), wear clothes that you would want to meet Jesus in. It can be cute and stylish but not designed to turn a guy on." If a girl uses just a little common sense, she can dress modestly. She realizes that what looks good on fashion models doesn't always look good on her. As she chooses her clothes, she asks God to give her concern for the spiritual welfare of the guys she's around. Yes, we are free in Christ to dress as we like, but true freedom limits itself in consideration of others.

Choose Companions Carefully

Young people must learn that the company they keep will greatly affect their ability to live out their moral convictions and adhere to their standards. Why? Because the need for approval is so strong during the adolescent years. If kids don't receive approval from their parents, they will seek it from their peers. Regrettably, peer approval for most teens revolves around conformity to the values of the group. In their search for approval, teens may go along with the standard of their peer group even though it violates their own personal moral standard.

The apostle Paul recognized the tremendous problem of peer pressure. In 1 Corinthians 5:9 he says, "I have written you in my letter not to associate with sexually immoral people." When you hang around and associate with immoral people, you are strongly influenced to become immoral yourself. In confirmation of Paul's words, one teenage girl said:

> If everyone is having premarital sex and talking about it, your conscience becomes numbed and you no longer feel the conviction against it. In fact, your friends encourage it. You begin to feel the pressure after so long. The girls make you feel that you aren't very attractive and aren't worth much, and the guys make you feel like a wimp because you're not experienced like others. After so much of that from the crowd, you say, what the heck, and do it! Even so, you know it was wrong, but peer pressure overruled. At that point, you laid down your morals and turned your back on God's commandments.

Of course, peer pressure doesn't always have to be negative. If the morals of the group involve doing what is right, a peer group can be a great source of support for the young person who wants to live a godly life. As one student said:

> I know that my friends have a great influence on who I am and also on what my values are. Godly friends can be a real source of encouragement when struggling with sexual desires.

The issue for kids comes down to choosing friends carefully. They should avoid continuous contact with peers who do not share their basic values and convictions. And they should choose to develop deeper friendships with those who share their values and convictions.

Whether we like it or not, we tend to become like the people we hang around with. Jesus stressed the importance of role modeling in Luke 6:40 when he says that a student shall be like his teacher. To a great extent, a young person's friends often have as much influence as a teacher, so it is important to choose those relationships carefully.

It is also important that Christian youth be involved in some kind of support group. Hebrews 10:25 tells us not to give up the habit of meeting together with other believers. Galatians 6:2 admonishes us to help carry one another's burdens. Meeting regularly with like-minded people is helpful and encouraging. A supportive group, such as a church youth group or Bible study at school, will reinforce a student's commitment to a godly lifestyle. As one young woman wrote:

> I have never engaged in premarital sex. It was largely due to my Christian upbringing. Throughout my adolescence and college years I had a strong network of friends and fellow church members who provided the support and caring needed through those unsure times. The care and intimacy derived from those special people have given me enough security and love to save the act of sexual intercourse for the person I choose to become one with in marriage.

In a world where it seems as if everyone is saying yes to premarital sexual involvement, it is strategic for kids to bond together with others who are saying no. Reinforcement of convictions from peers can help kids face sexual pressure.

Seek Close Relationships; Delay "Going Steady"

Going steady too early almost always causes sexual problems for an adolescent couple. All too often kids go steady because it is convenient and comforting — it's nice to know that they have someone to be with at every event and at all the times in between. But in most cases it is best to avoid going steady at all until a person is mature enough to consider marriage.

When a boy and girl go steady, the temptation is strong to lower their guard. They start frequenting the same places, doing the same things. They begin taking each other for granted, and it becomes almost impossible to resist physical intimacy. In fact, research indicates that teens who go steady for more than six months almost always become sexually intimate. The power of sexual attraction is such that any two mutually attracted people who spend large amounts of time alone are tempted to express their feelings through intercourse. The problem is aggravated when the going steady begins at a relatively early age.

I recommend that kids spend most of their dating time on double or group dates and avoid exclusive one-on-one relationships until they are older and seriously contemplating finding a person to marry.

The physical contact and affection kids seek in romantic relationships is not wrong in itself. We all need love and physical affection. The primary context where physical touch is learned is in the family. Children can learn the affectionate use of touch by seeing their parents express love to each other and to their kids. When young people experience intimacy through hugging and affectionate touching in the family, it is much easier for them to control themselves in a dating situation.

In addition to the family, close nondating friendships also can fill the need for intimacy in young people. One young woman gives the following advice for meeting intimacy and affection needs:

> Cultivate close intimate friendships with the same or opposite sex. Being able to share honestly and openly is one of our greatest needs, and to ignore it because we feel it can come only through a dating relationship is to give up one of life's most important experiences, that of intimate friendship.
>
> Give and receive physical affection from your friends. It is possible to alleviate this by hugs, pats on the back, handshakes, or whatever form of affection you feel comfortable with. Don't get caught up in the myth that all affection is sexual or the lie that sexual activity is the only way to quench the need for physical affection.

Encourage your young people to both *be* and *find* good friends who meet their needs for intimacy without tempting to violate their convictions.

Seek the Wisdom of Others

Kids growing up need role models who demonstrate what Christian love, marriage, and sexual love are all about. Ideally, parents are the primary source of this positive modeling for most Christian young people. But even when parents are fulfilling that role, your kids should be encouraged to look for other godly role models—those who will give them good advice and help develop and strengthen their convictions.

Scripture teaches us that there is wisdom in the advice of many godly people. Sometimes, confused by our emotional involvement in a situation, we need someone else to help us see things more objectively. Sometimes we have blind spots in our ways of thinking and acting. Sometimes we just need someone to act as a sounding board for us: to let us discuss our ideas and feelings, give us feedback, and advise us about possible courses of action. Our kids are no different.

In seeking advice, young people need to search out those they respect—mature Christians who know and care about them. In addition to parents, other candidates for good advice may be youth leaders, pastors, and lay leaders at church. One thing kids need to be aware of is the difference between seeking advice and seeking confirmation. To seek confirmation means to go to someone who will agree with you about what you have already decided. To seek advice means to go to someone you respect because of his or her walk with the Lord and ask that person for guidance.

Of course, when kids seek advice it doesn't necessarily mean they have to follow the advice given. Ultimate responsibility for decision making belongs to the individual who seeks counsel.

Seeking advice about premarital sexual activity can help young people form and uphold their convictions as the counselor assists them in thinking through what God's Word has to say about the subject. Seeking godly advice also can be of great value to a person who has been involved in premarital sex, has confessed and received forgiveness for that sin, and yet continues to feel guilt because of it.

Ask God to Help

Most young people who have developed convictions and standards to successfully cope with sexual pressures acknowledge the importance of asking God for help. None of the strategies for saying no suggested in this book will be effective if students do not recognize their need for God's help. They don't have to go it alone in this difficult area when they realize that God wants to help them. These students attest to that fact:

> I asked God to help me control my passions and to show me how to have a relationship without sex. He helped me to avoid situations that were conducive to sexual response.

◆ ◆ ◆

> We both knew we couldn't do it on our own, but that we had to rely on the self-control of Christ. We finally took it to the Lord in prayer and got down on our knees each time we met, because we had tried everything else!

◆ ◆ ◆

> Although it may seem that your sexual impulses cannot be controlled, there is one certain way to help you restrain: Give your life completely to Jesus Christ. Ask him to come into your heart and be the Lord of every corner of your life, including being the Lord of your sexual nature and desires.

◆ ◆ ◆

Admit to God that you need his help in conquering your sexual desires. Prayer is one of the biggest helps there is.

Obviously, the idea of asking God for help presumes a life-changing relationship with him through Jesus Christ. Although the solution to youth sexual problems requires more than evangelism, evangelism must be central in any strategy to wait until marriage for sex. I have found that when young people realize their need for help in dealing with their sexuality, they are also very open to Christ's invitation to personal relationship.

Young people need to know that without God's help they are likely to fail in the area of sex, but with his help they can be victorious over sexual temptation. I have often told kids, "God is more concerned about your sex life than you are." You see, God didn't just give us difficult-to-follow sexual rules and regulations and then abandon us. Of course not. He also promised his help and power because he wants us to succeed. Being a morally responsible person requires effort, but God provides the strength needed.

We must encourage our young people to utilize prayer as the first step to a sexual lifestyle that is honoring to God. They must admit their frailty and depend on his supernatural power to reserve their active sexuality for marriage.

We also must encourage young people to go beyond merely a "please help me" relationship with God. They should be satisfied with just asking for his help to avoid sexual involvement. Ultimately, their goal should be to learn and to follow his will in all things, including potential sexual relationships. The deeper their relationship becomes with the heavenly Father, the more help they will receive for living a moral, Christian lifestyle.

◆ ◆ ◆

All these resources for convictions and commitment to wait are vital. But how do they translate these standards into action? When kids are out with each other in dating activities, how should they conduct themselves? In other words, what do the convictions, conscience, and commitment to wait look like on Saturday night? In the next chapter, we will help you help your kids determine healthy dating guidelines which are in harmony with their convictions.

CHAPTER 20

HELP KIDS DETERMINE STANDARDS FOR DATING

HELPING YOUNG PEOPLE establish a foundation of convictions and conscience and make a commitment to abstinence is very important. But there is another step we must take in encouraging our kids to say no to premarital sex. We must help them set standards for how they will interact with the opposite sex in a dating relationship. This is the nuts and bolts stage of living out their convictions for, and commitment to moral purity. Bottom line, we need to help them set specific standards for what they will and will not do on a date.

Several students wrote to me about the importance of standards for dating:

> Sexual desires are practically impossible to harness once let loose. It is important to stop the process before it begins.

> Set your standards. Write down what you will and will not do on a date.

◆ ◆ ◆

> You must determine where you want to end . . . before you begin.

◆ ◆ ◆

> Set your standards now, not when you're deep into a relationship. Set them according to what is right in the eyes of God.

◆ ◆ ◆

I have to live by my own convictions, and for me this has meant setting strict standards in the area of purity.

Dating standards are like a fire escape: The time to look for it is long before the building catches on fire. Daniel found this to be true. When faced with overwhelming odds to compromise his moral convictions, this teenager already had decided: "Daniel made up his mind that he would not defile himself with the king's choice food or with the wine which he drank; so he sought permission from the commander of the officials that he might not defile himself" (Dan. 1:8, NASB).

Young people need to be encouraged to set limits for sexual activity before they go out on a date, even before any relationship begins. As someone has said, "It is much easier to break no standard than it is to break some standard. Don't just slide; decide!" If a person waits to set his or her standards until their hormones are aroused, they'll probably "blow it."

Each Christian young person should sit down and set standards about how far he or she intends to go on a date. It is best if this process is completed long before he or she comes close to involvement in any compromising situations. What are some guidelines for setting sexual standards? For Christians, the answer is clear: Begin with God's principles as presented in his Word. How do Christian young people "draw the line"? Here are some examples:

I have made a commitment not to have any kind of physical relationship with a man before I'm married. Not even kissing. It seems odd to people in this day and age, because sex is taken so lightly and kissing is just for fun. But how can I think thoughts that are "pure and honorable and lovely" (Phil. 4:8) when I am pressed close to someone's chest? How can I possibly set my mind on "things above" (Col. 3:2) when someone's mouth feels so warm on mine?

◆ ◆ ◆

Abstinence is the best preventative. You cannot finish something you never start. Refraining from even nominal physical contact until permanent commitment has been made may be the best for you.

This is the standard I adopted before I married: I will treat a woman on a date the same way I want some other man to treat the woman I will someday marry. In other words, I decided ahead of time to act on dates in such a way that I would never be afraid of my wife meeting any of my former dates.

I also recommend that young people share their standards with their dates. It's amazing how it clears the air for a couple to discuss dating standards as they begin a relationship. Doing so also minimizes the frustration and anger caused by false expectations. For example, if a young woman doesn't let her date know her standards early on, she had better be prepared for a furious response when the guy who tries to violate her standards gets stopped. It's so much better for each person concerned to share his or her standards openly from the beginning. It also develops a kind of accountability. When the other person knows what the standards are, it's not quite so easy for the first one to forget them either.

Once they've set their standards, young people should be encouraged to stick to them, even when they think they've met "Mr." or "Ms. Right." Setting standards ahead of time and sticking to them may not be easy, but it's worth it.

I strongly recommend that young people make themselves accountable to other people regarding their dating behavior. Making yourself accountable to another person is a valuable way to strengthen self-discipline and control sexual desires.

The word accountable means "able to answer for one's conduct." To make yourself accountable to someone means to share honestly with that person, on a regular basis, areas of your life in which you are struggling. For example, a young man might go to someone and share his struggles with sexual desire for his girlfriend. He might ask that person, "Would you hold me accountable in the area of sexual temptation with my girlfriend?" He might share specific things that he does or does not want to see happen in their relationship and re- quest that he be asked periodically (perhaps after each date) to report on how he's doing.

WHEN SHOULD THEY START DATING?

One big question we parents must face is when to let our kids start dating. Many adolescents begin quite young, as early as age eleven or twelve. But just because "everybody else is dating" (which they are not at eleven or twelve) is no reason to let your kids start dating then. You need to do what is best for your kids.

The time to date has come when you as a parent are confident that your child is mature enough to date responsibly. This means your child is ready to set some standards along the lines we will discuss in the paragraphs ahead—and stick to those standards. If your young person is not ready for committing to standards, he or she is not ready to say no to the pressures toward premarital sex. And such a child should certainly not be out dating.

HOW TO MAINTAIN CONTROL WHEN DATING

Here are a number of practical suggestions for helping young people curb sexual drives and temptations when in a dating relationship. You may want to go over this section point by point with your young people, encouraging them to determine their own standards.[1]

Date Only Those with the Same Convictions.

One of the principal standards for dating relationships you will want to instill in your child is that he or she should not date a non-Christian. Second Corinthians 6:14 is clear: "Do not be yoked together with unbelievers. For what do righteousness and wickedness have in common? Or what fellowship can light have with darkness?" A Christian dating a non-Christian is dangerous for at least two reasons.

First, everyone a person dates is, however remotely, a possible candidate for marriage. And there is no question that a believer should never marry an unbeliever. Since a person will marry someone he or she has dated, it only makes sense that the people your kids date meet at least the most basic requirement of a marriage partner—that of being a Christian.

Second, even if there is no intention of marriage, a non-Christian does not share a Christian's convictions and standards. There are moral non-Christians, to be sure, but even with the best intentions, dating non-Christians can lead to immorality. This dilemma is best handled by avoiding the situation altogether and not dating non-Christians.

The people your children date should not only be Christians but have the same convictions. They should have the same understanding of the importance of serving and walking with God and living according to his standards. Your children will have much more fun—and be safe—if they are spiritually compatible with those they date.

In helping your young person determine whom to date, teach him or her by example and by instruction to go beyond the surface when evaluating people. Kids seem to focus on three qualities when judging the desirability of a potential date: looks, personality, and popularity. But looks and popularity are extremely superficial and do not say much about the person. Even personality fails to reveal much about such important inner qualities as character and convictions.

This young woman's sad story clearly illustrates the importance of young people restricting their dating to people who share their convictions about moral purity:

It's not a pretty picture. It's not a TV soap opera, either. The reality of pregnancy outside marriage is scary and lonely. At twenty-four, I'm single and eight months pregnant. To have premarital sex was my choice one hot June night, forcing many decisions I thought I would never have to make. Those decisions have radically changed my life.

Perhaps the biggest surprise is that I am a born-again Christian who loves the Lord. How did this happen? It all started when I made a choice to date a non-Christian. "There's nothing wrong with just dating," I reasoned.

I was honest with my boyfriend in sharing the importance of my relationship with Jesus. He knew I was a Christian and he knew that I believed sex was for marriage. Rick thought I was outdated and couldn't believe I had never spent the night with a guy. However, he knew where I stood and didn't push me.

Twice in the eight months before I got pregnant I told him I thought we should break our relationship off. The Holy Spirit was convicting me like crazy. I knew 2 Corinthians 6:14: "Do not be yoked together with unbelievers. . . ." But Rick would say, "Just because I don't have the same beliefs doesn't mean we don't get along and have a great time together."

To me, Christianity wasn't just a belief, it was a way of life; yet what he said seemed to be true enough. Once when I said I would never marry a non-Christian, he said he didn't want to get married, but he did want to date me.

Without ever intending to, I was slowly falling in love. Almost every evening he worked out at the health club where I was employed. This made it convenient to see him every day, and we spent extra time together on weekends. We enjoyed many of the same activities, and we talked honestly and openly with each other on most issues. I felt the freedom to be myself when I was around him. Having previously dated a Christian who expected nothing less than perfection, this was a refreshing relationship.

During that time I was slowly becoming more and more comfortable with Rick. Without wanting to admit it, it was also the beginning of compromise. From all outward appearances, there was no indication that I was pushing God aside. I was still active in our church and remained in fellowship. The longer we dated, and the more attracted to him I became, the easier it was to let my guard down. A good-night kiss that put me on cloud nine during our first month of dating turned into hours of passionate kissing in front of his fireplace. I started to justify staying at his house on occasion, due to the half-hour drive home.

I was slipping, making small allowances for further advance in our relationship. Oh, I knew it wasn't right, and I knew it wasn't the relationship that God would want for me, yet I wasn't strong enough to end it. I felt apathetic toward God, and I didn't feel like saying no to Rick. Compromise had weakened me. By the time we had intercourse, it was so easy to let down the final defense.

Romans 12:1 says we are to offer our bodies as living sacrifices, holy and pleasing to God. In verse two, Paul continues by telling us not to conform to the world. I always knew what was right. I knew that my dating Rick was not God's will—that's clear from Scripture. I initially justified it because the relationship wasn't that important to me. Then, when I could not use that justification any longer, I simply decided not to care. At that point I wasn't afraid of sinning. My reason for not committing fornication was I was afraid I would get pregnant. And that's exactly what I got—pregnant.

I was horrified and resentful. "Why me, God? It's not as though I'm some tramp who sleeps around and deserves this." My reaction was the opposite of many of my married friends. I didn't want anyone to find out. There would be no congratulations or celebrations, no birth announcements or baby showers, only fear. I became angry and spiteful toward God. I thought, *Now I can have sex without the worry. I'll show you, God. Since I'm already pregnant, what have I got to lose?* With that fear gone, I saw no reason to be accountable to God. Faced with the alternative of an unwanted pregnancy, however, I knew that I, not God, had jumped the gun.

Many tough decisions had to be made. Most important, I needed to get right with God again. I needed not only the forgiveness that God grants when we ask for it, but also I needed to become steadfast in the Word and to trust in God again. I decided to leave my great job, wonderful church, and network of friends. I moved to another state and lived with friends who have become like family to me and who also love the Lord. I also came to realize that an unwanted pregnancy on my part did not equal an unwanted child. I opted for adoption.

"Why me, God?" Because I knew better but was disobedient anyway. "Why wait until marriage?" I believe it's a simple answer, and there need be no other reason: because God tells us to wait. He tells us that, not to be a party pooper, but because he loves us and ultimately knows what is best for us. My feelings got in the way. However, whether we like it or not, we are to be obedient to God. Feelings can color the way we see things. They, rather than the Word of God, become the benchmark.

Over the past several months, I have been dealing with the consequences of this particular sin. I have also seen, as never before, the goodness of God. Ephesians 1:7-8 has become a reality through many tough days and decisions: "In him we have redemption through his blood, the forgiveness of sins, in accordance with the riches of God's grace that he lavished on us with all wisdom and understanding." I purpose to choose God's way.

It is crucial that your young people date only those who have convictions similar to their own. In this story, the young woman made the mistake of justifying dating a non-Christian and then began compromising to his level of morality. The Scripture that talks about "be not unequally yoked" was disobeyed, and she ultimately had to deal with the consequences of her decision.

That Scripture applies not only to dating non-Christians but also to dating Christians who do not share the same convictions. If you really want to control the sexual area of your life, then be careful not only about your own lifestyle but also about the lifestyle of those you date. If you date others who are like-minded, there will be a commitment to encourage and be accountable to each other. However, if the person you date has lower moral standards than yours, you may easily find yourself compromising to their level rather than upholding your own convictions.

Set Dating Goals.

A recent survey of dating practices among teens showed that "by age seventeen, intercourse is an accepted, if not an expected, part of dating relationships."[2] For that and other reasons, it is important for young people to have objectives and goals for their lives and for their dating relationships. I like what one girl wrote to her boyfriend:

What do you say we make a list—together, I mean—of the things we would really like to see accomplished in our lives? I think we could be great accountability partners for each other, don't you? Let's help each other be all that God created us to be.

Researchers have discovered that a serious commitment to "religion," with the sense of purpose it gives, makes a noticeable difference in the sexual activity of teens. A good relationship with Mom and Dad also makes a difference. For those who have that kind of relationship, I encourage them to interact in establishing dating goals. Obviously, parents should not dictate these goals for their children, but their counsel and assistance can be invaluable. Once the goals have been decided, Mom and Dad can play a key part as members of a young person's accountability team. For example, if a young person decides on an 11 P.M. date curfew, then he can say to his parents, "Mom and Dad, I want you to hold me accountable for getting home on time."

For years, one of the things I have continuously stressed with my three daughters and my son is that I prefer to view dating (or spending time with the opposite sex) as a relationship that has tremendous responsibilities to the other person.

Here are some suggested dating goals for young people:

1. Be accepting of the other person by honoring his or her God-given dignity. (This gives a person a sense of security.)
2. Build up the other person by showing appreciation for that person's uniqueness, gifts, and abilities. (This gives a person a sense of significance.)
3. Encourage the fulfillment of the other person's goals. (Part of that encouragement would be to hold the other person accountable in the fulfillment of those goals.)
4. Be accountable to the other person for fulfilling your own goals according to God's principles. (This develops your self-discipline.)
5. In every situation, try to reflect Jesus Christ in your attitudes and actions.

Here are a couple of suggested personal desires for dating:

1. I desire that my dating partner become a better person as the result of knowing me and us spending time together.
2. I desire that my dating partner develop a closer relationship with Jesus Christ as a result of our dating relationship.

No matter what your young people are doing—whether sharing activities and feelings or expressing legitimate affection—the real purpose in a dating relationship should be to build up the other person, to minister to the other person. The primary desire should be that the dating partner will respond positively to these efforts and, as a result, walk more closely with the Lord.

Make Definite Plans for Dates.

The best way to implement standards for relating to a dating partner is to plan carefully. It's not only smart to be creative in planning dates, but it's also a lot of fun. Before young people go out on a date, they should know where they're going to go and what they're going to do. It is easiest to stay out of trouble on dates when you make them creative, make them fun, and stay out of situations that can lead to problems. Plan your dating life carefully. Here is some advice from some kids who are learning to plan ahead:

> Before going out on a date you should have it well planned. Plan so that there will be little space where you can get into trouble sexually.
>
> ◆ ◆ ◆
>
> Don't spend long periods of time together without anything to occupy your time.
>
> ◆ ◆ ◆
>
> We found we needed to do things with other unmarried couples. It was so nice to spend a quiet evening at home, but all too often when the lights and music got soft it was easy to get carried away.
>
> ◆ ◆ ◆
>
> Don't stray from the original plan of what you will do, or where you will go on a date. Impulsive changes of plans usually spell trouble.
>
> ◆ ◆ ◆
>
> Be very careful of the things you do on a date. Stay away from listening to suggestive music. Be careful of what movies you see on a date. You may not think it makes much difference, but it really does. It's just that much easier to go ahead with what you've already seen (or heard).

A date should always involve activity that will provide good opportunity for conversation, since that is the best way to get to know someone. This is especially true of a first date. A movie or a concert does not provide much time for conversation. Playing catch, riding bikes, skating, or hiking together is more conducive to conversation. A first date in which two people can talk together at length gives them a chance to explore common interests and tastes, how their senses of humor compare, and other areas of personality and character.

When planning a date, your young people should keep in mind the goals which have already been set. Such planning should be seen not only as a way to avoid sexual involvement, but also as a means of bringing about growth in the other person and in oneself.

Communicate Openly about Sex.

Have you ever wished that someone else could read your mind—that someone could know your thoughts, feelings, and opinions about something without you making the effort to explain them? Often we are afraid of self-disclosure, afraid that the other person may not accept us if we tell him or her how we really feel about something.

A young person who does not communicate clearly his or her convictions about sexual involvement may get into trouble. Kids can avoid a lot of confusion and misunderstanding by pointedly telling dating partners how they feel about sexual involvement. Here's what two students wrote:

> The most important thing for a couple to do is talk about their views on premarital sex. It may seem a little embarrassing, but it is essential to know how each person feels. If one person doesn't think that having sex before marriage is wrong at all, then their whole relationship should be reevaluated. Chances are, if both are Christians and want to please the Lord, they will agree that premarital sex is wrong.
>
> ◆ ◆ ◆
>
> Make your boundaries known to each other. Be honest when you see a problem coming. Remember, the ball is always in your court. You bring up the subject. You start being honest and your partner will begin to feel comfortable sharing as well.

One young person suggested that couples discuss their limits and values when they are not "in the mood" in order to avoid later problems. Good idea. In the midst of arousal it's easy to rationalize away the standards we have set when in a calmer frame of mind. Discussion of standards needs to be done at a time and a place where both people can be objective in evaluating their limits. Then, once standards are set, they need to be followed totally. There must be a commitment to the standards. As another student comments, "Unless we both were committed to God's principles and to his will before we got into the tempting situation, we were almost sure to fail."

Include Prayer.

Here is a prayer one student prays before each date:

Dear Lord,

Trusting you for strength, I promise to keep myself pure for the person I am to marry by abstaining from sex and from any other physical expressions that do not honor you.

Such a prayer, prayed before each date, could certainly help to keep a person's dating life on the right track. The attitude conveyed here is one of recognizing that there will be temptation, and that the strength to resist temptation must come from the Lord. This student is ready to take God up on his promise: "Commit everything you do to the Lord. Trust him, and he will help you" (Ps. 37:5, NLT).

A student from UCLA described the power of committing a date to Christ through prayer. He went to Biola University to pick up his date. He let her in the car and went around to get in on his side. He looked over and her head was bowed.

"What are you doing?" he said.

"Praying," she replied.

The guy told me, "Josh, she ruined everything I had planned for that evening!"

One young person commented on the value of prayer *during* a date:

Reading the Bible and praying together is one way to spend time alone without having to worry about sexual temptation. The benefits are obvious: a spiritual bond is created; the couple grows closer to God; and more biblical knowledge is gained.

I often suggest to kids that they begin and end their dates with a brief time of prayer. Starting off the date with prayer will give them the opportunity to commit their date to the Lord together and ask his guidance on it. Knowing that they will be ending the date in prayer will give greater motivation to keep their words and actions such that they won't need to be ashamed before God.

Incorporating prayer into one's date life can add a new dimension of depth and security to a relationship. An eighteen-year-old girl describes her experience:

I am familiar with the temptations that can arise in a dating relationship. I'm just as exposed to the sin around me in high school as anyone else. However, because I am in fellowship with Jesus Christ, my standards of living and conduct are different, and I do not participate in events that may cause a separation between God and myself. As a spiritual leader, my boyfriend Todd begins our moments alone with a time for God and for sharing with each other what the Lord is doing in our lives. It's exciting! After a good time of fellowship and prayer, we enjoy holding hands and spending silent moments together with a peace, knowing that we are not entering into the boundaries of impurity.

Although I want to encourage teens to pray together, I also need to warn them to be cautious. Prayer can be extremely intimate. In fact, nothing in this world is more intimate than going to our heavenly Father in prayer. When this kind of intimacy begins to be expressed in a male-female relationship under proper control, it can be edifying, but it carries a definite risk. If there is a vulnerability to the sexual, it is easy to move from the spiritual intimacy of prayer to physical intimacy. I've known enough young people who have said they originally became so close through prayer that the next thing they knew they were becoming physically intimate. Be careful. It's a very fine line.

Here are a few keys to share with your kids about using prayer effectively in a dating relationship:

1. Be brief.
Commit your goals and desires for your time together to the Lord, but remember that spending extended amounts of time alone together in prayer may create a degree of intimacy that you are not able to handle.

2. Be positive.
Express your love for the Lord and your desire to please him in all you do. Thank the Lord for positive Christlike qualities that you appreciate in each other and for the things that he is teaching you through your relationship.

3. Pray for the needs of others.
Couples sometimes have a tendency to make their prayer life so introspective that they forget there are other people with needs also. Praying for others will help to create a healthy, outward focus for your relationship.

4. Be careful of your physical contact when praying.
Remembering that prayer will naturally create a sense of intimacy between you, it is wise to avoid a lot of physical contact during prayer. You may wish simply to hold hands or not to touch each other at all.

5. Don't pray about your negative feelings or your sexual struggles.
This is not the place to verbalize needs such as, "I feel lonely. I want to be loved. I want to be held" or "I really want to make love to my girlfriend even though I know it's wrong" or "I so desire my boyfriend but not until it's the way the Bible says it must be." You need to be honest with the Lord about your negative feelings and struggles with sexual desire, but that kind of honesty needs to take place in the privacy of your time alone with him.

Keeping guidelines like these in mind, allow God to build prayer into your dating life as a natural expression of your commitment to him individually and as a couple.

Avoid Being Alone.
Imagine that a girl's parents are out of town for the weekend and have given her permission to entertain her boyfriend in their home. After a candlelight dinner has soothed their hunger pangs, the two find their way to a comfy sofa in front of a blazing fire. Feelings of romance run high, and soon they find themselves saying, "Let's do it. It seems so right."

High school seniors who date spend an average of 14.5 hours a week alone with their date.[3] That's a recipe for moral disaster. Proverbs 6:27 tells us in effect that if you play with fire you're going to get burned. The same principle applies to controlling dating situations. A lot of time alone together is more than most kids can handle. Research shows that the first act of sex doesn't happen most often in a car, but at the home of one of the couple when parents are away (usually between three and five in the afternoon).[4]

Situations like this are an open invitation to trouble. The way for kids to handle that kind of temptation is not to put themselves in it in the first place. They need to avoid potentially compromising situations, such as parking alone in the dark for long periods of time, watching sexually oriented films or videos, or being at a date's house while parents are away or asleep.

Young people need to think through their goals ahead of time and determine what kinds of activities they want to do. One adult said this in retrospect:

"Do nothing in private that you wouldn't do in public." That advice once seemed a bit stiff to me, unrealistic, even prudish and unreasonable. It even seemed to suggest that what you did when alone depended on how brazen you were prepared to be in public. Looking back now on my experience and that of other Christian friends, such advice seems much more sensible than I then thought.

Parents can help their adolescents minimize compromising situations. When your son or daughter asks to have a date at the house when you are away, you have the right to say no. Ironically, we are often afraid to give the kids the keys to the car for a date, but we leave the front door wide open.

Don't be afraid to ask your kids where they are going, what their plans are, and when they will be back. Set reasonable curfews and let them know what you expect from them in their dating. By holding them accountable you also provide them with clear answers to pressures from their dating partners. When pressured they can simply give a reply such as, "I can't have you come over after school today. My parents don't allow me to have friends over when they're not home" or "I'm sorry, but my parents are expected home in a few minutes." Parents can give kids an out by setting boundaries.

Young people should not assume they are strong enough to handle compromising situations. The temptations of being completely alone can be too much for even the strongest Christians. Below is the story of one college student who learned this lesson the hard way.

During my freshman year, I began dating Brad, one of the leaders in a Christian movement on campus. Because both of us were involved in the group's music ministry we spent a great deal of time together planning music for our weekly meetings and other special events. One thing led to another and soon we were an "item."

At our high-pressure university, most of our time was spent studying. Because I had a single room in a house full of other girls from this Christian group, it seemed like the perfect place for Brad and me to study. It wasn't. "Study breaks," as any college student knows, are a required part of a good study time. For Brad and me, study breaks went from running down to the kitchen for a Coke, to talking and hand-holding in my room, to kissing and so on. I don't really re-member how we justified everything that happened in that room, but I remember that we tried to.

I remember standing in front of 100 college students on a Friday night and leading singing, with Brad right behind me playing the guitar, and I was pretend-ing that I was right with God. I remember leading a Bible study on holiness with my disciples, while I was writhing inside with shame. I remember sharing the gos-pel with many students who were probably purer in the realm of the physical than I was. I remember how the power of the Holy Spirit began to ebb from my life. And I remember I hated myself.

I took a one-year leave of absence from college and moved 3,000 miles away from school and my hypocrisy and my sin. During that time, just like a baby, I learned to walk with God again. I learned that he could forgive me for my selfish-ness and my sin. And I learned that his commandments are meant for our good.

Set Aside the Physical and Focus on Building the Relationship.

Once couples become sexually involved, their priorities often shift away from the spiritual, emotional, and social sides of the relationship and focus on the physical. Couples who desire godly relationships need to set aside the physical/ sexual part and focus on building the other aspects of their relationship. One young person wrote:

When you begin to develop a relationship, try to start out on a friendship level. Generally, you would never consider taking advantage of a friend. Moreover, you would tend to relate to the person in a spiritual or emotional way. This is impor-tant. A couple needs to know each other spiritually and emotionally so that later problems can be properly resolved.

If young people sense that the physical has become too great a part of their date life, they may need to evaluate the relationship honestly. One young woman advises asking these questions:

Are you really seeking ways to strengthen your relationship? Are you seeking to help your boyfriend grow spiritually and emotionally? Is your sexual relationship drawing the two of you closer together or pulling you apart? Do you think that your relationship is stronger now than it was before you were sexually involved?

Another young woman points out that putting sexual involvement on the shelf can bring about several positive benefits:

1. It will put a new spark in the fire! Withholding yourselves sexually from each other will give you something to look forward to in the future.
2. A commitment not to engage in premarital sex will please the Lord and thus will begin to eliminate much of the guilt you may be feeling.
3. It will help build a foundation of commitment because you will have made a commitment to continue seeing each other even though your sexual relations have changed.
4. It will motivate you to discover new areas in each other's personality you have not yet explored.

Focusing away from the sexual aspects will definitely alter a relationship. If the relationship is based on nothing more than sexual chemistry, a couple probably will break up. But if there is a good foundation of love and respect, the relationship will become stronger as the couple gets to know each other's person rather than each other's body.

Though our society tells us otherwise, it is possible to have a fulfilling date life without sex. In fact, over the long run, it is easier, as this young woman discovered:

I am nineteen years old and have dated several different guys during high school. At present I have been dating a fantastic Christian guy for the past two years. We have only held hands and I have never kissed anyone, let alone engaged in any kind of sexual relationship. Most people today feel that this kind of lifestyle is crazy and just plain stupid. Don't misunderstand me. This kind of dating relationship is not easy, but it's by far the best. I don't know any girl who has had more fun in her teenage dating life than I have. I have dated the neatest Christian guys who respected me and took me out for the sole purpose of having fun and getting to know me better.

EQUIP YOUR KIDS WITH "ESCAPE ROUTES"

No matter how carefully young people plan, prepare, and pray for their dating experiences, there may be occasions when they find themselves seemingly trapped in a morally unhealthy relationship or situation. We have not adequately prepared them for dating until we have equipped them to find ways out of such predicaments. Here are several "escape routes" I suggest to kids.

Make a Commitment to God.

An unhealthy situation should always direct a young person back to reaffirming his or her commitment to God and to purity. The problem may have come up because his or her convictions or commitment was compromised at some point. Challenge your kids to use bad situations to reaffirm their resolve to obey God and keep him first in their relationships. One young woman wrote me about such a commitment:

> I knew what I had to do. I had to give Ken back to the Lord and put Jesus first, where he should have been all along. I knew I had to do this, but I was so afraid. For over a year I had been holding on to Ken and putting all of my faith in him only; I had a dream that I would one day become more to Ken emotionally than I was physically. Yet how could I become more to Ken, when I had let myself become so much less?

This girl recognized that, as a Christian, she had to give Jesus his rightful first place in her life. As a young person becomes involved in close relationships he or she is tempted to make a boyfriend or girlfriend the center of his or her life. When that happens, activities, thoughts, and decisions all begin to revolve around that "one special person." This is especially dangerous if that special person begins to pressure his or her date for sex. If the teen's desire to please his or her date has taken precedence over the desire to please God, he or she will often give in to the pressure, perhaps out of fear of losing the person's love.

Yet no matter how much we love another person — even in marriage — Jesus Christ must always be our first love and the highest priority of our lives. When he is the center of our lives, everything else will fall into its proper place. For example, young people can evaluate their dating life and relationships with the opposite sex by asking, "Would this be pleasing to God?" If God has first place in their lives, they will not engage in any activity that would displease him.

If God is no longer first in a young person's life, the first escape route from a problem situation is to recommit his or her life to God, trusting him to work out what is best. If a student has become sexually involved, he or she needs to give that over to the Lord, make a commitment before him to end sexual activity, and depend on God for the power and ability to carry out that commitment. One young man advises his peers:

I challenge you to give God a chance to work in your relationship. Make a commitment to him to stop being sexually involved and to wait for the right time with the right person. If you and your girlfriend really are in love, then your love for each other will only grow stronger and deeper as you build your relationship on the Lord and save sex for its proper context. If your relationship doesn't survive without the physical part, then it obviously wasn't right and wasn't God's best for you. And why settle for anything less than the best?

Break Off the Relationship.

Pat first had sex when she was sixteen. She became a Christian the next year and, although she eventually learned that sex outside marriage was wrong, she was often frustrated by her inability to break an established habit pattern of exchanging sex for love. Finally, Pat decided to stop dating for a couple of years so she could get her thoughts together. It was a time of incredible spiritual growth, and it seemed that God gave her victory in an area that had been a thorn in the flesh for so long.

Pat's story illustrates the fact that sometimes, when kids find themselves unable to break an established habit involving some level of moral compromise, the best thing to do is to stop dating for a while. This is more than just fleeing the immediate situation. It involves breaking off any ungodly relationship altogether and not dating until the young person develops strong, godly convictions and gains the spiritual and emotional maturity needed to put those convictions into practice.

There is a kind of catch-22 in this area. The person who most needs to back away from a dating relationship is the young person who is most insecure and immature. Yet an immature person will have a hard time recognizing and acknowledging his or her immaturity, while more mature people will be able to admit their weaknesses. This is where good advice can be invaluable—advice from a respected older person who can discern maturity levels in various areas of a student's life. If a person is too immature to make wise decisions and cannot resist peer pressure, then the best thing that person can do is to back away from a dating relationship until he or she can develop the needed maturity.

Another part of the catch-22 is that backing away from ungodly dating relationships and ungodly friendships is very difficult for an immature person. Insecurity is one reason a person becomes hooked in a dating relationship. This often causes one to hang on even when being hurt. It's like the battered wife who hangs in there with her husband. Despite the negative environment, there is still some sense of security that she fears losing if she leaves him.

In a parenting situation, tough love may be needed. For the student's own good, parents may need to prohibit their son or daughter from dating for a time. Tough love has two aspects that must balance each other: love and authority. Tough love exercises authority, but tough love also demonstrates acceptance and appreciation. Parents shouldn't be "tough" until they have first demonstrated love.

A young person who has been sexually active may be filled with confusion and guilt and will need to allow God to work a healing process in his or her life. This nondating time can be a rich experience of developing intimacy with the Lord, experiencing his love and forgiveness, and cultivating convictions about his standards. One girl gives this advice to her friends:

If you have already had sex, don't despair. Don't feel that the Lord is through with you and there is no hope now since this has happened. If you've sinned, you need to ask the Lord's forgiveness, but you also need to forgive yourself. Although you can't change the past, if the Lord has forgiven you, there's nothing to do but forget it and go forward. By forward I mean, break off your sinful relationship. That would be the first step toward true repentance—turning away from your sin. Don't feel tied to your boyfriend just because you've already given yourself to him. Don't feel that you're bound to him, and no one else is going to want you now. I don't know what the Lord has planned for you, but if you seek his will for your life, he promises to show it to you. You'll just have to trust God that whatever man he may bring into your life later will be as forgiving and understanding as he is concerning your past.

Romans 8:28 promises that all things work together for good to them who love God and are called according to his purpose. That's a pretty reliable promise, coming from God. Don't let the devil continue to trip you up with sin. After all, that's just what he wants to do: mess up your life. Ephesians 3:20 says God is able to do exceedingly abundantly above all that we ask or think, according to the power that works in us. Give him that chance.

Look for the Way of Escape.
The Bible is clear about temptation: "No temptation has seized you except what is common to man. And God is faithful; he will not let you be tempted beyond what you can bear. But when you are tempted, he will also provide a way out so

that you can stand up under it" (1 Cor. 10:13). In other words, no temptation or trial will come to us that is beyond human experience or beyond what we can bear. There is always a way of escape from temptation. Your kids may sometimes feel like they are trapped in tempting situations, but they are only trapped when they make disobedient choices.

Your young people must realize that they have a way of escape in any situation. It is the power to say no. When someone they are dating suggests—or insists—on parking alone, going to the backseat of the car, going home when parents are gone, etc., the way of escape has already been provided. God gives them the power and privilege of saying no.

God will always give us strength equal to the temptation. But the best way out is to escape before the compromising situation develops. The most effective way of escape, of course, is simply to learn to say no when faced with temptation. Obedience is difficult, but the rewards far outweigh the temporary pleasures of disobedience.

Make a Fast, Strategic Exit.

Controlling youthful sexual desires in volatile situations often means doing one of two things: escaping from the situation or breaking off the relationship. Since kids don't usually like breaking off relationships, let's look at a less drastic option, the option of making a strategic exit. Your kids need to know that in situations of temptation or compromise, physically walking away may be God's superhighway of escape.

I often tell kids, "If you can't handle the situation, get out of there. Run as fast as you can!" I relate the Old Testament story of Joseph being tempted by Potiphar's wife (see Gen. 39:7-12). Recognizing the danger of the temptation, Joseph left everything and ran away from danger. Sometimes that's the best way. A girl may have to say, "I won't be a party to this. Take me home right now, or I will call my parents to come get me." A guy may have to say, "I can't stay for this activity. If you want to stay, you will have to find your own way home."

This is the message of a number of Bible verses relating to temptation and compromise. First Corinthians 6:18 instructs: "Flee from sexual immorality." Second Timothy 2:22 says: "Flee the evil desires of youth." James 4:7 tells us that if we resist the devil, he will have to flee from us. The goal is not to see how much evil we can tolerate without stepping over the line. The plan is to get as far away from evil as possible. As one student wrote:

Stand clear of tempting circumstances. Never place confidence in the flesh. In other words, never deceive yourself by assuming that you have control over the degree of your involvement with your dates. Since fire burns, wise men avoid it.

◆ ◆ ◆

What happens when your child ignores the escape routes? What do you do when he or she crosses the lines of conviction, conscience, and commitment to become involved in premarital sex at some level? How should you respond? Where do you go from here? We will answer these questions in the next chapter.

CHAPTER 21

OFFER FORGIVENESS AND PROVIDE HOPE WHEN KIDS BLOW IT

WE LIVE IN A DAY of so-called sexual liberation, when society tells our young people that morality doesn't matter. "If it feels good, it's OK to do it." Despite being told there's no reason to feel guilty, sexual guilt among young people is increasing. I meet so many young people who want to be forgiven. Here are the words of just one of them:

> I had sex with my boyfriend, thinking I owed it to him. Later, when I learned I was pregnant, he blew up and said I should get an abortion—that it was all my fault. So, to save my parents heartache and to keep Matt, I had an abortion. Now Matt has left me. How can God love me after all I have done? I'm just so confused. Can God really love and forgive me?

How do we help our kids who say, "I've blown it, I've been involved sexually" or "I've lost my virginity, so what's the use of saying no anymore?" or "After all I've done, how can God love or forgive me?" What do we say? What do we do? Do we simply quote Bible verses about God's forgiveness and send them on their way?

I think we need to recognize that people with sexual guilt may have serious difficulties with the concept of forgiveness. For example, some have problems believing that God can or will forgive them. Others are either unable or unwilling to accept his forgiveness. And few can forgive themselves. As a result, there are many Christian young people who have asked for God's forgiveness—and are forgiven—yet who go through life without experiencing the benefits of that forgiveness.

I believe that whatever help we provide must be in the context of loving relationships. Whether as parents, pastors, youth leaders, or teachers, it is not enough to talk about forgiveness. We must live it.

THE GIFT OF FORGIVENESS

We must begin by accepting and forgiving those who are seeking God's forgiveness. This should be our first step. We can never help anyone we cannot accept. To tell someone about God's forgiveness is meaningless unless we ourselves show acceptance. Especially for parents, acceptance begins with forgiveness.

Do you have a son or daughter who is struggling with the guilt of sexual misconduct? What about young persons in your youth group or congregation? Do you want to help them experience the power of God's forgiveness and cleansing? Then, first of all, be forgiving yourself. Here are three helpful principles:

1. Take the Initiative.

Have you ever questioned yourself, "Why should I forgive her? She hasn't even said she's sorry!" God's love compels us to take the initiative by offering forgiveness. "This is real love. It is not that we loved God, but that he loved us and sent his Son as a sacrifice to take away our sins" (1 John 4:10, NLT). If God had waited for us to repent and ask his forgiveness before reaching out to us, we would still be lost. But "God showed his great love for us by sending Christ to die for us while we were still sinners" (Rom. 5:8, NLT). He took the first step—paying the death penalty for our sins—and then offered us his pardon.

As God's children, we must follow our heavenly Father's example and take the initiative. God wants us to reach out to our hurting sons and daughters, parishioners, and students. Forgiveness takes the initiative.

2. Try to Restore Relationships.

The goal of forgiveness is reconciliation. So often when young people become involved sexually, the relationship with their parents is either strained or broken. God wants parents to assume responsibility for their part in the collapse of the relationship and to initiate reconciliation.

Did you know that God doesn't want you to worship if you have a broken relationship with your children that you haven't tried to make right? Jesus said, "If you are offering your gift at the altar and there remember that your brother [son, daughter] has something against you, leave your gift there in front of the altar. First go and be reconciled to your brother [son, daughter]; then come and offer your gift" (Matt. 5:23-24).

How many parents would show up for church next Sunday if they followed Jesus' instructions? Regardless of who is "at fault," it is so important to restore your relationship with the hurting young person. If parents wait for their child to ask forgiveness first, reconciliation may never happen. Forgiveness seeks reconciliation.

3. Be Genuinely Forgiving.

Forgiveness means to release someone from a debt. It's not the same as saying, "Oh, that's all right," when someone says he's sorry. Forgiveness recognizes that a wrong has been done but is willing to accept and forget anyway.

So many parents say they have forgiven, but they continue to hold the past over the heads of their children. "I forgive you . . . but I won't forget." Forgiveness means not keeping a scorecard, not saying something like, "There you go again." God said he puts all our sins behind him. He has buried them in the deepest ocean, and, as Corrie ten Boom liked to say, he puts up a No Fishing sign. This is what God does when he forgives us. We must do the same when we forgive our young people. Be genuinely forgiving.

By offering genuine acceptance and forgiveness to young people who are desperately seeking God's forgiveness, we provide them with a credible basis for understanding God's forgiveness. This truth is effective to the extent that we demonstrate it.

A PICTURE OF GOD'S FORGIVENESS

Young people generally see God through parents and church leaders. They project their image of us onto God. This is particularly true of parents. If we are forgiving, it is relatively easy for our children to conceive of God as forgiving. If we are stern and unforgiving, it may be difficult for our children to imagine a God who loves and forgives.

The actions and attitudes of parents can be barriers standing in the way of their children ever receiving and accepting God's forgiveness. For example, a young woman I counseled several years ago was severely handicapped in her ability to experience forgiveness because of her relationship with her parents, particularly her father. Tracy explains:

My mother was an alcoholic and was never really there for me. I was the youngest of five children and, in a way, my sister Donna, who was two and a half years older, kind of became my mother. My father was never there for me either except for discipline—strict discipline. You know, "belt-on-the-table" type stuff. I had no relationship with him. I've got pictures where I have my arm around him, trying to show him affection, and he is just sitting there. I was scared to death of my father, but I still wanted his attention.

Tracy's autocratic father, with his lack of caring and affection, would have a serious effect on her future relationships with others, especially men. Tracy continues:

As I grew up, I was always getting sick or hurt, trying to get attention. My sister Donna was like that, too. I remember a day when we both bashed her arm with a stick. She hit it for a while and then made me do it too. We kept at it until her arm was actually broken. But my father looked at it and said, "No. It's not broken. It's fine. Sure, you got a big old welt and bruise, but it's fine."

Most of the time my sister Donna could get away with anything. She was always the "black sheep" type, getting busted for drugs and stuff. But my folks believed everything she said. When it was me, they always thought I was a liar. I hated it. All my life I hated it, but I could tell them anything. They never knew I was on drugs. They never had a clue. I don't know if Donna told them I was a liar or what, but they always said to me, "Tracy, you're lying to us." I wasn't a liar; that's what was real weird.

Tracy became involved in drugs at the age of ten when she began to smoke marijuana. By the age of twelve she was popping "uppers" and "downers" regularly. At fourteen she had her first sexual experience with a childhood boyfriend. She was not sexually involved again until she was sixteen, when after a single act of intercourse with another boy, she became pregnant.

Her mother, who had recently accepted Christ, and her unbelieving father insisted she have an abortion. Tracy was devastated. Following the abortion, she spent the next three months crying almost constantly, hating her parents, grieving for her baby, and suffering severe depression.

Several months later, after her father's conversion to Christ and after watching the spiritual growth of her mother, Tracy realized her own spiritual need and invited Christ into her life. For the next two years she concentrated on growing as a Christian. She generally avoided men and seldom dated.

Then Tracy enrolled in a Christian college and became active in the antiabortion, pro-life movement. As she shared her testimony publicly, she felt other Christians judging her. This had a negative effect on her Christian walk.

Tracy began dating a Christian student, who asked her to marry him. Although a wedding date had not been set, the couple was given a book on Christian marriage. After reading it, Tracy's boyfriend began pressuring her for sex. Finally one night he forced himself on her physically. That virtual rape was a traumatic experience for her. She lost the limited self-esteem she had built up since becoming a Christian.

Over the next three years, Tracy had unsatisfying relationships with seven different men. In most cases, sexual intimacy terminated the relationship.

I would start a relationship. The guy would start trying things and I would try to stop it. But I would end up sleeping with him and then walk away. I wanted affection. I wanted to feel accepted. But whenever I became physically involved, I wouldn't feel accepted at all. I'd feel dirty.

It was like originally the guy's opinion would be, "Oh, you're so wonderful. You walk with God. You're so on fire. You minister here and there." And then he would find out my background, which is no secret. In front of large pro-life audiences, I told my background. But once a guy knew about me, he would begin pushing me to have sex, and that made me feel I wasn't OK, that I wasn't a new creature, that I was just fooling myself into thinking I was a good girl.

I began to think, *Well, these are Christian guys, who have a relationship with God, and they obviously don't respect me or they wouldn't try things. They think I'm nothing, that I have no worth or value. Maybe this is all I'm worth.*

Our young people all want to be accepted. Acceptance is a God-given need that must be met before they can ever feel a sense of security. The problem for most of them is that they look to the wrong things for their acceptance. Like Tracy, they often look to other people or to sexual involvement for their acceptance. It never works.

I decided I might as well go back to being what I used to be. I intended to go back to drugs and everything. But first I went and slept with this guy who wasn't a

Christian. I was torn to pieces inside. In that encounter, I realized that wasn't me. That wasn't my nature any longer. I knew it was wrong. It wasn't something I really wanted to do, but somehow I just hadn't found the answer yet.

I was still reading the Bible. I was active in the church. Everybody who didn't know my background respected me and thought I was a really wonderful person.

Actually it was having Christians judging me that pulled me away. As that kept getting worse, I pulled back from the church. There was this really neat guy whose parents found out about my abortion and who ordered him to stop going out with me. Here was a twenty-two-year-old man and his parents were telling him, "You can't see this girl." Out of obedience to them, we broke off the relationship.

How important it is for parents and church leaders to show acceptance and forgiveness to young people. Tragically, well-meaning but unforgiving Christian people have pushed more than one young person "over the edge."

Next I was deeply hurt by a guy with blond hair and blue eyes. He'd been talking marriage until he found out about my background. One night he sat me down and told me he couldn't accept my background or me. He said, "I want to, but I can't." I kept asking him to forgive me. But he said, "No. There's nothing to forgive." And he just walked away from me. I was devastated.

I was so hurt and angry I decided I would find a young man with blond hair and blue eyes who looked like this guy, sleep with him, and become pregnant. And then people would blame it on the guy who had hurt me so much. I would never say that it was his child, but it would look like him. And so I did exactly that and became pregnant—but I miscarried.

Tracy spent the next two years in and out of depression. She was ready to give up on God completely, when she met Dave. Dave was also a Christian. After a month of dating, they were engaged. Then, when they became physically involved, Tracy fell apart. Unable to handle it anymore, she broke off the relationship.

It was at that point I became suicidal. But the day I was preparing to kill myself, I thought of my nieces and nephews. A picture went through my mind of my brothers and sister telling them that Aunt Tracy had killed herself. I began to think I mustn't do this, because my nieces and nephews would grow up thinking, Christianity doesn't work. Look at Aunt Tracy!

At that moment the phone rang. It was my older brother who had left home when I was only eight years old. He knew nothing of what was going on in my life, but he said, "Tracy, you're suicidal, right? You're thinking you have no hope." I couldn't believe it. This was my older brother whom I'd never really known.

I said, "Wait a minute; are you serious?" He told me he and his wife had been praying just moments before, and God had shown them exactly what I was going through. Then I knew that Christianity did work, and I knew that God was real and God was capable of changing me. I had begged him to do it for years, but I still was missing something, and I didn't understand what that was.

What Tracy was missing was a true understanding of God's forgiveness and acceptance. She had gone through counseling before, but it was mostly self-help kinds of therapy, trying to make her feel better about herself. But feeling better about herself didn't change anything because her concept of God was still wrong. Like so many people, Tracy's concept of God was very much affected by her relationship with her father. Whenever she pictured God, she saw him in her father's image. To her, God was autocratic, unforgiving, and distant. Clearly, without a change in her concept of God, she would never be free to understand and accept his forgiveness.

Her view of God began to change when she began talking with my friend, Dick Day, a Christian counselor.

I listened to Dick Day talking about repentance and about changing my attitude about God. I began to have an understanding of who God is; that he loved me and wanted me; and why he paid for my sins. I had heard those things before, but I finally understood them. It was almost as if the veil was lifted.

I learned about God's character. He is righteous and holy. And righteousness cannot fellowship with or relate to unrighteousness. When God sent his Son to die for us he did this to satisfy his character, because the "wages of sin is death." But I also realized that because of Jesus' death, God's character was satisfied where I was concerned. It was so fresh to understand that God loved me unconditionally and gave his Son so I could be forgiven and cleansed.

I used to hear people talk about being hidden, or covered, by Jesus. People would hold a little "Jesus thing" and say that God sees Jesus but he doesn't see them. But that kind of thinking didn't help me to stop my sin. It seemed I was back there behind Jesus, still being as ugly and gross as I had always been, with no power to stop.

Slowly I began to understand that because of Jesus' death, I wasn't just "covered," I was forgiven.

For Tracy it was the turning point. As her concept of God began to change, so did her understanding of his forgiveness.

I began to see my infinite worth and value to God. He created me—who I am and how I am. God didn't need me, but because of his love he wanted me. And because he wanted me, he provided a way for me to repent—to confess not only my sin, but also to confess that it is forgiven. And that was incredible.

I have had a hard time praying and believing—for myself. I could always pray that God would move mountains for somebody else and believed he could do anything. But for me, I couldn't see it. I couldn't see that he could do anything for me. So, I would pray for myself, totally doubting that anything would ever happen for me.

But when I realized that God wanted me, not just to cover my sin, not just to make me "look" okay, but to cleanse everything and love me—it gave me a whole new concept. From then on I had a new concept about prayer, about God and about myself.

When Dick first met Tracy, she was anxious, depressed, inhibited, subjective, passive, and hostile. Three months later she was calm, lighthearted, socially expressive, objective, and tolerant of herself and others. As a result of Tracy's new understanding of God's acceptance and forgiveness, she has a new self-image. She sees herself as God sees her, a person created in his image with infinite worth and value. Because she now sees herself differently, Tracy is also beginning to see other people differently. She is even beginning to see her father differently.

Over the years, since my father became a Christian, he has been changing. But I didn't see it. I had this picture of my father, like I once had of God, that I had projected on him for so long, because of the past. So, when he was changing, I couldn't see it.

Seeing herself as God sees her also has given Tracy a new concept of sex, making possible a different kind of relationship with men. Sex is no longer needed as the basis for relating. Forgiven and cleansed, Tracy has become free to begin a new relationship with Dave. For both of them, this is a new beginning.

> Before this, we didn't really have a relationship. Although we loved each other, we didn't really know each other as people. We just had this physical desire and affection for one another. We knew each other somewhat, but the physical had just taken over.
>
> After understanding God's character and after repenting, we came back together. But it's totally different. Now Dave and I have the freedom to talk, to communicate, to understand who each of us is really. While I was in counseling with Dick Day, we became reengaged.
>
> This time I am free to make the kind of commitment I was never able to make before. Until now, I couldn't trust God and I couldn't trust Dave. Those other times I'd been engaged, I couldn't really make that commitment of my whole self. I could just commit my body.

Tracy no longer needs sex as a basis for love and acceptance. She is free to love and be loved as a total person. This young woman, who has lived through years of sexual guilt, has finally experienced the liberating power of God's forgiveness and cleansing grace. The beautiful thing about developing a healthy self-image—that is, seeing yourself as God sees you, and therefore being able to forgive yourself as God forgives you—is that you will then be able to be a channel of God's love and forgiveness to others.

After experiencing tremendous difficulties in relating to men, Tracy is now free to commit herself completely to a marriage relationship. She and Dave were married, and their relationship is growing. It is based on a proper understanding of who God is and what love and forgiveness are all about.

What helped Tracy most in her forgiveness/growth process? The love and acceptance given her by other Christians. They didn't just talk about God's love, acceptance, and forgiveness. They lived it.

BIBLICAL INSIGHTS FOR THOSE WHO SEEK FORGIVENESS

What hope can we offer to a young person who feels like "damaged goods"? Can lost virginity ever be restored? Can that person ever find deliverance from the emotional pain that keeps him or her in bondage? Does the abundant life that Jesus promises really apply to him or her?

Now that you know how important it is to accept and forgive those who seek God's forgiveness, here are some biblical insights you might share with young people who have sinned sexually.

First, let's consider one important figure in the Old Testament, David. If anyone has ever "blown it," he sure did. He had everything going for him. He was the king. God's hand of blessing was on him. He was a "five-point student on a four-point system." And then he saw Bathsheba.

Now David didn't just look at this beautiful woman. He stared. And the moment you begin to stare, you're hooked. David got himself hooked. After learning that her husband, Uriah, was fighting the Ammonites with the Israeli army, David sent for Bathsheba. If that wasn't bad enough, the Bible says, he had sex with her (see 2 Sam. 11:4). And she became pregnant.

David knew he was in trouble, so he devised a cover-up. He sent for Uriah, hoping that while he was home, the soldier would sleep with his wife. But David's plan didn't work. Uriah spent his first night back in Jerusalem sleeping in the palace servant quarters. How frustrated David must have been. He even tried to talk Uriah into going home to his wife and "enjoying himself." But Uriah refused, unwilling to leave his men. In desperation David got Uriah drunk (2 Sam. 11:13), hoping he would then go home and make love to his wife.

When none of this worked, David ordered Uriah sent to the front lines, where he was killed. What began with a stare led not only to adultery and an unwanted pregnancy but to murder. David really blew it.

But consider what happened next. David admitted his sin and asked God for forgiveness:

> Troubles without number surround me; my sins have overtaken me, and I cannot see. They are more than the hairs of my head, and my heart fails within me. (Ps. 40:12)
>
> Have mercy on me, O God, according to your unfailing love; according to your great compassion blot out my transgressions. Wash away all my iniquity and cleanse me from my sin. For I know my transgressions, and my sin is always before me. Against you, you only, have I sinned and done what is evil in your sight, so that you are proved right when you speak and justified when you judge. . . .

Cleanse me with hyssop, and I will be clean; wash me, and I will be whiter than snow. Let me hear joy and gladness; let the bones you have crushed rejoice. Hide your face from my sins and blot out all my iniquity. Create in me a pure heart, O God, and renew a steadfast spirit within me. . . . . Restore to me the joy of your salvation and grant me a willing spirit, to sustain me. Then I will teach transgressors your ways, and sinners will turn back to you. (Ps. 51:1-4, 7-10, 12-13)

Here was a man who had killed someone, believing that if he allowed God to forgive and cleanse him, he would once again be used to bring sinners to the Lord. Is there any sin so terrible that God cannot forgive it? No, not even sexual sin, not even murder. Any young person who doubts this needs to immerse himself or herself in Psalm 51.

Steps to Forgiveness
If you know of a young person who has "blown it" through sexual sin, encourage him or her to walk through these steps with you.

1. Admit your sin.
It is so easy to blame other people or our circumstances for our sins. That's as old as Adam and Eve. So many people say, "God, I've sinned . . . but I loved her! . . . but I was vulnerable! . . . but I had needs!" God can't work in your life if you insist on saying, "I have sinned, but . . ." According to 1 John 1:9, we must confess our sin. To confess means to agree with God about your sin. The first step on the way to forgiveness is to admit our sin to God. "God, I've sinned, period."

True repentance means more than just feeling sorry for what we have done or regretting that we are going to suffer the negative consequences of the sin. Repentance occurs when we feel so sick about what we've done that we don't ever want to do it again. True repentance acknowledges that we sinned against our Creator.

2. Accept God's forgiveness.
Read 1 John 1:9: "If we confess our sins, he is faithful and just and will forgive us our sins and purify us from all" — all means everything, including sexual immorality — "from all unrighteousness." Also read Hebrews 10:11-12: For all time "one sacrifice for sins." And read Colossians 2:12-14, where you will see that "he forgave us all our sins."

If you were the only person alive, Christ still would have died for you. You may have heard that before, but do you believe it? If you were the only person alive, you would stand in the place of Adam. You would sin, just as Adam did. And God would provide a Redeemer for you, just as he did for Adam (see Gen. 3:15).

In living the Christian life, we fail every day. Yet every day God is waiting to forgive us. Accepting the fact that we are sinners, that we sin, doesn't mean we should wallow in unworthiness. God wants to lift us up and set us free.

Some people, however, are sure that God could never forgive them because they have sinned too much or for too long. A seventeen-year-old high school girl asked after her abortion, "How can God really love and forgive me?" She didn't yet realize the significance of Christ's death on the cross and how it related to her. If only she could grasp the Good News of forgiveness. The Good News, the gospel, is that Jesus didn't come to save righteous people. He came to save sinners. He isn't interested in your proving to him how good you are. His message is forgiveness! The record is wiped clean.

Once I owned a Volkswagen Rabbit, which turned out to be a dud on the mountain roads where I lived at the time. So I had a turbocharger put on—and convinced my wife it made the car safer. That same day I was driving into town on a long straightaway. A motorcyclist was ahead of me, not going too fast, so I decided to pass and pulled out. Well, he figured he wasn't going to let some Rabbit pass him, so he stepped on the gas. There I was with a new turbo, and I thought I might as well test it. I floored it, and it worked. I passed the motorcycle and was doing 85 mph as the straightaway ended, and I hit my brakes for the curve.

Two curves later, the biggest red lights I've ever seen flashed in my rearview mirror. A cop pulled me and the cyclist over and ticketed both of us.

When I went to pay the ticket the clerk said, "You don't need to pay this if you take a three-hour driver's safety class." So I did and went back to the clerk with the little slip signed by the driving instructor. I gave it to the clerk, who said as she took it, "Your record is wiped clean."

After I was back in the car it hit me. My record is wiped clean. It was a powerful reminder of what Jesus Christ did on the cross with my sins. He wiped my slate clean. He canceled my debt and made it possible for me to be reconciled to God.

3. Show fruits of repentance.

Matthew 3:8 says, "Produce fruit in keeping with repentance." Repentance means turning around, changing one's mind. At this point you need to look at your life and your relationship. Ask God what fruit of repentance you need to show. It might be breaking off a relationship. It might be making major lifestyle changes. It might be not frequenting certain types of places again or not watching certain kinds of movies or TV programs. It also might be limiting your dates to double-dating situations. It could be any one of a number of other things, anything that enables you to stay on course.

4. Forgive yourself.

Early in my Christian life I would confess my sins to God, acknowledge his forgiveness—but then get down on myself. *McDowell, how could you have done that? What makes you think God can use you after what you did? Sure, God forgives you, but . . .* Such thoughts would set me off on a major guilt trip.

My problem was that, although I knew God could forgive me, I didn't always forgive myself. Somehow I thought I had to earn the right to forgive myself. I had to prove I was worthy. I couldn't make mistakes and then minister in his name. Isn't it interesting that we can be harder on ourselves than God is?

However, refusing to forgive ourselves can be a form of pride. We think we should be beyond sin. We refuse to accept ourselves as we really are—fallible human beings who are capable of blowing it, not just once, but again and again. In not forgiving ourselves, we are implying that Jesus Christ's death on the cross is not sufficient for all our sins. We are saying, "God, I'm a better judge of what can be forgiven than you are." What an insult to almighty God!

The real issue in forgiving ourselves is not how many times or how badly we blow it. The real issue is how you and I respond when we do sin. For example, one day in a restaurant I hurt a brother in Christ deeply by saying something I should never have said. On the way home I realized the impact of my uncalled for, off-the-wall remark. Immediately I confessed my sin to God. I also realized I needed to return to the restaurant and confess my sin to the one I had hurt.

So I turned around, found this brother and said, "What I said was wrong, and I know I hurt you. I've confessed it to God, and I've come back to ask your forgiveness. Will you forgive me?"

To my amazement he said, "No. I won't forgive you. Someone in your position shouldn't have said that."

I went home frustrated and confused. Soon I was off on another of my guilt trips, asking myself, "How could you have said that? How can anyone in Christian work hurt a brother like that? How can God use you now?" My self-chastisement almost sounded like a new hymn about the misery of personal guilt. "Oh, Woe Is Me."

Do you see what I was doing? I was making forgiveness from a brother the prerequisite for being able to forgive myself. I was letting someone else's response control my life and relationship with God.

Then the Holy Spirit started working on me. "Just a minute, Josh. You're not handling this right. You can make one of two responses: You can wallow around in guilt, focus on your failings—or you can realize that Jesus died for this situation, confess it to God and the one you hurt [which I had done], and get on with your life, having learned something."

After wrestling awhile with the alternatives, I confessed the whole thing to God one more time, and then I added, "And Father, I forgive me too." I determined to do all I could from then on to heal the relationship with my wounded brother, but not to allow his response to impair my assurance of God's forgiveness for me.

As time went on I repeatedly went out of my way to express love to the person I had hurt. One day about a year later, I said to my wife, "You know, I think the relationship is healed. The hurt seems to be gone, and from all appearances I think he has forgiven me. In fact, the relationship seems better than ever before."

One of the things that hurts God the most is for someone to reject or "cheapen" his grace. God's grace comes out of his loving heart: "For God so loved the world that he gave his only Son" (John 3:16, NLT). Although we don't deserve it, because of the Father's love, Jesus Christ came down to earth and died on the cross for us. When we refuse to forgive ourselves, we actually are throwing God's loving grace right back in his face.

No matter who you are, if God's grace can't cover that sin in your life, it can't cover any sin. Confession is agreeing with God, not only about the wrong done, but also about what he has done in forgiving. I suspect that to reject forgiveness is more grieving to God than the original act; it is a denial of God's grace for which he paid so dearly.

5. Don't let Satan deceive you.

Satan will try to make you feel condemned. But if you know Jesus Christ personally as Savior and Lord, you can never be condemned. Romans 8:1 says, "So now there is no condemnation for those who belong to Christ Jesus" (NLT).

Be sure, however, to discern the difference between condemnation and conviction. When sin enters your life, the Holy Spirit doesn't work to condemn you, but he does work to convict you. When you respond to God's conviction in your life through the Holy Spirit, you are drawn to Christ and the result is joy. Condemnation, on the other hand, pulls you away from Christ and leads to despair. Discern the difference between condemnation and conviction.

So, if you've "blown it"—even in terms of sexual sin—this is what you need to do to experience forgiveness and cleansing: Admit your sin to God; repent, which means change; acknowledge God's forgiveness; forgive yourself; and don't let Satan prevent you from experiencing the full benefits of God's forgiveness.

WHAT CAN BE DONE ABOUT LOST VIRGINITY?

No one can regain his or her physical virginity. That's lost forever. But I really believe that one's spiritual and emotional virginity can be regained. This is a message of encouragement and hope you can share with young people who are despondent over their lost virginity.

"Don't let the world around you squeeze you into its own mould, but let God re-make you so that your . . . mind is changed" (Rom. 12:2, Phillips). The negative experiences of our lives have squeezed us into their mold. The only way to be cleansed to the point of emotional virginity is to let God remold our minds from within. To do that, God has provided three resources: his truth—to understand who he is and who we are; his Holy Spirit—to illuminate his truth and to bring it to fruition in our lives; and his people—to express his love and forgiveness in relationships.

Tracy learned God's truth in relationship with his people. When the Holy Spirit illuminated God's truth for her, Tracy experienced restoration of her emotional and spiritual virginity. This has given Tracy a fresh start. Another young person had a similar experience:

> If you are already involved in sexual immorality, it isn't too late. God will forgive you and help you begin a relationship that is pleasing in his sight. No matter what you've done, no matter how many times you've done it, Jesus Christ has the capacity to heal, to cleanse, and to purify.

Young people who are sexually active today need a new beginning. Most college students, even those from Christian homes, are not innocent in the area of sex, and that is becoming increasingly true for high school students. Many young people already have gone "all the way" sexually or at least further than they may want to admit.

The problem is that sexual sin can cause a person to take one's eyes off Christ's love and forgiveness and begin to lose all hope of ever again living a chaste lifestyle. This young person has resigned himself or herself to a life of promiscuity, sometimes just because of one bad experience. "After what I've done, what difference does it make? It doesn't matter anymore." If a young person has yielded to sexual pressures, it is all too easy to adopt the attitude of the escaped convict who is fleeing a death sentence for murder: "I've got nothing to lose!"

Without knowing the reality of God's forgiveness and restoration, many young people assume that because of their past the future is already lost. We need to understand that one crime does not doom a person to the life of a criminal. It's never too late to begin saying no.

It all begins with forgiveness. Forgiveness is not a license for sexual permissiveness, but rather an opportunity to make a fresh start. With God we can have a new beginning. We don't have to feel trapped into continuing down a particular wrong-way path. Through forgiveness, God can make possible the choice of a new path in which we can walk according to his principles.

Remember the story of Jesus and the woman caught in adultery? Jesus said, "He that is without sin . . . , let him first cast a stone" (John 8:7, KJV). Because he extended forgiveness and acceptance, I'm sure that woman never forgot his request to "go, and sin no more" (John 8:11, KJV). I keep a little sign on my desk which says, "Remember, today is the first day of the rest of your life." There's always a new beginning.

A young newlywed wrote to me:

> My fiancé and I knew we had to get out of our sexual immorality. With God's help we did not engage in sex during the nine months until our wedding. The first time we made love after our wedding, tears of joy streamed down my face. I experienced the true beauty of the sexual relationship as God intended it. Choose to enjoy that special sexual relationship that God has designed to be exhilarating and refreshing within marriage. Choose to wait.

When we understand God's perspective on sex, we realize why sex should be experienced only within the sanctity and security of a total commitment of marriage. We can understand why it is important to say no to premarital sexual involvement.

We must recognize and respect God-designed limits. Maximum enjoyment of sex comes when God's guidelines are followed, his protective commandments are obeyed, and his sexual boundaries are observed.

HOPE LIVES ON

For the young person who is struggling under the pain of sexual sin and lost virginity, I can think of no more hopeful words than those of Dr. John Diggs. Perhaps you know of a young person who needs to read this letter:

You're thinking, "I've already blown it. There is no point in me even thinking about 'saving myself' for my future spouse."

Don't despair. Hope lives on.

Whatever mistakes you've made can be frozen in time. Whatever patterns of behavior you have established can be changed. If you have been involved in a sexual relationship, you can stop. Now. If you have an STD, you can get treatment. And avoid getting another one. If you have already had a child without getting married, you can make sure that his or her brother or sister comes into a stable home, after you get married. If you have had an abortion, you can avoid repeating that painful event in the future and seek healing for the deep hurt you have already endured.

As a doctor, I have seen the anguish that goes along with unmarried sex—the diseases, the pregnancies, the destructive behaviors, the sense of worthlessness, the sense of being used. Because so many people are suffering, some have come to consider this suffering as normal. People on talk shows almost brag about this anguish. *The Jerry Springer Show* comes to mind. It is not normal. After the fifteen minutes of fame have passed, there are serious problems left behind. These sex-related problems are an unnecessary distress. As a father, I long to fix these problems when I see them in today's young people. I realize that the only effective "fixing" is to avoid them in the first place.

First, stop doing what you are doing. It may be easier said than done, but it is more important to be done than said. Resistance from your boyfriend or girlfriend is possible. On the other hand, you may find that they agree with you. If not, then their insistence on sex for the relationship to continue may tell you a great deal about what they think about your relationship.

Second, pledge to yourself, to your family, and to your future spouse that you will wait until the wedding night. Why? That is the key to having a successful marriage. Sexual baggage brought into the marriage is a threat to the marriage, not a benefit.

Third, don't be afraid to tell your friends about your decision. They will respect you for having the guts to go against the grain, for being counterculture with a cause. And your future spouse will respect you for saving marital intimacy for marriage.

This change in attitude will make you more attractive to the opposite sex, not less. They will know that you take relationships seriously, that you take your sexuality seriously, that you can be trusted, and that you can become disease-free.

If you have already made mistakes that have left you with an incurable STD, that is something your future spouse will have to deal with. That will be a small barrier compared to the benefit of being with someone like you who maintains their self-respect and integrity. Renew your life, and renew your actions. Invest in your future. Good things will come.[1]

CHAPTER 1: WHY DOES TRUE LOVE WAIT?

1. Jacqueline F. de Gaston, Larry Jensen, and Stan Weed, "A Closer Look at Adolescent Sexual Activity," *Journal of Youth and Adolescence* 24, no. 4 (1995): 469–474.

2. Kathleen Kelleher, "Talking to Teens about Sex—It's in the Details," *Los Angeles Times,* 29 January 2001, sec. A, p. 4.

3. Lifeway True Love Waits News Media Center, "The National Longitudinal Study of Adolescent Health," March 30, 2001; <www.lifeway.com/tlw/trends.asp>.

4. L. Kann et al., "Youth Risk Behavior Surveillance—United States," *Morbidity and Mortality Weekly Report* 44, SS-1 (March 24, 1995): 11.

5. Judi Hasson, "Campaign Aims to Steer Girls onto Right Path," *USA Today*, 21 November 1996, sec. A, p. 3.

6. Jane Gadd, "Sex Talk Is Easy When It's Teen to Teen," *National News*, 5 March 1996, sec. A, p. 6.

7. Melissa Healy, "Clinton Frees $250 Million for Sex Abstinence Teaching," *Los Angeles Times*, 1 March 1997, sec. A, p. 12.

8. Hollis L. Engel, "Americans Lead List in Sex Survey," *USA Today*, 24 May 1996.

9. Susan Okie, "Teenage Chlamydia Cases Alarm Experts," *The Washington Post*, 3 September 1997.

10. M. B. Fletcher, "The Adolescent Experience: Sex Happens" (paper presented at the Southern Baptist Ethics Conference, Nashville, Tenn., February 3, 1992), 4.

11. S. L. Hofferth, J. R. Kahn, and W. Baldwin, "Premarital Sexual Activity among U.S. Teenager Women over the Past Three Decades," *Family Planning Perspective* 19 (1987): 45–53.

12. The Institute of Medicine, *The Hidden Epidemic: Confronting Sexually Transmitted Diseases,* ed. Thomas R. Eng and William T. Butler (Washington, D.C.: National Academy Press, 1997): 104.

13. Andrea E. Bonny, M.D., and Frank M. Biro, M.D., "Recognizing and Treating STDs in Adolescent Girls," *Contemporary Pediatrics* (March 1998): 123.

14. R. W. Blum and P. M. Rinehart, *Reducing the Risk: Connections That Make a Difference in the Lives of Youth* (Minneapolis, Minn.: Division of General Pediatrics and Adolescent Health, University of Minnesota, 1997), 14.

15. Norvel Glenn and Elizabeth Marquardt, "Hooking Up, Hanging Out, and Hoping for Mr. Right: College Women on Dating and Mating Today," *Independent Women's Forum* (July 26, 2001): 2.

16. Oregon Health Division News Release, "New Findings Show Fewer Teens Engaging

in Sexual Activity," March 29, 2001; <www.ohd.hr.state.or.us/news/2001/329ccfh.htm>.

17. Centers for Disease Control News Release, "Teen Sex Down New Study Shows," May 1997; <www.cdc.gov/od/oc/media/pressrel/teensex.htm>.
18. Ibid.
19. National Center for Health Statistics Press Release, "Teen Sex Down New Study Shows," May 1, 1997; <www.hhs.gov/news/press/1997pres/970501.html>.
20. Joshua Mann, M.D., Joe S. McIlhaney Jr., M.D., and Curtis C. Stine, M.D., *Building Heathy Futures: Tools for Helping Adolescents Avoid or Delay the Onset of Sexual Activity* (Austin, Tex.: The Medical Institute, 2000): 5.
21. "The Naked Truth," *Newsweek* (May 8, 2000): 58.
22. Centers for Disease Control, "Youth Risk Behavior Surveillance—United States, 1997," *Morbidity and Mortality Weekly Report* 47, SS-3 (August 14, 1998): 1–89.
23. The Alan Guttmacher Institute, "Teenage Pregnancy Overall Trends and State by State Information," April 1999; <www.agi-usa.org/pubs/teen_preg_stats.html>.
24. Glenn and Marquardt, "Hooking Up, Hanging Out," 2, quoted in Karen S. Peterson, "College Women Find the Non-Dating Game Confusing," *USA Today*, 26 July 2001, sec. A, p. 1.
25. Jerry Abejo, "Citing Drop in Teen Pregnancy, Report Credits Range of Factors," *The Philadelphia Inquirer,* 25 April 2001; <inq.philly.com>.
26. The Council of Economic Advisers, *Teens and Their Parents in the Twenty-first Century: An Examination of Trends in Teen Behavior and the Role of Parental Involvement,* The White House Conference on Teenagers: Raising Responsible and Resourceful Youth, Washington, D.C., May 2000, 17.
27. Laurie Goodstein and Marjorie Connelly, "Teen-Age Poll Finds Support for Tradition," *New York Times*, 30 April 1998.
28. Oregon Health Division News Release, "New Findings Show Fewer Teens Engaging in Sexual Activity," March 29, 2001; <www.ohd.hr.state.or.us/news/2001/329ccfh.htm>.
29. Kaiser Family Foundation and *YM* magazine, "National Survey of Teens: Teens Talk about Dating, Intimacy, and Their Sexual Experiences," Kaiser Family Foundation and *YM* magazine, "National Survey of Teens: Teens Talk about Dating, Intimacy, and Their Sexual Experiences," *YM* magazine (May 1998): 5.
30. Susan Sprecher and Pamela C. Regan, "College Virgins: How Men and Women Perceive Their Sexual Status," *The Journal of Sex Research* 33, no. 10 (1996): 3–15.
31. International Communications Research, "The Cautious Generation? Teens Tell Us about Sex, Virginity, and 'The Talk' " (a summary of findings from two nationally representative surveys of teenagers conducted by the National Campaign to Prevent Teen Pregnancy, International Communications Research, April 27, 2000), 2.
32. Ibid., 5.
33. P. Beaman and H. Bruckner, "Power in Numbers: Peer Effects on Adolescent Girls'

Sexual Debut and Pregnancy" (Washington, D.C.: The National Campaign to Prevent Teen Pregnancy, 1999).

34. International Communications Research, "Not Just Another Thing to Do—Teens Talk about Sex, Regret, and the Influence of Their Parents" (a summary of findings from a nationally representative survey by International Communications Research, June 30, 2000), 1.

35. Ibid.

36. Ibid.

37. de Gaston, Jensen, and Weed, "Adolescent Sexual Activity," 465.

38. Lynn Smith, "90s Family: Giving Girls the Ability to Say No," *Los Angeles Times,* 28 April 1996, sec. E, pp. 3–4.

39. Michael Ebert, "Caught," *Citizen* (April 18, 1994): 3.

40. Tom McNichol, "Sex Can Wait," *USA Weekend*, 25–27 March 1994, pp. 4–6.

41. de Gaston, Jensen, and Weed, "Adolescent Sexual Activity," 473.

42. "Norplant," Narr. Diane Sawyer, *Prime Time America,* ABC, December 15, 1992.

43. Originally published in Josh McDowell, *How to Help Your Child Say NO to Sexual Pressure* (Waco, Tex.: Word, 1987), 141–2.

CHAPTER 2: ADOLESCENT PREMARITAL SEX

1. Joshua Mann, M.D., Joe S. McIlhaney Jr., M.D., and Curtis C. Stine, M.D., *Building Healthy Futures: Tools for Helping Adolescents Avoid or Delay the Onset of Sexual Activity.* (Austin, Tex.: The Medical Institute, 2000): 19.

2. Heather Farish, Family Research Council Press Release, "The Whole Story on Sex," March 29, 2001 (Washington, D.C.: Family Research Council).

3. American Social Health Association, *Sexually Transmitted Diseases in America: How Many Cases and at What Cost?* (Menlo Park, Calif.: Kaiser Family Foundation, 1998).

4. Kaiser Family Foundation and *YM* magazine, "National Survey of Teens: Teens Talk about Dating, Intimacy, and Their Sexual Experiences," *YM* magazine (May 1998): 12.

5. Ibid.

6. The Medical Institute, "National Guidelines for Sexuality and Character Education" (Austin, Tex.: The Medical Institute, 1996): 5.

7. M. G. Powell and J. Wright, "Counseling Young Women: An STD Update," *Treating Female Patient* 7, no. 3 (1993): 10.

8. Kaiser Family Foundation, *Sexually Transmitted Diseases in America: How Many Cases and at What Cost?* (Menlo Park, Calif.: Kaiser Family Foundation, 1998); <www.kff.org/content/archive/1445/std_rel.pdf>.

9. Shari Roan, "Common Sexually Transmitted Diseases," *Los Angeles Times*, 10 October 1995.

10. Department of Health and Human Services HHS News, "Scientific Review Panel

Confirms Condoms Are Effective Against HIV/AIDS, but Epidemiological Studies Are Insufficient for Other STDs," July 20, 2001; <www.hhs.gov/news/press/2001pres/20010720.html>.

11. Sexuality Information and Education Council of the United States, "Fact Sheet: Sexually Transmitted Diseases in the United States," *SIECUS Report* 25, no. 3 (1997).

12. The Medical Institute, "Supporting Evidence from Recent Studies That Reveal the Necessity of Healthier, More Responsible Sexual Behavior and Education" *Sexual Health Update* 5, no. 2 (winter 1997): 2.

13. The Institute of Medicine, *The Hidden Epidemic—Confronting Sexually Transmitted Disease,* ed. Thomas R. Eng and William T. Butler (Washington, D.C.: National Academy Press, 1997): 33.

14. D. H. Kedes et al., "The Prevalence of Serum Antibody to Human Herpesvirus 8 (Kaposi Sarcoma—Associated Herpesvirus) among HIV-Seropositive and High-Risk HIV-Seronegative Women," *Journal of the American Medical Society* 277, no. 6 (1997): 478–81.

15. Adapted from P. D. Hitchcock, *AIDS Patient Care* 10 (1996): 79–85.

16. John R. Diggs Jr., M.D., *Physical Consequences of Premarital Sex* (Sioux Falls, S. Dak.: Abstinence Clearinghouse, 2000), 1.

17. Patricia Hersch, "Teen Epidemic—Sexually Transmitted Diseases Are Ravaging Our Children," *American Health* (May 1991): 44.

18. American Social Health Association, *Sexually Transmitted Disease in America.*

19. W. Cates et al., "Estimates of the Incidence and Prevalence of Sexually Transmitted Diseases in the United States," *Sexually Transmitted Diseases* 26 (supplement 1999): 2–7.

20. The Institute of Medicine, *Hidden Epidemic,* 312.

21. Cates et al., "Estimates of the Incidence and Prevalence."

22. World Health Organization, *Sexually Transmitted Diseases (STDs)—Fact Sheet* (Department of HIV/AIDS, April 1996).

23. Patricia Donovan, "Family Planning Clinics: Facing Higher Costs and Sicker Patients," *Family Planning Perspectives* (September 10, 1991): 198–202.

24. Cates et al., "Estimates of the Incidence and Prevalence."

25. House Committee on Commerce, Ronald O. Valdiserri, M.D. speaking to the Subcommittee on Health and Environment on cervical cancer, *Congressional Record* (16 March 1999), 18–22.

26. Ibid.

27. The Medical Institute, "Abstinence and 'Safer Sex' Sexuality Education: A Comparison" (Austin, Tex.: The Medical Institute): 20.

28. Sexuality Information and Education Council of the United States, "Sexually Transmitted Diseases."

29. The Medical Institute, "Abstinence and 'Safer Sex,' " 20.

30. Ibid.

31. Ibid.

32. Ibid.

33. Michelle Ingrassia, "Virgin Cool," *Newsweek* (October 17, 1994): 61.

34. The Medical Institute, "Safe Sex?" (Austin, Tex.: The Medical Institute, 1999), documented slide presentation.

35. Centers for Disease Control, "Sexual Behavior among High School Students—United States, 1990,"*Morbidity and Mortality Weekly Report* 40, nos. 51–52 (January 3, 1992): 885–8.

36. Centers for Disease Control, STD statistics, *1993 Sexually Transmitted Diseases Surveillance Report,* (May 1993).

37. Jennifer Kornreich, "The Risks of Young Love: Sexually Transmitted Diseases Common in Teenagers," MSNBC, March 20, 2001; <www.msnbc.com/news/529857.asp>.

38. The Institute of Medicine, *Hidden Epidemic,* 177.

39. Molly Masland, "The Sex Ed Dilemma: Beyond the Birds and the Bees," MSNBC, March 20, 2001; <www.msnbc.com/news/535245.asp>.

40. Centers for Disease Control, "Premarital Sexual Experience Among Adolescent Women—United States, 1970–1988," *Morbidity and Mortality Weekly Report* 39, no. 51 (January 1991): 929–32.

41. The Medical Institute, "Sexuality and Character Education," 5.

42. Centers for Disease Control, Division of STD Prevention, *Sexually Transmitted Disease Surveillance 1995* (September 1996): 43.

43. M. A. Shafer, C. E. Irwin, and R. L. Sweet, "Acute Salpingitis in the Adolescent Female," *Journal of Pediatrics* 100 (1982): 339–50.

44. Kornreich, "Risks of Young Love."

45. The Institute of Medicine, *Hidden Epidemic,* 39.

46. Joe S. McIlhaney Jr., M.D., *Sex: What You Don't Know Can Kill You* (Grand Rapids: Baker, 1997), 23.

47. The Institute of Medicine, *Hidden Epidemic,* 37.

48. R. Rolfs, E. Galaid, and A. Zaidi, "Pelvic Inflammatory Disease: Trends in Hospitalizations and Office Visits, 1979 through 1988," *American Journal of Obstetrics and Gynecology* 166 (1992): 983.

49. A. P. Acquavella, M.D., A. Rubin, M.D., and L. J. D'Angelo, M.D., "The Coincident Diagnosis of Pelvic Inflammatory Disease and Pregnancy: Are They Compatible?" (Washington, D.C.: Washington Hospital Center, 1998).

50. McIlhaney, *What You Don't Know,* 20.

51. The Institute of Medicine, *Hidden Epidemic,* 5.

52. McIlhaney, *What You Don't Know,* 20.

53. Sheryl Gay Stolberg, "U.S. Awakes to Epidemic of Sexual Diseases," *New York Times*, 9 March 1998.

54. D. Rusk et al., "Analysis of Invasive Squamous Cell Carcinoma of the Vulva and

Vulvar Intraepithelial Neoplasia for the Presence of Human Papilloma Virus DNA," *American Journal of Obstetrics and Gynecology* 77 (1991): 918.

55. The Institute of Medicine, *Hidden Epidemic,* 5.

56. Mark J. Messing, M.D., and Donald G. Gallup, M.D., "Carcinoma of the Vulva in Young Women," *American Journal of Obstetrics and Gynecology* 86, no. 1 (July 1995): 51.

57. Thomas E. Elkins, M.D., "Infectious Aspects of Contraceptive Practices" (paper, University of Michigan Medical Center, 1992), 9.

58. Ibid.

59. House Committee, Valdiserri, 18–22.

60. The Institute of Medicine, *Hidden Epidemic,* 10.

61. T. S. Quinn, Review of *The Hidden Epidemic: Confronting Sexually Transmitted Diseases*, The Institute of Medicine, ed. Thomas R. Eng and William T. Butler, 1997, *New England Journal of Medicine* 337, no. 16 (October 16, 1997): 1177–8.

62. Elkins, "Infectious Aspects," 10.

63. The Institute of Medicine, *Hidden Epidemic,* 10.

64. The Medical Institute, "Sexuality and Character Education," 5.

65. McIlhaney, *What You Don't Know*, 79.

66. "Troubling Teen Sex Trend," *USA Today,* 27 December 2000, sec. A, p. 10.

67. M. B. Fletcher, "The Adolescent Experience: Sex Happens" (paper presented at the Southern Baptist Ethics Conference, Nashville, Tenn., February 3, 1992), 9.

68. Kornreich, "Risks of Young Love."

69. "Troubling Teen Sex Trend."

70. The Council of Economic Advisers, *Teens and Their Parents in the Twenty-first Century: An Examination of Trends in Teen Behavior and the Role of Parental Involvement,* The White House Conference on Teenagers: Raising Responsible and Resourceful Youth, Washington, D.C., May 2000, 17.

71. Abbylin Sellers, *The Sexual Abstinence Message Causes Positive Changes in Adolescent Behavior: A Circumstantial Review of Relevant Studies* (Santa Barbara, Calif.: Westmont College, 1998).

72. S. K. Henshaw, "U.S. Teenage Pregnancy Statistics with Comparative Statistics for Women Aged 20–24," The Alan Guttmacher Institute, March 5, 2001; <www.agi-usa.org/pubs/teen_preg_sr_0699.html>.

73. Centers for Disease Control, "Declines in Teenage Birth Rates, 1991–1997: National and State Patterns," *National Vital Statistics Reports* 47, no. 12 (December, 1998).

74. Henshaw, "Pregnancy Statistics."

75. Centers for Disease Control, "Abortion Surveillance: Preliminary Analysis—United States," January 7 1997; <www.cdc.gov/mmwr/preview/mmwrhtml/mm4851a3.htm>.

76. Kornreich, "Risks of Young Love."

77. Kari Petrie, "High School Student Says Abstinence Efforts Fail," Women's E-News, September 29, 2001; <www.womensenews.org/article.cfm/dyn/aid/478/context/archive>.

78. R. A. Maynard, ed., *Kids Having Kids: A Robin Hood Foundation Special Report on the Costs of Adolescent Childbearing* (New York: Robin Hood Foundation, 1996): 1–2.

79. Family Research Council, *Free to Be Family* (1992): 28–29.

80. Maggie Gallagher, "Elegy for Father's Day," *Investment Business Daily,* 14 June 1996, p. 6.

81. Eva M. Clayton, "Teenage Pregnancy, " *Congressional Record* (27 February 1996).

82. Maynard, *Kids Having Kids,* 1–2.

83. Mann, McIlhaney, and Stine, *Building Healthy Futures*, 19.

84. A. Bachu, "Trends in Premarital Childbearing: 1930–1994." *Current Population Reports* (Washington, D.C: U.S. Census Bureau, 1999): 23–197.

85. Lynn Smith, "What's the Matter with Kids Today? Their Parents," *Los Angeles Times*, 19 May 1996, sec. E, p. 3.

86. Karen Peterson, "Birth Rate Drops for Teens," *USA Today*, 22 September 1995, sec. D, p. 2.

87. Michael Gartner, "Surprise! Programs Help Close Race Gap," *USA Today*, 5 December 1995, sec. A, p. 11.

88. Mark Potok, "Out-of-Wedlock Childbirth Rising," *USA Today*, 8 November 1995, sec. A, p. 2.

89. Ibid.

90. Linda Kinamine, "Numbers of Two-Parent Families Up," *USA Today*, 16 October 1995, sec. A, p. 1.

CHAPTER 3: ADOLESCENT PREMARITAL SEX: THE HIGH COST TO SOCIETY

1. C. Murray, "The Coming White Underclass," *Wall Street Journal*, 29 October 1993, sec. A, p. 14.

2. Joshua Mann, M.D, Joe S. McIlhaney Jr., M.D., and Curtis C. Stine, M.D., *Building Healthy Futures: Tools for Helping Adolescents Avoid or Delay the Onset of Sexual Activity* (Austin, Tex.: The Medical Institute, 2000): 4.

3. The Medical Institute, "Abstinence and 'Safer Sex' Sexuality Education: A Comparison" (Austin, Tex.: The Medical Institute, 1999): 20.

4. Heather Farish, Family Research Council Press Release, "The Whole Story on Sex," Family Research Council: Press Room, March 29, 2000 (Washington, D.C.: Family Research Council).

5. R. A. Maynard, ed., *Kids Having Kids: A Robin Hood Foundation Special Report on the Costs of Adolescent Childbearing* (New York: Robin Hood Foundation, 1996), 11–14.

6. Ibid., 1–2.

7. S. D. Hoffman, E. M. Foster, and F. F. Furstenberg, "Reevaluating the Costs of Teenager Childbearing," *Demography* 30 (1993): 1–13.

8. Lynn Smith, "What's the Matter with Kids Today? Their Parents," *Los Angeles Times*, 19 May 1996, sec. E, p. 3.

9. "The Riddle of Prematurity," *The Female Patient* 19 (April 1994): 67–77.

10. I. Kallings et al., "Current and Previous Vaginal Candidiasis," Third International Symposium on Vaginosis/Vaginitis, Madeira, Jan. 25–29, 1994), 11.

11. *Medical Tribune* (June 16, 1994): 8.

12. Diane Duston, "Sons of Teen Moms 3 Times More Likely to Wind Up in Jail," *South Coast Today,* 13 June 1996; <www.s-t.com/daily/06-96/06-14-96/a02wn018.htm>.

13. Maynard, *Kids Having Kids,* 7–11.

14. Bureau of the Census, "Marital Status and Living Arrangements, 1991," *Current Population Reports,* Bureau of the Census (Washington, D.C., 1991), no. 450.

15. William Galston and Elaine Kamarck, "A Progressive Family Policy for the 1990s," in *Mandate for Change*, ed. Will Marshall and Martin Schram (New York: Berkeley, 1993).

16. Maynard, *Kids Having Kids,* 7–11, 17.

17. Duston, "Sons of Teen Moms."

18. Maynard, *Kids Having Kids,* 7–11, 14.

19. Ibid., 3.

20. Centers for Disease Control, "Abortion Surveillance: Preliminary Analysis—United States, 1997," January 7, 2000; <www.cdc.gov/mmwr/preview/mmwrhtml/mm4851a3.htm>.

21. Budget of the United States Government, 1999.

22. Joe S. McIlhaney Jr., M.D., *Sex: What You Don't Know Can Kill You* (Grand Rapids: Baker, 1997), 59.

23. Alan Guttmacher Institute, "Sex and the American Teenager" (New York: Alan Guttmacher Institute, 1994): 7.

24. Susan Richardson, "An Overlooked Weapon in the Battle of Teen Pregnancy: Self-Esteem," *Austin American-Statesman*, 5 March 1998.

25. Maynard, *Kids Having Kids,* 7–14, 19–20.

CHAPTER 4: THE PHYSICAL REASONS

1. Francesca Lyman, "Coming of age too soon?" MSNBC, March 2, 2001; <www.msnbc.com/news/537410.asp>

2. Suzanne Fields, "Condom nation," *The Washington Times: National Weekly Edition,* 27 April 1997.

3. Josh McDowell, *Why Wait: What You Need to Know about the Teen Sexuality Crisis* (Nashville, Tenn.: Thomas Nelson, 1987), 79.

4. Kaiser Family Foundation and *YM* magazine, "National Survey of Teens: Teens Talk about Dating, Intimacy, and Their Sexual Experiences," *YM* magazine (May 1998): 1–2.

5. Ibid., 5.

6. Sarah Crichton, "Sexual Correctness: Has It Gone Too Far?" *Newsweek* (October 25, 1993): 4.

7. Andrea E. Bonny, M.D. and Frank M. Biro, M.D., "Recognizing and Treating STDs in Adolescent Girls," *Contemporary Pediatrics* (March 1998): 139.
8. "Kaiser Family Foundation and *YM* magazine, "National Survey of Teens," 5.
9. D. P. Orr et al., "Factors Associated with Condom Use among Sexually Active Female Adolescents," *American Academy of Pediatrics* 120 (1992): 311.
10. Anne Pandolf, "Teen Sex from Drug Use: Odds Are Greater If Teenagers Use Alcohol, Drugs," *ABC News,* December 7, 1999; <abcnews.go.com/sections/living/DailyNews/teensex991207.html>.
11. Centers for Disease Control and Prevention, "Summary of Notifiable Diseases—United States, 1997," *Morbidity and Mortality Weekly Report* 48 (1998): 1–81.
12. L. Kann et al., "Youth Risk Behavior Surveillance—United States," *Morbidity and Mortality Weekly Report* 44, SS-1 (March 24, 1995): 11.
13. Pandolfi, "Teen Sex from Drug Use."
14. J. Thomas Fitch, M.D., "How Effective Are Condoms in Preventing Pregnancy and STDs in Adolescents?" (Austin, Tex.: The Medical Institute, July 1997): 2–4.
15. The Medical Institute, "Safe Sex?" (Austin, Tex.: The Medical Institute, 1999), documented slide presentation.
16. Tom Luster and Stephen A. Small, "Sexual Abuse History and Number of Sex Partners among Female Adolescents," *Family Planning Perspectives* 29 (1997): 204–11.
17. The Institute of Medicine, *The Hidden Epidemic: Confronting Sexually Transmitted Diseases,* ed. Thomas R. Eng and William T. Butler (Washington, D.C.: National Academy Press, 1997): 8.
18. Al Neuharth, "Can Rally for Kids Curb Abuse, Neglect?" *USA Today,* 31 May 1996, sec. A, p. 13.
19. Elizabeth Mehren, "The Throwaways," *Los Angeles Times,* 12 April 1996, sec. E, p. 3.
20. Elizabeth Mehren, "As Bad As They Wanna Be," *Los Angeles Times,* 17 May 1996, sec. E, p. 3.
21. Deborah Sharp, "Advocates Divided on Anti-Pedophile Bill," *USA Today,* 9 May 1996, sec. A, p. 2.
22. Bruce Frankel, "Report: Child Abuse Estimates Low," *USA Today,* 7 December 1995, sec. A, p. 3.
23. D. Boyer and D. Fine, "Sexual Abuse as a Factor in Adolescent Pregnancy and Child Maltreatment," *Family Planning Perspectives* 24 (1992): 5.
24. "Study: Up to 20 Percent of Boys Sexually Abused," *Modesto (Calif.) Bee,* 2 December 1998, sec. A, p. 5.

CHAPTER 5: THE ENVIRONMENTAL REASONS
1. Lance Morrow, "Fifteen Cheers for Abstinence," *Time* (October 2, 1995): 90.
2. Paul David Tripp, "The Way of the Wise: Teaching Teenagers about Sex," *The Journal of Biblical Counseling* 13, no. 3 (spring 1995): 36.

3. Anita Manning, "Teen Girls No Longer Enjoy an Age of Innocence," *USA Today*, 6 October 1997, sec. D, p. 4.

4. M.B. Fletcher, "The Adolescent Experience: Sex Happens" (paper presented at the Southern Baptist Ethics Conference, Nashville, Tenn., February 3, 1992), 9.

5. Haddon Robinson, ed., "CT Classic: Sex, Marriage and Divorce," *Christianity Today* (December 14, 1992).

6. Joe S. McIlhaney Jr., M.D., *Sex: What You Don't Know Can Kill You* (Grand Rapids: Baker, 1997), 92–93.

7. Samantha Levine, "The Perils of Young Romance," *U.S. News and World Report* (August 13, 2001).

8. Tamara Henry, "Campus Crime Climbs," *USA Today*, 22 April 1996, sec. D, p. 1.

9. L. Klingaman and J. R. Vicary, "Risk Factors Associated with Date Rape and Sexual Assault of Adolescent Girls" (poster presentation at the Society for Research on Adolescence, Washington, D.C., March 19–22, 1992): 31–2.

10. S. L. Rosenthal and S. S. Cohen, "Primary Prevention of Sexually Transmitted Disease: Self-Efficacy in the Context of Sexual Coercion," *Adolescent and Pediatric Gynecology* (1994): 66.

11. Department of Health and Human Services' National Center for Health Statistics, *1995 National Survey of Family Growth, U.S.* (Washington, D.C.: 1995).

12. Joshua Mann, M.D., Joe S. McIlhaney, Jr., M.D., and Curtis C. Stine, M.D., *Building Heathy Futures: Tools for Helping Adolescents Avoid or Delay the Onset of Sexual Activity* (Austin, Tex.: The Medical Institute, 2000): 24.

13. P. Koss, "The Women's Mental Health Research Agenda—Violence against Women," *American Psychology*, 45 (1990): 374.

14. Klingaman and Vicary, "Risk Factors."

15. John Bacon, "Nation Line—Rape Victim Controversy," *USA Today*, 11 March 1997, sec. A, p. 3.

16. Fletcher, "Adolescent Experience," 9.

CHAPTER 6: THE MEDIA'S ROLE

1. Alice Fryling, "Why Wait for Sex?" *InterVarsity Christian Fellowship of the USA Student Leadership Journal* (spring 1995): 1.

2. Abbylin Sellers, *The Sexual Abstinence Message Causes Positive Changes in Adolescent Behavior: A Circumstantial Review of Relevant Studies* (Santa Barbara, Calif.: Westmont College, 1998), 1–3.

3. G. Gerbner, *Women and Minorities: A Study in Casting and Fate* (a report to the Screen Actors Guild and the American Federation of Radio and Television Artists, June 1993), 3.

4. J. Davies, "The Impact of the Mass Media upon the Health of Early Adolescents," *Journal of Health Education* (supplement 1993): 28–34.

5. Ibid.

6. Carnegie Corporation of New York, *A Matter of Time: Risk and Opportunity in the Nonschool Hours* (a report of the Task Force on Youth Development and Community Programs, Carnegie Corporation of New York, December 1992), 29.

7. American Psychological Association Commission on Violence and Youth, *Violence and Youth: Psychology's Response: Summary Report of the APA Commission on Violence and Youth* (Washington, D.C.: American Psychological Association, 1993: 32.

8. Research Division of MEE Productions, Inc., *The MEE Report: Reaching the Hip-Hop Generation* (Philadelphia, Pa.: MEE Productions, Inc., 1992): xii.

9. U.S. Congress, House, Office of Technology Assessment, *Adolescent Health, Volume II: Background and the Effectiveness of Selected Prevention and Treatment Services,* sess. OTA-H-466, (Washington, D.C.: GPO, November 1991), II–90.

10. Davies, "Impact of the Mass Media," 28–34.

11. M. Morgan, "Television and School Performance," in *Adolescent Medicine: Adolescents and the Media* (Philadelphia: Hanley & Belfus, 1993), 607–22.

12. J. D. Klein et al., "Adolescents' Risky Behavior and Mass Media Use," *Pediatrics* 92, no. 1 (1993): 24–31.

13. J. W. Grube and L. Wallack, "Television Beer Advertising and Drinking: Knowledge, Beliefs, and Intentions among School Children," *American Journal of Public Health* 84, no. 2 (1994): 254–9.

14. Bradley S. Greenberg et al., "Sex Content on Soaps and Prime-Time Television Series Most Viewed by Adolescents," in *Media, Sex and the Adolescent*, ed. Bradley S. Greenberg, Jane D. Brown, and Nancy L. Buerkel-Rothfuss (Cresskill, N.J.: Hampton, 1993), 29–44.

15. Bradley S. Greenberg, "Content Trends in Media Sex," in *Media, Children and the Family: Social Scientific, Psychodynamic, and Clinical Perspectives* (Hillsdale, N.J.: Lawrence Erlbaum, 1994), 165–82.

16. Greenberg, Brown, and Buerkel-Rothfuss, *Media, Sex, and the Adolescent*, 182.

17. Bradley S. Greenberg, "Race Differences in Television and Movie Behaviors," in *Media, Sex and the Adolescent,* ed. Greenberg, Brown, and Buerkel-Rothfuss, 45–152.

18. Bradley S. Greenberg and R. Linsangan, "Gender Differences in Adolescents' Media Use, Exposure to Sexual Content and Parental Mediation," in *Media, Sex and the Adolescent*, ed. Greenberg, Brown, and Buerkel-Rothfuss, 134–44.

19. A. Soderman, Bradley S. Greenberg, and R. Lingsangan, "Pregnant and Non-Pregnant Adolescents' Television and Movie Experiences," in *Media, Sex and the Adolescent*, ed. Greenberg, Brown, and Buerkel-Rothfuss, 163–73.

20. Bradley S. Greenberg, R. Linsangan, and A. Soderman, "Adolescents' Reactions to Television Sex," in *Media, Sex and the Adolescent,* ed. Greenberg, Brown, and Buerkel-Rothfuss, 196–224.

21. J. Bryant, "Effects of Massive Exposure to Sexually Oriented Prime-Time Television Programming on Adolescents' Moral Judgement," in *Media, Children and the Family*, 183–95.

22. Bill Keveney, "There's More Sex on TV, but Little About Risks," *USA Today,* 7 February 2001, sec. D, p. 6.

23. Kaiser Family Foundation, "Sex on TV," a biennial report (Menlo Park, Calif.: Kaiser Family Foundation, January 2001): 2.

24. Gene Edward Veith, "Crass Wasteland," *World* (March 3, 2001): 14.

25. Kaiser Family Foundation, "Sex on TV," 2.

26. Ibid., 5.

27. Ibid., 8.

28. Veith, "Crass Wasteland," 14.

29. Ibid.

30. Ibid.

31. N. L. Buerkel-Rothfuss and J. S. Strouse, "Media Exposure and Perceptions of Sexual Behaviors: the Cultivation Hypothesis Moves to the Bedroom," in *Media, Sex and the Adolescent*, ed. Greenberg, Brown, and Buerkel-Rothfuss, 225–247.

32. Bryant, "Effects of Massive Exposure," 183–95.

33. J. S. Strouse and N. L. Buerkel-Rothfuss, "Media Exposure and the Sexual Attitudes and Behaviors of College Students" in *Media, Sex and the Adolescent,* ed. Greenberg, Brown, and Buerkel-Rothfuss, 277–92.

34. David Whitman, Paul Glastris, and Brendan I. Koerner, "Was It Good for Us?" *U.S. News and World Report* (May 19, 1997): 59.

35. S. L. Rosenthal and S. S. Cohen, "Primary Prevention of Sexually Transmitted Disease: Self-Efficacy in the Context of Sexual Coercion," *Adolescent and Pediatric Gynecology* (1994): 87.

36. J. Arnett, "The Soundtrack of Recklessness: Musical Preferences and Reckless Behavior among Adolescents," *Journal of Adolescent Research* 7, no. 3 (1993): 313–31.

37. The Institute of Medicine, *The Hidden Epidemic: Confronting Sexually Transmitted Diseases,* ed. Thomas R. Eng and William T. Butler (Washington, D.C.: National Academy Press, 1997): 9.

38. Alan Bash, "Ample Sexual Content in 8 P.M. 'Family Hour,' " *USA Today*, 12 December 1996, sec. D, p. 3.

39. Bradley S. Greenberg and R. W. Busselle, *Soap Operas and Sexual Activity* (a report prepared for the Kaiser Family Foundation and presented at the Soap Summit, October 21, 1994).

40. Whitman, Glastris, and Koerner, "Was It Good for Us?" 59.

41. Veith, "Crass Wasteland," 14.

CHAPTER 7: THE EMOTIONAL REASONS

1. Kathleen Kelleher, "Talking to Teens about Sex—It's in the Details," *Los Angeles Times,* 29 January 2001.

2. Laurence Steinberg, "Failure Outside the Classroom," *The Wall Street Journal*, 11 July 1996, p. 10.

3. R. W. Blum and P.M. Rinehart, *Reducing the Risk: Connections That Make a Difference in the Lives of Youth* (Minneapolis, Minn.: University of Minnesota Division of General Pediatrics and Adolescent Health, 1997), 15, 17, 19.

4. Ann Landers, "Sorry, Ladies: Cuddling Second in Sex Survey," *Los Angeles Times*, 25 November 1995.

5. Kaiser Family Foundation and *YM* magazine, "National Survey of Teens: Teens Talk about Dating, Intimacy, and Their Sexual Experiences," *YM* magazine (May 1998).

6. Department of Health and Human Services, National Center for Health Statistics, *Monthly Vital Statistics Report for 1998,* 13.

7. Ibid.

8. Jim Okerblom, "Single Parents Head over 30% of Families with Minor Children," *San Diego Union,* 10 January 1995, sec. A, p. 11.

9. Linda Kinamine, "Numbers of Two-Parent Families Up," *USA Today*, 16 October 1995.

10. Dennis Rainey, submitted to Josh McDowell for Biola University graduation speech, May 13, 1998.

11. Barbara Ehrenreich, "In Defense of Splitting Up," *Time* (April 8, 1996): 80.

12. David Blankenhorn, June 16, 1995 essay, published in *Summit Ministries: The Journal* (August 1995): 3.

13. Karen Peterson, "Saying 'No' to the Notion of No-Fault Divorce," *USA Today*, 25 January 1996, sec. D, p. 1.

14. Karen Peterson, "Some Parents Worse Off When Parent Marries Again," *USA Today*, 4 January 1996, sec. D, p. 1.

15. Ibid.

16. Maggie Gallagher, "Elegy for Father's Day," *International Business Daily,* 14 June 1996.

17. Peterson, "No-Fault Divorce."

18. A. J. Norton and L. F. Miller, "Marriage, Divorce, and Remarriage in the 1990s," *Current Population Reports* (Washington, D.C.: GPO, 1992): 23.

19. David Popenoe, "The Controversial Truth: Two-Parent Families Are Better," *New York Times*, 26 December 1992.

20. The Horatio Alger Association of Distinguished Americans, "The State of Our Nation's Youth," August 7, 2001; <www.horatioalger.org/pubmat/surpro.htm>.

21. Dennis Rainey, *One Home at a Time* (Colorado Springs: Focus on the Family, 1997), 25.

22. Ibid.

23. William J. Bennett, "The Index of Leading Cultural Indicators," a joint publication of Empower America, The Heritage Foundation, and Free Congress Foundation (Washington, D.C.: Heritage Foundation, 1993), 1: 27.

24. Alan Guttmacher Institute, *Sex and America's Teenagers* (New York: Alan Guttmacher Institute, 1994).

25. Lisa Collier Cool, "The Dreaded Talk," *Ladies Home Journal* (March 2001).

26. YMCA of the USA, "Talking with Teens: The YMCA Teen and Parent Survey Final Report," *The YMCA–2000 Strong Family Survey* (New York: Global Strategy Group, 2000): 5.

27. Ibid., 1.

28. Report by The Council of Economic Advisers, *Teens and Their Parents in the Twenty-first Century: An Examination of Trends in Teen Behavior and the Role of Parental Involvement,* The White House Conference on Teenagers: Raising Responsible and Resourceful Youth, Washington, D.C., May 2000, 18.

29. Ibid., 21.

30. Michael Resnick et al., "Protecting Adolescents from Harm: Findings from the National Longitudinal Study on Adolescent Health," *Journal of the American Medical Association* (September 1997), as reported in the report by The Council of Economic Advisers, *Teens and Their Parents in the Twenty-first Century: An Examination of Trends in Teen Behavior and the Role of Parental Involvement,* The White House Conference on Teenagers: Raising Responsible and Resourceful Youth, Washington, D.C., May 2000, 23.

31. Kaiser Family Foundation and *YM* magazine, "National Survey of Teens: Teens Talk about Dating, Intimacy, and Their Sexual Experiences," *YM* magazine (May 1998): 11.

32. International Communications Research, "Not Just Another Thing to Do—Teens Talk about Sex, Regret, and the Influence of Their Parents" (a summary of findings from a nationally representative survey by International Communications Research, June 30, 2000), 1.

CHAPTER 8: THE RELATIONAL REASONS

1. Nancy Hellmich, "Cheating, Sex and Kids' Scruples," *USA Today*, 1 February 1990, sec. D, p. 1.

2. Nancy Gibbs, "How Should We Teach Our Children about Sex?" *Time* (May 24, 1993): 63.

3. Josh McDowell and Dick Day, *Why Wait? What You Need to Know about the Teen Sexuality Crisis* (San Bernadino, Calif: Here's Life Publishers, 1987).

4. "The 1994 Churched Youth Survey" (Dallas: Josh McDowell Ministry, 1994): 62.

5. Kaiser Family Foundation and *YM* magazine, "National Survey of Teens: Teens Talk about Dating, Intimacy, and Their Sexual Experiences," *YM* magazine (May 1998): 5.

6. Ibid.

7. Ibid.

8. Liana R. Clark, M.D., "Teen Sex Blues," *The Journal of the American Medical Association* 273, no. 24 (June 28, 1995): 1969–70.

CHAPTER 9: THE PSYCHOLOGICAL REASONS

1. Ann Landers, "Study Finds Girls Regret Having Sex," *Austin American-Statesman,* 20 October 1996, sec. E, p. 2.
2. Kaiser Family Foundation and *YM* magazine, "National Survey of Teens: Teens Talk about Dating, Intimacy, and Their Sexual Experiences," *YM* magazine (May 1998).
3. International Communications Research, "Not Just Another Thing to Do—Teens Talk about Sex, Regret, and the Influence of Their Parents" (a summary of findings from a nationally representative survey by International Communications Research, June 30, 2000): 1.
4. P. Beaman and H. Bruckner, *Power in Numbers: Peer Effects on Adolescent Girls' Sexual Debut and Pregnancy* (Washington, D.C.: The National Campaign to Prevent Teen Pregnancy; 1999).
5. S. C. Carvajal et al., "Psychological Predictors of Delay of First Sexual Intercourse by Adolescents," *Health Psychology* 18 (1999): 443–52.
6. S. A. Small and T. Luster, "Adolescent Sexual Activity: An Ecological, Risk-Factor Approach," *Journal of Marriage and the Family* 56 (1994): 181–2.
7. Jacqueline F. de Gaston, Larry Jensen, and Stan Weed, "A Closer Look at Adolescent Sexual Activity," *Journal of Youth and Adolescence* 24, no. 4 (1995): 465.
8. Nancy Gibbs, "How Should We Teach Our Children about Sex?" *Time* (May 24, 1993): 63.
9. Michael D. Benson, M.D. and Edward J. Torpy, "Sexual Behavior in Junior High School Students," *Obstetrics Gynecology* 85 (1995): 279.
10. R. W. Blum and P.M. Rinehart, *Reducing the Risk: Connections That Make a Difference in the Lives of Youth* (Minneapolis, Minn.: University of Minnesota Division of General Pediatrics and Adolescent Health, 1997), 22.
11. Ibid., 22–23.
12. Ibid., 24.

CHAPTER 10: ABSTINENCE

1. William R. Bright, "Love: The Major Emphasis, or Dialogue between a Single Staff Member and God's Word" (a message to the staff of Campus Crusade for Christ, Orlando, Fla., 1997).

CHAPTER 11: THE PHYSICAL REASONS TO WAIT

1. Heather Farish, "Better U.S. Teens Abstain Than Opt for European Way," *Houston Chronicle,* 16 February 1999.
2. Agneta Andersson-Ellstrom, Lars Forssman, and Ian Milsom, "The Relationship between Knowledge about Sexually Transmitted Diseases and Actual Sexual Behaviour in a Group of Teenage Girls," *Genitourinary Medicine* 72 (1996): 32–6.
3. Committee on Adolescent Health Care, American College of Obstetricians and Gyne-

cologists, "Condom Availability for Adolescents," *Journal of Adolescent Health* 18 (1996): 380–3.

4. Joe S. McIlhaney Jr., M.D., *Sex: What You Don't Know Can Kill You* (Grand Rapids: Baker, 1997), 22.

5. R. T. Michael et al., *Sex in America* (New York: Little, Brown and Company, 1994), 187.

6. The Institute of Medicine, *The Hidden Epidemic: Confronting Sexually Transmitted Diseases,* ed. Thomas R. Eng and William T. Butler (Washington, D.C.: National Academy Press, 1997): 39.

7. W. Cates et al., "Estimates of the Incidence and Prevalence of Sexually Transmitted Diseases in the United States," *Sexually Transmitted Diseases* (supplement, April 1999): 2–7.

8. Department of Health, Education, and Welfare and Centers for Disease Control, Venereal Disease Program, "Syphilis, a Synopsis," *PHS Publication* no. 16601968.

9. The Institute of Medicine, *Hidden Epidemic,* 6.

10. Lawrence K. Altman, "3 Million HIV Infections Added Worldwide in '96," *Denver Post,* 28 November 1996, sec. A, p. 24.

11. Joint United Nations Program on HIV/AIDS, *Report on the Global HIV/AIDS Epidemic* (Geneva, Switzerland: December 1997).

12. "Stats, Stats, Stats," *The Pastor's Weekly Briefing* 3, no. 21 (May 26, 1995): 2.

13. Doug Levy, "Gene Variant May Affect Anxiety Level," *USA Today,* 29 November 1996, sec. D, p. 4.

14. The Institute of Medicine, *Hidden Epidemic,* 39.

15. "HIV Prevention Act of 1997," *Washington Watch Policy Update* 8, no. 5 (March 14, 1997): 3.

16. Centers for Disease Control, *HIV/AIDS Surveillance Report* 7, no. 2 (December 1995): 126–31.

17. "Around the U.S.," *Dallas Morning News,* 2 December 1994, sec. A, p. 10.

18. "AIDS Top Killer of 25–44's," *Moscow Times,* 2 February 1995, p. 5.

19. "Staying Current: Straight Talk about AIDS/STDs," *The Newsletter of AIDS Information Ministries,* A Program of Teen Choices, Inc. 10, no. 1 (spring 1997): 1.

20. Ibid., 3.

21. Robin DeRosa, "HIV Study," *USA Today,* 9 February 1998, sec. B, p. 8.

22. P. J. J. Boyer, "HIV Infection in Pregnancy," *Pediatric Annual* 22, no. 7 (1993): 406.

23. "Arm Yourself against AIDS," MSNBC, June 29, 2000; <http:/msnbc.com/modules/quizzes/loadquiz.htm>.

24. "HIV Prevention Act of 1997," *Washington Watch Policy Update.*

25. D. Michaels and C. Levine, "Estimates of the Number of Motherless Youth Orphaned by AIDS in the United States," *Journal of the American Medical Association* 268 (1992): 3456.

26. World Health Organization and Joint United Nations Program on HIV/AIDS, *Global*

Summary of the Hiv/Aids Epidemic, End 1999 (Geneva, Switzerland: World Health Organization and Joint United Nations Program on HIV/AIDS, 1999): 5.

27. Office of National AIDS Policy, "Youth and HIV/AIDS: An American Agenda," March 1996; <www.niaid.nih.gov/publications/dateline/full/0996.htm>.

28. Ibid.

29. "Adolescent Sexuality: Is Just Saying 'No' Enough?" *Obstetrics/Gynecology Nurse Forum* 3, no. 2 (April 1995): 4.

30. The Medical Institute, "Safe Sex?" (Austin, Tex.: The Medical Institute, 1999), documented slide presentation.

31. *Seventeen* (May 1990): 149–51.

32. A. Goldstein, "D. C. Unveils Anti-AIDS campaign—1 in 45 City Teens Infected with Virus, Study Estimates," *Washington Post*, 13 May 1992, sec. A, pp. 1–4.

33. The Alan Guttmacher Institute, "Sexually Transmitted Diseases (STDs) in the United States," *Facts in Brief* (September 1993).

34. Kim Painter, "Cautious Optimism for AIDS Patients," *USA Today*, 27 January 1997, sec. D, p. 4.

35. Judi Hasson, "Campaign Aims to Steer Girls onto Right Path," *USA Today*, 21 November 1996, sec. A, p. 3.

36. A. Lazzarin et al., "Man to Woman Sexual Transmission of the Human Immunodeficiency Virus: Risk Factors Related to Sexual Behavior, Man's Infectiousness, and Women's Susceptibility," *Archives of Internal Medicine* 151 (1991): 2411.

37. Sheryl Gay Stolberg, "U.S. Awakes to Epidemic of Sexual Diseases," *New York Times*, 9 March 1998, p. 18.

38. William Archer III, M.D., *Sexual Health Update Newsletter* 1, no. 4 (September 1993): 1.

39. McIlhaney, *What You Don't Know*, 30.

40. M. C. Dickerson et al., "The Causal Role for Genital Ulcer Disease As a Risk Factor for Transmission of Human Immunodeficiency Virus: An Application of the Bradford Hill Criteria," *Sexually Transmitted Diseases* 23 (1996): 429–40.

41. The Institute of Medicine, *Hidden Epidemic*, 7.

42. Ibid.

43. Department of Health and Human Services Press Release, "AIDS Falls from Top Ten Causes of Death: Teen Births, Infant Mortality, Homicide All Decline," October 7, 1998.

44. Sexuality Information and Education Council of the U.S., "Fact Sheet: Sexually Transmitted Diseases in the United States," *Siecus Report* 25, no. 3 (1997).

45. The Medical Institute, "Chlamydia Trachomatis: The Most Common Bacterial Sexually Transmitted Disease in the United States," *Sexual Health Update Newsletter* 3, no. 3 (fall 1995).

46. John R. Diggs Jr., M.D., *Chlamydia* (Sious Falls, S. Dak.: Abstinence Clearinghouse, 2000), 1.

47. Ibid.

48. Michael et al., *Sex in America,* 182.

49. S. D. Hillis, "PID Prevention: Clinical and Societal Stakes," *Hospital Practice* (April 1994): 121–30.

50. "Staying Current," 4.

51. Centers for Disease Control, "Sexually Transmitted Disease Surveillance, 1995," *Morbidity and Mortality Weekly Report* 45 (September 1996): 53.

52. Stolberg, "U.S. Awakes."

53. Ibid.

54. Jennifer Kornreich, "The Risks of Young Love: Sexually Transmitted Diseases Common in Teenagers," MSNBC, March 20, 2001; <www.msnbc.com/news/529857.asp>.

55. McIlhaney, *What You Don't Know,* 23.

56. John Diggs, "A Perspective on the Medical Implications of Virginity Pledge among Teens," *The Physicians Consortium* (January 5, 2001).

57. Shari Roan, "Common Sexually Transmitted Diseases," *Los Angeles Times,* 10 October 1995.

58. The Institute of Medicine, *Hidden Epidemic,* 39.

59. Barbara Kantrowitz, "The Dangers of Doing It," *Newsweek* (summer/fall 1990): 56–7.

60. Susan Okie, "Teenage Chlamydia Cases Alarm Experts," *Washington Post,* 3 September 1997, p. 49.

61. Ibid.

62. Ibid.

63. Ibid.

64. The Institute of Medicine, *Hidden Epidemic,* 39.

65. McIlhaney, *What You Don't Know,* 23.

66. Stolberg, "U.S. Awakes," 18.

67. Sexuality Information and Education Council, "Fact Sheet."

68. Andrea E. Bonny, M.D., and Frank M. Biro, M.D., "Recognizing and Treating STDs in Adolescent Girls," *Contemporary Pediatrics* (March 1998): 126.

69. Hillis, "PID Prevention," 121–30.

70. A. E. Washington and P. Katz, "Cost of and Payment Source for Pelvic Inflammatory Disease," *Journal of the American Medical Association* 266, no. 18 (1991): 2565–9.

71. The Medical Institute, "Chlamydia Trachomatis."

72. Hillis, "PID Prevention," 121–30.

73. McIlhaney, *What You Don't Know,* 25.

74. The Institute of Medicine, *Hidden Epidemic,* 5.

75. Bonny and Biro, "Recognizing and Treating STDs," 133.

76. Sexuality Information and Education Council, "Fact Sheet."

77. L. Westrom, "Incidence, Prevalence, and Trends of Acute Pelvic Inflammatory Disease and Its Consequences in Industrialized Countries," *American Journal of Obstetrics and Gynecology* 138: 880–92.

78. Ibid.

79. The Institute of Medicine, *Hidden Epidemic,* 5.

80. V.P. Smetnik and L.G. Tumilovitch, *Non-Surgical Gynecology* (St. Petersburg: Sotis Publishing, 1995).

81. Sexuality Information and Education Council, "Fact Sheet."

82. McIlhaney, *What You Don't Know*, 30.

83. Ibid., 33.

84. John R. Diggs Jr., M.D., *Gonorrhea* (Sioux Falls, S. Dak.: Abstinence Clearinghouse, 2000), 1.

85. Mike Toner, "Resisting Arrest," *Atlanta Journal-Constitution,* 20 January 1996, sec. G, p. 1.

86. McIlhaney, *What You Don't Know,* 30.

87. Sexuality Information and Education Council, "Fact Sheet."

88. Toner, "Resisting Arrest."

89. House, Ronald O. Valdiserri, M.D., speaking for the Committee on Commerce to the Subcommittee on Health and Environment on Cervical Cancer (16 March 1999), 9.

90. Ibid.

91. Ibid.

92. Betsy Bates, "STD Reinfection Reflects Failure to Modify Lifestyle," *Ob-Gyn News,* 15.

93. Bonny and Biro, "Recognizing and Treating STDs," 119, 123, 131.

94. Kornreich, "Risks of Young Love."

95. House, Valdiserri, 11.

96. Ibid., 13.

97. Bates, "STD Reinfection," 15.

98. "Making life choices," *Health and Sexuality* 2, no. 2 (1991): 3, quoted in *Medical Aspects of Human Sexuality* (August 1991): 132.

99. Diggs, *Gonorrhea.*

100. John R. Diggs Jr., M.D., *Herpes Simplex* (Sioux Falls, S. Dak.: Abstinence Clearinghouse, 2000), 1.

101. W. E. Lafferty et al., "Herpes Simplex Virus Type I As a Cause of Genital Herpes: Impact on Surveillance and Prevention," *Journal of Infectious Diseases* 181 (April 2000): 1454–7.

102. Lafferty, "Herpes Simplex."

103. D. Fleming et al., "Herpes Simplex Virus Type 2 in the United States, 1976–1994," *New England Journal of Medicine* 337, no. 16 (October 1997): 1105–11.

104. William Archer III, M.D., *Sexual Health Update Newsletter* 1, no. 4 (September 1993): 1.

105. Division of Health, Wisconsin Department of Health and Social Services, "Women and VD," 1994.

106. Fleming et al., "Herpes Simplex," 1105–11.

107. Ibid.

108. McIlhaney, *What You Don't Know*, 42–3.

109. R. W. Blum and P. M. Rinehart, *Reducing the Risk: Connections That Make a Difference in the Lives of Youth* (Minneapolis, Minn.: University of Minnesota Division of General Pediatrics and Adolescent Health, 1997), 7.

110. Anita Manning, "Genital Herpes Infections Up 30% Since Late '70s," *USA Today*, 16 October 1997, sec. D, p. 3.

111. The Institute of Medicine, *Hidden Epidemic,* 39.

112. Ibid.

113. Manning, "Genital Herpes," 3.

114. The Institute of Medicine, *Hidden Epidemic,* 49–54.

115. Ibid.

116. William Archer III, M.D., *Sexual Health Update Newsletter* 5, no. 2 (winter 1997): 2.

117. Ibid., 9, no. 1 (spring 2001): 8.

118. J. A. Kulhanjian et al., "Identification of Women at Unsuspected Risk of Primary Infection with Herpes Simplex Virus Type 2 during Pregnancy," *New England Journal of Medicine* 326 (April 2, 1992): 916–20.

119. The Medical Institute, "Safe Sex?"

120. J. Benedetti, J. Zeh, and L. Corey, "Clinical Observation of Genital Herpes Simplex Virus Infection Decreases in Frequency over Time," *Annals of Internal Medicine* 131 (1999): 14–20.

121. Fleming et al., "Herpes Simplex," 1105–11.

122. House, Valdiserri, 6.

123. Ibid.

124. William Archer III, M.D., *Sexual Health Update Newsletter* 5, no. 2 (winter 1997): 2.

125. National Institutes of Health Consensus Development Program, "Cervical Cancer," *Consensus Development Statements* 14, no. 1 (April 1–3, 1996); <odp.od.nih.gov/consensus/cons/102/102_intro.htm>.

126. R. Whitley et al., "A Controlled Trial Comparing Vidarabine with Acyclovir in Neonatal Herpes Simplex Virus Infection: Infectious Diseases Collaborative Antiviral Study Group," *New England Journal of Medicine* 324 (1991): 444–9.

127. Kulhanjian et al., "Identification of Women," 1105.

128. William Archer III, M.D., *Sexual Health Update Newsletter* 9, no. 1 (spring 2001).

129. House, Valdiserri, 3.

130. The Medical Institute, "Safe Sex?"

131. House, Valdiserri, 18.

132. National Institutes of Health, "Cervical Cancer."
133. The Institute of Medicine, *Hidden Epidemic.*
134. John R. Diggs Jr., M.D., *Human Papilloma Virus* (Sioux Falls, S. Dak.: Abstinence Clearinghouse, 2001), 1.
135. Ibid.
136. McIlhaney, *What You Don't Know*, 34.
137. National Institutes of Health, "Cervical Cancer."
138. Jim Zach, M.D., University of Wisconsin Stephens Point Health Center (revised February 1990), 2–3.
139. American Social Health Association, "Some Questions and Answers about Genital Warts," 1990.
140. Kaiser Family Foundation, *National Survey of Fifteen to Seventeen Year Olds: What Teens Know and Don't (But Should) about Sexually Transmitted Diseases* (Menlo Park, Calif.: International Communications Research, December 2, 1998): 8.
141. House, Valdiserri, 3.
142. I. A. Koutsky and N. B. Kiviat, "Genital Human Papillomavirus," in K. K. Holmes et al., eds., *Sexually Transmitted Diseases* (New York: McGraw-Hill, 1999), 347–59.
143. W. Cates et al., "Estimates of the Incidence and Prevalence of Sexually Transmitted Diseases in the United States," *Sexually Transmitted Diseases* (April 1999 supplement): 2–7.
144. Koutsky and Kiviat, "Genital Human Papillomavirus."
145. Abstinence Clearinghouse, *Abstinence Clearinghouse Fact Sheet on Human Papilloma Virus.*
146. Ibid.
147. National Institutes of Health, "Cervical Cancer."
148. William Archer III, M.D., *Sexual Health Update Newsletter* 7, no. 3 (fall 1999).
149. Ibid.
150. Blum and Rinehart, *Reducing the Risk,* 5.
151. William Archer III, M.D., *Sexual Health Update Newsletter* 3, no. 1 (March 1994): 1.
152. The Medical Institute, "Listing of Sexually Transmitted Diseases," 1994; <www.w-cpc.org/sexuality/std.html>.
153. House, Valdiserri, 3.
154. Y. F. Ho et al., "Natural History of Cervicovaginal Papillomavirus Infection in Young Women," *New England Journal of Medicine* 338 (1998): 423–8.
155. Ibid.
156. Patricia Hersch, "Sexually Transmitted Diseases Are Ravaging Our Children, Teen Epidemic," *American Health* (May 1991): 44.
157. Diggs, "Virginity Pledge."

158. House, Valdiserri, 3–5.

159. Diggs, "Virginity Pledge."

160. McIlhaney, *What You Don't Know*, 8.

161. Zach, 2–3.

162. McIlhaney, *What You Don't Know*, 34, 36.

163. The Institute of Health, *Hidden Epidemic,* 43.

164 American Cancer Society, "Cancer Facts and Figures 1999: Selected Cancers," February 21, 2000; <www.cancer.org/statistics/cff99/selectedcancers.html>.

165. Suzanne D. Vernon, Elizabeth R. Unger, and William C. Reeves, "Human Papillomavirus and Anogenital Cancer," *New England Journal of Medicine* 338, no. 13 (March 26, 1998): 921.

166. Linda Alexander et al., *The Tip of the Iceberg: How Big Is the STD Epidemic in the U.S.?* (Kaiser Family Foundation, December 2, 1998), 22.

167. M. Sugase and T. Matsukura, "Distinct Manifestations of Human Papillomaviruses in the Vagina," *International Journal of Cancer* 72 (1997): 412–415.

168. William Archer III, M.D., *Sexual Health Update Newsletter* 8, no. 1 (spring 2000): 1.

169. L. A. G. Ries et al., eds., *SEER Cancer Statistics Review, 1973–1996* (Bethesda, Md.: National Cancer Institute, 1999).

170. P. A. Poletti, A. Halfon, and M. C. Marti, "Papillomavirus and Anal Carcinoma," *International Journal of Colorectal Diseases* 13 (1998): 108–11.

171. L. D. Ke et al., "Expression of Human Papillomavirus E7 mRNA in Human Oral and Cervical Neoplasia and Cell Lines," *Oral Oncology* 35 (1999): 415–20.

172. Smetnik and Tumilovitch, *Non-Surgical Gynecology,* 182.

173. Blum and Rinehart, *Reducing the Risk,* 5.

174. Eva Rylander, M.D., et al., "The Absence of Vaginal Human Papillomavirus 16 DNA in Women Who Have Not Experienced Sexual Intercourse," *Obstetrics Gynecology* 83 (May 1994): 735–7.

175. C. Fairley et al., "The Absence of Genital Human Papillomavirus DNA in Virginal Women," *International Journal of STDs and AIDS* 3 (1992): 414–7.

176. William Archer III, M.D., *Sexual Health Update Newsletter* 8, no. 1 (spring 2000): 1

177. American Social Health Association, "Some Questions."

178. McIlhaney, *What You Don't Know*, 40.

179. Diggs, "Virginity Pledge."

180. McIlhaney, *What You Don't Know*, 49.

181. Centers for Disease Control, "Ten Leading Nationally Notifiable Diseases—U.S., 1995," *Morbidity and Mortality Weekly Report* 45 (1996): 883–4.

182. Stolberg, "U.S. Awakes," 12.

183. House, Valdiserri, 14.

184. Ibid., 24.

185. Smetnik and Tumilovitch, *Non-Surgical Gynecology.*

186. House, Valdiserri, 22.

187. McIlhaney, *What You Don't Know,* 54–5.

188. Smetnik and Tumilovitch, *Non-Surgical Gynecology.*

189. J. M. Walboomers et al., "Human Papillomavirus Is a Necessary Cause of Invasive Cervical Cancer Worldwide," *Journal of Pathology* 189 (1999): 12–19, quoted in *Sexual Health Update Newsletter* 8, no. 1 (spring 2000): 1–2.

190. American Social Health Association, *Sexually Transmitted Diseases in America: How Many Cases and at What Cost?* (Menlo Park, Calif.: Kaiser Family Foundation, 1998), quoted in *Sexual Health Update Newsletter* 8, no. 1 (spring 2000): 1–2.

191. L. A. Koutsky and N. B. Kiviat, "Genital Human Papillomavirus," in K. K. Holmes, P. A. Mardh, and P. F. Sparling et al., eds., *Sexually Transmitted Dieseases* (New York: McGraw Hill, 1999), 347–59, quoted in *Sexual Health Update Newsletter* 8, no. 1 (spring 2000): 1–2.

192. G. Y. Ho et al., "Natural History of Cervicovaginal Papillomavirus Infection in Young Women," *New England Journal of Medicine* 338 (1998): 423–8, quoted in *Sexual Health Update Newsletter* 8, no. 1 (spring 2000): 1–2.

193. J. H. Jamison et al., "Spectrum of Genital Human Papillomavirus Infection in a Female Adolescent Population," *Sexually Transmitted Diseases* 22 (1995): 236–43, quoted in *Sexual Health Update Newsletter* 8, no. 1 (spring 2000): 1–2.

194. The Institute of Medicine, *Hidden Epidemic,* p. 5.

195. Michael Gartner, "Politics Always at Issue on Abortion," *USA Today,* 2 April 1996, sec. A, p. 13.

196. Patricia Edmonds and Desda Moss, "Abortion Battle at Stalemate," *USA Today,* 23 January 1996, sec. A, p. 3.

197. "Abortions Performed in Canada on the Rise," *Christianity Today* 6, no. 10 (October 1995).

198. "Abortion and Breast Cancer Linked in Report," *World* (October 26, 1996): 18.

199. Geoffrey Cowley and Mary Hager, "Breast Cancer: Is Abortion a Factor?" *Newsweek* (October 21, 1996): 73.

200. Jennifer Warren, "For Aborted Fetuses, a Question of Pain," *Los Angeles Times,* 4 January 1998, sec. A, p. 3.

201. Steve Schwalm, "The Coercion of Abortion by Men," New London Day, CT. AR98B6LF, 1998.

202. Vincent M. Rue, "More Psychological Harm Than Quoted," *Los Angeles Times,* 22 September 1995, p. 10.

CHAPTER 12: THE EMOTIONAL REASONS TO WAIT

1. Bill Mattox, "Rebuilding a Marriage Culture: Why Capturing Young People's Imagination is Key," *Family Policy* (May 1997).

2. Drew Reid Kerr, "Celibacy Is Sexier Than Sex: Two Out of Three Women Would Rather Be a Virgin If Married Today," *Redbook* Press Release, August 1994; <redbook.women.com>.

3. Michelle Healy, "Sex and the Teenage Girl: Curiosity Wins," *USA Today*, 28 December 1999, quoted by *CultureWatch*, Focus on the Family, January 3–7, 2000.

CHAPTER 13: THE RELATIONAL REASONS TO WAIT

1. Robert Michael et al., *Sex in America: A Definitive Survey* (Boston: Little, Brown and Company, 1994); E. O. Laumann et al., *The Social Organization of Sexuality: Sexual Practices in the United States* (Chicago: University of Chicago Press, 1994), quoted in *U.S. News and World Report* (May 19, 1997): 59.
2. Concerned Women for America, "Happily Never After," *Family Voice* November/ December, 1999; <cwfa.org/library/_familyvoice/1999-11/06-13c.shtml>.
3. Michael A. Fletcher, "For Better or Worse, Marriage Hits a Low," *Washington Post*, 2 July 1999, sec. A, p. 1.
4. Karen S. Peterson, "At 20, a Soul Mate Is a Cool Concept," *USA Today*, 13 June 2001, sec. A, p. 1.
5. Ibid.
6. Patrick Rizzo, "Fewer Americans Than Ever Getting Married—Study," Yahoo News, July 3, 1999; <groups.yahoo.com/group/abet/message/100>.
7. Larry Bumpass and Hsien-Hen Lu, "Trends in Cohabitation and Implications for Children's Family Contexts," Center for Demography, University of Wisconsin, Madison, Wis., 1998; David Popenoe and Barbara Dafoe Whitehead, "The State of Our Unions: The Social Health of Marriage in America" (State University of New Jersey, Piscataway, N.J., The National Marriage Project, June 1999).
8. Wendy D. Manning and Daniel T. Lichter, "Parental Cohabitation and Children's Economic Well-being," *Journal of Marriage and the Family* 58 (1996): 998–1010; David Popenoe and Barbara Dafoe Whitehead, "The State of Our Unions: The Social Health of Marriage in America" (State University of New Jersey, Piscataway, N.J., The National Marriage Project, June 1999).
9. David Popenoe and Barbara Dafoe Whitehead, "The State of Our Unions: The Social Health of Marriage in America" (State University of New Jersey, Piscataway, N.J., The National Marriage Project, June 1999), quoted in John Witte Jr., *From Sacrament to Contract: Marriage, Religion, and Law in the Western Tradition* (Louisville.: John Knox, 1997), 209.
10. David Popenoe and Barbara Dafoe Whitehead, "The State of Our Unions: The Social Health of Marriage in America" (State University of New Jersey, Piscataway, N.J., The National Marriage Project, June 1999).
11. Larry Bumpass, James A. Sweet, and Andrew Cherlin, "The Role of Cohabitation in Declining Rates of Marriage," *Journal of Marriage and the Family* 53 (1991): 913–27.
12. Ibid.
13. Elizabeth Thomson and Ugo Colella, "Cohabitation and Marital Stability: Quality or Commitment?" *Journal of Marriage and the Family* 54 (1992): 259–67.
14. Joshua Mann, M.D., Joe S. McIlhaney Jr., M.D., and Curtis C. Stine, M.D., *Building*

Healthy Futures: Tools for Helping Adolescents Avoid or Delay the Onset of Sexual Activity (Austin, Tex.: The Medical Institute, 2000), 18–19.

15. Bumpass, Sweet, and Cherlin, "Role of Cohabitation."

16. Thomson and Colella, "Cohabitation and Marital Stability."

17. Alfred DeMaris and K. Vaninadha Rao, "Premarital Cohabitation and Subsequent Marital Stability in the United States: A Reassessment," *Journal of Marriage and the Family* 54 (1992): 178.

18. Larry Bumpass and James A. Sweet, "National Estimates of Cohabitation," *Demography* 24 (1989): 615–25.

19. R. T. Michael et al., *Sex in America* (New York: Little, Brown and Company, 1994).

20. Concerned Women for America, "Happily Never After."

21. Edward O. Laumann et al., *The Organization of Sexuality: Sexual Practices in the United States* (Chicago: University of Chicago Press, 1994): 363–5.

22. Joan R. Kahn and Kathryn London, "Premarital Sex and the Risk of Divorce," *Journal of Marriage and the Family* 53 (1991): 845–55.

CHAPTER 14: THE SPIRITUAL REASONS TO WAIT

1. Originally published in Josh McDowell, *Givers, Takers, and Other Kinds of Lovers* (Wheaton, Ill.: Tyndale, 1981): 19–21.

2. Paul Tripp, "The Way of the Wise: Teaching Teenagers about Sex," *The Journal of Biblical Counseling*, 13, no. 3 (spring 1995): 36.

3. Ibid., 42.

CHAPTER 15: WHY "SAFE SEX" ISN'T SAFE

1. Amy Stephens, "The Kaiser Report: Truth or Dare?" October 23, 2000; <www.family.org/cforum/editorials/a0015083.html>.

2. John R. Diggs Jr., M.D., "Why the Sex Experts Are Wrong," Family Research Council: Press Room, March 29, 2001; <www.frc.org/get/ar00h1.cfm?CFID=3371&CFTOKEN=91154837>.

3. "A Response to *Morbidity and Mortality Weekly Report*, 'Update: Barrier Protection against HIV and Other Sexually Transmitted Diseases, August 6, 1993,' " *Sexual Health Update Newsletter* 2, no. 1 (December 1993).

4. Susan Weller, "A Meta-Analysis of Condom Effectiveness in Reducing Sexually Transmitted HIV," *Social Science and Medicine* 36 (1993): 12.

5. Joe S. McIlhaney Jr., M.D., *Sex: What You Don't Know Can Kill You* (Grand Rapids: Baker, 1997), 63–4.

6. "A Response," *Sexual Health Update Newsletter*.

7. The Medical Institute, "Safe Sex?" (Austin, Tex.: The Medical Institute, 1999), documented slide presentation.

8. University of Texas Medical Branch News Release, "Data Show Condoms Only 69 Percent Effective Against HIV," June 7, 1993.

9. Weller, "Condom Effectiveness."

10. Elise F. Jones and Jacqueline Darroch Forest, "Contraceptive Failure Rates Based on the 1988 National Survey of Family Growth," *Family Planning Perspectives* 24 (1992): 12.

11. Ibid., 16.

12. John R. Diggs Jr., M.D., letter to author, 26 January 2001.

13. Henry J. Redd, " 'Safe Sex' Sex-Ed a Delusion: Abstinence, Moral Curricula Cut Sexual Activity, Pregnancy, STDs," *Ledger*, 4 September 1992.

14. Weller, "Condom Effectiveness," 12.

15. Ibid.

16. The Medical Institute, "Safe Sex?"

17. Steve Sternberg, "Little Evidence of Condom Protection against Some STDs," *USA Today*, 20 July 2001, sec. A, p. 9.

18. K. L. Noller, *Obstetrician/Gynecology Clinical Alert* (September 1992).

19. Diggs, letter to author.

20. James Trussell, David Lee Warner, and Robert A. Hatcher, "Condom Slippage and Breakage Rates," *Family Planning Perspectives*, 24 (1992): 20.

21. C. Michael Roland, ed., editorial, *Rubber Chemistry and Technology for the National Research Laboratory* (June 25, 1992).

22. W. Cates and K. M. Stone, Family Planning, "Sexually Transmitted Diseases and Contraceptive Choice: A Literature Update—Part 1," *Family Planning Perspectives* 24, no. 2 (March/April 1992): 75–84.

23. The Medical Institute, *Sexual Health Update Newsletter*, 8, no. 3 (fall 2000): 4.

24. McIlhaney, *What You Don't Know*, 85–7.

25. Alan Mozes, "Do Condoms and Seat Belts Promote Risk Taking?" Excite News, January 28, 2000; <news.excite.com/news/r/000128/18/health-psc>.

26. Dominque Hausser and P. A. Michaud, "Does a Condom-Promoting Strategy (the Swiss STOP-AIDS Campaign) Modify Sexual Behavior among Adolescents?" *Pediatrics* (April 1994): 582.

27. Brian Morris, M.D., "How Safe are Safes? Efficacy and Effectiveness of Condoms in Preventing STDs," *Canadian Family Physician* 39 (April 1993): 819.

28. John D. Hartigan, "The Disastrous Results of Condom Distribution Programs," *Family Research Council* (March 29, 2001).

29. R. W. Blum and P. M. Rinehart, *Reducing the Risk: Connections That Make a Difference in the Lives of Youth* (Minneapolis, Minn.: University of Minnesota Division of General Pediatrics and Adolescent Health, 1997), 5.

30. M. A. Schuster, R. M. Bell, and D. E. Kanouse, "The Sexual Practices of Adolescent Virgins: Genital Sexual Activities of High School Students Who Have Never Had Vaginal Intercourse," *American Journal of Public Health* 86, no. 11 (November 1996).

31. Heather Farish, "The Whole Story on Sex," Family Research Council: Press Room, March 29, 2001.

32. The Alan Guttmacher Institute, *Sex and America's Teenagers* (New York: The Alan Guttmacher Institute, 1994), 24.

33. J. Green et al., "Detection of Human Papillomavirus DNA by PCR in Semen from Patients with and without Penile Warts," *Genitourinary Medicine* 67 (June 1991): 207–10; G. Ilaria et al., "Detection of HIV-1 DNA Sequences in Pre-Ejaculatory Fluid," *Lancet* 340 (December 12, 1992): 1469; G. Kotwal et al., "Detection of Hepatitis C Virus-Specific Antigens in Semen from Non-A, Non-B Hepatitis Patients," *Digestive Diseases and Sciences* 37, no. 5 (May 1992): 641–4; A. van den Brule et al., "Detection of *Chlamydia trachomatis* in Semen of Artificial Insemi- nation Donors by the Polymerase Chain Reaction," *Fertility and Sterility* 59, no. 5 (May 1993): 1098–1103; R. Cone et al., "Frequent Detection of Genital Herpes Simplex Virus DNA by Polymerase Chain Reaction Among Pregnant Women," *Journal of the American Medical Association* 272, no. 10 (September 14, 1994): 792–6.

34. Joshua Mann, M.D., Joe S. McIlhaney Jr., M.D., and Curtis C. Stine, M.D., *Building Healthy Futures: Tools for Helping Adolescents Avoid or Delay the Onset of Sexual Activity* (Austin, Tex.: The Medical Institute, 2000), 17.

35. Editorial, "Short Takes: Advertising Abstinence," *The Atlanta Journal and Constitu- tion*, 22 February 1997, sec. A, p. 12.

36. Tom McNichol, "Sex Can Wait," *USA Weekend*, 25–27 March 1994, p. 4–6.

37. Tom W. Smith, "Attitudes toward Sexual Permissiveness: Trends, Correlates, and Behavioral Connections" (Chicago: University of Chicago National Opinion Research Center, 1992), 66.

38. Smith, "Sexual Permissiveness," 66.

39. Family Research Council, *National Family Values: A Survey of Adults* (a voter/con- sumer research poll for the Family Research Council, May 1994).

40. Larry Hugick and Jennifer Leonard, "Sex in America," *The Gallup Poll News Service* 56, no. 22 (October 6, 1991): 5.

41. SIECUS and Roper Starch Organization, "Teens Talk about Sex: Adolescent Sexu- ality in the '90s" (SIECUS and Roper Starch Organization, April 11, 1995): 25.

42. Gracie S. Hsu, "Abstinence: The New Sexual Revolution," *The Orange County Reg- ister Opinion*, 27 July 1994.

43. Centers for Disease Control, *Morbidity and Mortality Weekly Report* 45 (1996): 883–4.

44. Damiel Q. Haney, "Kids Growing Careful? U.S. Teens Having Sex Less, Using Con- doms More," ABC News, July 10, 2000; <abcnews.go.com/sections/living/ DailyNews/aids_teens0710.html>.

45. Freya L. Sonenstein, Ph.D., *National Survey of Adolescent Males* (Washington, D.C.: The Urban Initiative, 1995).

46. Centers for Disease Control, *National Survey of Family Growth, 1996* (Hyattsville, Mass.: Department of Health and Human Services, 1996).

47. Dale Stone, letter to author.

CHAPTER 16: DEVELOP A NURTURING RELATIONSHIP WITH KIDS

1. Melissa Grace, "Teen Pregnancies Raising Crime Costs," *Santa Barbara (Calif.) News-Press*, 22 June 1996.

2. Ibid.

3. Michael D. Resnick et al., "Protecting Adolescents from Harm: Findings from the National Longitudinal Study on Adolescent Health," *Journal of the American Medical Association* 278, no. 10 (September 10, 1997): 823–32.

4. Summarized in Joshua Mann M.D., Joe S. McIlhaney Jr., M.D., and Curtis C. Stine, M.D., *Building Heathy Futures: Tools for Helping Adolescents Avoid or Delay the Onset of Sexual Activity,* (Austin, Tex.: The Medical Institute, 2000).

5. Kathleen Kelleher, "Talking to Teens about Sex—It's in the Details," *Los Angeles Times,* 29 January 2001, p. 14.

6. This section is adapted from Josh McDowell, *How to Help Your Child Say No to Sexual Pressure* (Waco, Tex.: Word, 1987), 45–54.

7. Ibid., 67–74.

CHAPTER 17: ENCOURAGE AN INTIMATE RELATIONSHIP WITH CHRIST

1. Previously published in Josh McDowell, *Why Wait: What You Need to Know about the Teen Sexuality Crisis* (Nashville, Tenn.: Thomas Nelson, 1987), 404–409.

CHAPTER 18: TEACH AND MODEL MORAL VALUES AT HOME

1. This section is adapted from Josh McDowell, *How to Help Your Child Say No to Sexual Pressure* (Waco, Tex.: Word, 1987), 57–66.

2. Ibid., 93–98.

3. International Communications Research, "Not Just Another Thing to Do—Teens Talk about Sex, Regret, and the Influence of Their Parents" (a summary of findings from a nationally representative survey by International Communications Research, June 30, 2000), 1.

4. Donna Rice Hughes, "For Parents Only," Kids Online, 2000; <www.protectkids.com/fc/4parentsonly.htm>.

5. Adapted from Josh McDowell, *Help Your Child Say No*, 99–111.

6. Paula Rinehart, "Losing Our Promiscuity," *Christianity Today* (July 10, 2000): 3.

7. Ibid., 3.

8. Joshua Mann, M.D., Joe S. McIlhaney Jr., M.D., and Curtis C. Stine, M.D., *Building Healthy Futures: Tools for Helping Adolescents Avoid or Delay the Onset of Sexual Activity* (Austin, Tex.: The Medical Institute, 2000): 23.

CHAPTER 19: HELP KIDS DEVELOP THE STRENGTH TO SAY NO

1. Ronnell Jones, "Nevada Ranks Second for Teen Pregnancy," *Nevada Appeal*, 31 January 1996, p. 8.
2. R. W. Blum and P. M. Rinehart, *Reducing the Risk: Connections That Make a Difference in the Lives of Youth* (Minneapolis, Minn.: University of Minnesota Division of General Pediatrics and Adolescent Health, 1997), 30.
3. Abbylin Sellers, *The Sexual Abstinence Message Causes Positive Changes in Adolescent Behavior: A Circumstantial Review of Relevant Studies* (Santa Barbara, Calif.: Westmont College, May 1998), 4–5.
4. Ibid., 5.
5. LifeWay Christian Resources, True Love Waits, "History: Highlights from Our Past," 2001; <http://www.lifeway.com/tlw/ldr_hist_home.asp>.
6. The Medical Institute, *Sexual Health Update Newsletter* 5, no. 2 (winter 1997): 3.
7. Ibid.
8. Ibid.
9. Ibid.
10. Ibid.
11. Kaiser Family Foundation and *YM* magazine, "National Survey of Teens: Teens Talk about Dating, Intimacy, and Their Sexual Experiences," *YM* magazine (2000): 6–7.
12. R. C. Sproul, "How Far Is Too Far?" 1994, author's notes from a conference talk.

CHAPTER 20: HELP KIDS DETERMINE STANDARDS FOR DATING

1. Adapted from Josh McDowell, *How to Help Your Child Say No to Sexual Pressure* (Waco, Tex.: Word, 1987), 112–23.
2. Kaiser Family Foundation and *YM* magazine, "National Survey of Teens: Teens Talk about Dating, Intimacy, and Their Sexual Experiences," *YM* magazine (May 1998): 5.
3. Cindy Hallard and Gary Visgaitis, "The Teenage Dating Game," *USA Today*, 25 September 1995, sec. D, p. 1.
4. Kathleen Kellehen, "Who's Minding the Kids? Keeping Them Busy after School," *Los Angeles Times*, 10 January 1996, sec. E, p. 3.

CHAPTER 21: OFFER FORGIVENESS AND PROVIDE HOPE WHEN KIDS BLOW IT

1. John Diggs, "A Perspective on the Medical Implications of Virginity Pledge among Teens," *The Physicians Consortium* (January 5, 2001).

ABOUT THE AUTHOR

JOSH MCDOWELL is an internationally known speaker, author, and traveling representative for Campus Crusade for Christ. He has written more than forty books. These include *Right from Wrong, More Than a Carpenter,* and *The New Tolerance*. Josh and his wife, Dottie, have four children and live in Lucas, Texas.